THE CHALLENGE OF REVOLUTION

The Challenge of Revolution

Contemporary Russia in Historical Perspective

VLADIMIR MAU

and

IRINA STARODUBROVSKAYA

OXFORD

UNIVERSITY PRESS

OXFORD

UNIVERSITY PRESS

Great Clarendon Street, Oxford OX2 6DP

Oxford University Press is a department of the University of Oxford.
It furthers the University's objective of excellence in research, scholarship,
and education by publishing worldwide in

Oxford New York

Athens Auckland Bangkok Bogotá Buenos Aires
Cape Town Chennai Dar es Salaam Delhi Florence Hong Kong Istanbul
Karachi Kolkata Kuala Lumpur Madrid Melbourne Mexico City Mumbai
Nairobi Paris São Paulo Shanghai Singapore Taipei Tokyo Toronto Warsaw
with associated companies in Berlin Ibadan

Oxford is a registered trade mark of Oxford University Press
in the UK and in certain other countries

Published in the United States
by Oxford University Press Inc., New York

© Vladimir Mau and Irina Starodubrovskaya 2001

The moral rights of the authors have been asserted
Database right Oxford University Press (maker)

First published 2001

British Library Cataloguing in Publication Data

Data available

Library of Congress Cataloging in Publication Data
Starodububrovskaya, Irina.
The challenge of revolution: contemporary Russia in historical perspective/Irina
Starodubrovskaya and Vladinir Mau.
p. cm.
Includes bibliographical references and index.
1. Russia (Federation)—Politics and government—1991- 2. Russia
(Federation)—Economic policy—1991- 3. Revolutions—Russia (Federation) I. Mau, V.A.
(Vladimir Aleksandrovich) II. Title.
JN6695.S735 2001 303.6'4'0947—dc21 00–046505
ISBN 0–19–924150–3

1 3 5 7 9 10 8 6 4 2

Typeset in Minion by
Cambrian Typesetters, Frimley, Surrey

Printed in Great Britain
on acid-free paper by
T.J. International Ltd.,
Padstow, Cornwall

This book is dedicated to
Mikhail Gorbachev *and* **Yegor Gaidar**
*—two leaders, whose actions made
the subject of this book possible.*

What we saw in *perestroyka* was not a violent revolution, but a peaceful reform process which excluded cataclysms and destruction of productive forces, distress and suffering of people.

(Gorbachev 1995: 480)

It depends on us whether *perestroyka* is creeping and superficial, or profound and revolutionary.

(Gorbachev 1995: 351)

I do believe that what we have witnessed was a revolution, comparable in its effect on the historical process with the Great French Revolution, the Russian Revolution of 1917, and the Chinese Revolution of 1949.

(Gaidar 1996: 8)

PREFACE

It was the best of times, it was the worst of times, it was the age of wisdom, it was the age of foolishness, it was the epoch of belief, it was the epoch of incredulity, it was the season of Light, it was the season of Darkness, it was the spring of hope, it was the winter of despair, we had everything before us, we had nothing before us, we were all going direct to Heaven, we were all going direct to the other way – in short, the period was so like the present period, that some of its noisiest authorities insisted on its being received, for good or for evil, in the superlative degree of comparison only.

(Charles Dickens, *A Tale of Two Cities*)

Before the mid-1980s it had never occurred to us that we might become interested in the theory of revolution. The idea for this book came about almost by accident.

It was in 1987 that the CPSU General Secretary, Mikhail Gorbachev, first declared *perestroyka* to be a revolution. At that time we were working at the Institute of Economics of the USSR Academy of Sciences. Gorbachev's remark aroused our interest, and so we tried to imagine what lay in store for our country if his declaration proved to be accurate. As working models we took two revolutions of which we had reasonable knowledge—the French Revolution of 1789 and the Russian Revolution of 1917. By comparing them and identifying their common features, we attempted to predict the outcome of *perestroyka* in the USSR. The results of our investigations, and the predictions we made on the strength of them, were presented in various academic papers and published in the journal *Kommunist* and the newspaper *Nezavisimaya gazeta* (see Mau and Starodubrovskaya 1990, 1991*a*, 1991*b*).

Any informed Westerners (and, currently, not only Westerners) who read our works at that time would most likely have been amused. We were unacquainted with foreign works on the theory of revolution (such literature was not readily available then), and we unwittingly almost completely reproduced the logic of the revolutionary process which Crane Brinton had described long before us in his well-known work *The Anatomy of Revolution*. Even the terms we used for some of the stages in the process coincided with his, such as 'dual power' and 'Thermidor'. However, although our research on the theory of revolution at that time proved to be largely a reinvention of the wheel, the prognoses we made on the basis of this research turned out to be much more interesting.

The following story is often recalled by those who were involved. One of the most important conclusions in our work was that the unity of forces which emerges at the onset of the revolutionary crisis is soon exhausted. There then follows a period of divergence and polarization, which inevitably leads to sharp clashes between the most conservative and the most radical forces in the revolution. One of the authors of this book, who had just gone to work in the Institute for Economic Policy (IEP), headed by Egor Gaidar, wrote a section in the IEP's Review in which he argued that a clash of this type was inevitable. The section bore the ominous title 'Economics and Politics in the Era Preceding the Dictatorship'.[1] He was subjected to merciless criticism at a discussion at the Institute in April 1991. His opponents argued that it was not permissible to make serious and responsible prognoses about current politics using primitive analogies with events long past. The circumstances did not provide any basis for drawing such unambiguous conclusions. The hypothesis could therefore in no way be considered scientifically grounded.

Then came August 1991, and this 'unscientific presupposition' threatened to become a reality. During these days it was by no means certain that the putsch by the conservative section of the party-state bureaucracy against Gorbachev and his policies would fail. The possibility of a bloody dictatorship seemed quite real.[2] None the less, when this author, previously criticized for his dubious predictions, turned up at the Institute, people flocked to congratulate him. In spite of the tense atmosphere of those days, the joke went around that he should be severely reprimanded for failing to give an exact date for the putsch he had predicted.

It was in those difficult days that we decided that, sooner or later, we would have to write a book on the revolution in Russia which fate had kindly decreed we should witness. However, these plans had to be put aside for several long years. The putsch failed, and the first post-communist government assumed power in Russia. The USSR broke up, and a most difficult period of radical reforms ensued. We were completely immersed in these turns of events, and had neither the time nor the energy for theoretical studies. As far as possible

---

[1] This title intentionally echoes that of Lenin's well-known article of 1919, 'Economics and Politics in the Era of the Dictatorship of the Proletariat' (see e.g. Lenin, *CW* xxx).

[2] In his memoirs Gaidar describes his initial reaction to the news of the putsch: 'I try to imagine the consequences of the coup. At that moment I have no doubts that it will lead to a change of power. That its authors will be able to hold on for a few months, maybe even years. But then what? I couldn't envisage any kind of "enlightened dictatorship" or a "Russian Pinochet". Blood would flow, as under Pinochet, and probably more freely. But it would all be in vain. The conspirators do not have a single sensible idea about how to tackle the disintegrating economy . . . Yes, they have a year or two, maybe even five. Ultimately, in historical terms, that is just a moment. But for those alive today? How many of them would make it through those years?' (Gaidar 1996: 73) At that time we all presumably felt something similar. We tried to convince ourselves and each other that the putschists could not hold on for more than six months, although we ourselves had no idea what to expect and what to prepare for.

we tried to be not mere observers, but active participants in the transformation of Russia, thereby confirming that well-known truth that it is much more interesting to make revolution than to write about it. One of us was an aide to Egor Gaidar in the government in 1992 and 1993, and for the rest of the time was Deputy Director of the Institute for the Economy in Transition (as the IEP had been renamed). The other worked for three years in the Moscow office of the World Bank, dealing with plans for international financial organizations to support economic reform in Russia. This gave us the opportunity of obtaining first-hand information on the real progress of the revolutionary changes in Russia in a variety of spheres—not only in the capital, but in the regions as well.

However, even during those extraordinarily eventful years this book remained at the back of our minds. While experiencing the twists and turns of the recent Russian revolution on an emotional level, we were simultaneously trying to work out what each of these events meant in terms of the logic of the revolutionary process, and how they should be assessed in the light of the theoretical principles we had worked out previously. Some time in 1995 we started to think about realizing our long-standing aim, once it had become clear that the revolutionary process in Russia was nearing completion. Then we were kindly invited to spend the Trinity term 1997 at Christ Church, Oxford. We decided that the time had come to get down to working in earnest on this book.

For a whole year we made a serious study of the theoretical literature on this problem. We familiarized ourselves with concrete studies of individual revolutions. This analysis merely strengthened our view that events in Russia were of the same order as during the periods of major change in the past. Moreover, much of what had previously been thought of as specifically Russian was actually to be found in previous revolutions. The more we studied the literature, the clearer it became that our book would not only be about Russia, but about a series of revolutionary upheavals, starting with the English Civil War of the 1640s. For Russia's experience can help us understand previous revolutions just as much as previous revolutions can help us understand events in Russia.

The first draft of this book was written in three months—exactly ten years after we first developed our interest in this problem. Reworking the manuscript took another year and a half. It would have taken even longer had it not been for the invaluable assistance we received from our friends and colleagues in Russia and abroad, who spent much time and effort helping our research, discussing our overall interpretation and the specific problems considered in the book, making constructive criticisms of our mistakes, and helping us hone our arguments.

As we prepared to work on this book, and even while we were in the process of writing it, we could not help wondering whether it was possible, in such a short period of time, fully to grasp a problem on which scholars had been working for years or even decades. Would it not be better to continue studying Russian economic and politico-economic processes—a familiar area in which we had built our academic reputations? As we were finding our bearings in completely new territory, we would inevitably feel like novices, with neither the necessary reputation, nor sufficient experience, nor, maybe, the breadth of vision which one acquires after long immersion in a particular problem. The fact that this book has appeared at all shows that we were able to banish these doubts. It seems to us that, for all these handicaps, we have one indisputable advantage over the overwhelming majority of students of revolutionary processes—we have lived through a revolution.

First-hand experience of a revolutionary period in a country's history gives one a unique insight. It is practically impossible to gain such an insight in states where life is proceeding steadily and peacefully, with a stable political system and a highly developed economy. Consequently, we have often found that events at crucial and extreme moments in the life of a society are judged against values and criteria formed in quite different circumstances. This is natural for researchers who have never themselves lived through a revolutionary breakdown. If you have yourself experienced despair at the impossibility of getting food to feed your family and a one-year-old child at the end of 1991, you have a better insight into how women in starving Paris felt in the 1790s. When you have seen how even the most ideologically committed reformers manœuvred and retreated after 1992 as the objective situation changed, breaking even the strongest of characters, it is easier to comprehend Cromwell's evolution and the vacillations of Robespierre. If you have seen how Gorbachev's *perestroyka* initially raised the spirits of society, before sending them crashing down into an abyss of chaos and disenchantment, it is easier to explain how the bright hopes of democracy and freedom gave way to the bloody dictatorships of the Jacobins or the Bolsheviks.

We would certainly not argue that experience of 'sensations' can substitute for a real knowledge of the facts and processes which characterized the revolutions of the past. However, social theory, including the theory of revolution, is neither only, nor even mainly, concerned with the collection and systematization of facts. It is primarily about interpreting them. It is no accident that discussions about the real significance of quite well-known events can continue for decades. The discussion on the rise of the gentry in the period preceding the English revolution is a striking example of this. We believe that a real experience of life in revolutionary conditions can assist in the interpretation of known facts. To be more specific, this experience allows one to distinguish what can happen in a revolutionary epoch from what necessarily cannot happen because it requires conditions of stability and predictability. At the same time, it allows one to identify events which can only take place in the course of a revolutionary crisis, or which would be highly improbable in a stable, virtually unchanging social environment.

Although the experience of the last ten years has had a substantial influence on our perception of why and how revolutions occur, that influence remains latent in this work. We have produced a scientific monograph, not the memoirs of participants in events or an essay on the theme of revolution. Only here, in our short Preface, have we allowed ourselves to depart from an analytical style to explain how this book came about and what it means to us.

During the writing of this book we have had support from many people and institutions. Discussions and comments from our colleagues were of great value for us. Interviews with decision-makers were very important to give this book a flavour of revolution. Institutions where we worked and wrote this book afforded good opportunities for this study, which was, of course, time-consuming.

Our first readers and reviewers were our parents, and their contribution cannot be overestimated.

We are indebted to prominent Russian politicians—Mikhail Gorbachev, Alexander Yakovlev, Egor Gaidar, and Gennadii Burbulis—who contributed to this book in two important respects: as politicians, whose political and intellectual work in the 1980s and '90s created the very subject of our research, and as the interviewees of this book. Among these four we have to emphasize the role of Egor Gaidar, our colleague and friend, with whom we have been discussing our research for the past decade.

The title of the book is due to Yelena Kalyuzhnova, and we express our gratitude to her.

We are grateful to our colleagues John Biggart, Archie Brown, Revold Entov, John Fleming, William Fleming, Lev Freinkman, Brigitte Granville, Philip Hanson, Michael Kaser, Tatiana Koval', Mari Kuraishi, Carol S. Leonard, Yurii Levada, Mary McAuley, Michael McFaul, Vitalii Melyantsev, Peter Oppenheimer, Margarita Pinegina, Alex Pravda, Sergei Sinel'nikov, Judith Shapiro, Angela Stent, Richard Stoneman, Eugenii Turuntsev, Haim Zaltsman, and many others, not all of whom we can mention here. They provided valuable comments and important pieces of information for our study. We shall never forget the late Alec Nove, with whom we discussed the ideas for this research.

We wish to thank those individuals who helped us to prepare an English translation of this manuscript. Francis King did a tremendous job translating the manuscript into English. John Biggart was the first careful reader of the translation, and his comments, both on substance and on language, were of great importance for the authors. Translation was sponsored by the Institute for the Economy in Transition (Moscow) and the US Agency for International Development.

We owe a debt of gratitude to Christ Church, which provided an excellent opportunity for research and the writing of this book during our stay in 1997 as Fowler Hamilton Visitors to Oxford. Numerous discussions with the faculty of Oxford University formed an important part of our work on the manuscript. Peter Oppenheimer was the key person for us during our stay in Oxford, and we are grateful to him for his support and generosity.

It was very difficult for our colleagues in Moscow to grant us leave of absence for such a long time in 1997, and we thank the Institute for the Economy in Transition and the Foundation for Enterprise Restructuring and Financial Institutions Development for their compassion and understanding.

Finally, we are grateful to Eugeniya Antonova, Viktor Avralov, Olga Golant, Marina Turuntseva, and Irina Ustinova, who provided us with research assistance.

CONTENTS

LIST OF FIGURES

LIST OF TABLES

Introduction

The dramatic events in the USSR and Eastern Europe in the late 1980s and early 1990s have posed some tricky questions for specialists on the theory of revolution. There can be no doubt that these countries were in the throes of revolutionary upheavals. This was clear from the radical changes in their political régimes, the scale and the systemic nature of the transformations which took place, and, in many cases, the importance of popular movements 'from below'. However, most of the conceptual approaches normally associated with the theory of revolution could not readily be applied to these crises. The predominant conceptions of revolution applied to backward, underdeveloped countries, the agrarian-bureaucratic monarchies of the past and present-day 'Third World' states. Many prominent students of revolution agreed with Samuel Huntington in assuming that both Western democracies and communist régimes enjoyed reserves of political stability and were not susceptible to revolutionary cataclysms.

Some specialists on the theory of revolution still clung to their traditional views on the stability of the Soviet-type régimes, even when the revolutionary nature of the changes in the communist world had become quite obvious (the Soviet leadership had already started to speak about change in such terms in 1987). Here, for example, are two judgements made by prominent specialists in the field in 1989:

> All political élites today in the world are subject to some measure of challenge for sheer incompetence, though many countries including the U.S.A. and the U.S.S.R. possess reasonably effective ways of removing the incumbents without endangering the political system itself. . . . It is *conceivable* in the future, though not in a future that anyone has yet imagined in a very plausible way, that the political systems of these societies, too, may be destroyed because of their inability to serve the needs of their societies. But there may well be little reason to look forward to such an event. . . . Both of these states and a large number of their more immediate satellites are too powerful and not oppressive enough for there to be any serious prospect of revolution within an imaginable future. This is partly because there is no serious need for a revolution in these societies within an imaginable future, not because both of these societies do not have many dreadful features . . ., but because the defects which they do display inside their borders are not the sort of defects which revolutions have yet shown any capacity to cure. . . . The real revolutionary ideologies in the world today are primitivist in inspiration (the villages of the world surrounding its cities) because the real revolutionary situations in the world today are primitive in character. (Dunn 1989: 22)

> By contrast [with the Third World], democratic polities in the First World, and a combination of Communist party patronage and coercive repression in the Second

World, have prevented the emergence of strong revolutionary movements (or else, as in Poland, have staved off outright seizures of power by such movements). The unraveling of Communist patronage systems in portions of the Second World may allow the future growth of oppositional movements there. These will often be ethnic separatist, however, rather than revolutionary; and it is hard to imagine that threatened Communist armies will crumble or retreat as patrimonial and colonial armies have done.[1] (Skocpol and Goodwin 1994: 274)

If we are to develop an adequate analysis of the recent revolutionary changes, we clearly need to go beyond McFaul's recognition that 'the Russian State and the surrounding states from the former Soviet Union and Eastern Europe have undergone monumental political, economic and social change in the past several years, rivalled only by the French Revolution or the Bolshevik Revolution in scope of consequence' (1996: 169). These new examples of revolutionary cataclysm cannot simply be slotted into the existing theoretical schema. This schema is unable to account for events which have taken place in relatively developed, highly urbanized, and educated societies. Our experience of recent revolutions obliges us to re-examine seriously how the subject is currently treated in our social sciences. One aim of this book is to explain at least some aspects of the revolutionary experience of the late 1980s and early 1990s in terms of theoretical conceptions of the phenomenon of revolution. We do not intend to try to solve this problem once and for all.

First, we have limited ourselves to examining the experience of Russia. Our analysis does not extend to the other former Soviet republics, nor to the countries of Eastern Europe. We believe that each case merits a separate analysis to determine the nature of the changes that took place, the extent to which these changes can be considered revolutionary, and the way each country's experience affects our overall theoretical conception. This cannot be done in one single study. Other works have already been published, dealing, for example, with Poland, where the social nature of the revolution as a movement 'from below' was evident much earlier and to a much greater degree.

Secondly, we do not intend to re-examine all the existing theories of revolution. Their diversity and complexity makes that impossible. Our main interest is in those aspects of the theory of revolution which need to be reconsidered in the light of the Russian experience, that is, where recent revolutionary changes either provide additional arguments in favour of a certain viewpoint or, conversely, clearly contradict it.

In other words, the main aim of this study is to show how the experience of one more major revolution—the revolutionary changes currently under way in Russia—affects the further development of the theory of revolution, which aspects of that theory need further elaboration, and which problems need to be reconsidered.

---

[1] The article in question first appeared in *Politics and Society*, Dec. 1989.

Is this a valid approach? In the 1970s, a view gained currency among students of revolution which did indeed call this entire approach into question. It was argued that a general theory of revolution, encompassing not only its socio-psychological and political aspects but also the basic, structural relations within society, could not be constructed. Theda Skocpol developed this case in some detail, arguing that 'if one is to take a social-structural approach toward explaining revolutions, one really must theorise in terms of various specific types of societies, for there is little or nothing of any significance that can be said about the political or socio-economic institutions of all kinds of known human societies lumped together. (Skocpol 1994*b*: 113). This view was put even more forcefully by Ellen Kay Trimberger, who wrote that 'there can be no general theory of revolution (or of social change) applicable to all societies at all times. Any general theorizing about the causes and consequences of different types of revolution is invalidated by the distinct historical and international contexts in which particular revolutions occur' (Trimberger 1978: 1).

This sort of approach rules out comparisons between the revolutions of the past—which took place in overwhelmingly agrarian societies with monarchical systems of government—and present-day revolutions in mature industrial societies with anti-democratic régimes. The levels of social development, class structure, institutional relations, international and domestic situations, and historical circumstances are all entirely different in the two classes of revolution that we wish to compare. Can there be a sensible basis on which to compare revolutions in such different societies?

We believe that there can be, but it does not consist in examining the specific internal structures of the societies in question. The key factor is in the ability of a society to react to disturbances in its external environment. We can draw an analogy here with the laws of natural selection in biology. Living organisms may be large or small, highly developed or organizationally simple, and distinguished by all kinds of anatomical or physiological features. None of this in itself is important. What matters is whether the specific characteristics of a given organism correspond to the peculiarities of its environment, and whether these living beings can adapt to changes in that environment. It is this ability or inability to adapt which, in the final analysis, determines whether an individual will survive, and whether a species will be preserved or become extinct.

Something similar can be said about social organisms. Societies may differ in terms of their property relations, social structure, political system, ideology, place in the international order, and many other respects. None the less, they may be compared in the extent to which their features correspond to the objective external and internal conditions in which they exist, and in their ability to adapt to change. As in biology, it is adaptability that is crucial here: either social institutions evolve to meet new demands, or the system collapses from within under the weight of accumulated contradictions, and development takes a revolutionary path. How useful this general approach is, and whether it must significantly enhance our theoretical understanding of revolution, our readers must judge for themselves.

Traditional approaches to the study of revolutions suffer from one major deficiency. Ideological, psychological, political, and social relations have always occupied a central place in the theory of revolution. The same cannot be said about questions of economic development and economic policy in the period of revolution. At best they have been explored in a few specialized works dealing with individual revolutions, and they have almost never been the subject of a comparative analysis. When such an important aspect of overall social relations is overlooked, the resulting picture is inevitably distorted. One cannot obtain a complete overview of how different relationships in society interact without considering the economic dimension.

The reasons for this omission may have to do with the fact that most studies of revolution have been undertaken by political scientists, who may not have been keen to venture beyond their sphere of competence. Yet the analysis of revolution raises many questions which cannot be adequately explained solely in terms of political or psychological relationships. Once we take account of economic processes, these difficulties can be resolved clearly and simply. In our study of the causes, course, and consequences of revolutions, we shall devote particular attention to questions of economic change and economic policy.

In this work we have another aim, additional to our concern to use the Russian experience to enrich our theoretical understanding. A recognition of the revolutionary nature of the changes under way in Russia is not just of theoretical interest—it is also vitally important if we are to understand what is happening there.

Two problems can arise from an inadequate grasp of the nature of events in Russia. First, if one attempts to explain these events within the logic of evolutionary development, many of the decisions and actions of Russian politicians in recent years are quite incomprehensible. Why destroy the Soviet Union, when the level of co-operation between the republics had reached 60–80 per cent? Why has privatization in Russia made virtually no contribution to the state budget when many countries, for example in Latin America, have successfully used privatization to solve their fiscal problems? Why was it necessary to implement the reforms through shock therapy rather than gradually, allowing economic agents to adapt to changing circumstances? Much of what took place seems to contradict common sense. A variety of explanations have been advanced, from the incompetence of Russian politicians to the machinations of international imperialism. However, decisions which at first glance seem to make no sense become quite comprehensible when viewed in terms of the logic of a revolutionary process. Our analysis shows that the problems which Russian politicians faced were characteristic of other revolutions, too. Moreover, they were often resolved in very similar ways.

Another problem arises when social scientists possess an inadequate understanding of the theory of revolution. For example, David Kotz presented developments in Russia as a 'revolution from above', as distinct from a 'revolution from below', which he characterized as follows: 'Many times in history socioeconomic systems have been swept away by revolutions from below. In such a classical revolution, the underprivileged victims of a social system rise up, defeat the old ruling group, overthrow the system by which that ruling group had ruled, and begin the difficult task of building a new system to replace the old. The French Revolution is the prototype of such a historical event in the modern world, and the Russian Revolution of 1917 is a twentieth-century example' (Kotz with Weir 1997: 153).

However, even the most superficial historical analysis shows that this interpretation cannot be applied to any revolution at all, let alone the French (1789) and the Bolshevik (1917) revolutions referred to by Kotz. All the revolutions mentioned above began with a crisis of the state and of the élite which sustained it. This was accompanied by actions 'from below' of both a revolutionary and counter-revolutionary nature, and ultimately a new élite emerged to reconstruct the state. This is very far from the image of the triumphal march of the popular masses forwards a glorious future. If events in 1990s Russia are compared with a superficial representation of past events, the result will obviously be theoretical confusion. We must therefore bring to bear a more sophisticated understanding of past revolutions if we are to acquire a more accurate picture of contemporary Russia.

The second task that the authors of this book have set themselves is therefore to examine how our understanding of Russian events can be enhanced by examining these events from the standpoint of the logic of revolutionary development. What are the real motives, given the revolutionary nature of the current period in Russia, of the various decisions and actions of Russian politicians?

Revolution is a subject to which modern economic and social theories cannot easily be applied. Most of the systems of social thought developing in the West are better suited to examining stable, balanced societies, and sharp change of any sort is seen as a deviation from the state of equilibrium. Such theories tend to regard revolutions as something negative, accidental, and always avoidable. These theories cannot cope with anything other than very small, evolutionary changes.

Students of events in Eastern Europe and the former USSR today inevitably come up against these difficulties, and have to acknowledge the 'shortcomings of western theory and knowledge: . . . Most established economic theory aims to explain marginal and incremental changes. It is therefore at best partial, and at worst misleading, in the context of sweeping, rapid changes in entire systems. . . . Similar difficulties beset our explanations of political change:

models that fit more or less adequately the representative systems of capitalist democracies leave unstated both the underlying institutional forms and conditions for drastic transformation'. (Nelson, Tilly, and Walker 1997: 2).

Those studying the sources and forms of social development are increasingly making use of institutional theory of the kind associated particularly with the work of Douglas North.[2] This theory is mainly concerned with the mechanisms by which social institutions influence the development process,[3] the consequences of this influence, and the factors which affect the ways in which the institutions themselves change. However, this theory is also mainly about evolutionary, gradual change. Sharp, revolutionary changes remain peripheral to this analysis. At most, revolutions are seen as an external factor, able in some way to influence the development of institutions (North 1990: 89–91). They are not seen as something produced within the institutional system itself in its interactions with other factors of social development.

Unlike the approaches considered above, Marxist theory regards revolution as an organic element of social progress, indeed, as the 'locomotive of history'. It is this capacity to describe dynamic processes, including sharp, discontinuous changes that has made Marxism hitherto one of the most attractive sociological theories. However, in Marxism elements of scientific analysis are so closely intertwined with utopianism, and so many aspects are laden with ideology, that Marxism can hardly provide the necessary instrument for a modern analysis of revolution.

It seems to us, therefore, that the social sciences have not yet managed to develop adequate methods for analysing dynamic and radical changes. Consequently, we have not felt obliged to stick to just one approach, one conceptual basis for analysing revolutionary processes. Neither our analytical methods nor our results fit neatly into the frameworks of Marxism, of the institutional school, or of any other existing theoretical schemas. We think this is one of the strengths of our work. Not only have attempts to study revolutions on the basis of existing theories proved incapable of predicting the revolutionary processes in Eastern Europe and the former Soviet Union, they have not even been able seriously to analyse these processes. This shows the inadequacy of the existing methodologies, and suggests that some 'experiment' in this field may prove to be fruitful.

There is another aspect of our methodology to which we should draw attention. Although we shall use and frequently compare the experience of various revolutions, we shall not produce the sort of comparative historical analysis often employed in studying revolutions. Such an approach requires

---

[2] A detailed exposition of this theory can be found, for example, in North (1990).

[3] North defines institutions as 'the rules of the game' within society (North 1990: 3). Examples of such institutions are laws, rules, and norms, as well as traditions and belief systems.

detailed comparisons of various revolutionary processes, the identification of common features and differences, regular patterns and chance elements (Skocpol 1994*b*: 113–14; Skocpol and Somers 1994). It was not our aim to test or prove a particular hypothesis by juxtaposing various revolutions. We wanted to analyse one revolutionary process—the one which has been taking place in Russia from 1985–2000. As we looked at each concrete problem, we made a comparison with past events either where this helped us gain a more precise understanding of what is happening in Russia now, or where the experience of Russia's recent revolution helped explain past events more fully. In our analyses of different problems we use the experience of numerous revolutions (including those 'from above' and 'from below', and the so-called 'Fascist revolutions'). However, we do not compare the recent Russian events with any of these revolutions in a detailed, systematic fashion.

At first sight, it might seem that whilst such an approach is capable of revealing analogies between various historical events, it can do nothing to explain their essence. However, this is not the case. Our analysis is not concerned with analogies between revolutions. These were observed long ago and have been described in detail by the first generation of students of revolution.[4] Our main concern is this: why is it that revolutionary processes, occurring in quite different historical periods and under various circumstances, have so much in common both in their initial causes, and in the mechanisms and stages through which they proceed? Prior to the current Russian revolution it was possible to refer to common social conditions in agrarian monarchies, and in developing countries undergoing a period of modernization. When such similar processes take place before our very eyes in a fairly developed society, these explanations can no longer be considered satisfactory. It is necessary to look for more general principles of social interaction which will allow us to uncover the sources of revolutionary crises, and the mechanics of development of the revolutionary process. This will help us understand why certain tendencies are so clearly reproduced in every revolution.

The methodological approach chosen for this book is in some respects more general, and in others more concrete, than is usual for modern works on the theory of revolution. We have tried not to proceed simply from a comparison of various revolutions, but to present a theoretical approach to the general logic of the revolutionary process which embraces both revolutionary events in the modernization process and revolutions in present-day society. In this respect our conclusions can claim to be more universal and general. At the same time, all the questions we have examined are aimed at elucidating the processes and phenomena characteristic of just one revolutionary process,

---

[4] For the three generations of students of revolution, see Goldstone (1980). The best-known work which uses analogy to analyse revolutions is Brinton (1965).

namely, the collapse of communism and the post-communist transformation in Russia. In doing this, we have made a detailed analysis of certain aspects of past revolutions which have often escaped the attention of researchers, but which have proved to be highly relevant in the light of the Russian experience.

1

Why Revolutions Happen

1.1 The study of revolution

The first problem faced by a student of 'revolutions' is that the concept itself is very nebulous. For more than sixty years specialists who have been working on the theory of revolution have been unable to agree either on how to define the concept, or even on whether 'revolution' should be treated as a separate object of analysis. This is not surprising. There are relatively few phenomena which can unquestionably be categorized as revolutions. The number of 'indisputable' revolutions in world history has been variously put at between three and ten. What is more, these revolutions occurred at such different times, and under such different economic, political, and cultural conditions, that similarity between them might be more likely to cause surprise and confusion than to provide a basis for academic analysis. There are also many phenomena which look much like revolutions in a whole range of ways, but which none the less do not quite resemble the 'classic' cases. This category greatly outnumbers the 'indisputable' revolutions.[1]

Students of revolution will often try to get round this problem by subsuming revolutions under more general concepts, such as collective violence,[2] or the collapse of the state.[3] They may differentiate between revolutionary

---

[1] Jack Goldstone has described the problems this situation poses as follows: 'Because there have been few events that fit the extreme sense of 'revolution', yet many cases of governments being overthrown or temporarily disabled, there have developed almost as many varied definitions of 'revolution' as there are analysts and cases of state crises' (1991: 8). Ted Robert Gurr has stated baldly the 'justification for the choice of political violence rather than revolution as the subject of study: the former is far more common than the latter' (1970: 21).

[2] In his work *Why Men Rebel*, Ted Robert Gurr included revolutions among his subject-matter as 'fundamental sociopolitical change accomplished through violence', along with other manifestations of violence such as resistance movements, seizures of power, uprisings, and riots (1970: 4).

[3] Jack Goldstone, in using this term, tries to solve the problem of definitions by resorting to vector algebra. He breaks down the concept of a political crisis into eight elements. Where a given element is present in a particular historical situation, it is marked with the number 1, and where it is absent, it is marked with a 0. This schema makes it formally possible to describe 128 different situations, from complete stability to the most extreme of revolutions (1991: 10–12).

situations and revolutionary outcomes.[4] Finally, they may limit themselves to comparisons of a few specific revolutions, believing a more general approach to be impossible.[5] All these tendencies are currently dominant, and have over-shadowed attempts to find any kind of universal approach to the study of revolution.

There are considerable and obvious differences, both in their degree of radicalism and in their impact on world history, between the 'classic' or 'great' revolutions and other events which in various respects resemble them. However much certain scholars may have tried to smooth over the differences or reduce them to purely quantitative parameters, the differences remain. Nobody would seriously try to compare the Russian Revolution of 1917 with the French revolution of 1830 or with the uprisings in the Spanish provinces in the 1640s. On the other hand, it is considered quite legitimate to compare the Russian Revolution with the English Revolution and Civil War of the seventeenth century, the French Revolution of 1789, or the Chinese or Mexi-can revolutions of the twentieth century, and those researching the subject frequently do so.

The question of the place of 'classic' revolutions in world history has become particularly relevant today. In recent years we have seen the collapse of the world communist system—a complex and variegated phenomenon which combined national liberation movements, seizures of political power, and radical social and economic transformations. Can this collapse be regarded as a revolutionary process? There is no unanimity on this, but some researchers would put recent events in Russia on the same level as the French Revolution of 1789 and the Bolshevik Revolution of 1917.[6]

To a certain extent in this book we go against the established tradition. We seek to examine the full-scale, classic revolutions. They have occurred rarely in world history, but they have left a permanent legacy. They have taken place at very different stages in the development of civilization, starting with pre-industrial England in the middle of the seventeenth century, and ending with Russia at the end of the twentieth century, in the age of information techno-logy and the conquest of space. We shall not ignore other modes of social

[4] Charles Tilly has counted 707 revolutionary situations in Europe alone from 1492 to 1991 (1993: 243). Revolutionary outcomes occurred far less frequently.

[5] The classic example of this sort of approach is the work of Theda Skocpol (See Skocpol 1979).

[6] One of the first to make this analogy—in 1990, exactly one year before the putsch which led to the break-up of the USSR—was Michael McFaul: 'The French Revolution crushed the monarchical order of 18th-century Europe, forever altering the principles of legitimate government. The Russian Revolution challenged the 19th-century system, polar-izing the world into a 70-year battle between capitalism and socialism.

'The maelstrom of events unfolding in the Soviet Union today can only be understood as a revolution of grandeur analogous to the great revolutions of France and Russia' (1990: 1).

transformation, but shall look at them to the extent that they either create the conditions for, or are the consequences of, the great revolutions.

The parameters we have set ourselves present some serious problems when we come to consider the causes of revolution. Is it possible to find any common features in the preconditions for events which took place at such different times, in such different places, and under such different circumstances? An affirmative answer of course presupposes that what these causes have in common can be defined on a fairly abstract level, and that in each country and each epoch they will have their own concrete manifestations. None the less, the similarities can be seen quite clearly. Revolutions take place in those countries which encounter fundamental challenges to which they are unaccustomed. These challenges may be a consequence of endogenous development processes, or of worldwide, global tendencies. The institutional structure of these countries and the psychological outlook of the population do not allow them to adapt flexibly to new challenges, and these inbuilt constraints prevent adaptation and cannot be removed in the course of evolutionary development. Where a system of social relations does not contain internal constraints which prevent society from reacting adequately to any challenges that arise, a process of accommodation will take place. It may be a fairly painful process, but the social system will not break down. Thus the principal factor determining the stability of the established structures and relations of a society is their adaptability, their ability to accommodate to a changing environment. This characterization is, of course, highly generalized and even to a certain extent tautological. It will be developed and made more concrete below.

1.2 Challenges and constraints

We certainly do not claim to be the first to adopt the approach outlined above. Among the first students of revolution, Ted Robert Gurr set out so-called theories of 'social change' which locate the cause of political violence in the inability of social and political institutions, customs, and norms to react flexibly to an objective process of change. According to these theories the end of adaptation marks the beginning of revolution (Gurr 1970: 53, 55–6).

Among more recent writers, Jack Goldstone makes the fullest use of this sort of approach. He associates revolutionary upheavals with cyclical waves of population growth. Although these waves have occurred periodically over centuries, the intervals between them have been so great that in each particular case this process has created completely new problems for the authorities and society, undermining the basis of the traditional order. Rising prices caused chaos in state finances and reduced the purchasing power of the population. Increasing competition between workers led to a fall in wages, increasing competition between peasants to an irrational division of land-holdings. Among the élite, jockeying for state positions became more intense. The rapid growth of urban areas created potential hotbeds of discontent, especially given a demographic shift towards a greater proportion of young people in the population. As a result, a typical pre-revolutionary situation would involve a crisis of state finances, intensifying conflict within the élite, and a sharp increase in the potential for mass disobedience. However, Goldstone is far from believing that population growth must always have catastrophic consequences:

What matters is whether the existing social and political institutions are flexible enough to move easily in response to such pressures. Where institutions are flexible, as in modern democratic states, pressures can usually be absorbed through electoral realignment and policy changes. Where institutions are relatively inflexible, as in hereditary monarchies or empires with traditional systems of taxation, élite recruitment and economic organization, the result is more likely to be revolution or rebellion. (1991: 36)

Other approaches to determining the causes of revolution also usually refer both to new challenges and to society's inability to adapt in order to meet them, although not in as systematic a way as Goldstone does. In Marxist studies of revolution the main stress is laid on the impossibility of fully developing new economic processes within the confines of the old social structure, when the existing relations of production become fetters on the development of productive forces. What we find most interesting in the Marxist approach is the attention it pays to economic processes, often overlooked by writers from other schools.

One economic problem which can become acute in a pre-revolutionary period, for example, is the growth of towns and the effect of this growth on the development of market relations. As Barrington Moore has noted in relation to both pre-revolutionary England and pre-revolutionary France, 'the key agricultural problem was to get the grain to the classes that ate bread but did not grow the wheat' (1966: 45). He also saw the growth of urban goods markets as one of the main indicators of the 'bourgeois commercial impulse'.[7] The need to provide the towns with foodstuffs and other items of consumption gave rise to problems which demanded a substantial modification of the system of local markets, and the use of market relations on a wider scale. The existing social structure was unable to adapt fully to this without fracturing. Another contributory factor was an increasing involvement in world trade.

---

[7] For example, at the end of the 18th century Paris consumed 206 million pounds of grain, 5,850,000 pounds of fresh butter, and 78 million eggs per year. Satisfying its annual demand for meat products required 100,000 head of beef cattle, 420,000 sheep, 30,000 cows, and 140,000 pigs. The city also needed to be supplied with numerous other foodstuffs, as well as other groceries and fuel (Dobrolyubsky 1930: 11).

This made the economic structures and social relations of individual countries increasingly dependent not on local, easily controllable circumstances, but on the fluctuations of the world market.[8]

In a polemic against the Marxist standpoint, Theda Skocpol and Ellen K. Trimberger argue that the decisive factors in the development of revolutionary crises are not internal, but external, and they include among such factors 'political-military pressures from more economically advanced countries abroad'. They present objective contradictions within the *ancien régime* as first and foremost '*political* contradictions centered in the structure and situation of states caught in cross-pressures between, on the one hand, military competitors on the international scene and, on the other hand, the constraints of the existing domestic economy and (in some cases) resistance by internal politically powerful class forces to efforts by the state to mobilize resources to meet international competition' (Skocpol and Trimberger 1994: 122).

Finally, many researchers have drawn attention to the role played by social barriers in bringing revolutionary situations to maturity. As a society develops, the new élite groups which emerge become dissatisfied with the traditional mechanisms of vertical mobility that hinder the career advancement of able people. It has been argued that a common feature of the Russian, Iranian, Mexican, and Chinese revolutions, which took place between 1905 and 1911, was that 'economic growth created new economically and technologically important, yet politically excluded, social groups' (Hart 1987: 11).

Existing studies provide ample material to illustrate not only the emergence of fundamentally new challenges and new demands which put pressure on the existing system of social relations as a whole and on the state structure in particular, but also how the inflexibility of established relations and institutions limits the possibilities of adapting to this changed situation. However, these studies are not systematic, inasmuch as they concentrate on one type of challenge or constraint, or on a limited historical period. Our intention is to examine the question from a more general standpoint.

First, for the sort of tensions which can lead to a revolutionary explosion to arise in a society, there must be both new challenges, and constraints to institutional and psychological adaptation to these challenges. The particular nature of these challenges or constraints may change substantially over time. Tendencies which gave rise to crises in the seventeenth and eighteenth centuries need not have the same significance today.[9] In today's circumstances,

---

[8] Assessing the situation in pre-revolutionary England, Immanuil Wallerstein observed that 'the very process of internal industrialization made England's internal structure more, not less, dependent on the vagaries of the world market' (1974: 274).

[9] Goldstone has a different understanding of this question. After an extraordinarily interesting and well-argued analysis of the role of population growth in destabilizing pre-industrial countries, he unexpectedly launches into a discussion of this factor as a substantial reason for the difficulties faced by the USA today (Goldstone 1991: 492).

the scientific-technological revolution and intense international competition can present new challenges demanding social adaptation, just as population growth did in pre-industrial countries.

The nature of the constraints upon change can also alter. A key point to bear in mind when examining current developments is that systems based on centralized administration are unable to adapt flexibly. This thesis is import-ant for our subsequent analysis, so we shall consider it in some detail. As a writer on cybernetics has put it,

> a system directed from the centre is characterized by a very rigid structure and a lack of plasticity. This is because adaptation to changes, whether they arise by chance (fluc-tuations), or as a result of the evolution of the system itself or of its environment, takes place not in the individual parts of the system but only at the central point of direc-tion. Centralized direction allows the system to be stabilized for a long time, by suppressing both fluctuations and evolutionary changes in individual parts of the system, without reconstructing it. But in the final analysis this can prove fatal for the system itself. The contradictions between the unchanging structure of the system and the changes connected with evolution can grow to global proportions. The recon-struction of the system that is required is too sharp and radical to be contained within the existing structure, and leads to its destruction, that is, to a transition to a qualita-tively new structure. (Lerner 1967: 287)

Secondly, in a society on the eve of revolution, the crisis will present not just one challenge with which the society cannot cope, but a whole complex of such challenges, both internal and external. The internal problems may be the result of new demographic, technological, economic, or social processes acting upon that society's mechanisms and its state administration. The exter-nal pressures may also be many and varied. They may arise not only from military threats from more developed states, but also from international competition, or the need to stabilize in response to external 'shocks', such as unexpected demand fluctuations on world markets, world economic crises, world military conflicts, and so forth. The relationship between these factors may be different in each particular case. It is therefore pointless to try to iden-tify one universal causal factor in a pre-revolutionary crisis. We need to explain the fact that at certain moments a society comes up against a whole complex of problems which demand far-reaching changes in the way it oper-ates. This is no coincidence, but a natural expression of crises of economic growth, which occur at very specific stages in the development of every coun-try. This question will be explored in greater detail in Chapter 2.

Thirdly, the types of inbuilt constraints can be just as many and varied, and they can also be divided into internal and external constraints. Internal constraints fall into the following basic categories.

Economic constraints are those economic forms and relations which are either quite unable to react to changing economic circumstances, or which react to them entirely inadequately. The urban guild system of the Middle

Ages and the village commune system[10] are the most obvious examples of these sorts of constraints. The highly monopolized economies of the developed countries at the end of the nineteenth century and the beginning of the twentieth were another type of structure with limited potential for adaptation. The lack of adaptability in the centralized planning system is discussed in Chapter 2.

Social constraints include the various formal and informal mechanisms which limit horizontal and vertical mobility. As new economic possibilities and demands arise, these constraints prevent the formal status of various members of society being brought into line with their real economic and social position. Systems of social estates and various forms of serfdom can be seen as examples of social constraints. The *nomenklatura* and residence registration systems, characteristic of the states of the 'socialist camp' in the twentieth century, can also be put into this category.

Political constraints take two basic forms. On the one hand, there may be no legal mechanisms for replacing the existing régime and its policies where they cannot react adequately to changes in domestic and external circumstances. On the other hand, it may be impossible for new, economically influential groups to secure political representation and acquire institutional opportunities to defend their interests. To a greater or lesser degree these constraints exist in any undemocratic society.

All the above-mentioned constraints have an institutional character. Societies also need to be able to adapt in the socio-cultural, psychological sphere. As Walter Rostow has observed about the process of modernization, 'Psychologically, men must transform or adapt the old culture in ways which make it compatible with modern activities and institutions. The face-to-face relations and warm, powerful family ties of traditional society must give way, in degree, to new, more impersonal systems of evaluation in which men are judged by the way they perform specialized functions in the society' (1971: 58–9). Psychological stereotypes, rooted in traditional society in the economic, political, cultural, and religious spheres, constitute obstacles to this sort of adaptation. Socio-cultural constraints not only have a substantial influence on the ability of society to adapt to change, but can also hinder the removal of institutional constraints. For example, a widely held belief in the divine right of kings might prevent the removal of political constraints and hamper moves towards democratization.

External constraints are particularly prevalent in colonial or semi-colonial countries. They also exist in formally independent countries where their

[10] As recently as the beginning of the 20th century there was a case in Russia where a village commune took legal action against one of its members who had taken the liberty of working on his own plot on a public holiday. This was in violation of the established tradition in that locale, and the court ruled for the commune (Pastukhov 1994: 138).

economies and politics are to a significant extent controlled from outside, by more developed states. The economies and politics of such countries are oriented towards interests imposed from without, rather than to their own interests, and this can prevent those societies from adjusting to solve new problems. Such factors were important in preparing the way for the American War of Independence, the Mexican Revolution, and 'Third World' revolutions.

1.3 Mechanisms for removing constraints

It would be a gross oversimplification to claim that revolution is the only way to overcome the constraints which prevent society from adapting to new challenges. In fact, in all countries the removal of constraints has taken place in a lengthy and contradictory process of development, involving a variety of mechanisms. These mechanisms, besides the revolutionary processes we are examining here, include reforms, revolutions 'from above', and the policies of occupying powers where the country has been conquered or defeated in war.

The most obvious counterweight to revolution as a means of transforming society is reform implemented by the established authorities. It is quite natural that the authorities themselves should seek to introduce reforms, since they more than anyone else feel the pressure of new circumstances and of increasing dissatisfaction among the population. There have been successful examples of such reforms, such as Colbert's in the France of Louis XIV, Peter the Great's in Russia at the end of the seventeenth and beginning of the eighteenth centuries, the complex of reforms implemented in Prussia between 1807 and 1814, and so on. These reforms were for the most part not aimed at undermining the foundations of the existing economic and political order. They were able to mobilize new developmental possibilities within the bounds of existing constraints, or even to remove certain constraints. Consequently the need for more radical changes could be postponed, and the viability of the system could be restored, at least temporarily. Such reforms have played a significant role in the histories of many states, particularly Russia and Germany, by increasing their capacity to adapt.

However, pre-revolutionary régimes have also tried to implement quite radical transformations. Historical studies have almost completely overturned the notion that these régimes were always conservative and reactionary. Charles I initiated large-scale improvements in the way Crown lands were farmed (e.g. by draining the East Anglian fens), and his 'ship money',[11]

---

[11] Ship money was a tax which had existed since Saxon times. It was levied in time of war on the ports and on the maritime towns, cities, and counties of England, and was revived by Charles I with an extended application to inland counties. It was a form of universal direct tax, payable not only by landowners, but townsfolk as well.

however much it was detested at the time, was the first attempt at establishing a modern system of taxation. The French authorities in the pre-revolutionary period actively tried to support the development of industry and agriculture, partly along English lines. Louis XVI attempted to reform the tax system and improve the system of state administration as a whole. Turgot's reforms, although they remained largely confined to paper, included a transformation of the tax system, free trade in grain, the removal of monopolies and the guild system in the towns, and freedom for workers to choose their place of work. The modernizing efforts of the Tsarist régime in Russia had a long history and are widely recognized. None the less, these efforts were not crowned with success and even, according to certain scholars, hastened the advent of revolution.[12]

The same paradox, which at first seems inexplicable, is also found in so-called 'revolutions from above', which have been identified by some writers as a separate category of revolution (see e.g. Trimberger 1978). A characteristic of such revolutions is a change of régime within the pre-existing élite. This entails a change in the political form of government, with the most radical representatives of the existing élite coming to power. The new authorities then proceed beyond political transformations and carry out reforms aimed at a more or less radical removal of the economic and social constraints on society's development. It has been argued that revolutions from above differ from other processes of reform or seizures of power in that the transformations which are pushed through are profound enough to result in the 'destruction of the dominant social group' (Trimberger 1978: 2).

However, almost any revolution will begin as a political revolution, and the change of power will be limited to the existing élite. But in some cases the ruling élite is able to hold on to power, whilst in other cases events slip out of its control, and the revolution turns into a movement 'from below'. The leaders of the Meiji Revolution in Japan (1868) were able to retain power and consolidate the changes they brought about. This did not prove possible, for example, in the French Revolution. As Cobban has noted, the French Revolution started from above, but continued under pressure from below, particularly from the poorest sections of the urban population (see Cobban 1968).

Ellen K. Trimberger, one of the main writers on the phenomenon of revolutions 'from above', argues that where such revolutions succeed, this is primarily becauase of the existence of a powerful bureaucratic apparatus

---

[12] As Brinton has observed, 'Nothing can be more erroneous than the picture of the old régime as an unregenerate tyranny, sweeping to its end in a climax of despotic indifference to the clamor of its abused subjects. Charles I was working to 'modernize' his government. . . . In both France and Russia, there is a series of attempted reforms. . . . It is true that these reforms were incomplete, that they were repealed or nullified by sabotage on the part of the privileged. But they are . . . an essential part of the process which issued in revolution in these countries' (1965: 51–2).

which is not directly linked to the interests of the dominant class, and which therefore in crisis situations is able to sacrifice the interests of that class and bring about profound social transformations.[13] However, if we continue our comparison between the Meiji Revolution and the French Revolution, we cannot help noticing how similar the actions of the authorities were in both cases. François Furet argues that in France the bourgeois revolution was already accomplished without any compromise with the *ancien régime* in 1789–91. Indeed, alongside the transformation of the political structure, that is, the formation of a representative authority and the transition from an absolute to a constitutional monarchy, the system of estates was destroyed and career opportunities were opened to those with ability, general equality before the law was established, and restrictions on the free movement of labour and on trade and enterprise were lifted. The supporters of counter-revolution among the aristocracy emigrated. The question of transforming property relations was, in reality, resolved: the requirement that peasants pay for their redemption from feudal duties existed only on paper. Peasant proprietors withheld the redemption payments envisaged in the decrees of 4–11 August 1789 *en masse*, and the subsequent decisions to release them from this obliga-tion were no more than a juridical recognition of this *fait accompli* (Furet 1981: 125, 127).

As far as the leaders of the Meiji Revolution are concerned, they also destroyed the feudal constraints on the development of trade and production in town and countryside, as well as the barriers to free movement of labour and choice of work. Status restrictions were removed, career opportunities were opened to those with ability, and equality before the law was established. Peasants were granted the right to own land. It could be argued that the Meiji Revolution was very radical in that it facilitated the destruction of the economic and social basis of the traditional aristocracy, the samurai. However, the samurai were a rather unusual dominant class. They lacked their own economic basis and lived on grants of rice from the state. The abolition of these grants was in some respects analogous to the sharp reduction in waste-ful and unproductive court expenditure, which was brought under control in

---

[13] Trimberger asserts that 'revolution from above was made possible in Tokugawa Japan and Ottoman Turkey because state and military bureaucrats were not merely the instru-ment of a dominant economic class. . . . Relatively autonomous bureaucrats are . . . inde-pendent of those classes which control the means of production. . . . Relatively autonomous bureaucrats must be free of connection and control by both internal and international class interests' (1978: 4). Theda Skocpol also considers this to be of the great-est importance for the success of a revolution 'from above': 'Trimberger emphasized that it was only because the reformers *were true bureaucrats*, without landed property or close ties to landowners, that they were willing to take radical steps in bringing about economic and social transformation' (Skocpol 1994: 42).

the initial phases of both the English and the French Revolutions. As for the social class which was really dominant in the countryside and which controlled the peasantry, its position was significantly enhanced by the Meiji Revolution. The class structure of traditional society did not radically break down: 'Bureaucrats in Japan ... agreed to share power with a precapitalist landed class' (Trimberger 1978: 10).

We can conclude from all of this that actions very similar both in their character and in their degree of radicalism had completely opposite results in different countries and under different circumstances. In one case they forestalled a worsening of the crisis and allowed full-scale revolution to be averted, in the other they were powerless to halt the revolutionary process, and may even have accelerated it. We may assume that this different outcome was determined by the different initial conditions in which the authorities began the transformation process. It is to these conditions that we shall now turn.

1.4 Economic development and social fragmentation

It has long been known that pre-revolutionary societies are highly fragmented, divided into many strata and groups opposed to one another. Tocqueville noted the extremely splintered nature of French society, in which 'the homogeneous crowd was divided by an enormous number of petty obstacles into a multitude of parts, each of which forms a special community, concerned with advancing its own interests and taking no part in life as a whole' (Tocqueville 1967: 153). He associated this with the rigid partitions between the estates, which divided society into small groups, alien and indifferent to one another. This phenomenon is also discussed in Jack Goldstone's study (Goldstone 1991), which relates it to population growth and the consequent intensification of competition for land, employment, and state positions. Several writers see pre-revolutionary fragmentation as a result of a breakdown of a single system of values, norms, rules, myths, faiths, symbols, moral codes, and so forth, arguing that 'agreement on social values and norms is the essence of social solidarity' (Rudolph Heberle, cited in Gurr 1970: 136), and that 'any society in which opposed myths are present is to a degree subject to disintegration and faction' (Pettee 1938: 42–5).

It seems to us that the central factor which brought about this high degree of splintering of social forces and interests was a fairly lengthy period of turbulent (for that time) economic development in the pre-revolutionary period, accompanied by the beginning of economic growth and significant structural changes. These processes have occurred in almost all the countries which have undergone full-scale revolutions. In France an active transformation of agriculture took place during the second half of the eighteenth century.[14] The period between 1760 and 1790 saw successful industrial development based on the adoption of the English experience, and is generally regarded as the first phase of the Industrial Revolution (see Fohlen 1973: 68–9). It is well known that there was active growth and industrial development from the end of the 1830s to the middle of the 1840s in Germany and the same is true of Russia in the 1890s and in 1908–13. It is more difficult to say whether this also holds true for England in the pre-revolutionary period, but even here some researchers, most notably John Nef, have situated the earliest phase of the Industrial Revolution in the pre-revolutionary period.[15] In his opinion, from the middle of the sixteenth century up to the beginning of the Civil War there was rapid industrial growth in several sectors and a steep increase in coal extraction.

In the non-European revolutions this is even more evident. In these cases the pre-revolutionary régimes followed an active policy of industrialization and breaking down traditional structures, mainly on the basis of a large-scale influx of foreign capital. In Mexico, for example, the rate of GNP growth between 1884 and 1900 was 8 per cent per annum, and there was active development of railway construction, mining, light industry, and agricultural exports (Bethell 1986: 28–9). In Iran, where the pre-revolutionary period coincided with the oil boom, progress was even more rapid. GNP growth rates, particularly when oil export income was substantial, were extraordinarily high: 8 per cent between 1962 and 1970, 14 per cent in 1972–3, and 30 per cent in 1973–4. The proportion of the population living in towns rose from approximately 28 per cent in 1950 to 47 per cent in 1976. In just twenty years the proportion of peasants and farm workers among the working population fell from 60 per cent to about 30 per cent (McDaniel 1991: 82, 131). This phenomenon of pre-revolutionary growth is analysed in Chapter 7, which is devoted to characteristic revolutionary economic trends.

In the years immediately preceding the outbreak of revolution, rapid growth generally gives way to crisis and decline. This may occur as a result of very poor harvests, or of fluctuations in the terms of international trade, or of political or military failures. Where a society and state are incapable of adapting to the new tendencies stemming from the preceding period of dynamic development, the consequences of these basically cyclical processes of crisis and decline are even more grave. Thus the need to supply foodstuffs to rapidly growing towns can aggravate the consequences of a poor harvest for the peas-

---

[14] 'In France, the beginning of the agricultural revolution was around 1750–60' (Cipolla 1973: 470).

[15] Characterizing the causes of the English Revolution, Nef observed that 'if it had not been for the increased tensions resulting from the early industrial revolution, a settlement might possibly have been reached on . . . other matters without a clash of arms' (1940: 151).

ants. As Barrington Moore noted in his discussion of the difficulties of supplying French cities with grain, 'the pull of a few big cities was felt mainly in times
of scarcity, and then as a disruptive factor' (Moore 1966: 45).[16] The causes of
the long, disastrous famine which immediately preceded the Mexican Revolution have been set out by John M. Hart: 'Mexican agriculture was vulnerable
because the government failed to devote sufficient funds to irrigation and
because of the displacement of peasant cultivators of staple foodstuffs by
export-oriented commercial agriculturalists' (Hart 1987: 165). The dynamics
of industrial production are also affected by outmoded institutional forms.
Some specialists have explained the negative trends in English industrial
production in the pre-revolutionary period partly as a result of excessive sale
of monopoly rights by Charles I and the *ancien régime*'s inadequate foreign
policy (Kosminsky and Levitsky 1954: i. 100–1).

Many researchers have noted the connection between economic growth,
economic development as a whole, and the ripening of the preconditions for
revolution. Mansur Olson, for example, regards rapid growth as the 'major
force leading toward revolution and instability' and as a 'profound destabilizing force' (Olson 1997: 216). Many have also noted the importance of crises
immediately before the outbreak of revolution. But the mechanism by which
economic dynamics can exacerbate the situation has been interpreted in various ways.

Within the Marxist tradition the mechanism is associated mainly with the
ripening of the preconditions for a new, capitalist society, and the emergence
of the bourgeoisie as a class which is economically important but deprived of
social and political rights.[17] There is a struggle between this new class and the
traditional, socially dominant aristocracy, which tries to block change by
supporting the *ancien régime*. This leads ultimately to a revolutionary explosion. However, it has been shown by the so-called 'revisionist'[18] school that in

---

[16] K. P. Dobrolyubsky described the ways in which French cities were supplied in those
circumstances thus: 'Under the old order, in years of famine the absolutist authorities
resorted to banning exports of grain, and reinforced supplies to the cities, especially Paris,
at the expense of the starving provinces (such as the Champagne region in the famine of
1709). They created emergency grain stores, regulated the grain trade, enforced grain sales
and even fixed its price by law' (1930: 14).

[17] This sort of approach was not exclusive to Marxists. Mansur Olson described the
process as follows: 'The fact that there will be some who gain disproportionately from
economic growth means that there will be a new distribution of economic power. But there
will be an (almost Marxian) 'contradiction' between this new distribution of economic
power and the old distribution of social prestige and political power' (1997: 217).

[18] 'The revisionist school' denotes those historians who questioned the Marxist approach
to revolutions on the basis of an analysis of a number of specific cases. They questioned the
notion of revolution as a mechanism of social progress, the idea that revolutions were objective and inevitable, the role of the class struggle in revolutions, and so on. This school
includes such noted students of revolution as Russell, Trevor-Roper, Furet, and Richet.

pre-revolutionary societies the middle (bourgeois) strata were not directly involved in industry or entrepreneurship, and could therefore hardly be regarded as the forerunners of capitalism. Moreover, it was certainly not always the case that the way 'up the social ladder' was closed to such people. The acquisition of landed property or state positions, as well as marriages between members of different strata and estates, made it possible to a large extent to circumvent the barriers to 'vertical mobility'.[19] As we have shown above, pre-revolutionary régimes have in most cases not been particularly conservative.

Other researchers consider that political 'stability and instability are ultimately dependent on a state of mind, a mood in a society' (Davies 1997a: 136). In their view, the conditions for revolution ripen as a result of popular disillusionment when expectations have been raised by a fairly lengthy period of economic and social development, which has then given way to a sharp decline.[20] However, this explanation is also open to question. As Theda Skocpol has correctly observed, a revolutionary crisis may be used by a revolutionary vanguard to mobilize the disaffected masses, but it cannot be created by that vanguard (1979: 16–18). How that crisis, which manifests itself primarily as a crisis of the state, arises in the first place requires special explanation.

It seems to us that there is nonetheless a direct link between economic changes and the ripening of the conditions for revolution. However, the connection is not as linear as the approaches considered above suggest. In order to understand the interdependencies which exist here, we shall examine in greater detail the effect of economic changes on the social structure of pre-revolutionary societies.

It is immediately obvious that processes of economic change have far-reaching effects on social organization, which moves ever further away from the stability characteristic of traditional systems, with their rigid social structure, held together by vertical links, in which the different types of social stratification do not come into conflict with one another. In traditional systems the position and incomes of each social stratum find their justification in the functions each is obliged to fulfil. This makes the system stable and legitimizes its existence not only in the eyes of the élite, but also in the eyes of the masses. The beginning of dynamic economic development changes the situation

---

[19] In the 18th century alone some 6,500 families acquired noble status. Guy Chaussinand-Nogaret (1985: 28) has calculated that they constituted one quarter of the total population of nobles in France.

[20] 'Revolutions are most likely to occur when a prolonged period of objective economic and social development is followed by a short period of sharp reversal. The all-important effect on the minds of people in a particular society is to produce, during the former period, an expectation of continued ability to satisfy needs—which continue to rise—and, during the latter, a mental state of anxiety and frustration when manifest reality breaks away from anticipated reality' (Davies 1997a: 136)

fundamentally. The bases of the traditional social structure are undermined, there is a large-scale redistribution of wealth, and new economically signific-ant social forces arise.

It is true that societies in a pre-revolutionary period have already moved quite some way from their traditional, patriarchal state, and the traditional relationships within them have been significantly eroded. This process of erosion accelerates sharply in the decades immediately preceding the revolu-tion. Knut Borchardt's characterization of the situation in Germany prior to 1848 could be applied to any pre-revolutionary country: 'The rapid reversals of fortune, the alternation of prosperity and disaster, helped to shake and loosen the traditional structure of the economy. Few remained unaffected by the redistribution of economic opportunities and of real and monetary prop-erty to which this contributed: all this reduced the weight of tradition and custom' (Borchardt 1973: 94).

However, this dynamic process takes place within traditional social confines. This means that social stratification by status and access to power cannot be brought into line with the new distribution of wealth. None the less, as we have noted, social mobility has not been completely blocked. The tradi-tional system gradually transforms itself under the pressure of the new circumstances, but does not completely disappear. Old and new elements coexist within it in a state of irreconcilable contradiction. The superimposi-tion of this new stratification, resulting from economic development, onto the traditional system of status gives rise to a specific phenomenon—the pre-revolutionary fragmentation of society.[21] This fragmentation is the result of the pressure of new processes brought about by economic growth, and, more generally, dynamic economic changes, on the inbuilt constraints within the social structure.

[21] Although both fragmentation and economic change are often looked at among the causes of revolution, their interconnections are examined very rarely. For this reason Arnold Feldman's article 'Violence and Volatility The Likelihood of Revolution' (Feldman 1964), which considers the question of the preconditions for revolution, is of great inter-est. The starting point for fragmentation, in Feldman's opinion, is differentiation in status systems associated with the process of industrialization, as a result of which a 'more or less tightly integrated and relatively undifferentiated social system is transformed gradually into a system which contains many separate and functionally specific subsystems' (119). The interrelations between the different status systems are extraordinarily complex, since, on the one hand, the 'newly differentiated systems are born out of strain and conflict and differentiation may separate conflicting norms like kinship obligations vs. market criteria for recruitment and evaluation of labour' (120), while, on the other hand, 'differentiated systems do intersect and interpenetrate' (121). Societies in such a situation have different, intersecting systems for distributing social status. The systems are internally coherent, but conflict with one another. Consequently, 'societies undergoing fragmentation are likely to be rife with status inconsistency among individuals and status ambiguity in comparisons of individuals and groups' (121). In Feldman's view, 'the over-all process of fragmentation contributes to a society's revolutionary potential' (121).

In a pre-revolutionary society not only the élite strata fragment, but also the mass of the population. Contradictions within as well as between groups become more acute. At the same time this fragmentation greatly complicates the system of economic and social interests, further breaking it down, exacerbating conflicts, and making it impossible to form stable social coalitions.

We can characterize the processes leading to the fragmentation of society in the pre-revolutionary period as follows.

First, there is an accumulation of wealth in the hands of new economic agents, while at least a part of the traditional aristocracy experiences serious economic problems. There is consequently a growing discrepancy between, on the one hand, social stratification by wealth, and on the other, stratification by status and access to power. A part of the new economic élite finds its way into the ranks of the highest castes, intensifying the contradictions within them and affecting the evolution of their interests. Another part, the so-called 'marginal élites', remains excluded from the advantages and privileges of the ruling élite, and poses a threat to the stability of the existing system.

Secondly, the role and function of traditional economic agents changes. Social stratification intensifies among the peasantry, leading to an increasing divergence of interests between the richer and poorer sections.[22] The landlords become more involved in the market[23] and therefore less inclined to conserve patriarchal relations with their peasants, protect them, or help them through hard times.[24] On the other hand, they are less willing to remain the obedient subjects of a suzerain who has untrammelled power. The system of vertical interdependence gradually begins to give way to horizontal connections.

---

[22] It is noteworthy that in relation to Russia this process was examined by Lenin in one of his first economic works, *The Development of Capitalism in Russia* (Lenin, *CW* iii).

[23] The reaction of landowners to a widening of the sphere of market relations will vary from country to country. The enclosures in England destroyed the traditionally established balance of rights and customs. Conversely, in France an increase in farm incomes was largely the result of resurrecting long-forgotten feudal obligations in the period of the so-called 'seigneurial reaction'. The contradictory nature of this process has stimulated discussion among specialists on the French Revolution about how the changes in French agriculture in the pre-revolutionary period should be interpreted. Were they an essentially retrograde 'seigneurial reaction', or were they a 'seigneurial modernization'—an appropriate commercial reaction to wider opportunities profitably to sell grain and other agricultural produce? In fact, this sort of contradictoriness is quite typical of a transitional epoch, in which the old and the new coexist and are closely intermingled.

[24] As Tocqueville observed, in the 14th century 'the peasant was more oppressed, but he received more assistance. And although the nobles sometimes treated him harshly, they never abandoned him to the whims of fate', whereas in the pre-revolutionary period, 'especially in years of famine it was evident that the ties of patronage and dependence, which had at one time bound the large landowner and peasant together, were weakened or broken' (1967: 210, 219). In relation to pre-revolutionary England it has also been observed that 'the ties grew thinner between lord and peasant' (Wallerstein 1974: 259).

Within the élite these processes lead to a variety of tensions and conflicts. On the one hand, there is pressure from those social strata whose real role does not correspond to their formal status. On the other hand, the conflict deepens within the ruling social group, who is divided into a multitude of groups and clans, and unable to unite around their common interests.[25] This fragmentation cuts across the traditional lines of demarcation within the élite of the old society, such as the aristocracy, gentry, knights, and nobles. Economic development has had various effects upon different members of each stratum, and their interests have become divergent, sometimes even directly opposed. Many writers have remarked upon a paradoxical feature of pre-revolutionary societies, that contradictions within a particular class or social stratum may be considerably sharper than contradictions between different classes and strata.

The well-known discussion as to whether pre-revolutionary England witnesses the elevation of the gentry and the ruination of the old aristocracy never reached a definite conclusion. However, it did show clearly that within both groups there was an active process of differentiation regarding property and approaches to economic activity. As Christopher Hill observed, 'The inflationary century before 1640 was a great watershed, in which, in all sections of the community, economic divisions were taking place. Some yeomen were thriving to gentility; others were being submerged. Some peers were accumulating vast estates; others were on the verge of bankruptcy' (Hill 1958a: 8). Additionally, part of the upper aristocracy was becoming involved in entrepreneurial activity.[26] Similarly, in pre-revolutionary France the aristocracy was becoming actively involved in commerce,[27] while the provincial gentry in the main remained a conservative force, with an interest in maintaining traditional relations. In many respects there were analogous phenomena in Russia at the beginning of the twentieth century. Overall the landowning class

---

[25] As François Furet observed of the French Revolution: 'these two phenomena—on the one hand, a heavy bourgeois pressure to enter an increasingly crowded and perhaps proportionally more selective field and, on the other, beyond the dividing line, the conflict among different sections of the nobility—do not contradict but complement each other' (1981: 107–8).

[26] The importance of the aristocracy at this period is due rather to their willingness to encourage and finance new ventures, which were regarded as risky and therefore failed to secure the backing of more cautious social groups. Since large-scale mining and metallurgy were still novelties in the Tudor period they took the lead in their expansion. Since oceanic trade and exploration were novelties they again played a prominent part (Stone 1957: 61).

[27] From the beginning of the 18th century the upper echelons of the aristocracy took an active part both in the creation of banking institutions and in the initial stages of industrialization. One of the most important textile factories in the pre-revolutionary period belonged to the Duc d'Orléans (see Fohlen 1973: 32, 64). According to Guy Chaussinand-Nogaret (1985: 123), the main capitalist enterprises in the most advanced sectors—cotton and metallurgy—belonged to nobles.

experienced significant difficulties in adapting to the processes of modernization, and its decline accelerated, especially after the 1905 revolution. At the
same time there were numerous exceptions to this rule. In western Ukraine,
for example, the landowners were fairly successful in commercializing agriculture (McDaniel 1991: 152–6). The unity of interests among the Russian
landed aristocracy was also eroded by its increasing involvement in industrial
activity. At the turn of the century 82 of the 102 largest landowners were sole
or joint owners of 500 industrial enterprises. Of 1,482 joint-stock companies
surveyed in 1901–2, no fewer than 800 were headed by descendants of the
nobility (Munting 1996: 339).

As we can see, there are numerous divisions within the élite, and they fit
together in a complex and variegated mosaic of forces and interests pulling in
different directions. There are economically powerful social groups excluded
from the élite, 'parvenus', who are not fully accepted by the traditional élite
(which itself has always been heterogeneous) but who in their turn are trying
to prevent any further influx; there is the flourishing section of the traditional
élite, the section facing ruin, and so on. That part of the old aristocracy which
has become involved in commerce may, for example, have many interests in
common with entrepreneurs from lowlier backgrounds,[28] but will be sepa-
rated from them by traditional caste barriers.

Redistribution of wealth is only one of the factors which can increase
tensions within the ranks of the élite. The gradual, ongoing transformation of
the machinery of the state, and the increased competition for privileges and
state positions resulting from population growth, also have a significant influence. These are not simply conflicts between individuals or clans. A complicated system of contradictory economic, political, and social interests
develops within the élite, and different groupings within the élite will have a
different configuration of interests.

The growing fragmentation of the population as a whole in the decades
preceding the revolution is no less important. This is associated with increasing social stratification, as people find their sources of livelihood linked either
to the traditional or to the new economic structures. Here again differences in
economic interests underlie the differentiation. A process of polarization
occurs within the peasantry, separating a richer upper stratum from the land-
less peasants. The traditional guild system is faced with competition from
factories and mills, and contradictions arise between the urban masters and
the new entrepreneurs. The positions of merchants, entrepreneurs, and
financiers become differentiated according to how closely their commercial

---

[28] 'The aristocrat, who was freed from the feudal obligation to protect the serf, provide
him with lodging, feed him in hard times and maintain him in possession of his land,
became an agricultural entrepreneur. He improved efficiency, increased production,
reduced costs, and proceeded to devour his weaker competitors' (Hamerow 1958: 47).

activities are associated with the interests of the existing régime. This again can sow the seeds of many conflicts. In his analysis of the mandates of the different estates to the French Estates-General in 1789, François Furet commented that many of them 'set rich and poor peasants at odds over the sharing of common pastures, shopkeepers and guild masters over freedom to work, bishops and priests over the democratization of the Church, nobility and clergy over the freedom of the press'. He came to the overall conclusion that a 'society of 'status' and 'rank' was supremely one of particularisms' (Furet 1981: 58). These factors had a substantial influence on the course of the revolutionary process. As Jack Goldstone has put it, 'revolutions . . . generally show a host of conflicts rooted in low-level social structures that more directly touch popular groups than conflicts involving the national government' (1991: 49).

1.5 Social fragmentation and revolution

A period of active economic development, with its concomitant fragmentation of society, leads to a severe weakening of the state. It becomes increasingly likely that the conflict between the new processes and the constraints that are woven into the social fabric will be resolved in a revolutionary way. This is not simply a matter of the existing authorities' inability to take decisive measures. There have been cases in history when pre-revolutionary régimes have had a very inadequate grasp of the tasks facing society and their actions have only made matters worse. There have, however, been examples of the opposite, when authorities in a pre-revolutionary period have grasped the need for changes and made active attempts to implement them.

Even so, conditions of growing crisis and social fragmentation provide an extremely unfavourable environment in which to bring about these changes. First, the authorities are unable to carry out long-range policies, because they are constantly obliged to use all available instruments to avert financial collapse, even where such measures conflict with their long-term goals.[29] Secondly, they are constantly bombarded with quite irreconcilable demands, as different sections of society and groups within the élite expect diametrically opposed measures from them. Any attempt to satisfy one section will

---

[29] Jack Goldstone describes the actions of Charles I prior to the English Revolution as follows: 'Many of these projects were highly commercial and progressive—rent increases to market levels on Crown lands, partnerships to enclose and exploit fens and forests, and sale of trading privileges for international and domestic commerce [from our authors' point of view the last action can hardly be considered progressive]. Other projects were conservative and feudal—tighter rules of wardship to bring revenue to the Crown, requirement of gentry to take up knighthood, and sales of tithes and offices. But all these policies had in common the search for increased revenues' (1991: 80–1).

inevitably lead to more active resistance on the part of all the others. In this complex mosaic of forces and interests, all pulling in different directions, no package of changes proposed by the existing authorities can gain social support. It is almost certain that the balance of interests 'against' will outweigh the balance of interests 'for'.[30]

Finding themselves in an increasingly hopeless situation, the authorities start to waver, at times going along with radical attitudes, at other times trying to take refuge within the familiar boundaries of the traditional system; sometimes being excessively rigid, and sometimes agreeing to senseless compromises.[31] As a result the régime becomes ever more vulnerable. It loses its base both among its traditional supporters and among the newer social strata, and becomes the object of general dissatisfaction, albeit for diametrically opposed reasons. State power continues to weaken.

In this sort of situation the options available to the existing régime for preserving social stability become very limited. The revolution in Iran and the collapse of the Soviet empire seem to have given an unambiguous answer to the question which for so long intrigued specialists on the theory of revolution: 'Had Charles I in 1640, Louis XVI in 1789, Nicholas II in 1917 or others had strong and reliable security forces which they were willing to use to repress dissidents, who can say with certainty that revolution would have broken out at that time, if at all?' (Hagopian 1974: 157) The army and police are not forces independent of society, its ruling ideas and attitudes. The upper echelon of the officer corps is one of the most important sections of the ruling élite, and a crisis within that élite cannot leave it untouched. Therefore if the existing régime loses social support and confidence among the élite, the possibility of using force to suppress unrest is greatly reduced.[32]

The start of the revolutionary process does not remove the innumerable conflicts and contradictions which exist within pre-revolutionary society. The new authorities, assuming power in the first stage of the revolution, the stage

---

[30] François Furet has stressed the role played in preparing the ground for the French Revolution by the lack of consensus within the élite on the direction of reform: 'Every action by the State provoked intense hostility in a large part of the ruling élites, which were never united, either in favour of enlightened despotism, for example, or in favour of liberal reforms' (1981: 113–14).

[31] In the absence of consensus among the élite, observed Furet, 'the action taken by the monarchy in dealing with the central problem of taxation wavered between despotism and capitulation' (1981: 113).

[32] It is only when a régime in a crisis remains able to manoeuvre, and to 'buy' the social support of at least a part of the discontented, that it can use force against the other part. The 1905 revolution in Russia is a prime example of this, although it is usually cited to show that it is possible to suppress a revolution by using forcible methods. The Tsarist régime was in no position to use force until it had made concessions to the principal political demands of the bourgeois parties. Only once it had regained bourgeois support, albeit temporarily, could the régime suppress the revolutionary movement 'from below'.

of the 'revolution from above', inherit the situation in which the *ancien régime* fell. Society remains fragmented, and the diversity of forces and interests undermines the possibility of any kind of long-range policy 'from above'. The different fates of the leaders of the Meiji Revolution in Japan on the one hand, and of the leaders of the first phase of the French Revolution on the other, were far more a consequence of the extent of social fragmentation caused by the preceding period of economic change than of the degree of radicalism of their programmes.

It has recently been shown that Japan before the Meiji Revolution was not in a state of complete stagnation, as had previously been thought. Current estimates suggest that between 1830 and 1860 the average per capita increase in GDP was between 0.1 and 0.15 per cent per annum (Melyantsev 1996: 245). Trade was developing in Japan, and a process of proto-industrialization was under way (see Hanley and Yamamura 1977). The problems faced by the Tokugawa shogunate in the mid-nineteenth century resembled other pre-revolutionary situations: 'Foreigners were seeking access to Japanese trade. Internally, finances were precarious, the traditional status system and grada-tions of wealth were in disarray, and popular uprisings were growing more frequent' (Goldstone 1991: 411).

None the less, the destabilizing effect on the traditional structures was less severe than in other countries under the *ancien régime*. There are at least three factors which can be cited in support of this hypothesis. First, although economic growth in Japan did not cease, the rates of growth were significantly lower than in France in the latter half of the eighteenth century, where they may have exceeded 0.6 per cent,[33] or even than in England in the middle of the seventeenth century, which have been estimated at between 0.2 and 0.23 per cent per annum (see Meyantsev 1996: 93, 248). Secondly, the level of economic development attained by Japan by the second half of the nineteenth century was substantially lower than that of France at the end of the eight-eenth century or even of England in the mid-seventeenth century. Japan's per capita GDP was about one third lower than the pre-revolutionary levels of France and England (see Table 2.2). Thirdly, the fact that Japan was closed to the outside world, its policy of isolationism, meant that instability on the world market could not affect its internal situation. A further demonstration that Japan's pre-revolutionary contradictions were less developed is that although the existing régime had been substantially weakened, its internal crisis was not deep enough for revolution to break out spontaneously. Power changed hands only as a result of an external threat. What has been said about Japan is even more applicable to other cases of successful 'revolution from above'. They all took place in less developed countries, where the traditional structures had not been seriously shaken by rapid economic development.

---

[33] This estimate is based on Melyantsev (1996: 248).

Thus there existed the possibility of effecting the transformations 'from above' while preserving the relative passivity and subordination of the masses, without their becoming involved in active politics.

In countries (such as France at the end of the eighteenth century) which were already more developed and were still developing rapidly, economic changes had affected the entire system of social relations from top to bottom. Consequently, various sections of society sought to involve themselves in the process of change, in order to defend their interests. In such circumstances, the 'revolution from above' inevitably faced an insoluble dilemma. To agree to repress the movement 'from below' would be to compromise with the *ancien régime*, and the revolution would be left defenceless against the forces of reaction. This was the course taken by the German revolution of 1848 and the Russian revolution of 1905, and it ultimately determined their defeat. However, to rely on mass activity would inevitably carry the revolution beyond the bounds acceptable to even the most radical sections of the old élite. A new stage would begin, the 'revolution from below'.

Fragmentation is not only the central factor determining the inevitability of revolution; it also has the most decisive effect upon the course of events. Recent writers have drawn attention to the extraordinary heterogeneity of the forces taking part in a revolution. It has been claimed of the English Revolution that 'the pattern of conflict is not one of sharp and clear divisions; instead myriad local struggles differently shaped the conflict in different locales' (Goldstone 1991: 81). This thesis has been applied particularly to the French revolution, in which many specialists have identified three quite different currents or even three simultaneous revolutions. There was a bourgeois revolution, also described as an 'élite revolution' or a 'revolution of the enlightenment', which advocated free enterprise. There was a peasant revolution to seize land for redistribution and for the restoration of the rights of village communes, which was equally hostile to the seigneurs and the bourgeois. There was also an egalitarian revolution of the urban poor, which rejected the right of private property, subordinating it to 'the just demands of society'.[34] We can see the same heterogeneity in Germany in 1848: 'The truth is that there was no German Revolution of 1848. There were, rather, several simultaneous German revolutions, each with its own ideology and objective, all combining their efforts to achieve the overthrow of an oppressive system of government' (Hamerow 1958: 260). Three currents can be identified here, too: a middle-class movement of bourgeois character, peasant revolts, and urban uprisings, in which artisans were the main force. The aims of these three forces differed substantially: 'To the bourgeois liberal it meant the establishment of a new nation of parliamentary government and material

---

[34] Such an approach to the French Revolution is quite widespread among present-day historians of the so-called revisionist school. See e.g. Hunecke (1970).

prosperity. To the guild master it meant the restoration of corporate control over industrial production. To the peasant it meant above all the abolition of manorialism and the redistribution of landed property' (ibid. 156). Nor were the tendencies outlined above internally homogeneous. As Goldstone observes, 'peasant conflicts often involve revolutionary and counterrevolutionary peasant villages pitted against each other, while urban conflicts involve various groups of workers and urban élites on opposite sides' (1991: 49).

Moreover, not all the forces which take part in the revolutionary process have an interest in breaking down the barriers which prevent society adapting to the new requirements of the time. Alongside the movement to destroy the constraints on further development, 'rebellious constraints' appear, in the form of actions by those social forces who, in defence of their economic and social interests, come out against the new measures, even those which were brought in by the *ancien régime*. It is necessary to note that these 'rebellious constraints' do not appear only on the counter-revolutionary side. They are a most important component of the revolutionary forces themselves.

The ideology of 'rebellious constraints' may be articulated by patriarchal peasants, urban artisans, or traditionalist clergy. They openly propagate their anti-modernist programme in the course of the revolution. When the German revolution of 1848 was in full swing, a declaration was placed before the Frankfurt Parliament containing the main demands of the urban artisans, the first point of which was: 'We declare ourselves most firmly opposed to industrial freedom, and we demand that it be abolished insofar as it exists in Germany by a special paragraph of the fundamental law of the nation' (Hamerow 1958: 143–4). The French Convention more than once considered the propositions that 'freedom of trade in grain is incompatible with the existence of the republic' and that 'foodstuffs are the property of the people' (Dobrolyubsky 1930: 20, 28).

This element of 'rebellious constraints' has appeared in various revolutions to a differing extent, although not one of them has managed to avoid it completely. It was least important in the English Revolution,[35] where only the movement of clubmen, in defence of traditional relations and values, can be put into this category. It was far more important in the course of the French Revolution, when the economic policy of the Jacobins was to a large extent determined by the demands of the urban and rural poor, who came out against free trade and the destruction of patriarchal relationships in the countryside.[36] 'Rebellious constraints' played a substantial role in the Mexican revolution of 1910 and the Iranian revolution of 1979.

---

[35] Trevor-Roper (1953), in effect, ascribes the ideology of rebellious constraints in the English Revolution to that section of the gentry whose position was getting worse.

[36] Analyzing the policies of the Jacobin Convention, Dobrolyubsky observed that 'all attempts to avoid introducing maximalist measures were futile: like the terror, they were imposed upon the Convention from below' (1930: 34).

Continuing fragmentation ensures that the state remains weak throughout the entire period of revolutionary transformations, as the fates of the succession of régimes depend entirely on temporary and unstable coalitions of the extraordinarily diverse forces taking part in the revolutionary process. Only when the revolutionary transformations have brought about the conditions for the emergence of a new élite, capable of acting as the basis for a stable state, does the revolutionary process reach its conclusion. A crucial feature of revolutions is that the transformation of society takes place under conditions where the state is weak, and unable to control the course of events and processes. François Furet's comment on the French Revolution can be taken as a universal description of the revolutionary process in general: 'The fact is that between 1789 and 1794 the revolutionary tide, though dammed up and channelled by groups that successively came to power—having first fallen in line with it—was never really controlled by anyone, because it was made up of too many opposing aims and interests' (Furet 1981: 124). The diversity of the forces participating in the revolution, and the spontaneous character of the transformation of social relations, ensure that the results of the revolutionary process will be ambiguous.

1.6 The results of the revolution and post-revolutionary development

The effect of a revolution on the historical development of one or another country is not only one of those problems on which consensus can never be reached, but a problem on which there are diametrically opposed, irreconcilable points of view. Revolutions can be seen as a complete break with the past, or as having had no important influence, with post-revolutionary development regarded as a direct continuation of pre-revolutionary development; as having opened up new prospects for social development, or as having slowed down those positive processes which had begun to develop in the pre-revolutionary period. The conceptual approach we set out in this book views revolutions as one of the mechanisms for overcoming the inbuilt constraints preventing society from adapting to new conditions. Consequently, the first question which arises is: to what extent does a revolution result in the removal of these constraints and the creation of the preconditions for further evolutionary development? There can be no simple and unambiguous answer to this question, as there are at least three possible outcomes.

1. The constraints may be removed by methods which allow the system as a whole to become more adaptable and able to respond to change, whatever the changes may be. In this case the preconditions are created for the long-term evolution of that society, and although the emergence of new problems in the future may lead to serious conflicts and tensions, they will be resolved

in a non-revolutionary fashion. This is the most favourable outcome of a revolution, but in practice no revolution has ever led entirely to such a result.

2. Only those constraints are removed which prevented the society from adapting to the specific circumstances which pushed it towards revolution. The system remains inflexible, and when fundamentally new problems arise its adaptability proves to be inadequate. A society in such circumstances shows a great deal of stability in the short and perhaps even medium term, but in the long term it will face new revolutionary upheavals.

3. In the course of the revolution some of the constraints may be removed, but others may be preserved or even strengthened. Additionally, the revolution itself may give rise to new constraints which did not exist under the *ancien régime*. In these circumstances the adaptive capacities of the post-revolutionary society prove inadequate, and the problem of inbuilt constraints persists into the post-revolutionary period. The likelihood of further revolutionary upheavals remains, but these are not inevitable since the constraints may be removed by other means.

The factors which influence the outcome of a revolution and determine the different degrees of adaptability of the post-revolutionary society are many and varied. We shall try to identify them in general terms, to demonstrate the interconnection between the preconditions and consequences of revolution.

All other things being equal, the likelihood that the existing constraints will be destroyed is directly proportional to the pressure of the new circumstances which make adaptation essential. Both in France as a result of the revolution of 1789, and in Russia as a result of the revolution of 1917, peasants tended to become 'middle' peasants. This did not fully remove the economic constraints upon further development. It did not create very favourable conditions for carrying through industrialization and achieving rapid economic growth, either in terms of the volume of the internal market, or by ensuring a supply of cheap labour for industry. For France this meant that French commodities could not compete with British ones, thus preserving British economic hegemony in Europe and throughout the world. However, there was at that time no threat of more dangerous consequences, such as the loss of national independence or relegation to the status of a third-rate power.

In Russia, the task of rapid industrialization in the early twentieth century was regarded as a matter of life and death. Although Stalin's well-known phrase[37] may have dramatized the situation somewhat, it was not far from the truth. The balance of forces which had emerged as a result of the revolution was changed violently in the course of Thermidor: the collectivization of agriculture allowed an almost unlimited redistribution of resources for the needs

---

[37] 'We are fifty or a hundred years behind the advanced countries. We must make good this distance in ten years. Either we do it, or we shall go under' (Stalin, *Works*, xiii. 41).

of industrialization. In Japan the problem of removing the barriers to industrialization was also solved fairly successfully, and 'it was the inescapable and potentially mortal nature of the challenge faced by Japan after 1853 which explains its subsequent pursuit of modernization with greater single-mindedness than post-1815 Europe' (Rostow 1971a: 71).

However, the rigid, single-minded nature of the post-revolutionary system is determined by the very urgency and obvious dangers of the problems the country faces, and by the concentration of all forces and the mobilization of all resources to solve them. In creating the possibility of accelerated development in the short term, the post-revolutionary system carries within itself the potential for new conflicts and upheavals. Thus, the stronger the pressure of new circumstances, the less likely it is that the system as a whole will acquire the flexibility and adaptability to deal with any further new developments and changes. It is also more likely that the second pattern outlined above for removing constraints will be followed.

Most important of all for securing the system's long-term adaptability is the removal of political constraints. However, any revolutionary process creates unfavourable conditions for doing this. The restoration of the state which marks the end of the revolution usually involves the establishment of a strong authoritarian régime, which is able to put an end to the anarchy and uncertainty of the revolutionary period and to return society to a state of equilibrium. This means that in one form or another, the political constraints will be preserved. To ensure that the country can move towards stable evolutionary development, it is of crucial importance when and how these constraints are removed.

In this regard it is instructive to compare the English and French Revolutions. Overall, the results of the French Revolution seem to represent a vastly more radical break with the past than do those of the English Revolution. One might therefore assume that the French Revolution provided far greater scope for social development. In reality, however, it was England that remained free from further revolutionary upheavals, whereas France subsequently underwent a whole series of revolutions. The explanation for this is that as a result of the English Revolution of the 1640s and 1650s and the 'Glorious Revolution' of 1688, a political system was established which was capable of self-development. It could adapt to changing circumstances in the country and reflect newly emergent political and economic interests. Therefore the country could continue its development along an evolutionary path, through reforms implemented 'from above' by the existing political régime. The outcome in France was quite the opposite. The revolution was unable to secure the removal of the political constraints or the establishment of a political order able to adapt to changing circumstances. Consequently France went through a long period of revolutions and social convulsions, and did not acquire a stable political system until the second half of the twentieth century.

The example given above illustrates very well the proposition that a revolution will remove inbuilt constraints to a degree that is inversely proportional to the rigidity of these constraints. In other words, the more thoroughly a system needs to be reconstructed in order to be able to adapt to new demands, the less likely it is that it will be reconstructed all at once, even if it undergoes what seems to be a radical revolutionary break with the past. The role of 'rebellious constraints' in the revolutionary process is also directly associated with the rigidity of the barriers to adaptation. The extent to which this element is active is to a large degree determined by the historical traditions of the country and the depth of the changes necessary for solving the problems faced by society.

Obviously, the rigidity of existing barriers is determined by the unique historical experience of each country. Douglas North and Robert Thomas have argued that as early as the fourteenth and fifteenth centuries historical circumstances determined the different extents of the power of the monarchs and the different principles underlying the tax systems in England and France, which were to be of crucial importance in their subsequent development:

In the former, parliament had been able to wrest control over taxing power from the monarch. In the latter, the chaos of the fifteenth century, in which all property rights were insecure, had led the Estates General to give up power over taxes to Charles VII in return for a promise of increased order and protection against marauding bands of mercenaries and English invaders. In the process of keeping his promise, the French king eliminated his close rivals, placing the Crown in a better position to demand a larger share of the social savings generated by government. (North and Thomas 1973: 98)

Consequently, in France political constraints were much more rigid than in England. The French kings had gained the possibility of regulating the lives of their subjects on a much greater scale, and this created barriers to adaptation in various spheres. By contrast, in England the citizens preserved a substantial degree of independence from the authorities, and this made for a fairly high level of flexibility in the system even in the pre-revolutionary period.

If we look at the way production was regulated, similar approaches were taken in both England and France, based on rigid controls over enterprises, support for the guild system, and corresponding restrictions on the extent of markets, the number of producers, production methods, prices, and wages. As John Nef has observed, '[during] the eighty years preceding the civil war, Elizabeth and her two Stuart successors did everything in their power to build up a comprehensive system of industrial regulations to cover the expanding manufactures of the country. Their objectives very closely resembled those of the French kings who were their contemporaries. They also sought to regulate wages in the national interest' (Nef 1940: 31). The main difference was that the French authorities were able to ensure compliance with their decisions on these matters, while in England for the most part the regulations existed only on paper. To quote Nef again: '[in] the early seventeenth century the power of the king and his advisers to enforce their will in matters of industrial production was undermined in England at the very time when it was greatly strengthened in France' (ibid. 38).

In other words, the extent of the 'inbuilt constraints' was quite different in the two countries. In England fairly moderate changes were all that was needed to secure the necessary adaptability, whereas in France an outwardly much more radical revolution was unable fully to achieve this end.

Finally, as far as the destruction of various types of inbuilt constraints is concerned, the consequences of 'revolution from above' and of 'revolution from below' can be quite different. The most obvious difference is in the effect upon socio-cultural constraints. Revolution 'from above' is usually unable to make any serious impact upon these. Since there is no large-scale involvement of the masses in bringing about change, they do not take part in the real struggles which would allow them to accumulate the experience necessary for overcoming centuries-old stereotypes.[38] Conversely, in a revolution 'from below' there is a significant advance in surmounting traditional socio-cultural stereotypes as the masses are brought into active politics, and extend their horizons beyond the usual confines of their everyday lives. A decisive break with the past, in both ideology and practice, which characterizes the radical phase of any social revolution plays an important role here. For example, the execution of the monarch, which happened in practically every great revolution, dealt a devastating blow to the idea of the divine origins of monarchical power.

As for economic barriers, either type of revolution may have a contradictory effect on them, although a revolution 'from above', which does not have to take direct account of the interests of the 'rebellious constraints', is likely to be more radical, at least in the short term. Conversely, the likelihood of removing political constraints in a revolution 'from above' even more remote than in revolutions 'from below'. Not only is power exercised by authoritarian means, but no stable political régime will be formed. This is a natural consequence of the narrowness and uncertainty of the social base of an administration that is established by a revolution 'from above'. Such a revolution bears the seeds of serious political cataclysms to come.

At the same time both kinds of revolutions usually succeed in removing social constraints, by destroying barriers to horizontal mobility and by opening up career opportunities to those with ability. Certain revolutions with a significant national-liberation component have also been successful in remov-

---

[38] 'A revolution from above which had not freed the peasant from tradition, paternalism, and submissive values had not educated him to recognize his own economic interests' (Trimberger 1978: 115).

ing external constraints, either by winning national independence or by significantly restricting the power of foreign countries to determine their conditions of economic and political development.

1.7 Other ways of removing constraints

Since revolutions do not usually sweep away all obstacles to development, it is interesting to look more closely at other ways of achieving this end. We have already analysed mechanisms, such as reforms and revolutions 'from above', which fall short of full-scale revolution. Constraints may be removed by a combination of the methods listed above. When a social revolution has suffered defeat, political reaction is usually accompanied by active attempts by the *ancien régime* to forestall any future revolutionary upheavals. Efforts are made to modernize 'from above', which differ substantially both from attempts at reform made in a pre-revolutionary period and from the type of 'revolution from above' we have been examining. The basic difference is that these reforms are obliged to accept as given the configuration of social forces which has emerged from the revolution, and to engage in active social manœuvring not only within the élite, but on a wider social basis.

After the 1848 revolution in Germany, the conservatives, having returned to power, hastened to complete the agrarian reform, because they 'saw in agriculture not only the foundation of national greatness, but also a counterweight to liberal industrialism' (Hamerow 1958: 219). They were obliged to look for a golden mean between the interests of growing entrepreneurialism and those of declining artisan production, and also to make a serious move towards satisfying the interests of the working class. The 1905 revolution in Russia also gave impetus to the régime's measures to reconstruct social relations, particularly to destroy the village communes which, against the Tsarist authorities' expectations, had turned out to be an active revolutionary force. Even so, these changes were usually no more than fairly limited reforms, and were accompanied by moves backwards in many areas where the revolution had achieved significant successes in removing barriers to further development. Despite this, the ability of the régime to manoeuvre and take account of the interests of various strata of the population increased, and so changes 'from above', aimed at adapting the existing structures and institutions to the changing balance of social forces, were able to play a substantial role in removing constraints.

The last way in which constraints to further development can be removed is when changes in social relations are imposed by external forces. This may occur through conquest by more developed countries, or may be imposed upon countries with a comparable level of development but with more archaic institutional structures. The Napoleonic Wars had this kind of effect by spreading the achievements of the French Revolution to a significant portion of the territory of Europe. In Germany, for example, 'it was the French Revolution which opened a new era in the development of Germany by violently thrusting upon it the tenets of liberalism, nationalism and industrial freedom' (Hawerow 1958: 22).

In such cases constraints are broken down by two interrelated processes. First, in the occupied territories the political and economic order of the victorious country is established. Secondly, it is often necessary, in order to mobilize support against the aggressor, to push through decisive reforms so that a particular society can 'compete' with the approaches adopted by the more advanced country. The complex of reforms adopted in Prussia in 1807–14,

TABLE 1.1. *Ways in which constraints can be removed*

Methods of removal	Characteristics	Options
Reforms	Constraints are removed by the existing authorities, supported (at least partially) by the traditional élite	The reforms are a result of strong state authorities recognizing new challenges
		Reforms implemented to response to a failed revolution
		Reforms implemented under threat of foreign conquest
Revolutions 'from above'	Constraints are removed by strong authorities, which changes their political basis and finds support among new social groups and strata	Implemented by a new government which has seized power
		Implemented by an existing government, or a new one established constitutionally
Revolutions 'from below'	Constraints are spontaneously removed while the state authorities are weak	Great, full-scale revolutions
		Minor, second-rank revolutions
Foreign military occupation	Constraints are removed by the occupying power establishing an order resembling that of the victorious country	

often regarded as a 'revolution from above', is a typical example of this. Serf-dom was abolished and the medieval constraints on the development of production and on horizontal and vertical social mobility were substantially slackened.

The different ways in which inbuilt constraints can be removed are presented in Table 1.1, which clarifies the role of 'revolutions from below'. There are many different ways in which constraints can be overcome, and sometimes it may be difficult to classify them. This table sets out the import-ant difference between 'revolutions from below' and other types of revolution. Only in 'revolutions from below' are constraints removed spontaneously. In all other situations the authorities initiate the changes. They remain able to control and regulate the course of the reforms, and to coordinate and correct their implementation.

2

Revolutions and Economic Growth:
General Approach

2.1 Revolution and economic growth: general approach

In the preceding chapter we showed the close association between economic growth and the development of the prerequisites for revolution. However, we used the term 'economic growth' in a narrow sense, to describe a period in which certain indices show an increase—particularly per capita GDP. This is how the term has been traditionally used. However, 'economic growth' can also be understood in a wider sense. It can describe a period in which economic conditions are constantly changing and fluctuating, in which the rate of growth of production exceeds the rate of population increase not at every given moment, but only when one looks at long-term trends. In such cases economic growth may be regarded as a process of transition between one stable state (pre-industrial agrarian society) and another (post-industrial society with a high per capita income) (see Gaidar 1997a: 297–8). Periods of crisis and depression constitute an organic part of that process. They clear out the outdated elements of the industrial structure, lead to the renewal of the productive apparatus, and thereby create the conditions for an economic upswing on a new technological basis.

In this chapter we shall examine the relationship between revolution and economic growth seen in the second, broader sense. This question has been discussed frequently in works on the theory of revolution, and various positions have been taken. It was traditionally thought that revolutions were primarily a feature of the early stages of economic growth, that is, of the transformation of traditional societies into industrial societies, commonly referred to as the process of modernization.[1] It was argued that 'revolution is characteristic of modernization' (Huntington 1968: 264) and that all the great

---

[1] According to the most widely adopted interpretation, this process includes 'long-term change spanning centuries and transforming 'traditional' society based on agricultural and artisanal production, personal relations of dependence, local loyalties, rural cultures, rigid social hierarchies, and religious world-views, into industrial class society with highly developed industrial technologies, secularized cultures, 'rational' bureaucratic impersonal socio-political orders, and political systems of mass participation' (Kershaw 1993: 148).

revolutionary cataclysms 'have occurred during the era of 'modernisation', in the last several hundred years of world history' (Skocpol 1994*b*: 113).

Most recently, however, a school of thought has been gaining ground which links revolutions first and foremost to cyclical processes. A good example of this interpretation is the work of Jack Goldstone on the early revolutions. One of the main conclusions of his analysis is that 'there is no evidence that the revolutions of 1640 in England and of 1789 in France were instrumental in removing blockages to economic development' (Goldstone 1991: 483). On that basis he draws this general conclusion: 'In presenting the great crises as triumphs of progress over institutional "blockages", rather than as cyclic crises that shook, but often failed to fundamentally change, rigid institutions and economies, the story has misread the nature of early modern revolutions and rebellions ' (ibid. 484). Goldstone finds the roots of present-day revolutionary processes in areas only indirectly linked to the problems of economic growth: 'In our days revolutions and state crises stem primarily from policies that create . . . mismatches though still, in part, from ecological pressures' (ibid. 477).

In our view, however, it is precisely in these early revolutions that the connection between revolutionary crisis and a transition to economic growth can be seen most clearly. If we look at the theoretical aspects of the problem, the factors which researchers have identified as being the causes of revolution and those which cause economic growth to begin almost completely coincide. Goldstone himself associates revolutionary crisis with the pressures exerted by a growing population upon economic and social structures which are unable to adapt, thereby echoing an earlier, path-breaking work in which it was argued that for stable economic growth to begin it is necessary that the institutional conditions be formed, and the 'predominant parameter shift which induced the institutional innovations . . . was population growth' (North and Thomas 1973: 8). North and Thomas see seventeenth-century England as the first country in which such conditions were formed.

According to another contemporary theorist, the causes of revolution are determined by competition between states in the world arena, and take shape in those relatively backward countries which experience political and military pressure from their more developed neighbours (Skocpol 1979). This theory reminds us of Rostow's interpretation of the causes of economic growth, in which he asserted that 'the initial impulse to economic modernization is generally seen to arise from basically non-economic motives; that is, a reaction to one form of external intrusion or another, real or feared, by the more powerful on the less powerful' (Rostow 1971*b*: 3). Rostow also argued that in the majority of cases (particularly in France and in several other countries undergoing belated modernization), revolution occurs when the prerequisites for a transition to stable economic growth are being formed (ibid. 55). Development in this period is already significantly different from the processes which characterize traditional societies: 'It's not inherently cyclical. It moves—against

resistances, irregularly, fitfully, often with setbacks—but it moves in an inter-
acting, self-reinforcing process towards the norms of modernity' (ibid. 62).

All of the arguments adduced above are quite consistent with the notion of
a connection between revolution and the modernization process. However,
there are at least two additional historical phenomena which are directly
related to revolution, but which clearly lie outside the modernization period.
One of them is the so-called 'fascist revolutions' of the 1920s and 1930s. The
Nazification of Germany, at least, took place in a developed industrial society
and cannot be fully accounted for in terms of modernization problems. It is
true that not all authors accept that fascist régimes, particularly the Nazis, can
be counted as revolutionary,[2] but such a view is widespread in the literature.
Again, the changes which have been occurring in Eastern Europe and the
former USSR since the mid-1980s are clearly revolutionary in character, and
at least in some cases deserve to be recognized as full-scale revolutions. It can
be argued that both in Germany in the first third of the twentieth century, and
in Russia at the end of that century, the modernization processes were incomplete. Even so, the technological basis, the social structure, and the mechanisms of state administration in those countries differed substantially both
from those of the agrarian-bureaucratic monarchies of pre-industrial Europe
and from those of the Third World dictatorships of recent times. What we
need is a theory which will explain the sources of those revolutionary
processes which cannot be attributed to modernization, if our understanding
of the reasons for revolutions is to be full and complete.

In the preceding chapter a connection was made between the causes of
revolution and an excessively rigid institutional structure which prevents society from adapting to a changing environment. Since economic growth inces-
santly creates new trends and new problems which require constant
adaptation, it is not surprising that economic growth can provoke social crises
which lead to revolutionary upheavals. We also know that revolutions become
rarer the closer the modernization process is to completion. There are several
reasons why this is so.

First, in many cases the basic barriers to adaptation are destroyed by various combinations of reforms and revolutions during the modernization
phase. Adaptations to new demands can then take place in an evolutionary
way. It is only in those countries where, for one reason or another, this has not
happened that further revolutionary upheavals are likely. Thus the manner in
which a country develops during its modernization phase is crucially important in determining the relative importance thereafter of evolutionary and
revolutionary adaptation mechanisms.

---

[2] It is noteworthy that those students of revolution who were contemporaries of the
fascist régimes regarded them as revolutionary. Crane Brinton, for example, wrote of the
'fascist revolutions' in Italy and Germany (1965: 21).

Secondly, despite the potentially conflictual nature of economic growth, it does not require radical changes in the institutional structure at every turn. Adaptation is not always a question of 'life or death'. Historical analysis allows us to identify three periods which we shall call 'crises of economic growth'. The first of these, which has attracted the most attention, occurred when the preconditions for a transition to stable economic growth were being formed and during the first stages of that growth. This was the crisis of early modernization. The second was the crisis of mature industrial society, and it occurred in the more advanced countries during the first third of the twentieth century. Finally, the beginnings of the third crisis can be traced to the 1970s and 1980s, and can be seen as the crisis of early post-modernization. Each of these 'crises of economic growth' precipitated the need for a fundamental change in the mode of operation of established social structures and relations.

2.2 The past: the crises of early modernization and mature industrial society

The crisis of early modernization arises in the initial phases of economic growth, before that process has acquired a stable character but when it has already shaken the traditional structures and used up all their potential for adaptation. As the data in Table 2.1 clearly show, before economic growth can become stable and self-sustaining, institutional constraints must somehow or other be removed, by reform or revolution. This table has been adapted from Rostow (1971*a*), and characterizes the development of the preconditions for a move to stable growth.

If we examine other theories of the transition to stable economic growth, the connections between this process and revolution become increasingly obvious. This is true both in terms of the formation of the preconditions (as was noted in the preceding chapter) and in terms of the consequences. In relation to England, as we have seen, authors such as Nef have argued that the first industrial revolution occurred over the preceding century (1540–1640). In the case of France, there are still widely divergent opinions about when such a transition took place—from the pre-revolutionary period (the latter half of the eighteenth century) to the 1850s (after the 1848 revolution). (A general account of the discussions on this subject can be found in Crouzet 1996 and Fohlen 1973).

However, this sort of general characterization does not allow us to determine with any precision at what stage in the transition to stable economic growth a revolutionary explosion is most likely to happen. Moreover, our data can lead to the conclusion that considerable variations are possible with regard to timing. Revolutions may occur before the prerequisites for stable

TABLE 2.1. *Dates of preconditions for take-off to steady growth*

Country	Initial date: long sweep	Initial date: short period	Take-off begins
England	1688 (Glorious Revolution)	1750	1780s
France	1660 (Colbert's reforms)	1789 (outbreak of revolution)	1830s (after 1830 revolution)
Germany (Prussia)	1730 (Friedrich Wilhelm I)	1815 (after 1807–14 reforms)	1850s (after 1848 revolution and completion of earlier agrarian reforms)
Russia	1696 (reforms of Peter the Great)	1861 (reforms of Alexander II)	1890s
Japan	1853 (Commodore Perry arrives in Tokyo Bay)	1868 (Meiji Revolution)	1880s
Mexico	1877 (pre-revolutionary régime of Purfirio Diaz)	1920 (Mexican revolution essentially over)	1940s

Source: Rostow (1971*a*: 55).

economic growth have been created (as in England), while they are being created (as in France and Mexico), or in the latter stages of that growth (as in Russia).

Even so, an economic analysis allows us more accurately to identify the 'danger zone' during which there is the greatest risk of revolutionary upheaval. If we compare the pre-revolutionary per capita GDP of those countries which underwent major revolutionary upheavals in the modernization stage, we notice an interesting pattern. In all cases per capita GDP falls within a fairly narrow band, of approximately 1,200 to 1,500 US dollars (at the value of the dollar in 1990). We do not have data for these countries for the actual year the revolution broke out, so we have to make do with the closest year for which information is available. In France in 1820 the figure was $1,218. We can assume that there had been little, if any, growth over the preceding thirty years of war and revolution. The figure for Germany in 1850, just after the revolution, was $1,476. Mexico in 1913, two years after the outbreak of revolution, was very close to this figure, at $1,467. Per capita GDP in Russia at the time of both the 1905 and 1917 revolutions was within this range—it was $1,218 in 1900 and $1,488 in 1913 (Maddison 1995: 194–206). Unfortunately we do not have comparable data for England in the first half of the seventeenth century. However, if we base our estimate on the figure for 1820

TABLE 2.2. *Per capita GDP during periods of revolution*

State	Year/s of outbreaks of revolution	GDP per capita (1990 US dollars)		Notes
England	1640	c.$1,200		Unpublished calculations by Vitality Melyantsev
USA	1774	$1,287	(1820)	American War of Independence
France	1789	$1,218	(1820)	
Germany	1848	$1,476	(1850)	
Japan	1868	$818	(1885)	Revolution 'from above'
Russia	1905	$1,218	(1900)	
Mexico	1911	$1,467	(1913)	
Russia	1917	$1,488	(1913)	
Turkey	1923	$561	(1922)	Revolution 'from above'
China	1911–49	$614	(1950)	Steady economic growth not achieved in post-revolutionary period

Source: Maddison (1995).

($1,765) and make a rough calculation of growth rates over the preceding period, we can presume that the figure for England was close to $1,200.

Moreover, some major national liberation movements, sometimes regarded as revolutions, which played an important part in modernizing their countries arose at around this sort of income level: for example, the American War of Independence (per capita GDP in 1820 was $1,287, close to the French figure) and the Garibaldi movement in Italy (per capita GDP in 1870 was $1,467). By contrast, if we look at revolutions 'from above', we see that per capita GDP is significantly lower. It was just $818 in Japan in 1885 (and presumably even lower in 1868), and in Turkey it was little more than $560 at the time that Ataturk came to power. Table 2.2 gives data on per capita GDP levels in periods of revolution.

Some countries moved into the 'danger zone' without any accompanying signs of crisis. These exceptions fall into three basic categories.

First, some (although not all) countries were, in Rostow's phrase, 'born free'. In other words, they originated in mass migrations out of the metropolitan countries to new territories opened up by the voyages of discovery, and had never experienced the limitations of medieval society. A typical example of such a society is Canada, which entered the 'danger zone' in the 1850s.

Secondly, there are a number of European, particularly Scandinavian, countries where the constraints of traditional society were very soft and modernization processes did not bring about large-scale crises. In these countries the period of socio-political turbulence more or less coincided with the

Napoleonic Wars, after which the processes of adaptation assumed a peaceful, evolutionary form.

Thirdly and finally, there are countries in which the constraints of traditional society proved unusually durable, and in which the relationships and links belonging to traditional society were not shaken by the initial period of modernization. A typical example would be Spain, where per capita GDP had only reached $1,376 in 1870. The characteristic features of a modernization crisis did not manifest themselves in Spain in that period, although there was considerable political instability.[3] This had very definite consequences for the country's subsequent economic development—a long period of stagnation during which Spain lagged behind more rapidly developing states.

As can be seen in Table 2.2, a notable feature of these crises of early modernization was that they occurred at widely differing times. The crises that we have considered alone cover a period of around three centuries. It is therefore not surprising that states which were late in embarking on the road to modernization were accumulating the preconditions for the first crisis at a time when the more developed states were already beginning to encounter the problems of mature industrial society.

The crisis of mature industrial society, unlike the crisis of modernization, has not been studied very thoroughly. Its central event, the Great Depression, is often explained in terms of chance or subjective factors, but these factors cannot possibly account for the scale of the changes which developed countries

---

[3] More accurately, it was at precisely that level of development, in 1868, that the events known as the 'September Revolution' occurred in Spain. This was essentially a *coup d'état*, one of a series of such coups (*pronunciamientos*) which were a feature of that country's 19th-century history, although it was the most far-reaching of them, with a significant effect on Spain's subsequent development. The fact that the socio-political instability of the crisis of early modernization was so protracted is one of the distinctive features of Spain's development over most of the 19th century.

First, economic growth occurred at very moderate rates, and this allowed the social system gradually to adapt to the new challenges of the time. Secondly, from the time of the Napoleonic Wars, the social constraints of traditional society had gradually been removed. This was also facilitated by the periodic *pronunciamientos*. In the course of these *coups d'état* certain important social problems were solved. Thirdly, a mechanism was discovered for overcoming the danger of the financial crisis which tends to accompany the disintegration of the traditional economic and political system. The government was able to extract considerable financial resources from the redistribution of state, municipal, and church lands to private owners. (This phased land reform lessened the danger of a food crisis, extended peasant holdings, and solved the social question of legalizing the new land owners.) Fourthly, following the defeat of Napoleon I, Spain hardly faced any external threats—the European powers refrained from exerting much pressure on a declining Spain.

However, the slow and inconsistent process by which constraints were removed had its price—up to the 1950s Spanish growth lagged noticeably behind that of many European countries, and the process of industrialization was delayed (see Carr 1980; Tortella 1996).

experienced thereafter. From the last third of the nineteenth century, self-regulating economic and social mechanisms based on free competition began to produce crises. The increasing concentration of production and related forms of monopolistic control, which gave excessive power to individual corporations operating in their own interests; the sharpening class struggle; the intensification of international conflict—all of these factors gave rise to a need for new forms of regulation, new approaches to the mechanisms by which society functioned. Adaptation to fundamentally new requirements became the order of the day.

The crisis of mature industrial society can be regarded as primarily a crisis of self-regulating mechanisms. Writers at the time interpreted the crisis in a variety of ways. Hayek, for example, regarded the system of independent planning by large industrial monopolies as the worst of all possible regulatory mechanisms. Such a policy, he wrote in 1944, 'puts the consumer at the mercy of the joint monopolist action of capitalists and workers in the best organised industries' (Hayek 1991: 30). Schumpeter, who anticipated the decline of capitalism, rejected the view that big business as such had a restraining effect on economic development, and saw the reason for decline in the dwindling role of enterprise. 'The perfectly bureaucratized giant industrial unit' he argued in 1942, 'not only ousts the small or medium-sized firm and "expropriates" its owners, but in the end it also ousts the entrepreneur and expropriates the bourgeoisie as a class' (Schumpeter 1970: 134).

Like the crisis of early modernization, the crisis of mature industrial society was accompanied by serious conflicts, upheavals, and cataclysms. The most striking responses to this crisis in developed countries were Roosevelt's 'New Deal' and the advent of the Nazi regime in Germany. This latter phenomenon, we believe, can legitimately be regarded as a revolution.[4] However, unlike the crisis of early modernization, the crisis of mature industrial society did not affect only those countries in which the preconditions for crisis had fully developed. The First World War and the Great Depression, events which in one way or another engulfed many countries on different continents, made for an internationalization and synchronization of the latter crisis. This crisis was artificially spread to countries in which a developed industrial society had not yet been established. These countries were obliged to respond to processes which had penetrated from abroad. The upheavals in Latin America (in Brazil, Argentina, Chile, Peru, etc.), which brought about substantial changes in the economic and political development models of those countries, and the Asian national liberation movements in such places as Turkey and Persia, were responses to such processes.

The crisis of mature industrial society was felt particularly acutely in those countries where it coincided with the crisis of early modernization, and made

---

[4] This question is considered in greater detail in Ch. 11.

TABLE 2.3. *Socio-political events in the crisis of mature industrialism*

Year	State	Event
1917	Russia	Monarchy falls; Bolshevik revolution
1918	Austria–Hungary	Monarchy falls; empire disintegrates
	Germany	November revolution
1919	Hungary	Revolution; Horthy dictatorship established
1919–23	Turkey	National movement led by Kemal (Ataturk); republic established, far-reaching reforms (revolution 'from above')
1921	Persia	Military coup
1922	Italy	Mussolini's Fascists come to power
1923	Spain	Coup d'état; military dictatorship established
	Germany	Communist uprising in Hamburg; Fascist putsch in Bavaria
1924	Great Britain	First Labour government formed
	Greece	Republic proclaimed
	Mongolia	Republic proclaimed
1926	Great Britain	General strike, over 2 million participants
	Poland	Military coup; Pilsudski dictatorship established
	Portugal	Military coup; Salazar dictatorship consolidated
1929	India	Civil disobedience campaign for independence begins
	USA	Wall Street crash
	Russia	Policy of accelerated industrialization and forced collectivization; Stalin's personal dictatorship established
1930	Brazil	Vargas's military coup; constitutional reform on Italian fascist model; policy of import-substituting industrialization
	Argentina	Military coup; régime turns towards fascism and 'corporativism'; policy of import-substituting industrialization
1931	Spain	Republic established
1933	Germany	Hitler appointed Chancellor
	Cuba	Military coup
	USA	Roosevelt proclaims 'New Deal'
1934	Latvia	Coup d'état, authoritarian nationalist dictatorship estblished
	Austria	Attempted Nazi coup
	China	Communist uprising—'Long March'—begins
1936	Chile	State of siege declared; political repression greatly intensified
	France	'Popular Front' (communists, socialists, radicals) win elections
	Spain	Civil war begins
	Japan	Attempted military coup
1939	Spain	Franco dictatorship established
		Outbreak of World War II

the latter much more difficult to overcome. Many states in the early stages of industrial development responded to the general instability and external shocks by moving to a model of so-called import-substituting industrialization. This model presupposed a closed internal market and an important role for the state in the economy. This took the form both of a substantial state sector and a high degree of dependence of private capital upon the state. Table 2.3 sets out some of the globally important political and economic changes which characterized the period crisis of the mature industrial society.

In the final analysis, the reaction to the crisis of mature industrial society in every country was to curtail spontaneity and strengthen the regulatory role of the state in all spheres of economic life. As Hayek observed, 'According to the views now dominant the question is no longer how we can make the best use of the spontaneous forces found in a free society. We have in effect undertaken to dispense with the forces which produced unforeseen results and to replace the impersonal and anonymous mechanism of the market by collective and "conscious" direction of all social forces to deliberately chosen goals' (Hayek 1991: 15).

The reaction to the crisis manifested itself most rapidly in the political sphere, during the inter-war period. It led first and foremost to a growth of anti-democratic tendencies. In several states in Europe, Asia, and Latin America there were revolutions and coups; governments and constitutions changed. In many cases dictatorial forms of government replaced democratic ones, and national liberation movements provided the basis for authoritarianism.[5] Moreover, even in those countries which remained politically stable, such as Britain, France, and the USA, there was growing sympathy for authoritarian forms of rule.

In the economic sphere the reaction was an increase in the scale of state regulation, including a greater role for state ownership, state orders, and administrative constraints on the directions in which business could develop. Additionally, to a large extent the state assumed responsibility for economic stability. It prevented the collapse of large corporations and banks and regulated the economy with a view to ironing out fluctuations. In the social sphere the state took on a greater role in ensuring social security and the provision of social services (health services, education, and so forth), and this gave rise to the post-war 'welfare state'. The state intervened more in regulating relations between labour and capital, and in ensuring social consensus.

This new role for the state was strikingly expressed in a sharp increase in state expenditure as a proportion of the national product. In Britain this rose from 10 per cent in 1880 to 24 per cent in 1929 and almost 30 per cent in 1938. The increase in Germany was even more remarkable—from 10 per cent to 31

---

[5] Samuel Huntington identifies the period from 1922 to 1942 as the 'first reverse wave'—that is, the rolling back of the 'first wave of democratization' (1991: 14–18).

per cent and 43 per cent over the same period. In France the proportion of state expenditure almost doubled between 1880 and 1938, and it approximately tripled in the USA and Japan. In 1950 the proportion in these various countries was between 20 and 35 per cent (Melyantsev 1996: 148).

Although the stabilizing influence of the state in the crisis of mature industrial society is undeniable, the consequences of state intervention were far from straightforward. Even in the USA, the country which to the greatest extent retained liberal values, the situation after the Second World War has been described thus: 'In the 1950s the entrepreneurial spirit was nearly dead. With memories of the Depression and World War II still vivid, we continued to look toward the institutions of big business and big government to protect us' (Naisbitt 1984: 164). This increased role for the state was the key factor which undermined the entrepreneurial spirit. 'More and more, we relied on government to provide for basic needs. Government's traditional function is to safeguard citizens. We also asked that it provide food, shelter, and jobs. But by the 1960s government's role had grown to testing toys and regulating the environment and much of the economy' (ibid. 144).

2.3 The present: the crisis of early post-modernization

It was during the 1950s that tendencies began to emerge which eventually led to fundamental changes in the way in which industrial societies functioned, and many processes were rejected which had developed under the influence of the crisis of mature industrial society. The mid-1950s, several authors have argued, marked the beginning of a transition to a new type of society, which they have variously labelled post-industrial, post-capitalist, or post-modern. In recent years, the term 'information society' has become current. 'A post-industrial economy is one in which both the number of people employed in manufacturing and the proportion of gross national product going to maufacturing industries have taken second place to the service sector, a service sector made up of information, not domestic, operatives' (Stonier 1983: 23–4). According to some calculations, in 1950 only 17 per cent of employees in the USA could be regarded as working in the information sector, whereas by the beginning of the 1980s the creation, processing, and dissemination of information accounted for 65 per cent of all people employed. At the same time only 12 per cent were directly involved in productive operations (Naisbitt 1984: 4–5). In developed countries overall, between one third and two fifths of all people in employment work in the information sector (Melyantsev 1996: 206).

In post-industrial society the forces making for economic development change: 'Just as labour and capital were the central variables in industrial development, so information and knowledge are the decisive variables in post-industrial society' (Bell 1980). This has many consequences for the way the economy and society as a whole function. Since it is people who are the bearers of this knowledge, investments in 'human capital', particularly in education, health care, and so forth, begin to play a vital role. The level of qualification required of workers increases, and work takes on a more creative character. According to some data, the proportion of workers engaged primarily in creative work increased from 33–41 per cent at the beginning of the 1960s to 45–50 per cent in the 1980s (Melyantev 1996: 185). At the same time the basis for the sort of work which predominates in mature industrial society is disappearing. As Alvin Toffler put it, 'fragmented, repetitive mindless work paid off for the company. Today computers can very often do that kind of work faster and better, and robots can do the dangerous work. The old forms of work are less and less profitable and productive. So there is an incentive to change them' (Toffler 1983: 33).

The transition to a new, post-industrial phase of development fundamentally changes the nature of economic activity and in particular it changes the structure of production. Information technology, high-technology industries using microprocessors and biotechnology, instrument-making, pharmaceuticals, and the aerospace sector become the main sources of economic growth. Their lead in development is accompanied by a relative decline in other sectors. Over recent decades many countries have seen an ongoing fall in the relative importance of agriculture. Between 1950 and 1990 the proportion of the working population involved in agriculture fell sharply in Germany, from 23.2 to 3.7 per cent; in Italy, from 43.2 to 8.8 per cent; in France, from 27.8 to 5.6 per cent; in the USA, from 12.7 to 2.8 per cent; in Japan, from 48.3 to 7.2 per cent. It is clear that at this stage there is no longer any possibility of further redistribution of the labour force from agriculture to other sectors (see Melyantsev 1996: 160, 162–3). Moreover, the process of reducing the numbers employed in industry has begun. Between 1973 and 1990 the rate of decline was approximately 0.2 per cent per annum in the developed countries (ibid. 160). 'There arose the complex phenomenon of de-industrialization of production and employment. In particular, there was a decline in traditional sectors, a growth of unemployment among industrial workers, and a degradation of former industrial centres' (ibid. 162).

Sharp increases in the price of energy and raw materials in the first half of the 1970s accelerated the crisis of the resource-consuming reproduction model. Combined with worsening ecological problems, this increased the pressure on economies towards the conservation of resources. The amount of energy used per dollar of GDP in the developed countries was reduced. Between 1973 and 1990 the rate of reduction was on average three times greater than in the preceding decades. In such countries as Japan, the USA, and Italy, the average annual rates of reduction in that period exceeded 2 per cent—in Japan, the figure was 2.7 per cent (ibid. 155–7).

These new economic tendencies began increasingly to conflict with the institutional structures laid down during the phase of mature industrialism. Mass production of industrial goods, the basis of industrialism, was administered effectively through large-scale hierarchical structures, ensuring economies of scale. This period was characterized by the development of gigantic industrial corporations with centralized management systems, a large, centrally administered state sector in the economies of many developed and developing countries, and widespread bureaucratized, hierarchical relationships in many other spheres of social life. The situation which develops in post-industrial society is quite different: 'In an information economy, rigid hierarchical structures slow down the information flow—just when greater speed and more flexibility are critically needed' (Naisbitt 1984: 212). This is what underlies the tendency towards decentralization, and the greater orientation towards horizontal links, which come into conflict with established hierarchical institutional structures.

The post-industrial economy is characterized by greater competition, which undermines relatively stable monopolistic and oligopolistic market structures. A number of factors are associated with this process.

First, new industrial countries have entered into the world market, having developed rapidly in the post-war period. By the beginning of 1982 the importation of foreign cars into the USA, particularly from Japan, meant that American firms had lost 30 per cent of their domestic car market (Eglau 1986: 201). Another example is provided by Xerox, whose domestic market share in the USA fell from more than 90 per cent to below 50 per cent in less than ten years (ibid. 161).

Secondly, the production process has become internationalized. Transnational corporations have developed which transcend national boundaries and use the advantages of the international division of labour. By the 1980s General Motors' latest model was being built in eight countries and assembled from parts made all over the world (Stonier: 1983: 27). Such corporations work for the world market and inevitably come into competition with each other, regardless of whether the national policies of any given country favour competition.

Thirdly, scientific and technological progress have accelerated as we move towards an information society, and this constantly gives rise to new spheres of competitive struggle. It is in the high-technology sectors that the range of goods produced changes most rapidly, with substantial price competition. The entry of Japanese producers into these markets often brought about a 20–30 per cent reduction in prices.

Fourthly and finally, a policy of protectionism has become less attractive, because it limits access to the latest scientific and technological achievements and thus hinders the free exchange of information as a whole. Average tariffs on the import of finished products into developed countries have fallen from

32–34 per cent at the beginning of the 1930s and 16–18 per cent in 1950 to 4 per cent in 1994 (Melyantsev 1996: 148).

This means that in order to be competitive and survive, it is necessary to be mobile and flexible, to be able to react quickly to changing market requirements, and to generate new ideas and introduce the latest technologies into production. Post-industrial society is experiencing a new upsurge in that entrepreneurial spirit which, according to the commentators of the time, had almost disappeared during the second crisis. Firms are placing greater value on employees' independence and initiative, and there are greater opportunities for these qualities to express themselves outside the established corporate structures.

This is related to the fact that in post-industrial society the viability of small businesses has increased in many respects. In 1950, 93,000 new companies were formed in the USA, whereas by the early 1980s that figure had risen to 600,000 (Naisbitt 1984: 6). As for Western Europe, some experts consider that its capacity to export during the crisis years of the 1970s and 1980s was sustained primarily by small business, and they compare this with the bureaucratic and state-regulated nature of large-scale production.[6] It is small business which in many countries is the main source of new employment, and in some cases, of important scientific and technological innovations.

The transition to a post-industrial economy is not a single act. It is a fairly lengthy process in which changes accumulate gradually. The phases of this process closely resemble the phases of economic growth in the establishment and development of industrial society identified by Rostow. These are: the creation of the preconditions for a take-off to steady growth; the take-off itself; the sweep into maturity; high mass consumption (see Rostow 1971a: 12). Dizard, for example, sees the progression towards post-industrial society as a three-stage process. First, there is the formation of the basic economic sectors for the production and dissemination of information. This is analogous to the transition to steady growth, which involved the industrialization of a limited number of sectors of the economy. Secondly, there is the spread of information services to other sectors of industry and government. This can be compared with the move towards technological maturity—the spread of industrialization to a wide range of sectors. Thirdly, there is the creation of a broad information network at the consumer level. Like the move towards a high level of mass consumption in the industrial epoch, this means that not only the productive, but also the consumer, sphere is transformed on a new technological basis (Dizard 1982).

---

[6] In the view of Hans Otto Eglau, the maintenance of European export levels was 'primarily to the credit of those small and middle-sized firms which mostly specialized in fairly narrow segments of the market and were oriented towards selling their produce in markets all over the world. Their size prevented them from becoming objects of state interference' (1986: 224).

At each of the stages we have considered, new needs can arise in various forms and with varying degrees of intensity. None the less, the general logic of the process strongly resembles the development of the conditions for the crisis of early modernization. The capacity of established institutions and relations to adapt to the growing tendencies of post-industrial society is gradually exhausted. The conditions for the crisis of early post-modernization are created. This poses the question: can the existing system adapt in an evolutionary way, or can transition only be achieved by a revolutionary break?

We still do not have sufficient data to be able to characterize in full the timescale and progress of the crisis of early post-modernization. Its most striking manifestations to date have been the economic crises of the mid-1970s to the early 1980s, in which the contradictions of early post-modernization were compounded by a sharp rise in energy prices. However, despite these economic cataclysms, the crisis of early post-modernization was not as closely synchronized as the crisis of mature industrialism had been. The process was more complex.

On the one hand, as post-industrial tendencies in developed countries were emerging, developing countries were playing a growing role on the industrial goods market as the international division of labour intensified. These countries were still going through or just completing the industrialization process, and retained the potential of industrialism. Similarly, the increase in world energy prices affected various groups of countries in different ways, depending on whether they were net importers or exporters of energy resources on the world market.

On the other hand, the increasing importance of information technology has a global character, and, as the process of world-wide integration gathers pace, it requires countries at varying levels of development to adapt. We can trace the relationship between the so-called third wave of democratization identified by Samuel Huntington from 1974 and the crisis of early post-modernization. Students of post-industrial societies have observed that the potential afforded by information technology will be most fully realized in democratic societies which uphold the principle of freedom of information (Dizard 1982). Between 1973 and 1990 the proportion of democratic states in the world has risen from less than 25 per cent to more than 45 per cent (Huntington 1991: 26). Moreover, this third wave of democratization has had a clearly expressed liberalizing character: 'The distinguishing feature of this wave, which began in the states of Southern Europe and spread to Latin America, Africa, South and South-east Asia, Eastern and Central Europe, is the close correlation and interdependence of political and economic reforms, the simultaneous establishment of democratic institutions and economic liberalization, and the transition to the market mechanism as the main regulator of economic activity' (Vorozheykina 1997: 96).

We can also suppose that where the crisis of early modernization coincides with the crisis of early post-modernization, the consequences will not be so dire as when it coincided with the crisis of mature industrialism. Those countries which have started industrializing seriously in the last few decades can take a more balanced and decentralized approach to this process, in which the state need not play such a substantial role. Greater reliance can be placed on private capital. This can include foreign investment, which will not have the same destructive social consequences that it had at the end of the nineteenth and beginning of the twentieth century. Moreover, from the outset these countries have no interest in carrying out import-substituting industrialization, but rather seek to become an organic part of the international division of labour. We do not yet have enough experience of this process to generalize very widely, but the example of China shows that backward countries can industrialize in present circumstances with less conflict and more organically than was the case during the late nineteenth and early twentieth centuries when the economies of the developed countries were highly monopolized, and their foreign policies aggressive.

In those countries which completed the process of industrialization at an earlier stage, the processes of adaptation take place with varying degrees of conflict and radicalism. These processes occur on various levels. Networks—connections between people, brought together by common goals and interests, arising outside of the formal hierarchies—become more prevalent.[7] Corporations look for ways of making greater use of their employees' creative potential, of decentralizing decision-making, and of increasing the flexibility of their own activities. However, these localized changes alone cannot fully bring about the necessary adaptation without substantial changes in state policy. In the 1980s almost all developed and several developing countries underwent a series of profound and painful reforms which reduced direct state intervention in the economy through privatization and deregulation. These changes were implemented against the background of a resurgent neo-liberal ideology, which stressed the advantages of private property, the free market, and competition as against state intervention and regulation. Indeed, the reforms carried out by Ronald Reagan in the USA and Margaret Thatcher in Britain were so radical that some authors regard them (without adequate foundation) as revolutions (see Jenkins 1987; Adonis and Hames 1994).

The process of adaptation to the new post-industrial realities is particularly difficult in those countries which took the path of import-substituting industrialization: 'The large-scale industrial sector, created in the years of forced

---

[7] 'Simply stated, networks are people talking to each other . . . Networks exist to foster self-help, to exchange information, to change society, to improve productivity and work life, and to share resources. They are structured to transmit information in a way that is quicker, more high tech, and more energy-efficient than any other process we know' (Naisbitt 1984: 215).

industrialization and oriented mainly towards domestic consumption, has proved uncompetitive in an open economy. This has inevitably led, to varying degrees, to de-industrialization with all its accompanying and serious social problems' (Vorozheykina 1997: 97). Overcoming the constraints contained within this system usually involves a long period of political and economic instability, several painful attempts at 'reform from above' aimed at liberalization and stabilization, and sometimes even political revolutions.

In the case of the states of Southeast Asia, the severe financial crisis which broke out in the summer of 1997 may also have been related to the difficulties of adapting to the challenges of post-industrialism. The economic and political systems of these countries, which took shape as a result of the rapid post-war development, combined features of industrial civilization with an orientation towards the production of goods and services of a post-industrial type. Large financial and industrial conglomerates, closely interlinked with the state, predominated both in economics and politics. This close link produced a situation which was in many respects analogous to the centrally administered industrial economies: the state in effect took on responsibility for the efficacy of decisions taken by the management of these firms.[8] The financial sector played a subordinate role in industrial projects and its function was primarily to serve their interests. The domestic market was closed or almost closed to foreign goods; the main emphasis was on attracting foreign capital, particularly in the form of share ownership. There was a very large number of small businesses, but they had little political influence, given the undemocratic political structures of these states. Social security was minimal. In other words, the successes of the countries dubbed 'Asian Tigers' were the result of their ability to make use of the advantages and specific features of a certain phase of socio-economic development—industrialism. Some experts have even suggested that the source of the strength of the Asian Tigers lay in economic policies reminiscent of those employed in the USSR under Stalin.[9]A list of important events in the criiss of early post-modernization is displayed in Table 2.4.

None the less, of all the states we have considered, only in the Soviet Union has the crisis of early post-modernization given rise to a full-blown revolution.[10] This means that in all the other countries affected by this crisis, the

---

[8] Describing the relationship between the state and firms, Christopher Lingle observed that 'rewards tended to go into private hands, whereas losses were covered through a taxpayer's fund' (Lingle 1998: 3).

[9] 'Asian growth, like that of the Soviet Union in its high-growth era, seems to be driven by extraordinary growth in inputs like labor and capital rather than by gains in efficiency' (Krugman 1997: 175).

[10] We stated earlier that we would not attempt to consider in detail whether the events surrounding the fall of the communist régimes in Eastern Europe and the former Soviet republics can be regarded as revolutions. In our opinion, communist régimes were

TABLE 2.4. *Socio-political events in the crisis of early post-modernization*

Year	State	Event
1973		Oil crisis, drastic increase in fuel prices
1974	Portugal	Revolution; dictatorship falls, democratic régime established
	Greece	Collapse of military dictatorship
1975	Spain	Franco dies; democratic processes begin
1978	People's Republic of China	Market economic reforms begin
1979	Iran	Islamic revolution
	Great Britain	Thatcher elected Prime Minister; liberal economic reforms begin
1980	Poland	Mass strikes begin; Solidarity trade union established
1981	USA	Reagan elected President; liberal economic reforms begin
1983	Argentina	Crisis and collapse of military régime
1985	USSR	Gorbachev elected CPSU General Secretary; *perestroyka* begins
	Brazil	Collapse of military régime; transition to democratic rule
	Uruguay	Collapse of military régime; transition to democratic rule
1986	Philippines	Marcos régime collapses; democratic government formed
1988	Taiwan	Policy of régime's gradual democratization adopted
	South Korea	Presidential elections; formation of a democratic régime.
1988–90	Chile	Pinochet resigns; democratization of régime.
1989	Poland	Communist régime collapses
	Hungary	Border with West opened
	Czechoslovakia	Communist régime collapses
	GDR	Berlin Wall falls
	Bulgaria	Democratic processes begin
	Romania	Communist régime collapses
1989–90	USSR	Democratic elections for People's Deputies; one-party system abolished; Gorbachev elected President
	Republic of South Africa	Dismantling of apartheid begins; racial segregation abolished.
1990	Mongolia	Break with communist system
	Germany	Reunification
1991	Albania	Communist régime collapses
	Ethiopia	Collapse of pro-communist dictatorship
	Eastern Europe	Warsaw Pact and Comecon dissolved
	USSR	Attempted *coup d'état*; disintegration of USSR
	Russia	CPSU activity suspended; liberal economic reforms begin
1993	Russia	Post-communist constitution adopted
1997	Asia	Financial crisis in Asian 'economic tigers'

main obstacles to adaptation had been removed in the course of their historical development, whereas the USSR lacked the capability to adapt and respond to the crisis period in an evolutionary way. In order to understand the peculiarities of the historical development of Russia (and subsequently the USSR), we need to look at the process whereby inbuilt constraints were broken down in other countries. We can then consider why this process was ineffective in the USSR.

2.4 Removing the constraints: various patterns

As we have seen, the manner in which the crisis of early modernization is overcome is of crucial importance in determining the prospects for evolutionary development in subsequent phases of the historical process. Various attempts to trace this connection have been made in studies on the theory of revolution. One of the best-known of these was undertaken by Barrington Moore. Moore identified three possible paths towards modern society: through bourgeois revolution to Western democracy (Britain, France, the USA); through 'revolution from above' to fascism (Germany, Japan); or through peasant revolution to communist dictatorship (Russia, China) (see Moore 1966). A critic of Moore's work has made the point that these three paths can also be interpreted as three consecutive stages in the transition to modernization, realized at different phases of historical development (see Skocpol 1994: 46–8).

This approach employs the conceputal framework that was developed, for example, in the works of Alexander Gerschenkron, who showed that 'in several very important respects the development of a backward country may, by the very virtue of backwardness, tend to differ fundamentally from that of an advanced country . . . the extent to which these attributes of backwardness occurred in individual instances appears to have varied directly with the degree of backwardness' (Gerschenkron 1962: 7.) According to this approach, countries can be divided into three categories: pioneers of industrialization, moderately economically backward, and profoundly economically backward. The pioneers of industrialization were England, and, to a certain extent, Belgium and France.[11] A typical example of 'moderate backwardness' was

imposed on many East European states from without, and for that reason once the external support was withdrawn, these régimes collapsed fairly simply and painlessly, without any major weakening of state power. However, in some cases, notably Poland, Bulgaria, and Romania, this question needs to be examined further.

[11] Gerschenkron (1969) counts France among the 'moderately backward' countries, whereas Crouzet (1996: 36) believes that French industrialization has features in common both with that of the pioneer countries (particularly England), and with that of countries which began industrializing later.

Germany; Italy and Austria also belonged to this category. Finally, Gerschenkron regards Russia and Japan as classical examples of profound economic backwardness, in that they embarked upon industrialization about three decades after Germany. Obviously, this classification applies to those countries which started to modernize before the 1920s and 1930s—that is, in our terms, before the end of the crisis of mature industrialism.

It should be borne in mind that the relationship between the type of revolution and the time at which a country began its modernization phase is not as direct as the authors considered above suggest. France and the USA, classified by Moore along with England as countries which underwent bourgeois revolutions, cannot be said without some qualifications to have modernized early.[12] 'Revolutions from above', in Moore's classification, were a feature both of Germany—a moderately backward country—and of Japan—a profoundly backward country. At the same time Russia, placed in the same category as Japan, had a peasant revolution. As for China, it is difficult to fit that country into this classification scheme at all because, as we have seen, modernization processes did not get fully under way there until a much later stage.

Even so, there is a close internal connection between the form of a given society's political and institutional transformation, and the timing of its economic modernization. The timing of a country's industrial revolution will determine the character of the new problems a society will encounter in that process, the type of inbuilt constraints hindering the necessary adaptation, and the intensity of the conflicts which attend the removal of these constraints.

Let us begin by considering those countries which pioneered industrialization. The conditions for industrial development were most favourable where the following features were present. First, there was a dynamically developing agricultural sector, able to feed the growing cities, furnish a cheap labour force for industrial enterprises and provide a market for industrial goods. Secondly, medieval regulatory systems had been dismantled and there were no economic and social restraints on the development of enterprise. Thirdly, there were foreign markets. Fourthly, state policy had to assist the development of production and provide favourable conditions for it.

For the entrepreneur in the early stages of industrialization, there was no great problem in finding external sources of finance. Industrialization mainly began in less capital-intensive sectors, the enterprises were not particularly large-scale, and they largely financed their own expansion. Crouzet, for example, noting that the 'French Industrial Revolution . . . has much in common with the experience of other "early industrializers", including Britain', identified the following common features in both countries' industrialization: 'The

---

[12] Most researchers date the industrial revolution in France from the 1830s, and in the USA from the 1850s, with the exception of New England, where it started at the end of the 18th century, and gathered pace in the 1820s and 1830s.

cotton industry was the first to mechanize on a large scale; the family firm or the small partnership were dominant; most of the new industrialists had earlier been either merchants or merchant-manufacturers or involved in traditional industry; the financing of firms' expansion was internal, through ploughing back of profits (Crouzet 1996: 36).

Up to 1848, groups with an interest in the transformation of agriculture, industrial expansion, and the removal of constraints to the development of these sectors showed themselves clearly in the revolutionary processes in those countries which were early to industrialize. They ensured favourable conditions for an industrial revolution. Demands for unlimited rights for private property, for freedom of enterprise, and for the abolition of all medieval barriers to the development of trade and industry were recurrent themes in the programmes of the revolutionary forces during this period. The greatest independence from state paternalism and exemption from interference in property relations was seen as the inalienable right of all economic actors. The only function allotted to the state was to create the most favourable conditions for the development of the national economy. At the same time, to ensure that this function was carried out adequately, it was vitally important to be able to control the operation of the state machine and its decision-making processes. The slogan of the American Revolution, 'No taxation without representation', could be applied to a greater or lesser extent to all revolutions of the time.

The success of industrialization depended to a great extent upon the degree to which revolutionary changes solved the problems outlined above. Many authors have associated England's pioneering role in the Industrial Revolution with the creation of favourable institutional conditions by the end of the seventeenth century, largely as a consequence of the previous revolutionary changes. For example, North and Thomas write,

By 1700 the institutional framework of England provided a hospitable environment for growth. The decay of industrial regulation and the declining power of guilds permitted mobility of labour and innovation in economic activity; this was later further encouraged by the Statute of Monopolies patent law. The mobility of capital was encouraged by joint stock companies, goldsmiths, coffee houses and the Bank of England, all of which lowered transaction costs in the capital market; and, perhaps most important, the supremacy of parliament and the embedding of property rights in the common law put political power in the hands of men anxious to exploit the new economic opportunities and provided the essential framework for a judicial system to protect and encourage productive economic activity.... The stage was now set for the industrial revolution. (North and Thomas 1973: 155–6)

The liberalizing tendency of revolutionary change could not be realized immediately or completely in all the countries which pioneered industrialization. Overall, however, sufficient scope for the development of enterprise was secured, and for the formation of a system of industrial relations sufficiently flexible to adapt to a variety of problems and demands. Therefore, for the countries which pioneered industrialization, the problem of securing an industrial structure capable of adaptation was largely solved in the course of the crisis of early modernization.

The moderately backward countries, however, experienced certain problems in the course of modernization. For them, as for the pioneers, industrialization came about in response to market stimuli, and within the bounds of institutions created by the market. But some constraints which hindered free economic activity continued to exert a braking effect on the process of industrialization. For example, in Germany prior to 1848 the construction of railways was hampered by administrative obstacles. These included constraints on the formation of limited companies,[13] as well as administrative regulation of the coal industry. The liberalization of industrial policy in the post-revolutionary period permitted a rapid acceleration of industrialization, which took place in the course of one of the most impressive investment booms of the nineteenth century.[14]

Assembling the resources necessary for industrialization posed a much bigger problem for the moderately backward countries than for the pioneer countries. There are a number of reasons why this was so: at the time when these countries embarked on industrialization, capital-intensive sectors such as metallurgy, engineering, and chemicals had already begun to play the leading role. Moreover, catching up required that the necessary industrial infrastructure be created more quickly. This precluded the possibility of relying solely on the evolutionary process of accumulating capital out of profits, as had been the case in earlier phases of industrialization.

The need to concentrate resources had a variety of structural consequences for the moderately backward countries, as can be seen from the example of Germany. First, it led to a change in the form and scale of enterprises: 'In branches like coal mining or steel making, heavy engineering, or chemicals, family firms increasingly gave way to enterprises organized as joint stock companies . . . In 1887 and 1907 four-fifths of the largest 100 industrial enterprises were joint stock companies' (Tilly 1996: 112). Secondly, banks assumed an entirely new role in the process of industrialization. Whereas in England the banks mainly catered for the short-term requirements of firms, in Germany an entirely new type of financial institution arose—the universal banks, concerned not only with the short-term, but also the investment, needs of industrial enterprises. These banks not only exercised effective financial

[13] Similar constraints also existed in countries which began industrialization at an earlier stage. However, they did not play such an important role, as capital was accumulated in a more evolutionary way.

[14] The earlier wave of industrialization, which started at the end of the 1830s, also occurred at a time when the state had temporarily reduced its intervention in railway construction in the first half of the 1840s. However, the creation of the *Zollverein* was no less important here.

control over the enterprises; they also had a significant influence on their strategy and tactics. Gerschenkron, along with many others, maintains that these banks became the main driving force of German industrialization. They facilitated major capital investments and even the founding of sizeable enterprises, particularly in the heavy industrial sector. Banks played a similar role in the industrialization of Austria, Italy, and certain other countries.

In this phase, the effectiveness of large-scale financial and industrial structures, able to regulate their markets to a significant extent[15] and to interact with the state, allowed the moderately backward countries to industrialize without constraints being removed as thoroughly as in the pioneer countries. There was no need fully to abolish vertical, hierarchical social relations, to make a clean break with state paternalism, or to defend freedom of competition. Therefore many moderately backward countries were able to adapt to the requirements of modernization without radical revolutions, through a gradual transformation of their structures by changes 'from above'. This meant that their state politics retained many more traditional features than was the case in the pioneer countries.

However, in this retarded condition there remained the potential for upheavals in the future. These countries had not carried through a thorough-going liberalization of their political and institutional structures. They had retained many of the inbuilt constraints of traditional society and recreated them in the industrialization phase. This meant that when the moderately backward countries faced the crisis of early modernization, they could not find the means of adapting to the changing conditions for economic growth. Since the prerequisites for evolutionary development were not fully present, this rendered those societies vulnerable to revolutionary upheaval. This became most apparent during the profound destabilization of the end of the 1920s and early 1930s, and in the so-called 'fascist revolutions'.

Germany's backwardness also played a significant role in the compromise that was reached between the ruling classes, the bourgeoisie, and the landowners, which, in Moore's view, was of crucial importance in the subsequent emergence of the Nazi régime. In England the conflict of interests between the landowners and the bourgeoisie over the question of agricultural protectionism ultimately led to a decisive victory for the new industrial class. In Germany this conflict was attenuated by policies of class compromise and this had far-reaching political and social consequences.[16] Moreover, at the time

---

[15] On this matter Gerschenkron has observed: 'The banks refused to tolerate fratricidal struggles among their children. From the vantage point of centralized control, they were at all times quick to perceive profitable opportunities of cartelization and amalgamation of industrial enterprises' (Gerschenkron 1962: 15).

[16] 'In 1880 Germany started on its road towards 'neo-mercantilism', towards 'state socialism' and, with its simultaneous colonial acquisitions, towards "imperialism"' (Gerschenkron 1962: 155).

this conflict—so vitally important for the future of the country—was under way, almost 50 per cent of the population of Germany was involved in agriculture, whereas in Britain the proportion was just 27 per cent. In making this comparison, Knut Borchard observed: 'In some ways Germany remained imprisoned in its role as a late developer' (Borchard 1973: 155).

In the profoundly economically backward countries an even more difficult situation arose. These countries had to solve the problem of developing mass production, while simultaneously creating a whole complex of interrelated sectors and large-scale infrastructural capital investments in a short period of time. Moreover, they undertook these tasks at a time when mature industrial society had entered a period of crisis. This meant that the necessary prerequisites for successful modernization in their case were different, and the process was even more conflictual than it had been for the earlier groups of countries.

First, the concentration of resources on such a scale was beyond the capacities of private economic agents. Therefore, 'the state, moved by its military interest, assumed the role of the primary agent propelling the economic progress in the country' (Gerschenkron 1962: 17). This meant that the independence of entrepreneurs from the state was no longer a precondition for successful economic expansion. On the contrary, it was closeness to the state and access to military orders that guaranteed stable economic development.

Secondly, it was essential to find sources of funds which could be channelled into catching up in industrial development. Realistically, the choice was not great: these funds either had to be squeezed out of the traditional economy, particularly the agricultural sector, or obtained from external sources of finance. In practice, one or another combination of these two sources was employed. Both methods involved a great deal of conflict. The agrarian sector was confronted by two mutually exclusive demands. On the one hand, successful industrialization required that agriculture should develop dynamically; on the other hand, the extraction of resources from agriculture greatly constrained the possibilities of developing the agricultural sector, and to a large extent reinforced its backwardness and inefficiency. This greatly aggravated the contradictions inherent in the industrialization process and the resulting social conflicts.[17]

Heavy reliance on foreign investment led to much the same consequences. Although this policy solved some of the problems of industrialization, it rendered the national economy dependent to an extraordinary degree on

---

[17] From this point of view, Gerschenkron was quite right to note the fundamental difference in the positions of Russian and French peasants during the industrialization period when he stated that 'the Russian peasant's attitude toward economic development was a great deal more negative than that of the French. The latter was hurt by certain forms of large-scale exploitation in agriculture, but he could watch economic development outside agriculture with equanimity and, in fact, with satisfaction. The Russian peasant was grievously affected by the industrialization of the country' (Gerschenkron 1968: 270).

external conditions. It subordinated the economy to aims and interests which were determined not by national priorities, but by the policies of foreign states and individual companies. This greatly augmented the importance of external challenges and constraints. It was therefore no accident that in most cases this phase of industrialization was accompanied by serious social conflicts, in the course of which a limit upon foreign intervention in the country's internal affairs was often demanded.

Thirdly, the need to concentrate resources could conflict with the need to destroy traditional systems of regulation and to ensure freedom of economic activity. Gerschenkron provides an interesting illustration of this thesis in a comparison of the tasks facing Turgot in pre-revolutionary France and Witte in pre-revolutionary Russia: 'We may assume, that Turgot's six edicts of 1776 would have gone far towards reducing discontent. A further arrangement concerning partial redemption of seigniorial rights probably would have greatly diminished the likelihood of successful revolution. A merely negative policy of abolition might well have sufficed. By contrast, Witte, in his economic policy, had to do a great deal more than simply remove obstructions from the path of economic progress' (Gerschenkron 1968: 274). Gerschenkron then examines Witte's support for measures to strengthen the medieval institution of the Russian peasant commune (*obshchina*), explaining that the commune's 'mutual guarantees' in the payment of state taxes made it possible to extract more resources from the peasant economy and augment state budget revenue. He also argues that the policy of breaking up the communes after the 1905 revolution constrained the state's fiscal options and weakened its capacity to support industrialization.

The industrialization process in profoundly backward countries therefore displays some important peculiarities. The first of these is that industrialization can be carried through with a much less thoroughgoing removal of the constraints left over from traditional society than was the case for the pioneer countries or even the moderately backward ones. The second is that the process is highly contradictory and conflict-ridden, in that it makes mutually incompatible demands on different sectors of the economy and upon economic agents. This leads to the emergence of new constraints in the process of removing the old ones. At the same time, the industrialization process has to take place in an unfavourable external environment, with the more developed countries adopting an aggressive policy aimed at carving up markets and subordinating the less-developed countries to their own interests. The third peculiarity is that the need for a large-scale redistribution of resources, the need to suppress social discontent, and the need to defend the country's interests on the world stage in the face of the aggressive policies of the more developed countries require a concentration of political power which leads practically everywhere to the establishment of authoritarian régimes. An actively modernizing régime does not permit itself such 'luxuries' as solicitude for the interests of those strata who are harmed by modernization. This results in an objective strengthening of the role of political constraints and reduces the likelihood that they will be removed in an evolutionary way.

The peculiarities of modernization in profoundly backward countries can give rise to two fundamentally different types of revolution. On the one hand, the more contradictory and conflictual nature of the process in these countries can result in greater mass participation and a stronger role for ideological 'rebellious constraints' during revolutionary cataclysms. On the other hand, the possibility of modernizing by actively transferring resources from traditional sectors to new ones, in the absence of a thoroughgoing removal of the constraints left over from traditional society, increases the chances of a successful revolution 'from above', while the masses remain passive. Thus the widespread anti-modernizing movement which was characteristic of the Mexican Revolution and the success of the Meiji Revolution in Japan can both be explained as characteristic attempts by profoundly backward countries to catch up.

However, as Gerschenkron has demonstrated, as profoundly backward countries develop economically, the relationship between different participants in the industrialization process changes. The leading role gradually passes from the state to the banks, and then at a later stage the enterprises begin to free themselves from the tutelage and direction of banking institutions and establish a more equal relationship with them (see Gerschenkron 1962: 21–2).

The industrialization of Japan was carried through in accordance with this logic. At first, the state played a central role in the process, creating many branches of industry from scratch. Up to 1880 virtually all the modern industrial enterprises had been organized by the state.[18] Moreover, the state made major capital investments in the development of Japan's infrastructure (see Black 1975: 172). However, as Japan's profound economic backwardness was overcome the task of supporting economic development increasingly passed to the economic agents themselves. In the 1880s the Japanese government sold off almost all the enterprises belonging to it, primarily to big bankers and financiers closely associated with the government (Trimberger 1978: 118–19). Thus, fully in keeping with the logic outlined by Gerschenkron, control over industry passed into the hands of the big banks. It was on the basis of this

---

[18] 'The Japanese government broke down feudal barriers to trade and industry, and then went on to build railways and telegraphs, open new coal mines and agricultural experiment stations; set up iron foundries, shipyards, and machine shops; import foreign equipment and experts to mechanise silk reeling and cotton spinning; and open model factories in cement, paper and glass' (Trimberger 1978: 118).

merging of banking institutions and industrial enterprises that gigantic multi-sector *zaibatsu* arose, which gradually extended their control over the entire economy.[19] In this respect the situation began increasingly to resemble Germany, where economic development had slowed down as a consequence of Germany's defeat in the First World War.

Although it had sold its industrial enterprises to private buyers, the Japanese state continued to play an active role in economic development. The government continued to provide financial support to industry through state orders, subsidies, tax breaks, and credits (Trimberger 1978: 119; Black 1975: 174). Moreover, the state retained a certain directing role in industrial development. The 'Memorandum on Industry', adopted in 1884, set out the general goals of industrial development over the coming decade (Black 1975: 171). The retention of a close link between industry and the state is also one of the characteristic features shared by Germany and Japan. It was therefore quite natural that, despite Japan's continuing lag behind Germany in its level of economic development, both countries took a similar route out of the economic difficulties of the 1930s. Both established militaristic régimes, with repressive domestic and expansionist foreign policies, and both moved from the use of (albeit imperfect) competitive market mechanisms to greater direct state intervention in the economy: 'At a time when economic conditions were precarious, government and business jointly attempted to curb competition through the control of output and prices and the allocation of markets and sales quotas. Such government sponsorship of cartels established the pattern of "administrative guidance"' (Black 1975: 172). Disagreement remains as to whether the régime established in Japan can be regarded as 'fascist',[20] although the many common features it shared with the Italian and German régimes are evident.

Thus, in many countries which had been developing in order to catch up, the manner in which the crisis of early modernization was overcome involved the retention of many substantial inbuilt constraints which hindered adaptation to new requirements. This led to serious political cataclysms during the crisis of mature industrial society. However, the remaining barriers were broken down, first by the fascist revolutions, and subsequently by defeat in the Second World War and during the ensuing occupations. Limitations on social mobility were removed, democratic political régimes were established, and the

---

[19] 'These large banks with close ties to state bureaucrats and to large private capitalists became uniquely characteristic of . . . zaibatsu capitalism in Japan' (Trimberger 1978: 118).

[20] Trimberger does not consider the régime established in Japan in the 1930s to be fascist. She argues that 'fascist movements failed to take political power in Japan . . . while they succeeded in Germany and Italy' (Trimberger 1978: 135). But Moore regards the Japanese régime as a variety of fascism. He notes, however, that it arose in a more natural way, and that it is much more difficult to demarcate the democratic and totalitarian phases in the political history of Japan than in that of Germany. (Moore 1966: 299, 304).

excesses of the monopolized economic structure were overcome. In this way, these countries acquired the potential to overcome the crisis of early post-modernization by adapting in an evolutionary way. In Russia, however, things developed differently.

2.5 Russia's 'special route' to modernization

Unlike Japan, Russia had a long tradition of supporting and developing enterprise, dating from the time of Peter the Great. Industrialization had been taking place spontaneously in Russia from the beginning of the nineteenth century in the production of textiles and sugar. Specialists on the question still disagree about the respective roles of the state and private initiative, but they would all concur that the state 'was enormously important in economic life to a degree extreme by the standards of much of Europe or North America' (Munting 1996: 334). As another writer expressed it, the 'state has usurped much of the role played by the English entrepreneurs' (McDaniel 1991: 73).

However, the direct involvement of the state in industrialization was basic-ally limited to the construction of railways. In order to encourage the development of industry a whole range of indirect measures were employed, directed at stimulating demand, creating favourable general economic conditions, and attracting foreign capital.[21] The state did not intend to replace the private entrepreneur with these measures: 'Although the government protected, subsidized, and rewarded private entrepreneurs, it was they ultimately who had to respond to the incentives and organize production' (McDaniel 1991: 72).

Thus the modernization process in Russia had many features common with modernization in both Japan and Germany. The similarity with Germany was that there were no drastic violent changes in the way the régime operated, and that, at least to a certain extent, it continued to rely on its traditional social supporters, particularly the landed aristocracy. As in Japan, Russia's modernization policies relied on the extraction of resources from the countryside (though in Japan the Meiji Revolution had permitted a more radical renewal of social relations). To an even greater extent than Japan,

---

[21] The most active industrialization processes in pre-revolutionary Russia are associated with S. Witte, the Minister of Finance from 1892 to 1903. The key elements of his economic policy were: a currency reform, ensuring the stability of a ruble freely convertible into gold; the rectification of the system of state finances (in which an important role was played by a spirits monopoly); active measures to attract foreign capital investments into Russia; the encouragement of railway construction as the driving force behind the country's economic growth; and the continuation and strengthening of protectionism, particularly in the conclusion of a customs agreement with Germany.

Russia relied on attracting resources from abroad.[22] Despite these similarities, Russia's development took quite a different course to that of Germany and Japan. The attempt to adapt to the challenges of modernization through changes 'from above' failed, and Russia underwent one of the most radical revolutions in European history. The result was a fundamental change in the model of modernization, as well as in the overall economic system.

Frequently the crisis which led to the 1917 revolution and the establishment of the Bolshevik dictatorship is explained in terms of to the catastrophic consequences of Russia's participation in the First World War. Indeed, this seems to be the most obvious factor, and it is referred to in almost all the analyses of Russian history in the first part of the twentieth century. For example, Skocpol writes, 'Had she been able to sit out World War I, Russia might have recapitulated the German experience of industrialization facilitated by bureaucratic guidance' (1994c: 139). This argument implies that the October Revolution in Russia was not a necessary phenomenon, but rather the consequence of an unfortunate concatenation of external circumstances. There are many arguments in favour of such a view.

Indeed, before the outbreak of the First World War Russia was developing according to the same pattern as that followed by Germany and Japan. The basic constraints upon industrial development were removed through the modernizing efforts of the Russian state (reforms 'from above') and the outcome of the 1905 revolution. The results of that revolution in many respects resemble those of the German revolution of 1848. Although both revolutions were defeated, they both enabled the policy of reforms 'from above' to become more radical, and made it possible to use the existing power structure to solve those economic and social problems which the revolution had tried to remove through pressure 'from below'. In Russia after the revolution of 1905 the bourgeoisie gained some opportunities to influence the policies of the Tsarist government. The bourgeoisie won the establishment of a quasi-constitutional monarchy. The government began to take active measures to destroy the remnants of medieval institutions and to create stable, favourable conditions for the development of enterprise.

At the same time, the leading role of the government in the process of economic development was substantially reduced, state investment in the economy fell, and state financial support for the development of industry was

---

[22] In Japan the proportion of financial resources from abroad was very high in the initial phase of modernization (around 50% between 1869 and 1884). However, it declined sharply in the phase of forced industrialization, down to 2–3% over the period 1885–1938. (Melyantsev 1996: 115). In Russia the proportion of foreign investment was substantially higher. Foreign capital accounted for 41% of new investment in the 1880s, 87% in 1903–5, and 50% in 1909–13 (McKay: 26–8). According to other estimates, around 40% of Russian industry was financed by foreign capital (Gregory 1982).

reduced. The role of foreign investment in economic development was gradually reduced to nothing.[23] As far as further modernization was concerned, the initiative passed increasingly to private economic agents. The transition to greater self-reliance certainly gathered pace. From the start of the twentieth century certain tendencies began to emerge in all countries engaged in industrialization to catch up. On the one hand, concentration of production when the internal market was shielded by protectionist policies allowed the process of monopolization to develop. From around 1900 cartel agreements began to exert a substantial influence on the development of industry.[24] On the other hand, the large banks were playing an increasingly important role in controlling industry (see Black 1975: 178). As Gerschenkron observed: 'it is true that, after 1905–06, the process of Russian westernization in the economic field proceeded continuously and smoothly, as never before' (1968: 277). It is, however, necessary to note that this process was only in its initial stage, and Russian industry remained much more dependent upon the state than, say, German industry.

The situation remained highly unstable. Russia's position was profoundly contradictory. It remained an agrarian country. Its working population exceeded 50 million, but only a little over three million were working for wages in factories or mines (Munting 1996: 331). Less than one fifth of the population was urbanized, and the livelihoods of around 80 per cent of the population depended directly upon agriculture (Grossman 1971: 12). But Russia had also become a major industrial power. By 1913, it stood in fourth place in terms of the total volume of industrial production, after the USA, Germany, and Great Britain, and was one of the major producers of the most important industrial goods (Munting 1996: 330, 334; incidentally, by 1860 Russia was in sixth place, overtaken by India and China). This sort of duality in Russia's situation necessarily caused sharp conflicts of interests, which weakened the social base of the régime and led to inconsistent and contradictory government policies.

Some writers consider that it was the limited nature of the transformations 'from above' which made a revolutionary explosion inevitable. For example, Tim McDaniel writes: 'The agrarian program was but one part of Stolypin's overall project for economic and political reform of the empire. His plans also

[23] 'Between the mid-1880s and 1900 foreign capital and management was a moving force in Russian industry. But after 1900 investment in Russian industry was done increasingly through Russian banks, in which foreigners could invest but not control. . . . Russian managers came to occupy more important positions within companies that had earlier been dominated by foreign managers' (Black 1975: 179).

[24] As one student of Russian industrialization has observed, 'high tariffs protected domestic inefficiency and enabled monopolistic practices to be adopted. Many cartels were formed about the turn of the century'. He goes on to mention the metals cartel Prodamet, the coal syndicate Produgol', and the Sugar Cartel (Munting 1996: 335).

included administrative rationalization, rebuilding the army and navy, the improvement of public education, social welfare measures for workers, and tax reform. Taken together, these changes might well have constituted a 'revolution from above', had they been enacted, but the land reform was the only significant aspect of the program to be realized' (McDaniel 1991: 77–8).

But even Stolypin's efforts to transform agriculture could only have been effective in the long term. In the transition period there remained wide scope for the peasants to adopt an ideology which would constitute a 'rebellious constraint', and move from passive to active forms of resistance to the destruction of the peasant commune. Additionally, the transition from an absolute to a quasi-constitutional monarchy did not proceed consistently, which meant that there remained a basis for sharper political conflicts. It was highly probable that, sooner or later, the role of the State Duma would have to be increased. Russia remained in the 'danger zone', without any guarantees that it would be able to effect long-term, strategic changes in an evolutionary way. In Gerschenkron's apposite phrase, 'the long run was cut short by the outbreak of World War I' (1968: 274).

Thus an explanation for the causes, course, and consequences of the 1917 revolution can be found in the simultaneous aggravation of three types of contradiction. First, there were the typical contradictions of the period of early industrialization. These stemmed from the difficulties of transforming an enormous peasant country, and were associated with the need for a fairly radical resolution of the agrarian problem. Secondly, there were the contradictions associated with the need of a profoundly backward country to catch up, a need which required the mobilization of financial resources and active redistribution from traditional to new industrial sectors of the economy. Finally, there were the contradictions stemming from the fact that the crisis of early modernization in Russia coincided with the emerging crisis of mature industrial society. This factor, in a country which had already come some way along the path of industrialization (Rostow 1971a: 119–21 argues that the revolution of 1905 marked the changeover from industrial revolution to progress towards technological maturity), and in which industry was highly concentrated and monopolized and closely connected to the state, could not fail to have an impact on the character of the pre-revolutionary crisis.

As we have seen, when a profoundly backward country embarks upon the process of modernization, economic development can be achieved with much less destruction of the inbuilt constraints left over from traditional society, with a much higher degree of state regulation, and with less extensive liberalization than in those countries which embarked on this process earlier. However, these anachronisms persisted in Russia at a time when, during the first three decades of the twentieth century, market economies experienced a crisis of self-regulation and greater state intervention was required. Thus, in Russia, tendencies which derived both from the traditional, patriarchal culture and from the contradictions of an up-to-date and actively developing industrial sector combined to reject private property and free competition and to support the dominant role of the state in the economy. It was this complex of ideas, and this dualism, which found its consistent manifestation in the ideology and practice of the Bolshevik party.

This is what makes it so difficult in the Bolshevik Revolution to distinguish between the ideology of those forces who were fighting for the removal of constraints on economic development and the ideology of 'rebellious constraints' discussed in the preceding chapter. The statism and collectivism of the Bolsheviks was very close to the collectivism of those semi-patriarchal strata of the population who were accustomed to paternalism and dependency and who rejected the values of industrial society. Their world was the so-called 'archaic socium', a holistic society with a vertical, pyramidal structure. The individual in such a society was an integral, inalienable part of the social whole (see Vishnevskii 1995: 216). McDaniel has cited the observations of a factory inspector, showing that at the turn of the century workers in the provinces were spontaneously advocating state socialism: 'They thought that the factory owner had no right to close the factory and that if he managed his affairs poorly the state would requisition it. They were also mistakenly of the opinion that the employer was obliged to provide work and housing for the entire local population. Further, they assumed that the authority could force the factory owner to raise their wages and use his profit to build more factories to increase employment' (McDaniel 1991:126).

These ideas had something in common with the most advanced social ideas of the time, expressed, for example, by someone as far removed from socialism as Henry Ford, the founder of the modern American car industry: 'The present system does not permit of the best service because it encourages every kind of waste—it keeps many men from getting the full return from service. And it is going nowhere. It is all a matter of better planning and adjustment taking the product of their labour from many people. It has no plan. Everything depends on the extent of planning and expediency' (Ford 1924: 2). Ideas of a society, organized and controlled 'from above' and administered according to the principles of rationality and justice, so popular in that period, coincided completely with the position of the Bolsheviks. We can concur entirely with the view that 'communism was thoroughly modern in its passionate conviction that good society can be only a society carefully designed, rationally managed and thoroughly industrialised. . . . Communism was modernity at its most determined mood and most decisive posture; modernity streamlined, purified of the last shred of the chaotic, the irrational, the spontaneous, the unpredictable' (Bauman 1993: 13).

Therefore, owing to the extraordinarily complex interaction between different types of contradiction and the dual nature of the Bolsheviks' actions, the revolution of 1917 cannot be characterized in simple terms. In its motive forces it was clearly, fundamentally, a peasant revolution, and in this respect it resembles other revolutions of the modernization phase, such as the French and the Mexican. When we consider its results, we also observe a number of consequences characteristic of many social revolutions of the modernization phase, such as the abolition of large landholdings and of the large landlords as a class. There are also certain characteristics which resemble the fascist revolutions of mature industrial societies, such as the establishment of a totalitarian regime and the subordination of the interests of production to the interests of the state.

However, the degree of state economic intervention which resulted from the Bolshevik Revolution was much more substantial than that achieved in the fascist states. In the Soviet Union all the processes of production and distribution were eventually completely taken over by the state. Private property relations were abolished. Control of the means of production came to be exercised by the *nomenklatura*,[25] a new ruling social stratum, or, some would argue, a class. The *nomenklatura*, whilst it did not enjoy formal property rights over the means of production, concentrated all powers of control over the means of production in its own hands. Clearly, this extent of state interference in economic processes was not historically inevitable. The objective bases for the rule of the *nomenklatura* arose out of the fact that the contradictions of Russia's effort to industrialize and to catch up were aggravated by the catastrophic destruction of productive forces during the First World War and the ensuing civil war. These contradictions were further complicated by the crisis of mature industrialism.

The consequences of the Bolshevik Revolution for Russia were mixed and contradictory. In the short term the main obstacles to forced industrialization were removed, and modern industrial production was established in an extremely short time. The USSR's economic potential proved sufficient to survive the most intense conflict with Germany in 1941–5 and emerge victorious. It remains a moot point whether the problems facing the country could have been solved without the use of the extreme measures which characterized the period from the end of the 1920s to the early 1940s. However, from the point of view of economic growth the industrial development of the Soviet Union was extraordinarily successful. Growth rates were unprecedented and

---

[25] The *nomenklatura* system has already been widely discussed in the scholarly literature (see e.g. Voslensky 1980). In short, the *nomenklatura* was the mechanism for vertical mobility and élite formation in Soviet-type states on the basis of: (1) promotion and selection for the leadership positions by the Communist Party hierarchy, usually among the party's own members; (2) preferential access to material goods and a better quality of life as one progressed up the *nomenklatura* hierarchy. The *nomenklatura* selection principle secured, restricted, and monopolized access to the ruling élite, leading to the formation of a closed caste, remote from society, which governed all processes and aspects of the social system. This caste itself was often referred to as the *nomenklatura*.

the Soviet Union was able to reduce the gap between itself and the developed countries, at a time when these countries were experiencing the most serious economic difficulties.

However, the problem of forced industrialization was solved using methods which accelerated the country's economic development for only a fairly limited period, which created obstacles to further progress, and which were extraordinarily resistant to adaptation. Consequently, the foundations which were laid were conducive neither to long-term growth nor to stable economic development. Once conditions for economic development changed, and the elements of the crisis of early post-modernization began to accumulate, Soviet society began to experience new difficulties. It was unable to deal with these within the constraints that had been created by the Bolshevik Revolution. The preconditions for a new revolutionary cataclysm began to mature in the USSR.

3

The Preconditions for Revolution in the USSR

3.1 The Soviet system and the contradictions of early post-modernization

Both Russian and foreign analysts have expressed the idea that the revolutionary events in Russia and the other countries of the Soviet bloc were a reaction to the new 'demands of the time', brought about by the processes of post-industrialization and post-modernization. Many of them have observed that 'command socialist economies collapsed when confronted with the external pressure to make a . . . leap to a higher level technique cluster, the information-computer technology' (Rosser and Rosser 1997: 221).

Zygmund Bauman, one of the first to introduce the term 'post-modern revolution', describes how the prerequisites for it are formed:

In its practical implementation, communism was a system one-sidedly adapted to the task of mobilizing social and natural resources in the name of modernization: the nineteenth-century, steam and iron ideal of modern plenty. It could—at least in its own conviction—compete with capitalists, but solely with capitalists engaged in the same pursuits. What it could not do and could not brace itself for doing was to match the performance of capitalist, market-centred society once that society abandoned its steel mills and coal mines and moved into the post-modern age . . . The post-modern challenge proved to be highly effective in speeding up the collapse of communism and assuring the triumph of anti-communist revolution[.] (Bauman 1993: 15, 17)

The Russian journalist and economist Otto Latsis has described this process in a very similar fashion. He states that

at the beginning of the twentieth century the task of modernization, of finding a way suited to Russian conditions from an agrarian to an industrial civilization, of building an industrial civilization, was resolved under the pretext of constructing socialism. This problem was solved in the worst possible way, in the most cruel and costly way, but it was solved. And while that problem was being solved, the system was viable. . . . The system broke down when the next task of civilization arose—the transition to a post-industrial civilization, which (and this became perfectly clear at some stage in the 1960s) this system could not resolve. (Latsis 1994: 47)

Indeed, from the 1960s onwards it became increasingly evident that the Soviet system was unable adequately to adapt to the changing requirements of economic development. This expressed itself quantitatively in a slowing rate

TABLE 3.1. *Indices of economic development, USSR, 1950–1985*
(average annual growth rates, %)

	1950–5	1956–60	1961–5	1966–70	1971–5	1976–80	1980–5
Official Soviet figures[a]							
GNP	–	–	6.5	7.4	6.3	4.2	3.3
National income	11.4	9.2	6.5	7.8	5.7	4.3	3.2
Gross industrial production	13.1	10.4	8.6	8.5	7.4	4.4	3.6
Gross agricultural production	4.0	5.9	2.2	3.9	2.5	1.7	1.0
CIA assessments[b]							
GNP				5.1	3.0	2.3	1.9
Gross industrial production				6.4	5.5	2.7	1.9
Gross agricultural production				3.6	–0.6	0.8	1.2

[a] Calculations based on *Narodnoe khozyaystvo SSSR 1922–1972* (1973: 56, 49, 127, 219, 321); *Narodnoe khozyaystvo SSSR za 70 let* (1987: 41, 51); *Narodnoe khozyaystvo SSSR v 1990 g.* (1990: 8); *Shagi Piatiletok* (1968: 89).
[b] Hanson (1992: 194–5).

of economic growth, as Table 3.1 illustrates. However, this process cannot in itself be regarded as a sufficient indicator of the inefficacy of the system. In practice post-industrial development is attended by a slowing rate of growth in all countries, at least when assessed by traditional criteria. The growing qualitative lag behind the developed countries, which expressed itself in a variety of ways, was of far greater significance.

Some researchers have argued that it is impossible for a system of the Soviet type to offer a wide consumer choice comparable with that of capitalist countries in the post-modern (some would say even late-modern) stage of development. Bauman sees this as the basic reason for the collapse of the communist régimes. Indeed, a centrally administered society, which rejects competition and individual freedom, necessarily aims at uniformity in people's needs. Moreover, the Soviet system's strategic aim of increasing its productive potential at the expense of the living standards of its population resulted in low personal incomes, which limited the possibility of choice. But even within these narrow confines consumer choice was restricted by a whole range of supplementary factors.

On the one hand, because imbalances remained from the period of rapid industrialization, the satisfaction of even the most basic needs could not be guaranteed. The significant backwardness of agriculture had not been overcome, so the supply of foodstuffs to the population remained a problem. From the beginning of the 1960s, even although around half of the population was still engaged in agriculture, the Soviet régime had to resort to large-scale purchases of grain and other foodstuffs from abroad. Annual grain imports, for example, were sometimes as high as 35–6 million metric tonnes. It was only after the radical economic reforms of the early 1990s that these purchases were quickly reduced to zero.

On the other hand, even when the volume of output was increasing, the possibility of consumer choice was undermined by the generalized nature of the shortages. At a time when in the developed market economies consumers were being offered an ever more diverse and individualized range of goods and services, in the Soviet economy the 'sellers' market' became increasingly dominant and entrenched. In order to deal with the worst aspects of the shortages, the Soviet authorities had to resort to importing consumer goods.

None the less, the inability of a society to deal with the challenges of post-modernization can hardly be reduced to the limited nature of consumer choice alone. What Belousov described as 'the exhaustion of the potential of the Soviet industrial model, of its ability to respond to changing goals and resource conditions of reproduction' was no less important (1994: 25). Janos Kornai's well-known study of the functioning of centrally administered economies showed that the lack of 'hard budget constraints' in those systems brings about an unlimited demand for investment resources. This leads to a capital-absorbing and resource-absorbing type of economic development, with a constant orientation towards extensive growth. The data in Table 3.2 show how resource consumption grew faster than GNP in

TABLE 3.2. *Growth of Gross National Product and energy consumption, USSR, 1940–85 (%)*

	1940–60	1961–70	1971–80	1981–5
GNP growth during period	116	66	20	10.4
Energy consumption growth during period	197	69	54	12.3

Source: Gaidar (1997a: 397).

the USSR, including the time at which resource conservation became a fundamental factor in economic development in the West.

It is therefore quite natural that economic growth in the industrial system established in the USSR was completely dependent upon the volume of primary resource extraction, with an inflated investment sector. Resource-consuming technologies became established in the sectors producing finished goods, while in the primary sectors, speeded-up, capital-intensive technologies were developed to boost the production of energy and raw materials (Belousov 1994: 26–7). For every unit of GDP in Russia in 1992, five times as much energy was used as in, say, Canada (Magun 1994: 151). The traditional sectors retained their dominance, stifling development in the most advanced areas of scientific and technical progress, such as computerization and new communications technology; current estimates are that in the sphere of telecommunications, the country has lagged behind by several decades.[1] The defence sector played a central role, not only because the status of a world superpower required this, but also because its development was not hampered by the mechanisms of central administration and planning.

The low innovative potential of the Soviet system was largely responsible for the technological backwardness of the investment and consumer sectors, the failure of attempts to conserve resources, and the fact that Soviet output was not competitive. In spite of the innumerable decisions that had been taken at all levels since 1937 to speed up the introduction of new science and technology in production, it proved to be impossible to achieve this on a mass scale. Any qualitatively new scientific and technical developments were generally used for military needs and had little influence on the level of civil production. As for the new technologies and new products which did appear in the non-military sector, their introduction involved considerable changes in existing patterns of co-operation and a temporary decline in the volume of output, and required better-trained personnel. All this caused enormous difficulties in the system of centralized planning and provided no significant incentives. Partial modifications of existing output were therefore always to be preferred to any major product innovation.

The problem of technical innovation was solved using the same mechanism as was used to satisfy consumer demand—mass imports, in this case of advanced equipment. However, the country was also unable either to get involved in the international division of labour, or to attain real independence from the world market.

The inability of the Soviet system to adapt to new global trends is even more striking when one considers that in certain areas, particularly those involved with 'human capital', the necessary conditions for successful post-modernization had

---

[1] Russia's lag in this sphere at present is estimated at between 25 and 30 years (Shul'tseva 1996: 118).

in fact been created. The level of education of the population, which is one of the most important prerequisites for the transition to post-modern development, had traditionally been high. The data show that the indices for education in Russia are 1.8–2.2 times higher than the average for countries of a comparable development level,[2] and are overall at much the same level as those of the most advanced countries. As for the quality of education, it compared favourably with that of countries not only at a similar level of development, but also with that of substantially more developed countries. The USSR also had fairly well-developed systems of social security and social services which, although not very efficient, none the less provided the minimum necessary standards in those areas.

In order to understand why the centralized system proved to be incapable of adapting to the conditions of post-modernization, we need to examine the whole complex of problems which faced Soviet society, and the alternative ways of solving them that were feasible within the confines of evolutionary development.

As in the case of the other revolutions we have analysed, the new problems faced by the USSR can be divided into domestic and external problems. External challenges arose out of the status of the USSR as a world superpower. The state not only had to bear the heavy costs of military expenditure and of providing assistance to 'friendly' countries, it also had to be able to present a viable alternative to the capitalist system, and compete with the achievements of the developed capitalist states. It was therefore vitally important for the country to demonstrate the capability for scientific and technical breakthroughs, if only in some of the most advanced sectors, such as space exploration.

The internal problems were brought about by two independent, but ultimately interconnected, processes. As a mature industrial society develops, the scale, complexity, and differentiation of its economic and social system all increase greatly. A more developed agglomeration of sectors and product lines gradually takes shape, as does a more complicated system of economic and social interests requiring co-ordination. Governing such a society requires quite different administrative forms and methods from those used to concentrate resources for industrialization: 'A polycentric system of administration is more compatible with the level of complexity and differentiation found in urban-industrial societies, amongst which Russia must be numbered . . . It is more efficient' (Vishnevsky 1995: 213). Problems associated with the fact that the administrative mechanisms were inadequate for the level of development of the industrial system first appeared, albeit in latent form, in the second half of the 1930s. They were, however, swept aside during wartime mobilization, but emerged again after the post-war economic restoration. Subsequently, as post-modernization processes developed, the problems became more acute.

---

[2] Calculated according to data in Gaidar (1997a: 517).

Another problem was the tendency towards post-modernization, which created in itself a need for mechanisms not only to co-ordinate an increasingly divergent system of interests, but also to ensure the dynamism of the economy. Significant structural changes, a torrent of innovations, and the transition to a resource-conserving model of economic growth all demanded flexibility, mobility, and the ability to change rapidly. Moreover, for the direction and form of these changes to be effective, information had to be able freely to circulate around the world without let or hindrance, and be widely accessible to interested parties.

It is clear that the political domination of the Communist Party of the Soviet Union (CPSU), the system of centralized planning, the largely extra-economic compulsion to work, the preservation of autarkic tendencies, and the senseless secrecy surrounding an enormous volume of information greatly restricted the feasiblity of adapting to new requirements. In fact, Soviet society had only two possible alternatives. One was to try to keep a rigidly centralized economy, and within its parameters redistribute resources to the most advanced sectors, strengthen controls on the movement of resources in order to balance supply and demand, and maintain administrative pressure from above to ensure dynamic development. The other was to increase the importance of decentralized incentives, which in their turn could help to realize centrally determined targets and permit the system to be more dynamically balanced on the micro-level. Both these approaches proved to be ineffective and unable to secure the system's adaptation to the processes of postmodernization.

3.2 Limits of adaptation mechanisms: mobilization and decentralization

As the economic system approached maturity, an increasing tendency towards hidden decentralization developed, preventing the economy from retaining its mobilized character. Formally, the rigidly centralized system hardly changed at all: it retained all its most basic attributes, such as state ownership of the means of production, centralized planning, centralized regulation of resource and finance flows, and centralized price-setting. The overall goals for economic and social development in each five-year period continued to be laid down in state plans, the targets of which were gradually disaggregated and handed down from on high to every enterprise. Incentives for the enterprise director and workforce continued to depend first and foremost on fulfilling the goals set in these targets, rather than on the financial results of their activities. The enterprise continued to be supplied from the centre, and relations between producers and consumers were established 'from above'. All the financial resources (profits) created by the enterprise but 'not needed' by it in order to fulfil its plan targets continued to be confiscated and redistributed from the centre. The activities of each enterprise continued to be controlled by a far-reaching bureaucratic apparatus. However, these formal procedures reflected less and less the real processes taking place within the administrative system, namely, an increasingly evident tendency towards decentralization.

Decentralization was occurring in the first instance as a result of the growth and development of the bureaucratic apparatus. This growth occurred partly because the system had become more complex to administer, but also because of a whole complex of other factors. These included pressure 'from below' to broaden the privileged strata and ensure vertical mobility, and the general belief at the time that any problem could be solved by creating new agencies for dealing with it. Thus the development of the Soviet system was accompanied by an ever-swelling bureaucratic apparatus and the appearance of more and more new ministries and authorities. The number of intermediate links between the federal administrative authorities at the highest level and the actual producers also increased.

In theory, this long bureaucratic chain was intended to ensure that the enterprises carried out as fully as possible those tasks which they had been allocated on the basis of the state's overall development goals. In practice, each of these administrative levels was concerned with achieving its own goals, which increasingly undermined any possibility of effective control 'from above'. Since the work of these authorities was judged on the basis of the successes of their own areas of responsibility, they increasingly turned into lobbyists for the specific interests of 'their' enterprises, pushing for larger allocations of resources and lower plan targets. A similar process affected both the sectorial and regional administrations, giving rise to such specific terms of the Soviet period as 'departmentalism' (*vedomstvennost'*) and 'localism' (*mestnichestvo*).

Under such circumstances, there were severe limitations on the ability of the state to transfer resources away from traditional sectors, the interests of which were defended by powerful lobbyists, towards the creation of new sectors, which had nobody to represent their interests. In practice, redistribution took place in a quite different direction: from enterprises which worked well to those that did not, from profitable sectors to loss-making ones. Although financial indicators are necessarily conditional where prices are established centrally, this situation led to dissatisfaction and pressure from high-income enterprises and regions for a more equitable distribution of resources.

There was an ongoing decentralization of information as the economic system became ever more complicated. The planning organs' assessments of the needs and capabilities of economic agents came increasingly to rely on information gleaned 'from below', from the enterprises themselves. It was technically impossible to verify the accuracy of this information. It is in the interests of enterprises in a centralized system to obtain the lowest possible plan targets and the greatest possible volume of resources to fulfil them. Consequently information was presented in a highly distorted fashion. Any attempts by the government organs to counteract this tendency, by raising plan targets above those suggested 'from below', on the one hand induced the enterprises to understate their capacity even more, and, on the other, resulted in the plan targets becoming increasingly voluntaristic. Disorganization worsened as a result. In the mature planned economy there were many widespread practices which came in for frequent criticism. These included 'planning from the achieved level' (determining targets for the forthcoming period on the basis of the results of the preceding one), which placed the enterprises which worked best in the worst situation; plan targets which had become contradictory by the time they reached the enterprises, and 'corrections to plan targets on the basis of actual results', which deprived the plan of its real function of forecasting. These were not the results of miscalculations by the planning organs, but the reaction of a system of centralized administration to processes of hidden decentralization.

Although the supply and marketing of materials and capital goods were formally centralized, hidden decentralization was developing in this area too. It appeared in two basic forms: a tendency to organize one's own supplies, and in the shadow economy. As a reaction to the increasingly ineffective centralized system of supply and its inability to deal with the 'dictatorship of the producer', enterprises strove as far as possible to supply themselves with everything they needed, from nuts and bolts to foodstuffs for their employees. Similar tendencies could be observed at higher levels, in different sectors and subsectors of the economy. As a result, instead of optimal specialization and an effective collaborative network laid down 'from above', there flourished a system of 'natural economy', along with an extraordinarily low level of specialization and standardization. In addition, there was an ever-increasing volume of exchange between enterprises outside of the centralized directives and limits, carried on semi-legally or illegally in order somehow or other to plug the gaps in the central supply system. The administrative organs, interested in reporting on the successful fulfilment of their plan targets, often simply turned a blind eye to this.

The growing conflict of interests between enterprises, sectoral and regional administrative organs, and the administrative structures on the federal level was exacerbated by the technical inability of the centralized planning system to ensure balanced development and an interconnected system of plan targets for each enterprise. This made the economy even more unstable. But these technical problems were not the main factor which limited the state's mobilization capacity in adapting to the new stage of development. The rigidly centralized economic administration precluded the creation of mechanisms to co-ordinate the increasingly developed system of economic and social interests formed by the breakdown of the economic system into a multitude of individual subjects on various levels, and to establish a complex network of interconnections between them.

These hidden decentralization processes undermined a planning system based on the principle of the economy as a 'single factory', and this led to the system's erosion. However, given the soft budget constraints, the lack of competition, and the continued formal orientation towards plan targets as the criterion for assessing the performance of enterprises, this decentralization did not result in any greater orientation to real demand. The 'dictatorship of the supplier' remained untouched. For this reason the outcome of the erosion of the planning system cannot be described in market terms. The outcome which emerged is best characterized as a conflicting symbiosis of monopolies of non-market origin, formed at different levels of an administrative hierarchy. Under these circumstances the planning system evolved towards the 'economics of concordance', constantly seeking compromises between the interests of different monopolies.[3]

Not all writers on this question believe that the mobilization model had no future after rapid industrialization. Michael Ellman and Vladimir Kontorovich, in their work *The Disintegration of the Soviet System*, take the view that administrative pressure in a centralized system plays the same role as competition in a market system, and argue that this lever could have continued to be successfully employed:

At the end of 1982, Andropov became General Secretary of the Communist Party, and economic growth resumed practically overnight. The chief reason for the improved performance of industry and the railroads was the new leader's policy of tightening discipline . . . The recovery of the Soviet economy from its 1979–82 decline showed that the traditional economic system was viable. The system reacted favourably to policies appropriate for it (such as tightening discipline) given its specific characteristics. (Ellman and Kontorovich 1992: 14–15)

---

[3] These tendencies were not unnoticed by researchers on the Soviet economy, who themselves coined this term. As Aven and Shironin observed: 'The current economic mechanism is substantially different both from the mechanism of the 1930s, and from the general normative model. Underlying this difference is the rapidly increasing complexity of the economic system . . . This means that the system of giving orders, the 'command economy', is unable to operate, and is gradually giving way to a system of agreements, a 'trade economy', in which the relations between top and bottom are not only, and not so much, relations of subordination. They are rather more relations of exchange. The resources, the 'arguments' used from above in this 'trade' are material and technical means, money, norms, various methods of encouraging directors, and so forth. The resources used from below are the fulfilment of production tasks (or the promise of such fulfilment), participation in periodic campaigns (particularly in agriculture), and so on' (Aven and Shironin 1987: 34).

It is fairly obvious that administrative pressure in the Soviet system could and did produce temporary improvements in economic performance. However, this does not mean that the system itself was viable and able to deal with the problems facing it. This can be seen from the more concrete studies produced by the same authors. First, the country was faced not only with quantitative tasks, but also with qualitatively new ones. The resumption of economic growth without fundamental changes in the nature of that growth cannot be regarded as positive. There were no qualitative advances in that period. As Kontorovich himself observes, the Andropov campaign to tighten discipline did not lead to any noticeable acceleration in technological advance (ibid. 233).

Secondly, even if administrative measures had a short-term positive effect, they usually had profoundly negative long-term consequences. Ellman and Kontorovich's analysis of the operation of rail transport provides a graphic example of this (ibid. 174–84). The increase in the load of goods trains, which was seen in this period as the most effective way of solving the haulage problem, did mean that freight deliveries could be speeded up to a certain extent. However, more accidents, and more wear and tear on locomotives and tracks, also ensued. There were additional losses because it took longer to make up a trainload, since administrative pressure meant that trains had to have more trucks, even on those routes where they were not needed. There was also a sharp rise in false accounting. Gradually the administrative campaign came to nought, owing to 'the diminishing returns to administrative pressure' (ibid. 182).

In the post-Stalin period the idea that the problems faced by the Soviet economy could be tackled by decentralization gained currency. This was not just a matter of rejecting the Stalinist legacy. There were inherent tendencies developing within the economy which were insistently pushing in that direction. The processes of hidden decentralization increasingly demanded to be recognized openly and to be taken into account in the running of the economy. The negative consequences of these processes were also insistently demanding correction.

To a certain extent the ideas of decentralization lay behind Nikita Khrushchev's change-over in 1957 to a system of territorial administration based on economic councils—*sovnarkhozy*. However, the most serious attempt to find a way out of the economic contradictions of the planned system in the USSR through decentralization was undertaken in the mid-1960s. The independence of industrial and agricultural enterprises was broadened, and there was a sharp reduction in the quantity of plan targets they were expected to fulfil. The performance of enterprises was increasingly assessed on the basis of their actual sales of their output and profits. Enterprises were given a greater degree of influence over the way surplus resources were to be used. The aim was set of moving towards 'wholesale trade in the means of production'. The financial obligations of the state and enterprises were declared to be separate, and a formulation taken from the 'Decree on Trusts' of the NEP period was used: 'the state is not responsible for the obligations of the enterprises, and the enterprises are not responsible for the obligations of the state'. However, the general boundaries of the centralized system were preserved, central planning retained its leading role, and the state continued to regulate prices and limit the extent to which enterprises could change their line of production. It was believed that the decentralization incentives which had been created would help attain on the micro-level the goals set by the state on the macro-level.

The results of this reform were mixed. On the one hand, the rate of growth increased, at least in the short term. Enterprises became more oriented towards their consumers, and paid more attention to bringing out new products. On the other hand, the reform showed the limited potential of decentralization when the foundations of a planned economy are retained. The 'egotistical' self-interest of economic subjects began to manifest itself more openly, without being checked by the 'hard budget constraints' of a market economy—the need for there to be effective demand for one's output, competition, and the threat of bankruptcy. Additionally, this self-interest was permitted to develop while prices remained fixed, bureaucratic interference 'from above' in the operation of enterprises continued, and supply and demand remained unbalanced. The result was that the contradiction between the 'planned' and 'market' elements in the economy became extremely sharp, leading to growing imbalance and tension within the system. The negative tendencies which resulted from the reform of 1965 can be put into the following general categories.

First, there arose the problem of producing 'profitable' and 'unprofitable' lines of output. Since prices were fixed centrally and did not reflect the real balance of supply and demand, whether it was advantageous to an enterprise to produce any given product bore no relation to whether or not that product was really wanted. Plan targets, based on the principle of 'social necessity', included the production of both profitable and planned loss-making lines. Therefore the enterprises' interest in raising profits by changing from less profitable to more profitable products, which in a market economy would have been a normal phenomenon, in the centralized system inevitably resulted in greater imbalances and shortages.

Secondly, the greater freedom for enterprises to dispose of their profits led to a larger proportion of resources being diverted towards consumption rather than investment. Given the low standard of living in the USSR, this can hardly be seen as a negative development. However, in an inflexible economic system any spontaneous shift of demand from the capital goods market to the consumer market inevitably leads to shortages on the consumer market.

Thirdly, partly because of the moves towards more expensive output and partly because of the growing imbalances on the consumer market, the rate of inflation increased. At present it is difficult to assess what role was played in this process was played by the artificial monopolization of the market, but it became increasingly obvious that the absence of competition had a important negative effect on the outcome of economic reform.

In this way, the behaviour of economic agents which would have been quite rational from the standpoint of market economics came into conflict with the external environment created by the system of central planning. The logic of the reform process tended inexorably towards increasing the regulatory role of the market. In the second half of the 1960s there were suggestions that state control of price formation be relaxed, that elements of market competition be intensified, and that enterprises be made more closely dependent on the financial results of their work (see Birman 1967; Rakitsky 1968).

But such far-reaching reforms, which to a large extent could have replaced economic control by the party *nomenklatura* with market control, were irreconcilable with the interests of a significant, and at that time the most powerful, part of that *nomenklatura*. Without substantial changes in property relations these reforms would not have destroyed its position as the ruling social stratum controlling the means of production. But these reforms would have meant a major shift in the balance of forces within that stratum, in favour of the factory directors and against the top party economic bureaucracy. Besides, the differentiation of interests within the *nomenklatura* at that time had not gone far enough and the position of the enterprise directors had not become strong enough for such a coup to take place.

Sensing a threat to its social interests, the bureaucracy from the outset used every means to try to prevent real change. Subsequent analysis of the course of the economic reform has led some to conclude that the positive developments in enterprise behaviour had more to do with hopeful anticipation of the promised changes than with any changes actually implemented, as these were blocked by the apparatus at all levels. The events in Czechoslovakia in 1968, which demonstrated in practice the possible political consequences of market-oriented changes, served as a pretext for discarding the reforms. Ideological control, which had been slackened to a certain extent when the reforms were being introduced, was tightened again. The pro-market economists who had laid the ideological basis for the economic reforms of 1965 were subjected to persecution.

Formally, bureaucratic control of the economy was restored, and all further changes, such as they were, followed the logic of improvements of the centralized system of administration: a search for the best planning indices, rationalization and unification of the basic structure of the administrative apparatus, and so forth. However, even the stunted version of the 1965 reform that was implemented gave a sharp fillip to the processes of hidden decentralization which were already under way. In the longer term it became inevitable that the role of the 'lower strata' of the bureaucracy, closest to the real flows of resources and finance, would be enhanced. Moreover, the reform generally promoted a restructuring of interests within the *nomenklatura*, not only vertically, but also horizontally. It sharpened the contradictions between those strata with an interest in retaining the redistributive mechanisms, and that part of the *nomenklatura* whose interests suffered as a result of large-scale redistributive processes.

Attempts were made to adapt the economy not only in the USSR, but also in the other states of the Eastern Bloc at this time, in the logic both of mobilization and of decentralization. However, even a cursory analysis shows that both the urgency of the new requirements, and the rigidity of the existing constraints, were much greater in the USSR than in the overwhelming majority of Eastern European states. Only the Soviet Union carried the burden of 'superpower' status, which necessitated a high level of military expenditure. Moreover, the very size of the country made the task of centralized administration extraordinarily complex. This meant that limitations in the technical competence of the planning organs had widespread repercussions. At the same time adaptation was more difficult owing to the greater rigidity of the mobilization mechanisms that had been created during the modernization phase, and to the more closed nature of the economy and society as a whole.

The countries of Eastern and Central Europe had more compact economies and a greater degree of contact with the outside world, and their centralized system, imposed from outside, was less deeply rooted. In their cases the adaptation processes, following one or another of the alternatives we have examined, produced greater results, and the reconstruction of relations within the ruling *nomenklatura* was generally accomplished in an evolutionary way. The GDR was relatively successful in establishing firm centralized control over economic development, whilst in practice ensuring that managers had fairly wide leeway for manoeuvring with resources. Hungary carried through substantial market reforms whilst retaining state ownership of the main means of production. Within the socialist camp both countries showed quite good results, and their experience gave rise to two opposed conceptions of how socialist economics could develop further. There was also stronger political pressure in the Eastern European countries to destroy the system altogether and break out of the confines of the 'socialist alternative'. However, any real or imagined attempt to do so was firmly suppressed by Soviet troops in 1968.

3.3 The régime becomes unstable

Although the Soviet system was unable to adapt to the new conditions of development, its potential for stability was far from exhausted. Rates of economic growth slowed sharply after the eighth five-year plan period (1966–70), but the régime was able to maintain social stability. The living standards of the bulk of

the population were sustained at a low but guaranteed level; the repressive apparatus of the state retained its efficacy, and people could still remember the large-
scale Stalinist repressions of the 1930s. In addition, society remained very much
closed, and the population was subject to ideological indoctrination, and so there
was very little awareness of living standards in more advanced countries. There
was no basis in society for any broadly based movement against the existing
régime, so protest remained limited to individuals.

Primary economic growth and dynamic structural changes, by shaking
traditional institutional structures, had prepared the revolutions of the
modernization phase. The oil boom of the 1970s had the same effect upon the
Soviet system. Highly efficient sources of oil and gas began to be exploited at
almost exactly the same time as the sharp rise in oil prices on the world
market in 1973. At first sight this seemed to create highly favourable circumstances for the Soviet régime, allowing it to use the 'cheap money' from oil
sales to cover the costs of the inefficiency of the centralized planned economy.
A source of funds had appeared which could be used to solve the domestic
and external problems confronting the Soviet system. In external relations, the
challenge was to consolidate the USSR's status as a superpower and to
continue competition with the West. It was in this period that military and
strategic parity with the USA was attained, at the cost of even greater military
burdens on the economy.[4] The task in domestic affairs was to try to use these
new sources of income to solve, artificially, problems which stemmed from the
very nature of Soviet society. Attempts were made to raise living standards and
regenerate the productive potential of industry. Capital investments in agriculture were increased with the aim of overcoming its backwardness and
undertaking large-scale land improvement schemes. There were mass imports
of foodstuffs and consumer goods in order to stabilize the consumer market.[5]

---

[4] According to some assessments, the share of defence spending in the USSR's GNP rose
from 13% in 1970 to 16% in 1980 (Ofer 1987: 1787–8). Mikhail Gorbachev assessed overall
Soviet military expenditure in the 1980s at around 20% of GNP.

[5] This process can be illustrated by the example of agricultural imports, the overall
volume of which increased several times in one decade, with certain individual items
increasing by 10 or even 100 times.

	1970	1975	1980
Total volume of agricultural imports (billions of US dollars, at prices for that year)	2.7	10.0	19.5
Imports of meat (thousands of tonnes)	165.0	515.0	821.0
Imports of edible fats (thousands of tonnes)	2.2	11.6	249.0

Source: Gaidar (1997*a*: 443).

However, this policy, for all its superficial appeal, had a series of consequences which irreparably undermined the stability of the Soviet system.

First, the Soviet authorities gambled on what Egor Gaidar has called 'inherently unreliable economic growth, based on oil revenues', a kind of 'essentially unstable, reversible development trajectory, based on resources whose accessibility could change sharply' (Gaidar 1997a: 451, 440). The country's dependence on foreign trade, that is, on the export of fuel, grew substantially, in order to permit the import of capital and consumer goods.[6] The proportion of fuel and energy sales among total USSR exports rose from 15.6 per cent in 1970 to 53.7 per cent in 1985. Financial stability, the maintenance of living standards, the development of the livestock industry using imported feeds, and the operation of enterprises using high-technology imported equipment—that is, the main factors ensuring economic and social stability in the USSR—all became crucially dependent on a stable level of export revenue.

The availability of this new source of income, which allowed the economy to be financed despite the limited capabilities of the existing institutional system, put an end to any serious attempts at reform in the economic and, particularly, the political spheres. The situation continued to deteriorate. The increased amount of financial resources did not lead to an economic upturn, and growth rates remained low. Despite the mass import of consumer goods, shortages on the consumer market continued to worsen. The tendency towards disintegration in the formally centralized economy gathered momentum. Any significant fall in external revenue would inevitably expose the full depth of the crisis and the collapse of the existing system.

Secondly, the much greater involvement of the USSR in foreign trade made it impossible to maintain the former degree of closure and isolation of society from the outside world. More intensive contacts developed with foreign countries, more people travelled abroad, and more information penetrated the country from outside. This undermined one of the most important sources of social stability under the Soviet régime. Soviet people could compare living standards, technological achievements, and social relations with those obtaining in the West, and this led to dissatisfaction. It made them feel that the prevailing social relations and living standards in their country compared unfavourably with what could be achieved under another social system. This feeling spread among the most advanced section of the ruling élite and significant parts of the intelligentsia, and then

---

[6] Comparing the situation in the USSR in 1970 and in 1985 from this point of view, Egor Gaidar observes: 'In 1970 (if we exclude trade with the Comecon countries, which were essentially non-market), the USSR was still a country with a fairly closed economy. It had economic structures which provided the high degree of self-sufficiency in resources typical of the socialist model. It was to a limited extent subject to the influence of developments on world markets. But by 1985 the role of external economic relations had increased sharply' (1997a: 444–5).

infected wider social circles. It gradually undermined belief in the correctness of the ruling ideology.

Thirdly, the influx of petrodollars, like the contacts with the West, accelerated the processes of restructuring within the ruling élite and the development of conflicting interests. These processes had already been actively under way for some time, since the end of the 1950s and the beginning of the 1960s.[7] The Khrushchev reforms had fostered the coalescence and increasing importance of the regional bureaucracy as an independent force within the élite. The economic reform of the mid-1960s had strengthened the position of enterprise managers.

Along with this differentiation within the ranks of the élite, the process of private appropriation of what were legally state resources intensified. Various observers have noted that during the 1960s state officeholders obtained increasing opportunities for treating their positions as their own private property. Additionally, in regarding 'their positions as their own private property, the Soviet élite was also enabled to regard that portion of state property and benefits to which their position gave them access as private property' (Pastukhov 1994: 27). This process necessarily influenced the real character of property relations which developed in Soviet society: 'Although total state property formally reigned supreme, various peculiar "shadow" processes were developing within it, and a kind of "bureaucratic market" arose. Within the protective shell of state . . . property, a hidden but no less real form of "quasi-private" or "proto-private" property was developing. Along with the accelerating degeneration of the *nomenklatura*, there was a tacit process of "pre-privatization" of property' (Gaidar 1997c: 93).

Available sources of information do not allow a detailed analysis of the effect of the oil boom. It is, however, clear that conflicts of interests within the ruling stratum became more acute, and the fragmentation of the élite was increasing. A number of factors played a role here. It is most likely that there was a more intensive accumulation of wealth in the hands of individual members of the *nomenklatura*, not necessarily in accordance with their formal positions in the then-existing hierarchy. These strata, in common with traders in the shadow economy, developed an interest in acquiring legal title to particular resources. The large-scale redistribution of resources earned by the export-oriented sectors to less efficient import-substituting branches greatly sharpened the contradiction between different territories and sectors, and increased the dissatisfaction of an influential part of the ruling élite with the redistributive activities of the state. It was in this period that representatives of different regions and branches of the economy began to argue in earnest

---

[7] 'In the post-Stalin period, especially after the formation of the *nomenklatura* system, clan structures flourished. There was increasing differentiation in the private interests of different representatives of the ruling class—a process which developed along territorial, sectoral, national, and other lines' (Badovsky 1994: 49).

about who was living at whose expense. The USSR lagged ever further behind the Western countries, and this became increasingly obvious with the extension of foreign contacts. Fairly broad sections of the élite, including the intelligentsia, some state officials, and representatives of the military-industrial complex, began to voice their protests.

As these conflicts developed, vertical mobility during the 1970s slowed down considerably. It has been calculated that before 1953, the dynamic of vertical mobility was eight years; between 1954 and 1961 it increased to nine years, in 1962–8 to eleven, in 1969–73 to fourteen, and between 1974 and 1984 to eighteen (Golovachev and Kosova 1996: 50). By the mid-1970s the influx of cadres from outside the *nomenklatura* was also sharply curtailed. In the Brezhnev period members of the party élite who had not previously been members of the *nomenklatura* comprised 6 per cent of the total, and in the top leadership, the government, and the regional élite nobody at all came from outside the *nomenklatura*. There was a significant renewal of cadres only in the parliamentary élite—over 50 per cent—but in the Soviet period the role of parliament was quite insignificant (Kryshtanovskaya 1995: 64). Overall, 'vertical mobility finally took the form of a slow progress by carefully regulated degrees up the career ladder, each movement upwards being subject to strict social control' (Golovachev and Kosova 1996: 51).

The operation of all these factors in the midst of an oil boom strengthened the centrifugal tendencies stemming from divergent interests, and provided the impetus for the initiation of reforms 'from above'. Analysts of the preconditions for *perestroyka* usually classify these contradictions in similar terms. Krasil'shchikov, for example, has identified the following social strata as having an interest in reforms:[8]

1. the industrial 'technical bureaucracy', who wanted to break free from the control of party functionaries;
2. liberal intellectuals, journalists, and some of the officials of the Ministries of Foreign Affairs and Foreign Trade, who had the greatest opportunities for contact with the West;
3. the heroes of the 'grey' and 'black' economy, who in many regions had merged with the local authorities and exercised a strong influence on local affairs, but were interested in a more 'independent' existence;
4. state and military officials, and technocrats in the military—industrial complex, who were well aware of the growing backwardness of Soviet military technology. (Krasil'schikov 1996: 78)

It would also appear that contradictions were developing within the party *nomenklatura*. According to Alexander Yakovlev, the regional party élite wanted 'on the one hand, independence and power, and on the other hand,

---

[8] Gaidar gives a very similar list (1997c: 114–15).

that the centre guarantee this power'. There is much evidence (including interviews given by Gorbachev and Yakovlev to the authors) to confirm that in the
1980s provincial party activists were far more supportive of the idea of reform
than was the central party apparatus, where the general opinion was that it
was necessary to 'tighten discipline, which has become lax at the local level'.

Analysing developments within society as a whole is even more difficult
than unravelling the contradictions within the élite. In order to understand
how the conditions for fragmentation might have developed, it is essential to
reject all notions of the Soviet people as an undifferentiated mass, in
contradistinction to the *nomenklatura* as a ruling class. In fact, the whole of
Soviet society was fairly rigidly structured, if not in relation to the means of
production, then certainly in relation to opportunities for consumption.
One's place in this structure was determined not simply by one's work, but
also by the territory in which one lived, the branch of the economy in which
one was engaged, and the size and strategic importance of the enterprise in
which one worked. The principles of stratification of Soviet society were
defined by special rules and mechanisms of supply. Following the criteria
outlined above, they determined fairly rigidly how far a person could satisfy
his or her needs. It was noted at the end of the 1980s that the purchasing
power of money, for example, depended to a great extent on the social status
of its owner: 'As a consequence of the ranking of territories, branches of the
economy, and jobs, and a corresponding distribution of benefits, the purchasing power of money increases as one moves from lower- to higher- status
employment, from low-ranked to high-ranked settlements, and from enterprises and institutions in low-prestige sectors to those in high-prestige ones'
(Kordonsky 1989: 45).

All the indications are that the oil boom, which led both to a growth of
money incomes and an influx of imported consumer goods, had a destabilizing effect upon this system. It was no longer possible to regulate these
processes according to the formal rules and co-ordinate the growth of nominal incomes with real access to material benefits. A reduction in the supply of
cheap resources and a fall in oil prices must also have had a destabilizing
impact. Besides, stratification on the basis of assessment 'from above' of the
importance of one or another form of work cannot be reconciled with any
other system of distributing material benefits, such as by actual work done or
by the success of an enterprise. The introduction of such systems would only
cause much sharper social conflicts and aggravate social fragmentation.

All of these contradictions became more acute with the exhaustion of the
model of growth based on oil revenues. At the end of the 1970s and beginning
of the 1980s there were numerous localized declines in output: for example,
in coal extraction (down by 2.7 per cent in 1979–81), rolled metal (down by
2.9 per cent in 1979–81), and rail freight traffic (down 2.3 per cent in 1979,
down 1 per cent in 1982) (Belousov 1994: 28). Although investment in the fuel

TABLE 3.3. *Export of oil and oil products from the USSR, 1980–1990*

	1980	1981	1982	1983	1984	1985	1986	1987	1988	1989	1990
Crude oil exports											
(million tonnes)	119	—	—	—	—	117	129	137	144	127	109
of which for											
hardcurrency	27.4	—	—	—	—	28.9	32.1	38.2	49.1	27.2	38.0
Oil products											
and synthetic											
and fuel											
(million tonnes)	41.3	—	—	—	—	49.7	56.8	59.2	61.0	57.4	50.0
of which for											
hardcurrency	22.3	—	—	—	—	30.6	37.2	38.4	40.5	34.6	33.3
Export of oil											
and oil products											
(billion roubles)	17.8	21.6	25.4	28.2	30.9	28.2	22.5	22.8	19.7	18.6	15.6

Source: Sinel′nikov (1995: 33).

and energy sector continued to grow rapidly (in 1985 it was twice the 1975 level), as did the proportion of total capital investments going to that sector, the growth in oil extraction stopped, and export volumes stabilized. Unfavourable movements in oil prices on the world market led to a gradual decline in export revenues. As Table 3.3 shows, their maximum level was achieved in 1983–4. Thereafter they declined steadily, even though export volumes increased up to 1988.

The first symptoms of the impending crisis were therefore becoming apparent in the first half of the 1980s:

In 1985, when Mikhail Gorbachev became leader of the country, the USSR's economic position appeared 'stagnantly' stable only superficially and at first sight. In fact the possibilities not only of development, but even of maintaining the current levels of production and consumption, depended entirely upon factors beyond his control—prices on the world oil and gas markets, the discovery of highly productive new sources of oil and gas, the possibility of obtaining long-term credits on world financial markets at low interest rates. However, the beginning of the decline in world market prices for oil, and the reduction in the absolute level of export revenues ($91.4 billion in 1983, $86.7 billion in 1985), showed that a miracle was not about to happen. (Gaidar 1997*a*: 450)

Yet another factor which increased dissatisfaction with the régime both among the élite and the population as a whole was the protracted war in Afghanistan. From the outset people considered it an unjust war: it brought about large casualties and clearly demonstrated that the Soviet Union was unfit to play the role of a superpower. The war discredited the existing political régime still further. This was confirmed in sociological surveys carried out at the end of the 1980s. In 1988, 63 per cent of the population considered the withdrawal of troops from Afghanistan to be among the most important events of that year (Levada 1997: 11). Almost three quarters of those asked agreed with Academician Andrei Sakharov's condemnation of the war as criminal, made at the First Congress of People's Deputies of the USSR (Nikitina 1997*a*: 38).

We can therefore argue that the pre-revolutionary processes in the USSR during the late twentieth century resembled the ripening of such conditions prior to other revolutions. The oil boom was the factor which destabilized the system and led to the fragmentation of interests both among the élite and amongst the population as a whole. The oil boom produced a sharp rise in the influx of resources from abroad, and its exhaustion sharply reduced the availability of those same resources. The Soviet Union, with its rigidly stratified society, was vulnerable to such large-scale fluctuations. Internal contradictions began to grow within that society, while centrifugal forces gathered strength. However, by contrast with other revolutions, in the Soviet case this process was to a considerable extent disguised. When the exhaustion of oil revenues, combined with the first attempts at reform, allowed these contradictions to manifest themselves, their scale and depth surprised almost everyone. Our analysis has enabled us to conclude that the fragmentation of the system did not stem from Gorbachev's policies. As in other revolutions, its causes are to be found in the economic conditions and in the actions of the '*ancien régime*' in the pre-revolutionary years.

3.4 The results of revolution: will the crisis of early post-modernization be overcome successfully?

Among the key aims determining the actions of governments at various stages of the revolution were modernization, renewal, and catching up with the advanced countries, from the 'acceleration of scientific and technical progress' of the Gorbachev era to the frequent attempts in recent years to create a favourable investment climate and finally return to economic growth. Has the revolution been successful in creating the conditions for faster development?

One very popular view is that the policies of the 1990s have done irreparable damage to the prospects of Russia's economic development. Those who hold this view rightly point out that the country has suffered a huge decline in production, one of the main victims of which has been the military-industrial complex, the most advanced sector in scientific and technical terms.[9] The

---

[9] 'Towards the end of the Soviet period up to 80% of all scientific research in the USSR was connected with the defence sector in one way or another. In addition around 70% of

budget crisis has dealt serious blows to expenditure on science and education. Many qualified workers are leaving these crisis-ridden sectors to perform low-skill functions in trade and the service sector. A massive deskilling of the workforce is taking place. The collapse of the USSR and of Comecon has led to the loss of many external markets, and this further restricts development possibilities.

On the strength of all this it has been claimed that 'the economic liberalism of the early 1990s in Russia became the banner not of modernization, but of anti-modernization, or, more precisely, of pseudo-modernization, in the interests of the Russian ... energy and metallurgy industries, and of other branches concerned with the extraction and primary processing of raw materials' (Krasil'shchikov 1996: 81). The advocates of this view argue that economic liberalism has had catastrophic consequences: 'In recent years, Russian society has increasingly fallen into a process of demodernization, in which structures of a feudal- bureaucratic and criminal nature have come to the surface' (Yanitsky 1997: 40). The alternative policy usually envisaged is the introduction of strict protectionism, an active state industrial policy directed towards identifying 'points of growth', and increased concentration and monopolization of the market via the creation of large companies with significant material and financial resources. In other words, what is advocated is a typical strategy for modernizing countries in pursuit of industrialization, as we saw above.

However, the Russian revolution of the end of the twentieth century is not an exception. All previous revolutions have resulted in a deterioration in the economic situation, the destruction of a significant part of productive capacity, and deskilling of workers. The Russian revolution of 1917 led to complete economic paralysis within three years, and a further five to seven years were needed before the pre-war volume of industrial and agricultural production was restored.[10] This did not prevent the post-1917 régime from subsequently carrying out rapid modernization. In other revolutions, between twelve and fifteen years were needed for production volumes to be restored to their pre-revolutionary level (Gaidar 1997a: 465). No revolution has ever brought about an immediate acceleration of modernization processes. Historians have noted

the scientific potential was concentrated in Russia. For a long time defence had been the main area in which the best achievements in high technology had been applied. All civilian electronic consumer goods, from computers to televisions, are manufactured in defence plants along with radar equipment and jet fighter planes. In 1993 80% of the output of the military-industrial complex was for civilian use. Military factories made 100% of the televisions and 80% of the refrigerators produced in Russia. It has been estimated overall that in 1993 around 30% of all civilian scientific research and design work was carried out in the military sector' (Nel'son and Kuzes 1996: 41).

[10] The output of industrial and agricultural production reached its pre-war level in 1926–7 (Grossman 1971: 21).

the short-term negative impact on economic development of both the English and the French Revolutions.[11] However, the medium-term consequences were quite different. Whilst post-revolutionary England became the first country in the world to undergo an industrial revolution, in France the revolution really did result in a slower rate of industrialization. Let us stress once again the conclusion reached in our preceding chapter: revolution cannot in itself lead to accelerated development. All it can do is to remove the institutional and socio-cultural barriers to such development.

Examining the consequences of the revolution in terms of the removal of the constraints which were holding back the post-modernizing development of the country, we reach conclusions which differ substantially from those outlined above. Some integral features of the Soviet system, such as the total-itarian political structure, central planning, and isolation from the outside world, have been eliminated. The unbearable burden of military expenditure has been reduced, production has been freed from constraints and pressure 'from above', chronic shortages have been overcome, and the 'seller's market' is gradually becoming a 'buyer's market'. As Vishnevsky has observed:

If we ignore for the present the moral aspects of the current process of redistribution, it is important and necessary to recognize that for all the incredible costs society is nonetheless being pushed in the direction suggested by history. The enormous, all-embracing mafia of the totalitarian state has been broken up into numerous pieces. Although they have retained many of their birthmarks, not one of them is in a posi-tion to regain its former unrestrained monopoly, and this changes things fundamen-tally. Society has changed from being vertical to being horizontal, from having one centre to having many, and from being constructed from above to being constructed from below. (Vishnevsky 1996: 66)

From this point of view the proposals for greater centralization in the recon-struction of the economy put forward by the critics of the radical transfor-mation under way in Russia, are a step towards re-establishing 'the all-embracing mafia of the totalitarian state' and other 'inbuilt constraints' which the experience of the last thirty years has shown to have hindered the development of the country.

Not all of the processes which have been taking place in the economy over the last decade can be regarded as negative from the point of view of post-modernization. Researchers who believe that the current transformation has had a negative effect on Russian development prospects often confuse 'de-industrialization' and 'de-modernization'. The relationship between them is

---

[11] Theda Skocpol claims that 'one can sensibly argue, that the direct and immediate impact of the English Revolution was to retard industrialisation and prevent democracy' (1994*a*: 39). The revolution and subsequent 20 years of war in France can be seen as a national catastrophe, which 'increased . . . backwardness and made it irremediable' (Fohlen 1973: 18).

96 *Preconditions for Revolution USSR**Preconditions for Revolution USSR*

not, however, a simple one. In the process of moving towards a post-industrial system, many developed and developing countries had to overcome serious difficulties arising from de-industrialization. Although this is a painful process, it cannot be regarded as purely negative from the standpoint of Russia's further development. As for the scientific and technical potential concentrated in the military-industrial complex, the problem is not straight-forward here either. The crisis of the so-called 'Asian Tiger economies' of 1997–8 has highlighted the contradiction, if not the incompatibility, between the post-industrial content and typically industrial form of these countries' economies. This is yet another argument in favour of the view that, from a historical standpoint, it would be futile to try to adopt the sort of model presented by the Soviet military-industrial complex. This could only delay Russia's recovery from the crisis.

Additionally, with the break-up of centralized control of the economy, spontaneous moves towards processes and proportions characteristic of post-modern society have begun. The proportion of economic activity represented by the service sector increased from 37 per cent in 1980 to 51 per cent in 1996. Despite the generally negative economic trends, levels of telephone and car ownership have continued to grow—areas in which the USSR lagged behind global trends to a very great extent. Between 1990 and 1997 the number of telephones per 100 families in the Russian Federation increased from 30 to 41.3, and the number of motor cars per 100 families from 18 to 35 (Goskomstat 1998*b*: 572, 595). There was also a rapid growth in computerization during the 1990s. Surveys have shown that 3 per cent of Russian households have home computers, and that in Moscow this figure is 10 per cent (Dubin 1997: 15). Modern communication methods are becoming more widespread. The telecommunications sector grew by 10 per cent in 1997 against an overall growth rate of 0.4 per cent, and this sector had also demonstrated stable growth in the preceding years. The number of mobile phones increased from 93.2 thousand in 1995 to 770 thousand in 1998 (Goskomstat 1998*b*: 570).

No less important are processes of change in the attitudes of the working population, which increasingly displays the motivation characteristic of the transition to post-industrial society. Research on the life strategies of young people has shown that they are less and less ready to sacrifice their health for their work, to carry out unskilled tasks which are below their abilities, to perform monotonous work, or to work in extreme climates. At the same time they are inclined to overcome the problems arising from studying at a 'difficult' institution, to perform highly responsible work, to retrain and to master new professions, and not to start families until they have reached a certain level of education and material and social status. They are also increasingly interested in the quality of life, such as the availability of housing and ecological conditions (Magun 1996: 306–17).

It is clear that young people's aims in life are based on a rejection both of the sort of work performed by many categories of worker in a mature industrial society (low-skilled, monotonous), and of the principles of social stratification which characterized the Soviet system: 'There was little chance for such strategies in the old Soviet economic system, where skilled work did not in itself, as a rule, guarantee the worker a high standard of living, and where improvements in living standards tended to be achieved largely at the cost of sacrifices in the conditions and content of work' (ibid. 317). Moreover, the aims of youth differ substantially from those of the population as a whole, mostly educated under the Soviet system, and for whom, according to the research, the values of active self-reliance, work and status attainments, and responsibility are not very important (Magun 1995: 137–51).

4

The Revolutionary Process

4.1 Regular patterns in the revolutionary process

Specialists on the theory of revolution have paid considerable attention to the causes, and, to some extent, the consequences of revolutionary upheavals. The actual course of events in revolutions, however, has generally been left for historians to deal with, and has not been treated in a theoretical way. An exception to this rule has been the schema of a revolutionary process worked out by the so-called 'natural historians'. The best-known work of this kind remains Crane Brinton's *The Anatomy of Revolution*, written in the 1930s. Brinton based his analysis of four revolutions—the English and French Revolutions, the Russian revolution of 1917, and the American War of Independence—on the notion of stages in a revolutionary process. He identified the following stages: initial phase of the revolution, directly associated with the fall of the *ancien régime*; the rule of the moderates; the reign of terror and virtue; and the Thermidor. These categories have subsequently been widely adopted by specialists and, with some modifications, have been used to describe a wider range of revolutions or, at least, have been used as the starting point for analysis of such phenomena as 'revolutions from above' and aborted revolutions, which Brinton did not include in his study.[1] In general, the initial phase of the revolution has received much less attention, and Brinton's schema has been reduced to a three-part formula: moderates–radicals–Thermidor. Criticisms of this approach have usually been based on the claim that the schema generalizes from the experience of the French Revolution. However, other approaches to the theory of revolution have not been widely adopted and have remained outside the mainstream of research.[2]

---

[1] Explaining that he was limiting himself to a study of just four successful revolutions of a 'popular' or 'democratic' nature, Brinton stressed that 'a complete sociology of revolutions would have to take account of other types of revolution, and notably of three: the revolution initiated by authoritarians, oligarchies or conservatives—that is, the 'Rightist' revolution; the territorial-nationalist revolution; and the abortive revolution' (1965: 21). A modification of this approach is used in such works as Hamerow (1958) and Trimberger (1978).

[2] For example, Hagopian proposes that the three-stage schema of the natural historians be replaced by a more general approach, based on the fact that 'each revolution gives birth to forces that tend to push it onward (hypertrophic forces), and forces that tend to wind it

The extent to which Brinton's schema is applicable has been discussed in greater detail by Samuel Huntington, who has identified two types of revolutionary process—Western and Eastern: 'In the "Western" pattern, the political institutions of the old régime collapse; this is followed by the mobilization of new groups into politics and then by the creation of new political institutions. The "Eastern" revolution, in contrast, begins with the mobilization of new groups into politics and the creation of new political institutions and ends with the violent overthrow of the institutions of the old order' (Huntington 1968: 266). Among the revolutions of the Western type one can include the English and French Revolutions, the Russian Revolution of the beginning of the century, the Mexican Revolution, the first stages of the Chinese Revolution and, among more recent cases, the Iranian Revolution. It is to these revolutions that Brinton's approach is most applicable: 'In general, the sequence of movement from one phase to the next is much more clearly demarcated in the Western revolution than in the Eastern type' (Huntington 1968: 266). However, this type of revolution may also be modified, for example, where there is active foreign interference in the course of the revolutionary process, such as that of the USA in Mexico.

In our view, Brinton's approach provides a satisfactory description of the course of the revolutionary process in the 'purer' examples of Western revolutions. His basic weakness is not that he imposes the pattern of the French Revolution upon a wider range of phenomena. The problem lies in the methodology adopted by Brinton and other 'natural historians'. He sets out more to describe the symptoms of the disease than to analyse why revolutions proceed along such similar trajectories. Any schema which limits itself to describing phenomena without uncovering their causes is always vulnerable to criticism. Therefore, in order to analyse how far the movement of the revolutionary process is universal, and to determine the trajectory of the 'revolutionary curve', we need to go beyond the selection of examples and look for the causes of these phenomena.

This task must be undertaken not only to confirm or refute any given conception. The question of regular patterns in the development of revolution leads us on to the much larger problem of the connections between the pre- and post-revolutionary states of society. This is part of the wider issue of whether the historical process can or cannot be interrupted. Unlike the question of the course of revolutions, this has always been a central problem for social sciences. Indeed, within the social sciences an entire spectrum of possible opinions can be found, ranging from interpretations of revolution as a complete break with the past, to the notion that revolution is unable to change

down (entropic forces). The interplay between these two kinds of forces could theoretically produce revolutions that run through three, four, five, six or even more clear and distinct phases' (1974: 246).

anything fundamental in the course of historical development.[3] In order to tackle this question, we have to look at the logic underlying the course of revolutionary processes. Otherwise, the answer will be little more than description, illustration, or a collection of examples of similarities and differences in the pre- and post-revolutionary policies of the authorities.

For this reason, our analysis of the revolutionary process has two aims. First, we want to uncover the logic of the development of revolution, to discover the reasons for the similarity of the 'revolutionary curve' in revolutions which have taken place at different times and in different circumstances. Secondly, we want to demonstrate the connection between the logic of the revolutionary process and the outcome of the revolution, in order to understand not only why the changes brought about are so unpredictable, but also what limits the extent of their radicalism. However, before we can begin to deal with these matters, we have to look at some preconceptions which often underlie theories of the revolutionary process and prevent people from understanding it properly.

The first of these preconceptions concerns the nature of the social forces participating in the revolutionary process. Many students of this question are still strongly influenced by the Marxist tradition, in which revolution is regarded as the highest form of class struggle. Consequently, they analyse the main forces taking part in this process in an excessively aggregated form, as social classes.[4] A typical approach would be to examine the interests and actions of the aristocracy, the bourgeoisie, the peasantry, the working class, and so forth. There is, however, no real basis for such an approach. As we showed in Chapter 1, society embarks upon revolution in a highly fragmented state, split up into small groups which cannot find a stable basis for unification. The basic element of the social structure is a much smaller unit than a class. This fragmentation persists throughout the course of the revolution, although the configuration of groups and interests may change more than once. This is because the effects of the revolutionary process on the economic and social position of particular social groups and strata can be complex, sharp, and unpredictable.

This kind of interpretation provides a better explanation of the dynamics of the revolutionary process than does aggregated class analysis. During the course of the revolution, pro-revolutionary coalitions come together in unstable combinations which subsequently break down and realign themselves. These combinations are not held together by any inherent common interest, but are brought together under the pressure of external circum-

---

[3] The first position is most typical of works in the Marxist tradition; the second is represented, for example, in the works of Tocqueville.

[4] Such an approach is characteristic of all the classic works in this area belonging broadly to the Marxist current, including the books by Barrington Moore, Theda Skocpol, and others.

stances. The collapse of each of these coalitions brings a change of régime. The emergence of social—primarily élite—groups with stable interests, rooted in the new property structures created by the revolution, marks the end of the revolutionary process.

Another preconception about the course of revolutions concerns the motives behind the actions of revolutionary governments. The role of ideology in determining the actions of revolutionaries, especially in the radical phase, tends to be exaggerated. Indeed, at first sight it does seem that almost all the radical changes brought about are directly derived from one or another revolutionary doctrine. However, on closer examination it becomes evident that the actions of revolutionary governments are determined by a far more complex set of causes, and that pragmatism is especially characteristic of those very revolutionary forces who at first sight seem most driven by ideology.

The basic factor determining the logic of the actions of a revolutionary government is not only, or even mainly, a vision of how social life could be reconstructed justly and efficiently. Rather it is the practical need to acquire a stable social base and to overcome economic difficulties. To deal with this problem, measures must be taken in two directions. On the one hand, the revolutionary government must find a way to finance the revolution, that is, to acquire a financial basis for its rule. On the other hand, it needs to support its own social base. It must work out how to create and sustain pro-revolutionary coalitions, the instability of which we have already noted, and it must determine their composition. These two conditions for the survival of a revolutionary government may often present contradictory but equally pressing demands. It is these requirements which will determine its policies on such questions as food supply, war, agriculture, and so forth.

Furthermore, as the number of revolutions in human history increases, the experience of revolutionary change becomes a significant factor in practical politics. A concern to avoid repeating the mistakes which toppled revolutionary governments in the past will often be more important than preserving the purity of ideological principles in determining what decisions are taken.

Even this very cursory list of the basic factors affecting the course of a revolution shows the vital role of economic processes in setting the trajectory of the 'revolutionary curve'. Throughout the course of the revolution there will be a financial and then a wider economic crisis, which will be the most important factor determining the actions of a revolutionary government. The effects of these economic changes on the position of different strata and groups will determine the configuration of the pro-revolutionary coalitions. Finally, the revolutionary process will reach completion only when, as a result of the redistribution of property and economic power, new élite groups are able to form. The similarities between the courses of revolutionary processes occurring at different times in different countries are largely a product of the common character of the economic cycle in revolutions.

In this chapter we shall not dwell on economic questions. Hitherto, they have been relatively neglected in the theory of revolution, so in order to demonstrate the existence of a revolutionary economic cycle, we have decided to analyse historical experience on a large scale and examine economic questions in Chapters 7, 8, and 9. We shall consider economic questions only briefly here, and then only where this is essential for our analysis of the political and social aspects of the revolutionary process.

4.2 The power and powerlessness of the moderates

In the traditional schema, the first stage after a revolutionary government has come to power is the rule of the moderates. If we look at the way this period is presented in the work of Brinton, we can see that it has quite a complex internal structure and contains a number of quite different sub-stages. It begins from the moment of general unity that Brinton dubbed 'the honeymoon', and identified as the initial stage of the revolution which lasts until the assumption of power by the moderates. It ends with a situation of dual power, which cannot be fully regarded as the rule of the moderates—in this period they are obliged to share power with radical forces. Our task is to examine how and why such a decisive change in the balance of power takes place, which leads ultimately to the fall of the moderates and the radicalization of the revolutionary process.

The initial moment of general unity after the victory of the first revolutionary assault has not received much attention from students of revolution, who tend to be more concerned with the subsequent revolutionary strife. There is no doubt about the ephemeral nature of the unity of the revolutionary forces. They are united in their dissatisfaction with the *ancien régime* and in the temporary upsurge of revolutionary enthusiasm, but they have quite different positive objectives. Brinton, with a certain sarcasm, described this period thus:

the party of the revolution has won. The muddy waters of doubt, debate and agitation are momentarily cleared. The revolution, hardly begun, seems over. In England after the Long Parliament has disposed of Strafford and wrung concessions from the King, in America after Concord, and that greatest of moral victories, Bunker Hill, in France after the fall of the Bastille, in Russia after the abdication, there is a brief period of joy and hope, the illusory but charming honeymoon of that impossible pair, the Real and the Ideal. (1965: 79)

It would be wrong to underestimate the importance of this period. Although it is short-lived, it leaves a legacy of illusions which survive it for a long time and which have a significant influence on the overall policy of the moderates. Since the *ancien régime* fell like a house of cards at the first assault of the revolutionary forces, the impression is created that it had no internal resources left and no serious support for its existence. The widespread consensus that the old order cannot be sustained is taken by the moderates to mean that there is agreement on the final goals of the struggle. They imagine the patriotic upsurge to be a lasting factor which can be relied upon in real politics. The illusion of unlimited goodwill, a firm belief that there is a wide coalition of revolutionary forces ready to support far-reaching changes, along with their control of a state apparatus which is, generally, loyal and still fairly functional, gives the new authorities a sense of omnipotence. Throughout the course of their rule, the moderates are unable completely to abandon these notions, even though they turn out to be ever further removed from reality. This substantially diminishes their ability to react effectively to any problems that arise.

Yet another factor which limits the moderates' freedom of manœuvre is their firm adherence to a particular programme of social reconstruction. In this respect they are far more doctrinaire than the radicals who follow them. The moderates' programme, formulated in the pre-revolutionary period, is usually based on the most advanced philosophical and religious ideas that had developed under the *ancien régime*, and is sanctified with the authority of the leading thinkers of the age. It takes on board the experience of other countries which have been more successful in responding to the demands of the time. Finally, it contains an economic doctrine of one sort or another.[5] This

---

[5] The basic programme of the 17th-century English revolutionaries combined a Protestant view of how to organize socio-political life with the traditions of British constitutionalism. The following sources can be identified as having exerted the greatest influence:

- the philosophical pragmatism of Sir Francis Bacon, who proposed a critical attitude to reality, and experience as the basis of knowledge;
- the juridical ideas of Sir Edward Coke, who systematized Common Law as it had been developed in England by the beginning of the 17th century, and stressed such features as the inviolability of property rights and the limitations placed on the power of the King by the traditions of the British constitution ('legislative power is exercised by the King in Parliament');
- Protestant ideology as the basis of protest against the absolutist-centralist aspirations of the monarchy as inscribed in the doctrines of Catholicism;
- the experience of the Dutch revolt in respect of its anti-absolutism in the political sphere and the policy of mercantilism (the encouragement of trade) in the economic sphere.

In France the programme for the reconstruction of society was strongly influenced by the philosophy of the Enlightenment, particularly such ideas as limiting the power of the monarch by the spirit of law, a social contract or some other natural mechanism, and the need to move from tyranny to an enlightened form of rule based on rights. The experience of British parliamentarism was actively assimilated. To an extent the American War of Independence also influenced the programme. Its economic ideas were based on the doctrines of the physiocrats, who proposed that arbitrary taxation be eschewed and

programme embodies the spirit of the age, and enjoys widespread social support in the pre-revolutionary period. Attempts by the most progressive politicians to implement this programme under the *ancien régime*, which usually foundered on the opposition of the conservatives, further strengthen the notion in society that there is no alternative to this particular course. It is as if this programme is literally fated to succeed. In practice, however, the result turns out to be quite the opposite.

The problem is that this programme of renewal was developed under the *ancien régime* and was not directly put into practice in that period. It contains a series of specific features which makes it inherently unfeasible, especially in a revolutionary society. First, it has a definite goal-oriented character. It describes a state of society which, from the standpoint of advanced ideas, would be desirable, but remains nebulous as to the concrete mechanisms whereby this ideal might be attained. Secondly, it contains the full complex of prejudices and limitations characteristic of the *ancien régime*, and tries somehow to combine all that was best in the old system with the new demands of the times. Thirdly, it is not oriented to the interests of specific social forces, but tries instead to embody certain abstract overall goals, reflecting notions of a fair, just, ideal social structure which could gain the support of everyone or almost everyone.

At the beginning of the revolution there is a broad unity of social forces. The impression this creates, that the normative state of society outlined in the programme can be attained quickly and easily, determines the moderates' behaviour after they come to power. At a time when the new authorities are not yet burdened with their own mistakes and still enjoy considerable room for manoeuvre, they devote themselves to trying to realize utopian goals with unsuitable means, relying upon illusory supporters. The results are wholly predictable. The French revolution of 1789 and the Russian revolution of 1917 provide very good examples of this. Both revolutions at their outset had to solve very pressing problems left over from the *ancien régime*. In France it was the financial crisis, in Russia the problems of peace and bread. In both cases the basic features of the moderates' policies display a remarkable similarity.

economic relations be liberalized. Overall the programme of changes in France, compared to that in England, was based on a more developed and elaborated system of ideas, including economic ideas. It displays much less evidence of a religious world-view, and a predominance of progressive, rather than traditionalist, elements.

The programme for transforming Russia at the beginning of the 20th century was strongly influenced by ideas originating in the crisis of advanced industrial countries. The rejection of liberalism, and the notion of a regulated market, were some of the most important sources of this economic ideology. Another basic component was socialist doctrine in its various guises. There was a clear understanding of the need to break with the remnants of archaic society and to bring the socio-economic and political structure of the country closer to the European model, for which the most important component was European parliamentarism.

First, there is a tendency to take mainly strategic, long-term measures. It is assumed, consciously or unconsciously, that the implementation of a programme of strategic measures can in itself stabilize socio-economic relations, and can overcome the very difficulties which caused the political crisis and a new government to come to power. 'It is not now a matter of combining those petty resources of stock-jobbing and fisk,' remarked Montesquieu, the Chairman of the Financial Committee of the French National Assembly; 'These talents, which have for so long been recommended and praised, will not succeed with us ... We need an all-embracing plan, a plan of financial renaissance' (cited in Fal'kner 1919: 23).[6] The Russian Provisional Government proposed to tackle in the same spirit the immediate problems of getting factories working and food supply, in accordance with its understanding of the strategic tasks of genuinely popular power. The declaration of Groman, who was responsible for supplying consumer goods to the population of Petrograd in that period, is very typical: 'I shall not distribute a single pair of shoes until the national economy as a whole has been regulated' (cited in Jasny 1972: 99). Not surprisingly, the authorities prove unable to take the immediate steps needed to overcome the crisis.

Secondly, there is an urge to base policies not on real interests, but on revolutionary enthusiasm and patriotism. We can see this very clearly by looking at the mechanisms the French National Assembly tried to use to resolve the pressing problem of financial stabilization. In principle, the deputies already had at their disposal a very coherent economic doctrine developed by the physiocrats. An important part of this doctrine was that the main burden of taxation should be shifted onto landed property. However, in practice, the government had great problems implementing this policy, and so postponed it until some time in the future. For the time being the principle of equal taxation for all estates was transformed into a principle of refusal to levy taxes at all. On 17 June 1789 a decision was taken to abolish taxes, including indirect taxes. In their place, the authorities proposed a 'simultaneous patriotic liability on every citizen of one quarter of his income, calculated on the basis of a voluntary and unverified declaration' (Smirnov 1921: 8). The financial consequences were entirely predictable. The principles guiding the Provisional Government in its attempts to solve the problems of food supply were very similar. Appealing to the people's revolutionary consciousness, the authorities proposed various schemes for self-taxation for the peasants. The extent of the liabilities were to be determined by local government organs and specially selected local inhabitants (the most 'responsible', 'respected', and 'hard-working'). At the same time several government economists imagined that, in

---

[6] It is notable that these words belong to someone who not only was one of the main financial authorities in the National Assembly, but who also belonged to the highest echelons of the aristocracy—one of its first representatives to join up with the Third Estate.

conditions of accelerating inflation, the peasants could be induced to sell their grain in exchange for certificates, whose value would be determined later, once the economic situation had stabilized.

Thirdly, there is an exaggerated belief that popular support will enable measures that under the *ancien régime* either did not work at all, or had negative results, to be employed effectively. When he convoked the Estates-General in 1789, King Louis XVI made Necker, the authoritative and popular financier, *de facto* head of the French government. A few years previously Necker had been dismissed for his attempts to make major changes to the financial system. In an attempt to find sources of finance for the new government in the first months of the revolution, Necker, with the support of the National Assembly, chose to make a new issue of state bonds. Such measures, which would have been natural for the financial administration of the *ancien régime*, had become extremely ineffectual even before the revolution. However, these traditional methods were combined with new expectations. Both the minister and the newly elected deputies were counting on the patriotism and revolutionary spirit of the population, which in the new circumstances was supposed to change its behaviour and give money to the new government. In fact, the government received less than 10 per cent of its planned revenue. In exactly the same way, the Provisional Government, in accordance with the then-widespread belief in the effectiveness of state monopolies, introduced a grain monopoly in full awareness of the failure of similar attempts by the Tsarist régime. The government was convinced that in the new circumstances the outcome would be quite different. When the politicians and propagandists of the time encountered an increase in social tension and active resistance to such measures by the peasants, they were incapable of going beyond responses like: 'What is the cause of . . . the trouble? There are many causes, but the main cause is in ourselves . . . The interests of the state are now our only interests. The government is no longer alien, but ours, a people's government' (*Prodovol'stvie i snabzhenie* 1917, no. 2: 3).

What is more, that unity of forces which constitutes the social base of the moderates begins to dissolve. Two processes are actively under way in this period. On the one hand, revolutionary society is rapidly being restructured. It becomes differentiated in line with the positive interests of the groupings involved in the initial bloc of social forces. On the other hand, the initial interests of the participants in the revolution become radicalized, and increasingly tend towards two opposite poles. We can label them roughly as 'party of the end of the revolution' and 'party of the radicalization of the revolution'.

In relation to the English Revolution these processes can be illustrated by looking at the balance of social forces represented in Parliament between 1641 and 1648. As Christopher Hill has noted, the greatest unity of forces in the Long Parliament was seen when it passed the bill of attainder against Strafford in May 1641, which only 59 members voted against. Six months later 148 members would vote against Parliament's petition of demands to the King, the Grand Remonstrance, and during the Civil War around 236 MPs associated themselves with the royalist party to a greater or lesser extent (of which about 100 had their estates in areas controlled by the royalist army) (Hill 1962: 111). David Underdown (1971) has also traced the realignment of forces among those parliamentarians who fought the King. He argues that from 1642–5 there were three basic groupings in Parliament: the 'party of peace', which wanted to reach agreement with the King on almost any terms; the 'party of war', which stood for the complete defeat of the King and a thoroughgoing reform of Church and state; and the 'middle group', which desired peace, but demanded further concessions from Charles on parliamentary control of the armed forces and the appointment of ministers. Each of these 'parties' had around thirty adherents, while the bulk of the parliamentarians were 'independents', who generally supported the middle group. In this period the middle group managed to make its aims the aims of the entire parliamentary party. The parties of Presbyterians and Independents in the Long Parliament formed in 1644–5. The first arose on the basis of the 'party of peace', which had been joined by individual members of the 'middle group', all opponents of the parliamentarian New Model Army and the parliamentary committees which exercised power on the local level, and all those who favoured a speedy agreement with the King on terms favourable to him. The second was essentially a union between the middle group and the radicals, with strong links to the army command. Underdown stresses that the lines of division were not so much religious as political, and makes a distinction between 'religious' and 'political' Presbyterians, and between 'religious' and 'political' independents. While the union with the middle group lasted, the independents could restrain both the Presbyterians and the radicals. But from the spring of 1647 disagreements began to develop between the army command, radicalized by pressure from below, and the middle group, which was moving to the 'right'. By autumn these disagreements had become sharper, and by the spring of 1648 a complete break loomed.

In France the broad coalition of social forces which had come together at the outset of the revolution began to crack as early as September 1789. A small group of former revolutionaries broke away. They were primarily members of the liberal nobility, disquieted at the general course of the revolution and, in particular, by the violent events of July: 'What united these *Monarchiens*, as they came to be called, was the desire to "put an end to the Revolution" ' (Furet 1996: 76). From then on the split began to gather pace. At the beginning of 1790 Count Mirabeau, one of the best-known participants in the revolution, set up active contact with the royal court, and in effect became a secret adviser to the King. In the spring and summer of 1791 there was a call for an end to the revolution from the so-called 'triumvirate'. This influential group of moderate politicians was adamant that the revolution should not be allowed to go any further.[7] A new crisis amongst the revolutionaries was brought about by increasingly sharp disagreements on the fate of the monarchy and by the revolutionary authorities opening fire on a peaceful demonstration of Parisians in the Champ-de-Mars. In July 1791 this led to a split in the Jacobin Club, the organization which had initially brought together a broad spectrum of opponents of absolutism. Some of its moderate members left the club and formed a new organization, which became known as the Feuillants. There was a parallel tendency towards conservatism in the actions of the authorities. In September 1791, after Louis XVI had sworn his allegiance to the constitution, the Legislative Assembly proclaimed an end to the revolution (Furet and Richet 1970: 97). However, this turned out to be premature. The growing conservative tendencies caused increasing dissatisfaction on the left. The divergence continued, and expressed itself in the opposition between the Montagne and the Gironde in the Legislative Assembly and the Convention. At the same time a more substantial factor in the development of the revolution appeared: the radical Parisian poor organized themselves. From August 1792 the Commune of Paris began to act as an independent centre of power. In addition, the forces of internal and external counter-revolution were consolidating and becoming active.

Other revolutions, too, were characterized by processes of realignment which increased divergence and polarization, and these processes were often even more complicated. A number of causal factors can be identified.

First, it was always likely that the interests of the participants in the revolutionary coalition would diverge, since their initial unity was artificial. It had been built around a negative rather than a positive programme. A variety of forces had united for one thing, to overthrow the old order, and once this had been achieved, the basis for unity disappeared. This has often been observed in the literature on various revolutions. In addition, the restructuring process is inevitably accelerated by the actions of the early revolutionary government itself. Although its policies are ostensibly in the general interest, in fact they have very different effects on different strata and groups. The requirements of some groups are satisfied, and for them the revolution is already completed. For other groups it is only beginning, particularly for those who took an active part in the overthrow of the *ancien régime* only to discover that in a number of respects their position has deteriorated substantially. The Manifesto of the Enragés, presented to the Convention after the victory of the Jacobins,

---

[7] On 17 May 1791 Duport made a speech at the National Assembly in which he said, 'The Revolution is over. It must be settled and protected by combating excesses. We must restrain equality, reduce liberty and settle opinion. The government must be strong, firm and stable' (cited in Furet 1996: 94). Barnave made the same point very strongly a few months later: 'They do us much harm when they continue the revolutionary movement indefinitely. At the present moment, gentlemen, you should feel that it is in the general interest that the revolution should stop' (cited in Manfred 1973: 26).

expresses these sentiments very clearly: 'For four years the rich have been enjoying the benefits of the revolution; the aristocracy of trade, more terrible than the old aristocracy, oppresses us, and we can see no end to their extortions' (Dobrolyubsky 1930: 29). The supporters of the *ancien régime* also begin to play an independent role—after the initial shock, they gradually consolidate themselves and return to political activity.

Secondly, economic problems get worse. This stems from the difficult financial and economic position bequeathed by the *ancien régime*, the complexity of adapting the economy to new economic regulators and a new demand structure, and also from the mistakes of the moderate government itself. The rate of economic deterioration varies from revolution to revolution. Where the moderates prove able for a while to stabilize the economic situation, their position can be temporarily strengthened. Where they fail to do this, the moderate government very soon departs from the historical arena. In France, the moderates ruled for a few years; in Russia in 1917 they lasted for just a few months.

Thirdly, a general radicalization of the masses takes place. The rapid growth of the Bolshevik party in Russia, from 25,000 to 300,000 between February and October 1917, provides an example of this process. What causes this sort of radicalization?

The initial period of the revolution is almost always attended by extraordinarily high expectations that the situation will improve, social justice will prevail, and the economy will flourish. The contrast between these expectations and reality is striking—the economic situation worsens and, in the view of important sections of society, the 'gains of the revolution' are unjustly distributed. This process of divergence between expectations and reality in the theory of revolution is known as 'relative deprivation', and is regarded as a most important precondition for mass violence.[8] It seems to us that this is the major factor in the radicalization of the masses. Objectively, the problems causing the situation to deteriorate may have nothing to do with the revolutionary process. They may be the result of, say, a poor harvest or the stresses of war. None the less, the blame for them is laid at the door of the revolutionary government, and general enthusiasm gives way to growing disenchantment. Ever more persistent rumours of forthcoming food and fuel shortages, and a growing sentiment that things were better before, are reliable indicators of the impending fall of the moderates.

All these processes taken together give rise to the situation that Crane Brinton characterizes as dual sovereignty, arguing that 'once the first stage in revolution is over, the struggle that arises between moderates and extremists comes to be a struggle between two rival government machines (1965: 134). In our view, that description is not quite accurate. The moderates' power is

---

[8] This approach is developed in Gurr (1971).

actually or potentially opposed from two sides—from the right as well as the left. The left demands that the revolution be widened, while the right believe that the revolution has given too many freedoms to the people, and that order needs to be restored. The centrist, middle line, which not so long ago seemed to suit everyone and to be able to reconcile all interests, now turns out to suit nobody. The basic values of democracy and freedom rapidly lose support, becoming associated with indecisiveness and softness. The 'most popular government' suddenly becomes most unpopular. It bears the responsibility for the worsening crisis, and loses all support.

The moderate government, realizing that its social basis is steadily erod- ing, starts to waver. It is frightened by the growth of radical sentiments and fears that the mass movement will get out of control. It uses force to try to suppress those who are calling for the revolutionary changes to be broad- ened—as in July 1791 when the demonstrators in the Champ-de-Mars were fired upon, or in July 1917 in Petrograd when demonstrations were put down by force. The sentiment grows among the moderates in favour of a compro- mise with the *ancien régime*, even if this means significant concessions. None the less, they are unable to break fully with the principles and values in the name of which, for them, the revolution was made. Nor can they abandon a programme which attempted to combine all that was best in the old order and the new. They are not prepared to establish a firm dictatorship. The lament of Alexander Kerensky, the head of the Russian Provisional Govern- ment in 1917, is typical: 'It is hard for me, because I struggle with the Bolshe- viks of the left and the Bolsheviks of the right, but people demand that I lean on one or the other . . . I want to take a middle road, and nobody will help me' (cited in Rabinowitch 1976: 115). The military commanders of the English Parliamentarian Army found themselves in a similar quandary— they wanted neither to fight the King, nor to make any significant compro- mises with him.

The economic policies of such governments will also tend to be inconsist- ent. In France the Legislative Assembly vacillated in its attempts to solve the agrarian question. The solemn promises of the Russian Provisional Govern- ment to maintain fixed prices for grain purchases throughout 1917 culmi- nated in those prices being doubled unexpectedly. The government will try to combine persuasion and price manipulation with threats of requisitioning and suchlike repressive measures, but it is not firm enough to carry these threats out in practice.

Naturally, this uncertainty and inconsistency does nothing to enhance the popularity of the moderate government, the position of which has already been substantially undermined. What is more, the situation continues to dete- riorate, economic problems worsen, domestic and foreign counter-revolution threaten, and mass dissatisfaction increases. A crisis, closely resembling that which very recently led to the fall of the *ancien régime*, gathers momentum.

The very inconsistency and contradictoriness of the moderates' policies in this period shows that they are no longer an independent force, but are vacillating between two extremes. We can cite further arguments in favour of the view that the moderates' social base is being eroded to the advantage of these extremes, and against the notion of dual power as a counterposition of moderates and radicals. First, the decisive conflict leading to the fall of the moderates usually takes place between forces to the left and the right of them. The second civil war in England, which broke out after Charles had refused to compromise with Parliament; the treachery of Dumouriez, who was prepared to send troops to Paris to restore the monarchy and the Constitution of 1791; the Kornilov revolt in Russia—in all of these cases provocations from the right posed a direct threat to the gains of the revolution, and in the final analysis led to the assumption of power by the radicals. In these circumstances the moderates continued to display indecisiveness, vacillation, and an inability to take the firm decisions required by the gravity of the situation. Secondly, if the moderates succeed in repressing the radical forces in the initial phase of the revolution, they are almost never able to hold on to power. The right consolidates itself, and the revolution suffers defeat. The German revolution of 1848 and the Russian revolution of 1905 provide two textbook examples of this.

Our analysis of the politics and circumstances of the period in which the moderates hold power allows us to draw certain conclusions as to the reasons for their weakness. These reasons form a complex web of subjective and objective factors. A society which embarks upon revolution is already so fragmented and heterogeneous that in all probability it could not hold to any single political line. Furthermore, at the very time when consolidation to defend the gains of the revolution and to deal with economic problems is becoming increasingly necessary, social restructuring and a differentiation of opposed interests are making themselves felt most strongly. These circumstances expose the weakness of the coalition created to counterbalance the 'tyranny' of the *ancien régime*. In addition, the moderate government itself is not well suited to survive against a multiplicity of aims and demands, is unable to manœuvre between different social groups and to form coalitions in support of its own social base. The forces which came to power on a temporary surge of unity and on the basis of the most advanced ideology developed under the *ancien régime* are, to the end, unable to rid themselves of the illusion that they can represent the interests of the whole of society. But the society whose interests they aspire to represent no longer exists. Instead, two opposing camps face each other, and compromise between them becomes increasingly impossible. It is the outcome of the clash between these two camps that will determine the future course of the revolution. The victory of the radicals means that the revolution has entered a new phase.

4.3 The radicals' quest for money and coalitions

When the radical forces assume power, they seem at first sight to be in a more difficult position than the moderates had been a few months or years previously. They are faced with internal and external counter-revolution, and are obliged to deal with even more serious economic difficulties. None the less, in a certain respect they have significant advantages over their predecessors. First, some social strata have already been cut off from the further development of the revolution as a result of the process of divergence. This significantly narrows the range of interests that the radicals have to harmonize. Secondly, these interests are consolidated from the outset by the need to resist the enemies of the revolution. Indeed, this 'negative' unifying factor lasts far longer than the unity which formed to overthrow the *ancien régime*. Thirdly, the radicals themselves are better adapted for acting in the real circumstances of divergent interests. They use a whole package of measures which unify society forcibly, from without, thereby allowing them to retain power.

The fact that the radicals are better able than the moderates to adapt to real circumstances is not because their programme of action is better suited to actual conditions. Although the radicals are able to break with the approach which seeks to combine all that is best in the old and new orders, their own ideology is just as utopian as that of the moderates, if not more so. The point is that ideology plays a different role in the radicals' politics. The practical programme of the moderates always flows logically from their more general notions and ideals. With the radicals that link is often not so direct. Either they expect the ideals of the revolution to be realized at some time in the future, or they very skilfully adapt the ideals themselves to the needs of the moment. The notion, widely held both by historians and by contemporaries, that the radicals are fanatical dogmatists who impose their wildly unrealistic ideas by fire and sword could not be further from the truth. Although the radicals do indeed subscribe to a fairly rigid set of dogmas, in practice these dogmas do not serve to check the government's actions. They are first and foremost an instrument to be applied externally upon society, and from that point of view can be regarded as an external ideology. The imposition of ideological dogmas on society (ideas which, incidentally, are always already present in social attitudes) is one of the levers for forcibly ensuring its unity.

A similar method is direct political force, and in the radical phase of the revolution it often takes the form of terror. The radicals reject the discredited democratic institutions of the moderate era, and are ready to use dictatorial, forcible methods to ensure social unity not merely occasionally, but continually and systematically. Intimidation of opponents becomes one of the most important methods for consolidating the radicals' power.

As far as their practical policies are concerned, in most cases the radicals display a profound pragmatism, and are much less hampered by their own programme and ideology than the moderates were. They are able to take account of the interests which actually exist and of the balance of social forces that has developed. Many of the key decisions taken by Cromwell in the English Revolution and by Robespierre in the French were forced upon them by events. Underdown, like many other historians of the English Revolution, has observed that very few leaders in the radical phase of that revolution actually shared the radical aspirations of their followers in the regiments and congregations, in deference to which they purged the Long Parliament, executed the King, abolished the House of Lords, and established the Commonwealth (Underdown 1971: 174). It is generally accepted that maximalist policies and the Terror were imposed upon the Jacobins 'from below'. By contrast, it is still widely held that for the Russian radicals in 1917 ideological doctrines played a decisive role in their practical policies. Let us examine how this claim fits in with the actions of the Bolsheviks in the first three years of their rule.

The Bolsheviks' contemporaries drew attention at the time to the contradictory nature of Bolshevik statements, and to their ability rapidly to revise their line and policies, even programmatic ones. This is also obvious if we compare the texts of the official party programmes of 1903 and 1919 with the real actions of the Bolshevik leadership after they took power in October 1917. Their programme of immediate measures in the event of taking power proposed a partial nationalization of industry and a transition to workers' self-management, the nationalization of land and a subsequent agrarian reform, and nationalization of the banks and major corporations, with protection for the rights of small investors. Major changes to this programme began to be made from the very first days after the Soviet government was formed. First, the Bolsheviks adopted the Socialist Revolutionaries' (SR) programme of agrarian reform by distributing parcels of land without immediate nationalization, which was more effective at winning the peasantry over to their side. Only after the civil war had begun, and it was necessary to provide the army and cities with food in order to stay in power, did the Bolsheviks start to rely on the rural poor, whose motivation was more one of consumption than of production. There followed the nationalization of land, the formation of Committees of the Rural Poor (with the redistribution of part of the richer peasants' lands among the poorer peasants), and requisitioning as a way of forcibly extracting the necessary foodstuffs.

The Bolsheviks' approach to the organization of industry was to change no less radically. The original syndicalist idea rapidly showed itself to be ineffective, both economically—factories did not work any better—and politically— it turned out that workers' self-management did not strengthen the Bolsheviks' position. It became clear that the independent organs of workers' administration quickly made common cause with enterprise owners in a united front against state interference. In the light of this experience, by the spring of 1918 the Bolsheviks had moved towards a decisive centralization of the administration of industry and towards nationalization, and began to implement Lenin's ideas about a 'single factory', which up until then had been disregarded. From this time on any attempts to return to syndicalism and workers' self-management were labelled as opportunist and rejected by the party leadership.

Of course, the most striking example of the Bolsheviks' 'flexibility' was their abandonment of the radicalism of the civil war and the transition to the 'New Economic Policy' (NEP) in the spring of 1921. Lenin claimed that the NEP had its ideological roots in certain ideas to be found in his writings at the end of 1917 and the beginning of 1918. This interpretation subsequently became standard among historians, particularly Soviet historians. In fact, the idea that NEP was already a mature, theoretically developed conception is incorrect. The decision to change direction was quite unexpected, and was taken in the course of the Tenth Communist Party Congress in response to the Kronstadt uprising. Until that moment the Congress had been considering how to consolidate the moneyless economy. The evidence suggests that the most important factor here was not programmatic considerations, but the experience of the French Revolution, to which the Bolshevik leadership had been giving some thought. In the preparatory materials to Lenin's works around this time there are constant passing references to '1794 versus 1921'. 'Pattern—French Revolution', he added (Lenin, *PSS*, xliii. 386, 387). And later again: 'Thermidor? Realistically, maybe yes. Will be? We'll see' (Lenin , *PSS*, xliii. 403). Not wishing to repeat the mistakes of the Robespierrists, which cost them their power and their heads, the Bolsheviks set out to meet the demands of the majority of the population.

It remains an open question how far the policy of 'war communism' was imposed by extreme circumstances, and how far these circumstances themselves created the conditions for the Bolsheviks to realize their own ideals. It cannot be denied that the Bolsheviks' ideas concerning the development of society influenced the ways they tried to solve the problems encountered after coming to power. However, it is necessary to see that their actions derived from a much wider range of circumstances.

First, as far as general approaches are concerned, the Bolsheviks' actions were fully in accordance with the logic of centralization which characterized the whole period from the time Russia entered the First World War. Articulating the dominant attitude of the time, even specialists working for the Tsarist régime would declare in 1916 that 'The war has made the state the predominant principle of social life, which all other aspects should serve', and remark that this 'organizational creativity . . . will leave its legacy to peacetime in one form or another' (Bukshpan 1916: 105; Doroshenko 1916: 567) In this period the state was already inclined to resort to administrative interference and repression, rather than opting for a more equal form of co-operation with industrial circles. Pal'chinsky, prominent in the Provisional Government of 1917, produced a programme of action which, had it been implemented, would have gone far beyond the Bolsheviks' economic ideology of that time. It envisaged mandatory appropriation and redistribution of production, compulsory state orders, the right to sequester enterprises, the introduction of an obligation to work, and a substantial curb on entrepreneurs' incomes.

Secondly, in their practical programme the Bolsheviks largely continued to use the methods to which the Tsarist and Provisional Governments, albeit less firmly and consistently, had resorted. The most obvious example was the state grain monopoly. Before the Bolsheviks took power the various attempts that had been made to apply this measure had not succeeded, for reasons which were fairly obvious: 'Under the *ancien régime*, when the Tsarist government did not shrink from using forcible and coercive measures, compulsory grain assessments . . . failed spectacularly. There was only one more thing the old government could have tried—to conduct indiscriminate searches through-out the countryside and confiscate grain by force at whatever cost. But even the Tsarist government could hardly have been that straightforward' (Sigov 1917). The Bolsheviks were that straightforward, and cleverly combined methods of compulsion with reliance on social forces which were appropriate to that kind of policy. The Provisional Government had already tried to extend the regulatory functions of the state, by creating state sugar and coal monopolies. It also made the first attempts to move towards planned regula-tion of the economy. The government was pursuing centralization so actively that some socialists even began to worry that the proletariat was losing its chance of bringing in state regulation to the class enemy.[9]

As well as applying more decisively the methods developed by previous Russian governments, the Bolsheviks also clearly studied foreign experience of state regulation, particularly the German experience. Lenin laid special stress on the continuous nature of Bolshevik policies, remarking that in this area 'the proletariat takes its weapon from the arsenal of capitalism, rather than "thinking it up" or "creating it from nothing"' (Lenin, *PSS* xxxiv. 310). Compulsory syndication, state supervision over the production and distribu-tion of both raw materials and finished goods, a general obligation to work— Lenin openly called for all these measures to be adopted from the German experience, although he gave them, naturally, what he believed to be a differ-ent class content. He even used a special term, 'integral socialism' (*tsel'nyi sotsializm*), meaning a combination of the German wartime economic system with Soviet power (Lenin, *PSS* xxxvi. 300).

[9] For more detail on the economic ideas and activities of the Tsarist and Provisional Governments, see Mau (1993); the chapter on the Provisional Government is entitled 'Half-way to War Communism'.

Thirdly, the policies adopted on the banking system were determined not least by the experience of the Paris Commune. The Commune had left the Bank of France in the hands of the bourgeoisie, and this was one of the reasons for its defeat. The Bolsheviks, who always paid a great deal of attention to the experience of previous revolutions, and knew how to draw lessons from them, were keen not to repeat the mistakes of the Commune. One of the first acts of the revolution was the armed occupation of the State Bank and of all private banks. The latter were nationalized, and then merged into a single People's Bank (Dalin 1983: 183).

Fourthly, the move to a moneyless economy was in many respects conditioned by the uncontrolled inflation of the preceding period, which had led to a loss of confidence in money. The peasants did not want to sell their produce for rapidly depreciating paper money, and the Bolsheviks were well aware of this. In May 1917 Lenin had written: 'The peasants are refusing to sell their grain for money, demanding instead tools, footwear, and clothing. This decision contains a mass of extraordinarily profound truth. The country has really come to such a state of collapse that we can now see in Russia, albeit to a lesser extent, what has been the case for a long time in other countries—money has lost its power' (Lenin, *PSS* xxxii. 98). There were other causes of a more practical nature. The régime was unable to ensure that enough banknotes were produced. In the midst of a deep crisis in industrial production and a severe food shortage it attempted to simplify the system of supply to the towns by providing foodstuffs to the entire population (with, for a time, differential entitlements depending on social class), rather than only to those with a source of income. All this meant that theoretical discussions on the fate of money were inextricably bound up with the dynamics of economic life. As Dalin has observed, after Kolchak had taken Kazan in the civil war and acquired a large part of the State Bank's gold reserve which had been evacuated there, those who advocated the withering away of money found their position strengthened (Dalin 1983: 189).

Fifthly, when circumstances dictated, the Bolsheviks were able to make a highly objective assessment of how far their ideal model diverged from the reality around them. While private trade in grain was ostensibly strictly forbidden and severely punished, in reality town-dwellers satisfied a large part of their foodstuff requirements through illegal trade. This was quite openly recognized by the Bolshevik leaders, who even took certain measures to give the peasants the opportunity to trade grain illegally.[10] The authorities recognized

---

[10] Examining these sorts of measures, Dalin observes that 'Lenin ordered that when determining the excess produce that peasants were obliged to surrender in food requisitions, the norms for personal consumption should be raised from 12 to 16 puds per head per year. This norm meant that peasant households had some grain left over and above their own consumption needs and their allotted quota for requisition. In one way or

that they were unable to satisfy even the most basic needs of the population, and therefore, while official supply became increasingly naturalized, money wages were retained and grew consistently. Under war communism wages were the main item of expenditure in the Russian state budget (Dalin 1983: 225–6). In many respects a similar attitude was taken towards the illegal trade in gold. The black market in gold was on such a wide scale in Moscow in 1920 and (to an even greater extent) in 1921 that the price of gold coin was registered in Soviet labour statistics.

Finally, we should note that Lenin's policies were frequently criticized by other socialists for being contrary to ideology. As early as 1918 the Left Communists adopted a very negative attitude to Lenin's conception of state capitalism, and protested against a mechanistic application of the experience of Imperial Germany or pre-revolutionary Russia, branding it a repudiation of 'the "commune-state" governed from below' (*Kommunist* 1918, no. 1: 18). The domestic and international authority of the Bolsheviks was also seriously undermined by their conclusion of a separate peace with Germany, which was regarded as a betrayal of the interests of the world revolution.[11] Some Left Socialists, such as Vladimir Bazarov and Alexander Bogdanov, argued that the ideology of war communism was diametrically opposed to the tasks of constructing a planned socialist society.[12]

One should not underestimate the reverse influence of the politics of war

another this surplus ended up on the market. Additionally, passengers were permitted to carry a certain quantity of food with them on trains' (1983: 231).

[11] 'The Bolsheviks reckoned that they could remain in power only if they guaranteed the peasants the peace that was promised in the first decree of Soviet power. For this reason it was necessary to conclude a separate peace with Germany. But to satisfy the demands of the peasants in this way was to betray the interests of the world proletariat and to postpone the world revolution, the 'complete guarantee' of the success of the socialist revolution. . . . Lenin and his supporters insisted on the necessity of a 'pause', even if this meant losing territory and revolutionary prestige. They repudiated the idea of a revolutionary war and immediate world revolution' (Kondrat'eva 1993: 67). These comments by Kondrat'eva provide an excellent illustration of how pragmatic the Bolsheviks could be when the retention of power conflicted with their general ideological principles.

[12] Bogdanov, who in 1917 was the first to use the phrase 'war communism of consumption', argued: 'Socialism is first and foremost a new type of co-operation: the comradely organization of production; war communism is first and foremost a special form of social consumption: the organization of mass parasitism and destruction, regulated in an authoritarian manner. The two should not be confused' (Bogdanov 1918: 87). Justifying the necessity of the policy of war communism after the transition to the NEP, Lenin made wide use of the very same terms employed by the critics of the policy of the preceding period: 'the economics of the besieged fortress', 'consumer communism'. This is very far from the language one would use to describe lofty ideals. At the same time, however, Lenin continued to regard the policies of the civil war period as an attempt at an immediate, albeit premature, transition to communism, and the NEP as a retreat. This ambivalence remained a feature of Lenin's attitude to this question right up to his death.

communism on the ideological positions of the Bolshevik party. The strategic line of moving rapidly to a moneyless economy, total socialization, and centralization was a product of war communist influence—it was much less typical of pre-revolutionary Bolshevism. The Bolsheviks did not abandon their view of war communism as '*an anticipation of the future, a future which has broken through into the present*' (Kritsman 1925: 75) when they made the transition to the NEP. Indeed this view continued to gather strength, and greatly influenced the choice of development paths for the country.

If ideology, however influential it might be, is not the decisive factor in determining the radicals' policies, then we need to consider what tasks the radicals really do accomplish. In our opinion, there are two basic tasks, both of which are highly pragmatic—securing a social basis for their own régime, and finding financial resources.

First and foremost, the radicals have to be constantly concerned with maintaining a balance of interests which will permit them to remain in power. Given the highly heterogeneous nature of the forces which take part in the revolution, the social basis of the radicals is extremely shaky and unstable. This means that the government must constantly manœuvre, take mutually acceptable decisions, create and recreate coalitions, and always be prepared to adapt its policy to new socio-political alignments. The actions of the Jacobins in France illustrate this very well. On the one hand, for all their firm intentions and frequent declarations to the contrary, they confirmed the regulation of prices for essential goods brought in by the Girondins, and later substantially extended the list of goods covered, often changing it in the light of circumstances. This was in the interests of two important social groups who had taken part in the revolution: the urban poor and a significant part of the peasantry, which was itself a purchaser of a substantial proportion of consumer goods. On the other hand, to balance this policy and obtain at least partial support from the entrepreneurs, the Jacobins persuaded the Convention to pass a measure introducing a 'maximum wage', vigorously suppressed strikes, and continued to uphold the law introduced by Chaumette at the outbreak of the revolution prohibiting the organization of trade unions.

The same can be said of the restrictions placed on the ability of large-scale farming to develop and consolidate itself. It was believed that large-scale agricultural production was more oriented towards personal gain than towards the satisfaction of the needs of the nation. Better able than small-scale production to withhold its produce from the market, large-scale farming enjoys greater opportunities to speculate, using its monopolistic position to raise prices in the towns. Some of the Jacobins themselves held such views.[13]

---

[13] Saint-Just, for example, believed that an ideal property structure would be one in which man 'can live independently' (Lefebvre 1964: 61).

But it was not for ideological reasons—or rather, not only for ideological reasons—that they were prepared to implement a corresponding package of measures. These measures were also particularly attractive to the radical government in that they catered to the interests of a number of social groups: a significant portion of the peasantry, the urban poor, and the merchant bourgeoisie. Restricting the large-scale private producer in the countryside freed the peasant from a dangerous competitor, strengthened the position of the urban merchants in obtaining agricultural products in the countryside (it partially alleviated the limitations resulting from the 'maximum'), and also, it was generally believed, made foodstuffs sold in the towns cheaper. But even in this case a certain freedom to develop large-scale production in the countryside remained. Restrictions on enclosures had been removed by the Constituent Assembly and the question was never reconsidered. In addition, the Jacobins had removed the limits on the size of agricultural enterprises and had even proclaimed the principle of 'freedom of agriculture'.

The active social manoeuvring of the Jacobins did not contradict their use of forcible methods against dissent, but complemented it. Although they resolutely persecuted both 'deviationists' and 'suspect' elements, the Jacobins were at the same time prepared to accede in practice to many of the demands of the social forces they faced. As historians have noted, when the Jacobins passed the 'Ventôse decrees',[14] which bore a distinctly populist character, one of their main concerns was to get the support, or at least the acquiescence, of the urban poor in the repression of the Hébertists, who had been advancing the demands of that stratum.

Thus in the radical phase of the revolution we find that in practice policies are based on a flexible assessment of the aims of different social groups. This presents an intractable problem for those researchers who are trying to establish the social and class nature of the radicals, to link their actions to neatly defined groups of interests. In Marxist literature, for example, it is common to describe the Jacobins' as 'petty-bourgeois'. However, when the requirements of day-to-day politics dictated, the Jacobins were able easily to transcend their 'petty-bourgeois nature'. For example, at the height of the Terror, they placed under their special protection the major bankers who had advanced them money to purchase foodstuffs abroad. The social basis of the Bolsheviks' policies during war communism was just as heterogeneous. Certain socialists who at that time had a negative attitude to the Bolsheviks argued that, overall, Bolshevism represented the interests of the speculators. Bazarov, for example, argued that 'speculation is not just something which has attached itself from outside; it penetrates the entire present system of state regulation through and through, it is its very soul. The speculator is not simply a parasite. He is also a

---

[14] The Ventôse decrees envisaged the confiscation of the property of enemies of the revolution and its distribution among the poor.

real support for the government, a hero who saves the authorities in critical situations' (Bazarov 1919: 356).

The radicals have to be concerned not only with their own social base—they must also continually hunt for resources to alleviate the financial crisis inherited from the moderates, to pay for the army, and to consolidate their own power. This is ultimately closely connected with ensuring social support, although on a day-to-day basis the two tasks may conflict. The new authorities have access to one fundamentally new source of income which was inaccessible to the *ancien régime*—the property of émigrés and other 'enemies of the revolution'. This property may, however, be used in two ways—either primarily as a means of maximizing income, regardless of the social consequences of its sale, or primarily to satisfy the interests of those social forces whose support is important to the government, involving the loss of part of the potential income. To an extent the resolution of this issue is always a compromise between these two goals, albeit a compromise with a definite bias towards one side or the other.

In the course of the English Revolution the financial issues manifestly predominated over social issues. This had become clear even before the radicals assumed power. The actions of the moderates in England differed substantially from those of analogous régimes in later revolutions, in that they were more conservative, less inclined to exotic experiments and innovations. There are a number of reasons for this, including the facts that the initial financial and social crisis was less profound, economic doctrine was relatively undeveloped, and the Long Parliament faced the immediate problem of fighting a war. The principal means for financing the revolution had been determined at the outbreak of the Civil War, and contained three basic elements: (1) the costs of the war were to be borne by the 'guilty parties'; active participants in the royalist cause were fined ('compositions'), and their lands were sequestered and sold; (2) loans were raised among entrepreneurs; and (3) the necessary taxes were introduced and collected. Cromwell's government did much to activate trade in real estate in general, and the market in landed property in particular. Although in a number of cases the government did offer certain benefits to particular groups of buyers, overall the desire for the maximum financial effect predominated. In many cases the new purchasers of the lands turned out to be their old owners, which, as far as historians can tell, did not worry the leadership of the republican army at all.

In France, too, at the start of the revolution there were two fundamentally different approaches to land reform: fiscal and social. The supporters of the former based their case on the need to realize the nation's assets with the maximum advantage to the country, in order to overcome the financial crisis as speedily as possible. To this end they proposed to restrict the possibility of subdividing the plots on offer, and to cut the time allowed to complete payment. The supporters of the latter approach argued that it was essential to offer favourable conditions for various sorts of people to acquire land, including the poorest sections of the peasantry, and this required a significant increase in the amount of time allowed for payment, as well as changes in the way this trade was organized. The constant vacillation of the moderates on this matter was one of the reasons why they lost support among the peasantry.

The Jacobins took active steps to simplify access to land resources, and strengthened the social aspect of land reform (part of the land was put aside for distribution to the poor). At the same time they significantly increased the amount of land available for redistribution by deciding to sequester and then sell the property not only of the Church, the Crown, and the counter-revolutionaries, but also of the so-called 'suspect' elements.[15] These measures attracted new supporters to the cause of the radicals and swelled the ranks of those willing to take up arms to defend the revolution, in order that the old owners should not return. Naturally enough, however, the financial interests of the government suffered as a result.

We can identify a number of reasons why the balance of social and financial tasks differed between the English and French Revolutions.

First, the scale of the movement 'from below' in the French Revolution was, overall much greater than that of the analogous actions of the 'lower orders' in the English Revolution. This has still not been fully explained. Historians have suggested various reasons. These include the greater importance of local authorities in England, which were little affected by the crisis compared to the state authorities; greater stratification among the peasantry, part of which had substantially improved its position by buying monastic lands in the sixteenth century;[16] and also the specific situation presented by the Civil War, which offered the dissatisfied population an immediate choice between King and Parliament. Whatever the reasons, in England the radicals were under much less pressure, and were not obliged to make such extensive concessions to secure social support as their French counterparts.

Secondly, during the radical phase France was compelled to defend itself against internal and external enemies, which meant that the maintenance of social unity was of critical importance. By contrast, during that phase England was conquering foreign territory. The social demands of the army—the most

---

[15] It would certainly be an inadmissible oversimplification to reduce the reasons for the decrees on 'suspect' elements to the need to resolve the financial difficulties of the radical government. However, it would seem that such considerations were taken into account. In the Thermidorian period the following phrase was attributed to the Jacobins: 'We are minting money on the Place de la Révolution' (see Dobrolyubsky 1930: 125).

[16] 'The ecclesiastical reform in England was accompanied by the confiscation of land belonging to the Catholic Church. As a result, alongside the class of major feudal landowners there emerged a significant stratum of self-reliant peasants known as yeomen. By the time of the English Revolution they, along with their families, numbered 800,000 out of a total population of 5 million' (Dalin 1983: 39).

active force when support was vital for the radicals—were to a considerable extent satisfied with Irish lands. Consequently, within England itself it was possible to devote more attention to the financial aspects of realizing the assets of the enemies of the revolution.

Thirdly, a vital difference was that whereas at the time of the Long Parliament and Cromwell inflationary financing had not yet been invented, the Jacobins made use of *assignats*. *Assignats*—state bonds linked to the price of land—had been introduced during the rule of the moderates. However, it was under the Jacobins that they fully acquired the functions of money. It was the use of paper money and the opportunities for inflationary financing which gave the revolutionary governments of France, especially the Jacobins, a significant freedom of manoeuvre unknown to the Long Parliament and Cromwell's government. Its role was fully recognized at the time: 'The *assignats* made the revolution, they led to the destruction of castes and privileges, they overturned the throne and created the republic; they armed and supplied those terrifying columns that bore the Tricolor beyond the Alps and Pyrenees; we owe them our freedom' (cited in Fal'kner 1919: p. xvii). With their hands unbound in the sphere of finance, the Jacobins could use more of the confiscated assets to deal with social problems.

Having analysed the actions of the radicals in various revolutions, we can now draw certain conclusions. The radicals come to power in conditions of crisis, when there is a pressing need to ensure social unity, and when the conflicts of interests within society have already been felt to the full. To achieve this unity, they use any means that come to hand: force, the imposition of general ideological nostrums, and active financial and social manoeuvring. The means that they choose, and the practical policy measures that they take, are determined not so much by their ideology as by the needs of the moment.[17] However, the steps taken by the radicals in response to immediate considerations, in order to maintain an unstable balance of interests, are crucial in determining the physiognomy of the post-revolutionary society. It is in this phase that new property relations are laid down, and the basis formed for the consolidation of new élite groups. It is this interconnection which helps us to understand why the results of the revolution are so unpredictable, and often so far removed from the revolutionaries' original intentions. Decisions as to the

---

[17] For this reason we cannot agree with Brinton's interpretation of the radical phase, which he called 'the reigns of terror and virtue'. Terror was used as one of the means of ensuring social unity in exceptional circumstances, when domestic and foreign counter-revolution was on the offensive, in a situation of increased danger for the revolutionary authorities. This was how circumstances developed in the course of the French Revolution and the Bolshevik Revolution. It is more difficult to discern a 'reign of terror' in England, unless we regard English policy in Ireland as terror. As far as 'virtue' is concerned, it seems to us that this is just one of the elements of the 'external ideology' imposed upon society, and is also intended to serve as an instrument for maintaining unity.

direction of change taken in the radical phase are not derived from pre-conceived ideas; rather they are taken under the influence of a given conjuncture. In the final analysis they are determined by the strength of pressure exerted by various groups of interests which must be satisfied if the régime is to remain in power. The ultimate outcome of this whole collection of decisions emerges spontaneously, as the sum of numerous divergent and often contradictory actions.

The interconnection between the radical phase and post-revolutionary development sets obvious limits to the scale of the changes which can be realized in the course of the revolution. As we have noted, there are two extreme positions on this question: one claims that revolution represents a radical break with the past, while the other starts from the premise that revolutions in general are incapable of changing anything in the course of historical development. However, neither interpretation adequately deals with the interconnection between pre- and post-revolutionary development. It seems to us that the limits of possible change are determined by the fact that during the radical phase manoeuvring takes place between the interests of various social groups which were formed in the pre-revolutionary period and which defined their position under the *ancien régime*. Therefore one of the most important outcomes of the revolution is that it brings the formal status of a range of social groups into line with their real position in pre-revolutionary society. English landlords secured unlimited rights over their land; in France petty peasant property received legal recognition and the Third Estate gained increased political representation of its interests, reflecting the growth of its economic influence—the preconditions for all these processes were in fact already being laid down in pre-revolutionary society.

If the long-term consequences of radical policies become clear only in the post-revolutionary period, their short-term results become apparent very quickly. It is possible to implement a policy based on political expediency, completely disregarding the logic of economic life, but only for a short time and at a fairly high cost. At the end of their time in power, the radicals become keenly aware of this cost, especially where they have employed administrative methods of economic regulation and inflationary financing. Both the Jacobins in 1794 and the Bolsheviks in 1920 were faced with economic collapse and paralysis, against which administrative methods had become ineffective. By this time the immediate threat to the gains of the revolution have also been overcome, and this removes the external factor maintaining the unity of diverse social forces. For the second time in the course of the revolution a very similar crisis develops, stemming from the worsening of economic difficulties and the exhaustion of the external threat which preserved social unity. This crisis heralds the end of the radical phase of the revolution. A familiar situation arises, in which the manoeuvrings of the régime result in general dissatisfaction. In France the '[economic] policy of the Robespierrists, who attempted to reconcile opposing interests in the name of strengthening the state power of the republic, disaffected the workers and the urban poor but did not satisfy the peasants, traders and manufacturers' (Dobrolyubsky 1930: 249). In Russia at the end of 1920 the Bolsheviks had to contend with the total opposition of the peasants, who comprised 80 per cent of the country's population. Then comes the Thermidor, the final phase of the revolutionary process. Its name derives from the coup of 9 Thermidor 1794 in France, which heralded the downfall of Robespierre.

4.4 The Thermidor, and mechanisms for ending the revolution

The end of the radicals' power signifies that the revolution has passed its peak, and that the revolutionary curve has begun its downward turn. However, the Thermidorian phase of any revolution does not lend itself readily to analysis. One problem is that it is very difficult to say when it begins and ends. In France the fall of the radicals was accompanied by a seizure of political power, and it can therefore be dated precisely, but other revolutions do not display the same clarity. In Bolshevik Russia a sharp change in political line was undertaken without a change of régime. Lenin characterized this as 'Thermidorizing oneself'.[18] As for England, the Thermidorian period, in Brinton's words, 'is not to be put with any preciseness' (1965: 206). It is no easier to put a date to the end of the Thermidor. As Huntington observed, in all Western revolutions it is easy to determine when they started, but difficult to ascertain when they ended (Huntington 1968: 272).

Another problem is that there is no agreement about the social content of the Thermidorian period. There was, for example, a very lively discussion around this subject in the 1920s, which had to do with the likely outcome of the Bolshevik Revolution. There were two contending positions: is the Thermidor necessarily a counter-revolutionary coup, accompanied by a sharp change in policy? Or is it the result of the internal degeneration of the radical government, in which the removal of some of the most odious figures makes no difference to the general tendency of that government's evolution?

The Mensheviks, along with some bourgeois writers, were convinced that the Bolshevik régime would inevitably fall and that a bourgeois government would come to power. They recognized that the Bolshevik leaders had studied the experience of the Jacobins, and were displaying both unprecedented harshness and unprecedented flexibility in order to keep political power in their hands. But, they argued, 'in practice the *dénouement* of the communist

---

[18] 'Working-class Jacobins are more astute and firm than bourgeois Jacobins, and had the courage and wisdom to Thermidorize themselves' (words of Lenin, cited in Sadoul 1924).

experiment may be postponed, but cannot be completely averted. And then the Russian 9 Thermidor, the collapse of the dictatorship, in which the destruction of the contradictions it has accumulated passes into the hands of the propertied classes in the form of a genuine bourgeois counter-revolution, is only a matter of time'. The only difference was that some, like Martov (a Left Menshevik), envisaged the politics of the Thermidor as 'an anti-democratic policy directed against the proletariat', whereas others, like Mirsky, thought that the Thermidorian liquidation of the Bolsheviks would lead Russia along the path to a democratic republic (Mirsky 1921; see also Martov 1921).

The position of Ustryalov, one of the authors of the *Smena vekh* (Change of Landmarks) collection of essays, was significantly different (Ustryalov 1921: 62–5). He saw the essence of the Thermidor not in the overthrow of the radical government, but in its gradual transformation in the direction of moderation, realism, and reliance on material interests: 'The Jacobins did not fall—for the most part they degenerated. As we know, they survived long after the Thermidor events, first as the government, and then as an influential party. Napoleon himself came from their midst' (Ibid. 66–7). Consequently, he envisaged a different fate for the Bolsheviks: 'After a while the French Jacobins proved unable to sense the new conditions of life—and perished. Neither Danton nor Robespierre had a flair for tactical flexibility. The present government in Moscow has been able in time to recognize the general change in the situation, the downturn in the revolutionary curve in the country and worldwide. It has recognized it, and has drawn the necessary conclusions' (ibid. 68). Many other researchers have also shown that, on the one hand, after the fall of the Hébertists the Jacobins began to soften their policies regulating trade and industry, while on the other hand, the Thermidorians did not make a sharp break with the policies of controlling prices, requisitioning, and rate setting. These and similar measures, albeit in attenuated form, were kept in place throughout the whole period of the Thermidorian Convention.

The political lines consciously chosen by one force or another are not, in our opinion, sufficient to determine whether the radicals' policies are abandoned or continued. Hitherto, our analysis of the politics of revolutionary governments has been based on the state of social relations which characterizes pre-revolutionary and revolutionary societies—that is, fragmentation, divergence of interests, and the instability of any alliances or coalitions that may form. In order to establish the similarities and differences between the Thermidor and other stages of the revolution, we must first of all look at whether social relations changed, and in what ways. It is possible to identify certain factors which distinguish the interests and attitudes of different social groups during Thermidor from those of the preceding stages.

Society in this period is generally characterized by social fatigue and a greater tendency among individuals and social groups to be concerned with their private interests which, in so far as the transformation of property relations has been completed, are increasingly firmly rooted in the economic structure of society. Certain social groups have achieved their particular aims, and have no interest in continuing the struggle. For example, both the French Revolution, and the Bolsheviks after the transition to the NEP, satisfied the interests of the peasantry. Other groups have exhausted their revolutionary energy and lost their leaders, and have therefore ceased to represent any serious threat to the authorities, who can now deal with them as and when they please. By 1795–6 the interests of the politically weakened urban poor in France could be disregarded. This disregard, combined with a passive attitude to the catastrophic collapse of the currency system, led to a serious deterioration in economic conditions and the outbreak of famine in Paris and certain other French cities. But, in contrast to the period of revolutionary upsurge, it did not bring about any further fundamental upheavals. The Bonapartist Lavallette described the situation in Paris in August 1794 in his memoirs as follows: 'The famine was appalling, there was extreme want, but the disempowered sovereign people hardly even dared complain. They were already just humble dirt, devoid of energy, still howling under the whip, but without even a thought of revolt' (cited in Dobrolyubsky 1930: 234). The hunger riots which broke out from time to time in Paris in this period were suppressed by force, and did not impel the authorities to do anything to improve the food supply. As for England, where the movement of the poor was always very limited, after the suppression of the Levellers in 1649 there was in practice no question of serious pressure 'from below'.

The active changes in property rights and the mechanisms of political power in the radical phase give impetus to the process of social restructuring, and particularly to the formation of new social groups. Although the élite created by the revolution is specific to each country, it usually includes the new owners of the property redistributed in the revolutionary period,[19] the new political élite brought forward on the wave of mass political activity, and the new army leadership established in the process of defending 'the gains of the revolution'. The Thermidor is the period when these groups consolidate themselves and struggle for spheres of influence and the acquisition of property. Society weakens, and the élite comes to the fore. It becomes more important in determining the policies of the authorities, and its different groups compete for control over the government.

During the Thermidor the government finds itself in a difficult situation. Society remains split—the interests of different strata and groups have not been satisfied to the same extent, and there is no consensus around a basic value system. Fragmentation has still not been overcome, but now it has a fundamentally different character. The interests with which the authorities

---

[19] The specific feature of the Bolshevik Revolution was that it did not sell off property, but nationalized it. The bureaucracy is often regarded as having been its collective owner.

now have to deal are rooted in the new economic structure of society. Consequently, they are better defined and more predictable, even though they remain very much in conflict with each other. Moreover, the interests of the élite begin to play a decisive role, and it is in this stratum that the government needs to secure its social base.

As we have noted above, the pre-revolutionary and revolutionary fragmentation of society results in a weakening of the state, and this is the most important distinguishing feature of the revolutionary process. The change in the nature of the fragmentation has a decisive effect on the ability of the state to pursue a long-range policy. The Thermidor is characterized by a gradual strengthening of the state, in that it is less dependent on current fluctuations in social attitudes, and it is able to maintain order, collect taxes, and generally perform the basic functions of a state. However, power remains extremely unstable. Different élite groups have strongly conflicting and even mutually exclusive interests, and there is still no basic consensus in society. The government is obliged constantly to manœuvre, to balance between various parts of the élite, to react flexibly to changes in the balance of forces within the élite. This causes frequent and often chaotic changes of political régime, or policy changes within the existing régimes. The type of politics which enables a government to remain in power by manœuvring between the interests of various social forces is called Bonapartism in Marxist phraseology. In the absence of any better term, that is the one we shall use to denote the specific mechanisms of state power outlined above.

Socio-political conditions during the Thermidor in some respects resemble, and in other respects differ from, the conditions of the radical phase. The similarity is that the Thermidorian régime, like its predecessors, is obliged actively to manoeuvre between various groups of interests, and can only survive by pursuing a Bonapartist policy. The differences are, first, that these groups for the most part belong to the élite; secondly, that they are gradually consolidating; and thirdly, that their interests are more clearly defined. The types of political leaders and political actions required in this period do not differ fundamentally from those of the preceding stage. It is therefore not surprising that in many revolutions (not only the Bolshevik, but also the English Revolution), the leaders of the radical phase have been able to adapt to the new circumstances.

The concurrent processes of the weakening of society, the consolidation of new élites, and the strengthening of the state gradually consolidate the political régime. At this point the revolutionary process is usually regarded as completed. Brinton, for example, takes this view. However, in this period the Thermidorian type of fragmentation has still not been overcome. For this reason, as the political régime consolidates itself, it is able to pull society together into a single whole only by the use of external force. The source of its power lies not in an organic link with an established basic system of social interests and values, but merely in the weakness and fatigue that is widespread throughout society. This also predetermines the form that this régime takes— a dictatorship. The inevitability of post-revolutionary dictatorship and its relationship with the specific structure of post-revolutionary society has been well described by Brinton: 'Dictatorship and revolutions are inevitably closely associated, because revolutions to a certain extent break down, or at least weaken, laws, customs, habits, beliefs which bind men together in society, and when laws, customs, habits, beliefs tie men together insufficiently, force must be used to remedy that insufficiency' (1965: 208). In the same way, the régime of personal dictatorship, whether it be that of Cromwell, Napoleon, or Stalin, flows naturally from the logic of the revolutionary process. The transition from the Thermidorian régime to that of the post-revolutionary dictatorship is often accompanied by a much more substantial break with the previous forms of government than the transition to the Thermidor, and also by the accession to power of new people.[20]

Subsequent political development is largely determined by how strong the dictatorship turns out to be. In most cases its ability to maintain the unity of society by force is limited. This is largely because one of the basic methods to ensure unity is to wage aggressive war, with the ostensible aim of spreading the gains of the revolution to other countries and territories. This further exhausts society's already limited resources. Fatigue accumulates, and a desire to return to the former, quieter way of life grows. The experience of revolutions shows that the stability of the dictatorship is undermined not only by defeat in these wars, as happened in France, but also by success, as in England.

The fall of the post-revolutionary dictatorship is usually accompanied by a restoration, which marks the end of the 'grand' revolutionary cycle. However, even the restoration does not mean that things will finally stabilize. The Thermidorian fragmentation remains and may even intensify, since the return of part of the old élite adds new contradictions to those already existing. To a greater or lesser extent the redistribution of property brought about by the revolution is called into question. In England this led to a partial restitution of land to its former owners. In France, Louis XVII on his accession to the throne immediately guaranteed the property rights resulting from the revolution, so no practical steps were taken in that direction. There was, however, much discussion about how to compensate members of the old élite, and the threat of redistribution remained for some time.

Society remains split for decades after the revolution, and cannot re-establish consensus around basic norms and values. The régime retains its Bonapartist character. Political instability, a lack of firm guarantees of property rights, and irreconcilable contradictions within the élite and in society as a

---

[20] In practice the only exception to this rule was England, where there was no clear distinction between the Thermidorian period and the post-revolutionary dictatorship.

whole also persist. In England this period of post-revolutionary stabilization ended with the 'Glorious Revolution' of 1688–9; in France it did not end until the revolution of 1830 (possibly not even until the revolution of 1848).

If the dictatorship proves sufficiently stable and capable of enforcing social unity for long enough, then processes take place within it which are very similar in their essence to the processes examined above, but substantially different in their form. The Stalin régime provides the most striking example of this.[21] In this case both the restoration and the politics of Bonapartism were avoided, at least in an open form. There was no manœuvring between the interests of different strata, but rather a forcible suppression of these interests. The mechanism for resolving social contradictions was the maintenance of a high degree of instability in the position of different social, national, and particularly élite groups, any one of which could at any time be subjected to mass repression. Right until the end of the Stalin dictatorship property relationships remained ill-defined, and the role of individual élite groups and the entire stratum of the bureaucracy in administering property and appropriating its products were not regularized. We can consider the period of post-revolutionary stabilization to have been completed only after the death of Stalin in 1953 and subsequent changes in the character of the political régime.

In any case, only after the end of the period of post-revolutionary stabilization, usually several decades after the end of the revolution, can the immediate consequences of the revolutionary cataclysms be regarded as overcome. Not until then does it become clear what long-term results the revolution has brought. Has it opened up new avenues for economic development, or has it put yet more barriers in its path? Can the established interests in society be brought into accord more readily, or have they remained irreconcilable? Is the new society more just and socially oriented than the *ancien régime*? The trends and processes which characterize post-revolutionary stabilization (or more accurately, post-revolutionary instability), both positive and negative, may turn out not to be integral to the society which emerges from the revolution.

---

[21] The reasons for the strength and durability of the Stalin dictatorship are examined in greater detail in Ch. 11.

5

The Revolutionary Process in Contemporary Russia

5.1. Revolution in Russia: *pro et contra*

Both Western and Russian experts have written in detail about the developments in Russia in 1985–2000. There is a wealth of academic literature, memoirs, and essays on this period. The events have been analysed both in terms of reform and of revolution. A fair number of works on Russia consider the ongoing developments to be revolutionary (e.g. Blumberg 1990; Galeotti 1997; Holmes 1997; Kotz with Weir 1997). This is, however, a highly contentious thesis which has been challenged with varying degrees of force, from the cautious—'there are grounds for hesitation' (McAuley 1992: 117)— to the categorical: 'no revolution can be found where there was none' (Pastukhov 1994: 114). The arguments of these opponents of the 'revolutionary thesis' can hardly be said to be systematic or particularly detailed. In some cases, diametrically opposed approaches are employed to support their cases. Nonetheless, it is possible to single out some common arguments underlying these various objections.

Often these arguments are rooted in an inadequate understanding of the 'classic form of the revolution', i.e. of a normative pattern to which Russia should conform. 'But there was no revolution, and totalitarianism was not crushed by hero-liberators, but died a natural death' (Pastukhov 1994: 110), runs one of the arguments employed. The so-called 'Western' revolutions (including the French Revolution, the Russian revolution of 1917, and the Mexican Revolution) are considered to have started with the collapse of the régime, and this is regarded as a distinguishing feature. According to Samuel Huntington, who first introduced the terms 'Western' and 'Eastern revolution', '[in] the "Western" pattern, the political institutions of the old régime collapse' (Huntington 1968: 266).[1] It is worth noting that diametrically opposed arguments are used against the 'revolutionary thesis': 'Would the central government have

---

[1] Some students of revolution drew attention to this as early as the 1930s: 'The revolution does not begin with the attack of a powerful new force upon the state. It simply begins with a sudden recognition by almost all the passive and active membership that the state no longer exists' (Pettee 1938: 100).

collapsed had it not been for the challenge from the outlying republics?'
(McAuley 1992: 117)

A similar notion is that the élite in Russia was not renewed to a great
enough extent to fit the classic concept of a revolution: '[the] social and
economic élites remained largely intact' (ibid. 118). However, research in
recent decades has shown that in earlier revolutions the renewal of the élite
was far less radical than is generally thought. It has long been common knowledge that this was the case in the English Revolution. It is well known that
many supporters of the King were able to buy back their confiscated estates.
Even in the French Revolution a significant part of the old élite was able to
preserve its position. Of the approximately 400,000 members of privileged
classes in France in 1789, 1,158 were executed and 16,431 emigrated. But even
in this case, many émigrés bought their confiscated lands through fronts,
making it possible for the old privileged classes to remain amongst the largest
landowners in the post-revolutionary period. In about half of France's
départements they continued to make up the majority of rich landowners. And
about 22.5 per cent of the new Napoleonic nobility had their origins in the
former privileged classes (Goldstone 1991: 296).

Finally, attempts to refute the 'revolutionary thesis' on the grounds that
events failed to ensure sufficient democratization are completely at odds with
historical experience. Revolution and democracy have always found it difficult
to coexist, and in this respect contemporary Russia has demonstrated a much
greater degree of democratic development than past revolutions, which 'tend
to produce not democracy but authoritarianism' (ibid. 483).

The view has also been expressed that these changes are not really epoch-
making: 'Unlike the revolutions of 1789 or 1917, there was no vision of a new
era opening for mankind. The new rulers did not offer grand ideas of a new
order but rather dwelt on the need to undo the mistakes of the past' (McAuley
1992: 118). Similar arguments have been presented to rebut the post-industrial
character of the changes: 'The emphasis in the economy at present is on *creating* a market system . . . a feature of early modernity' (Holmes 1993: 40). Several
comments are in order here. First, inside Russia, where hardly anybody remem-
bers life before the 1917 revolution, the transformations have meant a radical
break with the past. Secondly, it cannot be denied that the collapse of the
communist régimes in the USSR and the countries of Eastern Europe has
fundamentally changed the world system. A bi-polar world with two competing
social systems has been replaced by a world without a global military confrontation and without an alternative to the market economy. Thirdly and finally, the
free-for-all market of the early capitalist period should not be confused with the
peculiar renaissance of the market economy during the early post-modernization phase. The transformation of the communist system does not mark a
return to the past, but rather is part of a global process of democratization and
liberalization, characteristic of the latest developmental trends.

Much of the scepticism regarding the existence of revolutionary transformations in Russia is associated with the fact that most works on contemporary Russian history mention revolution only superficially and lack any conceptual analysis of the revolutionary process, or a definition of its nature and parameters. Various dates have been given for the beginning of the recent revolution in Russia, from the moment of Gorbachev's ascent to power (1985) to the collapse of the Soviet Union after the August putsch in 1991. Moreover, very different and often arbitrary criteria are used to pin down the starting date: the beginning of mass movements 'from below' (1989); the start of transformations in state property and the legislative underpinning of this process (1990);[2] Gorbachev's alliance with the radicals on the issue of reforming the USSR (the '9 + 1' negotiations in 1991) (Galeotti 1997). Clearly, all these approaches are based on different criteria and different interpretations of the essence of revolutionary processes in Russia. The issue of whether the revolutionary process has ended is equally ambiguous: is the revolution in Russia already finished or is the revolutionary epoch continuing?

Difficulties in analysing the contemporary Russian revolution are linked to two main factors. Despite drawing parallels with various past revolutions, most researchers have not attempted to apply a schema of the revolutionary process, derived from reference to the experience of earlier revolutions, to the analysis of contemporary Russia. In the logic of its development, the revolution in Russia is a typical 'Western' revolution, unfolding according to the same laws as other revolutions of this type. We hope to show that the principal processes described in the previous chapter were also followed by Russian events after 1985.

Of course, like any other revolution, the Russian revolution has some unique features in addition to its more generic ones. Three main specific features can be identified in the Russian events. First, there is the evolution from 'reform from above' to 'revolution from above' without violent change in the political régime during the 'Gorbachev era'. Secondly, there is the absence of mass violent action in general, and of revolutionary terror in particular. This changed the rules of the radical phase and led to a temporal disjunction between revolutionary transformations in the economic and political spheres. Thirdly, the protagonists were unwilling to acknowledge the revolutionary character of these changes, and had a negative attitude towards the very idea of revolution. If Labrousse is correct in his pronouncement that 'revolutions are made in spite of revolutionaries' (1969: 1), one would be hard put to find a more perfect example in support of his thesis than contemporary Russia.

In this chapter, we shall endeavour to analyse the course of the Russian revolution in terms of the general laws of the revolutionary process, pointing

---

[2] Curiously this criterion is used in two works; in one of them this is assessed positively, in the other negatively. See Hanson (1992); Kotz with Weir (1997).

out the specific features of the events in Russia as we do so. Our task is not to provide a detailed account of events (a rich literature already exists on the subject), but merely to determine the strategic line, the 'revolutionary curve', which helps to explain the logic and internal order of events; events which, at first glance, might appear to be a concatenation of circumstances and of the ambitions and idiosyncracies of individual leaders. Our analysis is based not only on available printed sources, but also on discussions of the issues with a number of leaders of the revolutionary movement in Russia (Mikhail Gorbachev, Alexander Yakovlev, Egor Gaidar, Gennady Burbulis) who were in a position to exert decisive influence on the development of events at various stages of the revolutionary process. (The role of these leaders and our inter- views with them are discussed in more detail in Chapter 6.)

5.2. Gorbachev: 'reforms from above'

From the end of the Stalin era, Soviet society displayed a certain cyclical devel- opment, in which periods of liberalization alternated with periods of tougher regulation in the economic and political sphere. This cycle derived from the alternatives available within the Soviet system: the mobilizing and decentral- izing alternatives reviewed in Chapter 3. Gorbachev's assumption of power in 1985 could well have marked the beginning of the next economic and polit- ical cycle, with predictable results: initial reforms leading to some rise in growth rates, but accompanied by greater imbalances and inflation, as a result of which reforms are rolled back and centralization is restored, at least formally. Gorbachev's first eighteen months as General Secretary were not inconsistent with such a scheme of events. The reforms undertaken were very similar to the course initiated by Yuri Andropov (in 1982–3) and in no way broke with the fundamental principles of the Soviet system. Moreover, in the initial period of reforms, the emphasis in many areas was placed on realizing the system's potential for mobilization.

In the economy, the proposal was to toughen discipline and order, and to tighten administrative control over the quality of production. At the same time, the twelfth five-year plan (1986—90) envisaged boosting the share of invest- ment in the national income; shifting investment priorities in favour of the machine-building sectors; acceleration of economic growth by mobilizing enterprises' internal reserves and by their fulfilment of more ambitious plans. The need for decentralization was not denied, but its application was limited to selected sectors, unrelated to the 'commanding heights': food and agriculture, light industry, and services. It was also proposed, in addition to administrative measures, to use material incentives more widely, e.g. collective and family contracts, to increase supply. There was no suggestion either of abandoning the principles of the centrally planned economy, or even of moving in the direction of the market-oriented countries of the socialist bloc (in particular Hungary). Foreign experts studying the developments in Russia noted at the time that serious market reforms were unlikely, and that improvements in the economy would be achieved by streamlining centralized control, cutting out layers of bureaucracy, and moving towards the style of centralized management characteristic of the German Democratic Republic (see e.g. Hanson 1992). At a meeting with secretaries of the Central Committees of Eastern European communist parties in 1985, Gorbachev is said to have proclaimed: 'Some of you look at the market as a lifesaver for your economies. But, comrades, you should not think about lifesavers but about the ship. And the ship is socialism' (quoted in Hanson 1992: 95). This, apparently, reflected his outlook on the world at the time.

In the social sphere, there was a clear emphasis on administrative methods. The best example was the anti-alcohol campaign, which aimed to overturn national alcohol consumption habits, ingrained over the centuries, by means of administrative pressure. These habits had undermined work discipline and resulted in negative demographic trends, such as a reduced life expectancy, and a high incidence of children with learning difficulties. As one writer on the Gorbachev period noted sarcastically: 'Gorbachev . . . instituted an anti-alcohol campaign, designed to wean Soviet citizens from the bottle and teach them instead the rewards of modernization' (Galeotti 1997: 58). Another example of administrative restrictions was the campaign against 'unearned' incomes, which was unleashed at the same time as the market-oriented law on self-employment was adopted. All these measures were replete with egregious administrative excesses, which made for huge queues for vodka, the destruction of valuable vineyards, and the 'tomato massacre' (the destruction of private tomato fields) in the Volgograd region, to name but a few.

There was no significant progress in political reform at this stage, which for the most part was limited to reshuffles of personnel which facilitated the rise to power of a new generation of younger and more energetic politicians. This process, started under Andropov, was radically intensified following Gorbachev's rise to power. At the same time, Gorbachev gradually moved away from the excesses of the previous period: easing the persecution of dissidents, relaxing censorship, permitting greater freedom in the exchange of opinions both within the party leadership and in society at large. This aspect of the reforms became known as the policy of *glasnost*, and was initiated as early as the beginning of 1986. However, at this time the political and ideological monopoly of the Communist Party of the Soviet Union (CPSU) remained sacrosanct, and was not questioned even by the most radical reformers on Gorbachev's team—some softening of the rigid régime was all that was on the agenda.

Thus, at least until the beginning of 1987, the Gorbachev team took no (or almost no) significant steps which could qualify as an attempt at reforming the existing order. None the less, by this point there were already significant factors obstructing a return to the traditional liberalization–centralization cycle. The most important of these was that in this society where cautious reforms were being attempted, some of the preconditions for revolution had already emerged.

First, the economic situation was bound to deteriorate as oil revenues dried up. The catastrophic fiscal consequences of the anti-alcohol campaign (the indirect tax on spirits was one of the main revenue items in the Union budget), the attempt to push ahead blindly for an acceleration of economic development and modernization of the national economy, along with other blunders, significantly aggravated economic difficulties. But they did not play a decisive role. The adjustment of the economy, as the flow of petrodollars dried up, was inevitably a painful process. At the same time, the mobilizing mechanisms, which were given priority during the early years of *perestroyka*, did not function well in the context of rigid fiscal constraints. Attempts at strengthening centralization inevitably ran up against financial obstacles.

Secondly, a major aspect of the Gorbachev team's policy was a sharp change in the direction of foreign policy. It pursued a course aimed at bringing the Cold War to an end, stopping the arms race and consequently cutting back on military expenditure. According to some accounts, similar moves were considered under Andropov, but were swiftly buried under pressure from the military leadership (Galeotti 1997: 61). As early as October 1985, Gorbachev came out with comprehensive proposals on nuclear arms reduction, and although at this time no significant measures were approved, there was a profound change in the style of relations with the West. This limited the scope of ideological arguments in favour of rolling back reforms, in so far as the 'external threat'—regularly used as a pretext for 'putting the screws on'—was now deemed to have receded.

Thirdly, while the methods of reforming the Soviet system in this period were entirely in keeping with the established model, the ideology started to change fundamentally. From the very beginning, Gorbachev sought to reconcile the Soviet system with humanitarian principles. The reassertion of these principles has been a feature of the post-war world, and is directly related to post-modernization processes. Activating the 'human factor' and creating opportunities for people to realize their potential were irreconcilably at odds with the mobilizing mechanisms, of which the violation of individual rights was an essential component. Without the use of coercion, mobilizing mechanisms simply ceased to function, as became apparent towards the end of 1986.

Fourthly, the first period of *perestroyka* revealed a fundamental contradiction in the position of the new leadership. On the one hand, the steps it took were extremely cautious, and aimed at avoiding any fundamental break with past traditions. On the other hand, the ascent of a new, dynamic leader gave rise to expectations in society, which far exceeded the real potential of the reforms. As a result, the reforms produced a social situation very much akin to the initial phase of a revolution, which Brinton describes as the 'honeymoon', and which in Russia was aptly named the 'rosy period':

By 1985 the USSR had reached the point where most members of the élites and counter-élites—ruling, opposition, and dissident—felt that the existing order could no longer be preserved. On this count everyone was united—reformers dreaming of democratic and market principles taking root in the country; modernizers convinced that technological reconstruction would cure all ills; 'revisionists' hoping for a transition to democratic socialism; and 'orthodox' believers in state socialism, who strove to rebuild a milder version of Stalinism, purged of its Khrushchevite and Brezhnevite elements. (Gordon and Pliskevich 1995: 317–18)[3]

In this situation the Gorbachev team, which had yet to embark on any revolutionary reforms, made a mistake which is typical of early revolutionary governments. They succumbed to the illusion that the problems facing the country could be resolved quickly, easily, and without conflict, and to the conviction that a fundamental consensus existed in society regarding the necessity for and direction of reforms ('We are all in the same boat', 'We are all on the same side of the barricade'). They imagined that the new régime's broad public support rendered it omnipotent, and therefore capable of reconciling the irreconcilable (such as *uskorenie*—acceleration—and *perestroyka*, or self-employment—individual entrepreneurship—and the fight against 'unearned income'). All of these features, typical for the early stage of the 'rule of the moderates', characterized the initial period of *perestroyka*.

As we saw in the previous chapter, early revolutionary governments usually view themselves as 'the most popular of governments', with a twofold consequence. On the one hand, this illusion drastically limits their ability to enact unpopular measures, even when the urgency of these measures is plain to see. On the other hand, they find themselves tied to a reform programme which had taken shape in the pre-revolutionary period when it had enjoyed mass public support. They are incapable of transcending the limitations of this programme, even when reality persistently demands this. The Gorbachev team, which had not yet taken the path of revolutionary reforms, was not so rigidly tied to the obligations of the 'most popular of governments'. However, public expectations drove it in this direction. As in any pre-revolutionary society, a programme prepared by experts and enjoying broad public support was ready to hand; it envisioned the building of 'democratic socialism' and a 'socially oriented market economy', or in other words, a combination of

---

[3] This description is very close to that given by historians with reference to the initial phase of other revolutions. For instance, Furet noted, '[It] did not matter that the urban masses' demands for regulation were contradictory to the *philosophers' laissez-faire*: that was a problem the future would pose, not the present' (Furet 1996: 57).

market and plan. Many members of Gorbachev's team were sympathetic to these views; Gorbachev himself was very interested in and actively propagated the ideas of the New Economic Policy (NEP). Any attempted shift in the direction of stronger centralization would have meant going against the expectations of the majority of the population, although for the 'reform government' itself this was by no means impossible.

The contradictions and problems contained from the outset in the Gorbachev reform programme, came to a head by 1987. The results for 1986 could be seen as supporting the chosen course: there was an increase in annual growth rates of national income, in industrial and agricultural output, and commodity circulation, while for the first time in many years returns on capital investment increased. However, 1987 gave the lie to the illusion that it was possible to rely on mobilization. Growth rates dropped dramatically: according to Western estimates GNP growth rates slowed from 4.1 per cent in 1986 to 1.3 per cent in 1987. The move towards increasing the share of capital accumulation in the national income proved unrealizable, as consumption continued to grow at still higher rates. Output of key machine-building products fell short of plan targets in two thirds of all cases. Foreign trade indicators deteriorated. In order to compensate for the loss in oil revenues in 1987, part of the gold reserves had to be sold off, but imports of consumer goods still had to be curtailed significantly.

It was not only the economic indicators, but also the general situation in the USSR which demonstrated that the potential of mobilization methods had been exhausted and that no effective reforms could be implemented by the *nomenklatura*. The country's leadership received more and more information revealing that nothing on the ground was changing; the local party bureaucracy was putting the brakes on any reform attempts.[4] According to early public opinion surveys, only 16 per cent of respondents believed that *perestroyka* was going successfully enough (see Ivanov 1988). The hopes placed in a renewal of cadres were not borne out. Gorbachev has said that he initially felt that the problem could be resolved 'by renewal, by bringing new cadres into circulation', and that the new generation of party functionaries would accept the proposed reform programme: 'In three years, he replaced party secretaries three or four times, especially at the city and district level, but the same blockheads kept coming back'. As Alexander Yakovlev pointed out, the officially approved reforms were regarded as something necessary for society, but not as something to be acted upon: 'In the party there was an estab-

---

[4] In his interview Gorbachev recalled that he travelled extensively throughout the country during this period, and received about 4,000 letters a day. From across the Soviet Union information came in that nothing was changing: 'Everything has remained the same; just as our district committee guys always controlled everything, and never let anyone put a foot out of line, so it has remained.'

lished pattern both of thinking and action. What does it matter that something has been said, written down, and officially approved? There has always been a certain order in the party, and that order should be adhered to.[5]

Within the ranks of the *nomenklatura* resistance grew to the personnel changes and the reforms, as became evident from the end of 1986. The January 1987 Plenum of the CPSU Central Committee was supposed to adopt fundamental political and cadre reforms. There was a real danger of Gorbachev losing power if he continued to pursue the reform course, as he himself was fully aware: 'And then I thought that we were heading for the Khrushchev scenario, when the Plenum would convene and tell us: "Guys, you're not ready yet; you don't have the least understanding of responsibility, of the country, of its role, or its position. That's quite enough, let's have somebody else. Enough is enough." '

5.3. Gorbachev: 'revolution from above'

With the exhaustion of the reformist approach becoming more and more obvious, an alternative was ever more openly considered: to look for support in public expectations, to embark on more radical reforms, and to start acting in accordance with the public's ideas about how to pull the country out of the crisis and revive it. However, this meant breaking with a significant section of the ruling élite, with the *nomenklatura*, and relying on other social strata and groups for support in conducting reforms. According to Gorbachev, he understood then 'that things would not work, and nothing would succeed, and that the only possible salvation lay with the people'. 'Reforms from above' developed into a 'revolution from above'. This process occurred in 1987–8, and displayed the following main characteristics.

Ordinary citizens were brought into the political process to a much greater extent. With their help the Gorbachev team attempted both to weaken the existing party *nomenklatura* and to remove the real power centres from the control of the party apparatus. A cautious call to support *perestroyka* 'from below' was made as early as the address of the Central Committee of the Communist Party to the Soviet people on the occasion of the seventieth anniversary of the Great October Socialist Revolution. The address, published in March 1987, contained some extremely unusual language for such a document: '*The Central Commit-*

---

[5] The same applied to the state authorities. Anders Åslund recalled: 'In the spring of 1986 Gorbachev issued a decree on agricultural reform. As a foreign diplomat, I went to *Gosagroprom* to find out how the decree was being implemented. However, top agricultural officials laughed derisively at my questions. They openly stated that nothing would change and that they simply paid no attention to Gorbachev's decrees' (Åslund 1996: 119).

tee appeals to the courage of the Soviet people. Ossified forms and methods are not easy to break. We need to fight for *perestroyka*, we need to defend *perestroyka*. What is required here is tenacity, resolve, and a principled approach' (CPSU 1987: 7). The authorities did not obstruct the development of public movements ('informal organizations'), which, according to available data, numbered 30,000 by the end of 1987 and 60,000 by the end of 1989 (Miller 1993: 102). Gradually, out of the numerous mostley 'informals' (*neformaly*) emerged alternative political parties in embryonic form.

Some measures were undertaken to involve enterprise workers in economic decision-making. The 1987 law on state enterprises introduced elections for directors by work collectives. The first cautious steps were made in developing non-state forms of property, first and foremost work collectives' property: lease-purchase enterprises, the co-operative movement, and 'people's enterprises'. Ultimately, all of this was not only aimed at achieving better economic results (these measures were in line with the most advanced economic ideas of the time), but also at winning political support.

From 1987, attempts were made to ensure that there were multi-candidate elections to party positions and to the soviets. On this basis, delegates were elected first to the Nineteenth Party Conference (1988), and later to the Congress of People's Deputies. Twenty per cent of republican and regional party leaders (34 people) suffered defeat in the elections to the Congress. The same fate befell many representatives of the military élite. The changes in the principles of cadre selection and appointment were fundamental: 'Elections as an alternative to *nomenklatura* appointment brought new leaders out into the political arena thanks to their personal qualities, rather than the established career maze' (Kryshtanovskaya 1995: 55).

Far-reaching reforms to the system of state institutions were put into effect. The traditional Supreme Soviet was transformed into a full-time parliament, and Gorbachev was elected its chairman. Later, the post of President of the USSR was established as head of the executive branch, with rather broad powers. The election of Gorbachev to this post in March 1990 completed the formation of an alternative power centre to the Politburo and the Central Committee of the CPSU. The removal in 1990 of Article 6 from the constitution, which had secured the leading role of the CPSU in Soviet society, adequately reflected the political changes which had taken place by that time. In general, one can accept Olga Kryshtanovskaya's assessment of political reform in this period: 'The political reform implemented by Gorbachev and his supporters not only significantly diminished the power of the CPSU, but also effectively signalled the fall of the *nomenklatura*' (Kryshtanovskaya 1995: 55).

The long-standing contradictions between different levels of the *nomenklatura* were deliberately exacerbated. The law on state enterprises, by establishing the principles of independence, self-management, and self-financing, directly set the interests of the managerial corps against those of higher levels of the bureaucracy. This was an obvious departure from the policy of stream-lining centralized control mechanisms, and reflected conceptual changes. This is how Gorbachev characterized the essence of the changes: 'With the law on enterprises it was necessary to empower work collectives and set them free, so that no central directorate could order them about, no ministry could order them about, since this was forbidden by law. For all attempts to do things from the top down, to change things one way or another, replacing ministries with committees, and committees with ministries, were futile. It was necessary to give confidence to the main tier of management, and then to enshrine that confidence in law'. A real battle developed around the implementation of the law. The top levels of the economic bureaucracy tried 'not to notice' the exist-ence of the law, continuing to exert influence on enterprises by administrative methods. Managers employed every means at their disposal in the struggle, entering into open conflict with higher administrative organs, and bringing in the press. The potential unity of the bureaucracy in opposition to reforms was successfully undermined.

Ideological bearings were changing ever more radically. Although the dogma of the people's 'socialist choice' remained inviolate, there was an ever greater emphasis on the difference between the existing social system and 'true socialism', for the sake of which the reforms were being carried out. Gradually the idea was introduced that protecting the existing system was not the same as protecting socialism. The limits of *glasnost'* were broadened, as an ever greater range of opinions was permitted, and ever more pointed criticism was made of 'the achievements of socialism'. It was in 1987 that, together with the term *glasnost* the term 'socialist pluralism'—a euphemism for freedom of speech—gained official currency.

But revolution has its own logic and that logic differs considerably from the logic of reform. The authorities, having ceased to rely upon the traditional ruling social stratum, found themselves under pressure from a much broader spectrum of conflicting interests and demands than had been the case during the evolutionary phase. Moreover, the position of Gorbachev's team was even more unstable than the position of any other régime at the early stage of a revolution. Usually the first revolutionary reforms occur during a period of broad unity of social forces. In this case the 'honeymoon period' had been exhausted in the earlier reform period, and the revolutionary measures accel-erated the fragmentation processes. More accurately, the first visible signs of fragmentation coincided in time with the development of the reforms into a revolution, and clearly manifested themselves in the second half of 1987 and the first half of 1988. The authorities, having only just decided to move towards meeting public expectations, discovered growing opposition both on the right and the left.

At the October 1987 Plenum of the CPSU Central Committee, the particular position of Boris Yeltsin, a candidate member of the Politburo, became clear. He criticized the pace of reforms and the official assessment of the situation in the country. His subsequent dismissal and the campaign against 'vanguardism' which followed the Plenum demonstrated that fragmentation processes were coming to the surface. What at first glance looked like the smothering of a nascent pluralism[6] in fact served as a catalyst for the development of a separate radical wing within *perestroyka*, which also acquired a strong, charismatic leader. Not every member of Gorbachev's team accepted the transition from 'reform from above' to 'revolution from above'. It did not take long for the conservatives to consolidate themselves. On 13 March 1988, *Sovetskaia Rossya* carried a letter by Nina Andreeva entitled 'I cannot forgo my principles', in which the political views of Politburo member Egor Ligachev were clearly visible. Three weeks later there followed a firm repudiation in a *Pravda* editorial (5 April 1988) which, it soon transpired, had been written by another Politburo member Alexander Yakovlev (see Andreeva 1988; 'Printsipy perestroyki' 1988). The appearance of these two articles and the three-week interval between them eloquently attested to the intense struggle that was taking place within the political leadership. The confrontation was all the more unexpected as it came not from the old guard, from whom Gorbachev had managed to free himself after coming to power, but from his comrades-in-arms.[7]

From the end of 1987, it was not just the political élite that was involved in the struggle. The grassroots movement, initially propelled by the political leadership, quickly acquired a momentum of its own. The organization of popular fronts in the Union republics proceeded apace. Gradually various economic and political forces became institutionalized. Ethnic conflicts and centrifugal trends in the USSR were on the rise.

The relationship between ethnic and social conflicts deserves special consideration. The predominance of the former throughout almost the whole period of the 'rule of the moderates' has led some researchers to view the developments in the country not as a social revolution, but as the collapse of an empire, drawing analogies with the collapse of Austria-Hungary. However, the centrifugal trends in the USSR were not primarily nationalist, but also social in nature. Even so, there were several factors which linked the fundamental political choices to the issue of national sovereignty.

First, the drive for independence was to a large extent determined by the ideas of republican leaders as to the direction and the pace of necessary reforms, and these ideas could differ from those of the Union leadership on

---

[6] According to Åslund, from this moment, 'Gorbachev ceased to be a supporter of radical reforms. In November 1987, he for the first time spoke out against the radicals who had "gone too far" ' (1996: 47).

[7] Yakovlev, in his interview, noted that up until 1987 he did not have any substantial disagreements with Ligachev.

both questions. Commentators have noted that the possibilities for developing a market economy, towards which the Baltic republics strove, were rather circumscribed as long as the all-Union system of material supplies was still in place. Political sovereignty for them was therefore an essential prerequisite for achieving radical reforms (Hanson 1992: 230). The fundamental differences between the economic models and political systems that have developed in the former Soviet republics since the collapse of the USSR fully confirms the importance of this factor in the drive for national independence.

Secondly, national movements were used by the regional party *nomenklaturas* to oppose reforms promoted by the centre. The most striking example of this were the Alma-Ata disturbances in December 1986, which started in response to the dismissal of the former Communist Party First Secretary Dinmukhamed Kunaev and his replacement with Gennady Kolbin, who was drafted in from Russia. According to Gorbachev, it was Kunaev, fearing the rise of Nursultan Nazarbaev (at that time Prime Minister, and from 1991 President of Kazakhstan), who had himself asked for a Russian to be sent to replace him. Then, taking advantage of the discontent caused by this appointment, Kunaev tried to organize mass unrest. Yakovlev bluntly described this event as 'a party revolt, the first revolt of a party *nomenklatura*, an attempt to test the waters'.

Thirdly, the national movements strengthened the power and influence of local élites, which until that time had had practically no political clout of their own. The legitimacy of the regional élites was consolidated by the introduction of a presidential post at the republican level and elections to representative organs. This was a logical progression in the process of exacerbating tensions within the *nomenklatura* and upgrading the role of lower strata as a counterbalance to the higher. However, in this case tensions were aggravated not in line with the wishes of the centre, as had been the case with the managerial corps, but against those wishes. The most striking example of this struggle was the 'tug-of-war' between the USSR and Russian leaderships, as they competed to bring enterprises under their respective jurisdictions. It is no coincidence that the events were frequently described in military terminology: 'the tax war', when Union and Russian leaders raced to lower profit tax in an attempt to win over enterprise work collectives to their side; 'the war of programmes', over the development of competing prescriptions for overcoming the crisis; 'the war of sovereignties', a kind of contest between all-Union and republican authorities to legitimize their positions.

This 'war' between the Union and Russian leadership contributed a great deal to the further acceleration of fragmentation and polarization in 1989–91, but overall the developments of this period were much more complex than a simple stand-off between the centre and the republics. Whilst a variety of public and political organizations and movements were being formed outside the party, schism was increasing within the CPSU. The splits within the CPSU took various forms: the uniting of rank-and-file party members with supporters of renewal in the top leadership in opposition to the party's middle level and the party apparatus; party members allying themselves with informal organizations which held opposing views; the formation within the party of non-statutory organizational structures; and the personification of different political lines by certain leaders. Indeed the peculiarity of the polarization of social forces in Russia was that a multi-party system arose not as a result of the emergence of a powerful political organization as an alternative to the CPSU, but through a schism within the CPSU.[8] Gorbachev had to admit this himself, when he stated at the Plenum of the CPSU Central Committee in April 1991 that representatives of not one but four or five parties were present at the meeting.

Politicized economic associations assumed an ever more active political role. They were better able than the newly created parties to reflect the interests of economically significant social strata, and were also involved in the implementation of economic decisions. They enjoyed tangible economic power thanks both to their influence on producers and their connections with the central and local authorities. Moreover, the Association of State Enterprises and the Peasants' Union, on the one hand, and the Scientific-Industrial Union and Association of Farms, on the other hand, held diametrically opposed views concerning the country's further development, and advocated fundamentally different economic policies.

Gradually, social conflicts, in addition to national ones, assumed a significance of their own. From 1989 there was a series of strikes, rallies, and demonstrations, which involved the population of various regions and the workers of various sectors of the economy. The most significant were the miners' strikes in July and October 1989, and then in March—April 1991. The purely economic demands of the strikers developed into political demands when the miners demanded independence from all-Union ministries and the freedom to set prices on what they produced. The final strikes put forward political demands, including the resignation of the government. In major cities mass pro-democracy rallies attracted tens and even hundreds of thousands of demonstrators.

However, the public was concerned not only with the problem of securing democratic reforms. In the context of a worsening economic crisis, the issue of economic reform became the key factor in the struggle for power. The existing régime was clearly unable to cope with the growing difficulties. In 1990, official statistics for the first time showed a drop in production, although according to a number of experts, this had already occurred in 1989 (see

---

[8] Oleg Vite, political writer and sociologist, remarked ironically that the newly emerging parties differed only in the time it took their members to recognize the necessity of breaking with the CPSU, and thus they could be named 'the March Democratic Party', 'the September Democratic Party', etc. (conversation with the authors).

Hanson 1992: 225). The law on state enterprises freed managers from administrative control, but failed to subject them to market controls such that enterprises became a law unto themselves. There was increased disruption in deliveries, and construction began to grind to a halt. The cash incomes of the population grew quickly. The budget deficit was constantly increasing, and the money supply was growing. In the context of fixed prices, this resulted in pervasive shortages of food products and other consumer goods. Empty shop shelves became a distinctive feature of major Russian cities. Food rationing became universal. In 1989, according to some sources, meat rationing had already been introduced in 40 per cent of regions; butter in 62 per cent; sugar in 92 per cent (Noren 1990: 225). By 1991 the situation had deteriorated even further. According to public opinion surveys, in April almost half of respondents could not find any staple foodstuffs on open sale. The July survey revealed that 70 per cent of respondents had, to some degree, experienced difficulties with converting their ration cards. Table 5.1 presents more detailed data.

Against the backdrop of deepening economic crisis, popular discontent grew, as disappointment followed the raised expectations of the 'rosy period'. Whereas in 1989 radical political reforms associated with the multi-candidate elections to the Congress of People's Deputies resulted in a brief burst of enthusiasm, by 1991 discontent had intensified considerably. There was a

TABLE 5.1. *Foodstuffs availability, USSR, 1991 (according to public opinion surveys; % of respondents)*

What food products do you currently see on open sale? (Apr. 1991)		Can you currently covert your ration cards or coupons freely and at any time? (July 1991)	
Meat sausages	12	Where I live there are no ration cards or coupons	8
		It is possible to convert all ration cards and coupons	11
Milk and milk products	23	Only a part of the ration cards or coupons can be freely converted	34
Butter	8	It is difficult to convert any ration cards or coupons	36
Vegetable oil	6	Hard to say	11
Flour, cereals	6		
Eggs	17		
Fish	7		
Saw nothing on open sale	48		
Hard to say	9		

Source: Nikitina (1997*c*: 48, 49).

TABLE 5.2. *Attitudes to the prospect of transition to a market economy and the pace of transition, USSR, 1990–1991 (%)*

	June 1990	July 1991
Favouring transition to market economy (total)	56	64
Favouring swift transition to market	18	23
Favouring gradual transition to market	38	41
Favouring a stronger plan system	24	19
Hard to say	20	16

Source: Sedov (1995: 24)

growth of radical views in society; trust in democratic values fell and charismatic political leaders gained popularity; there was active discussion of forthcoming 'hunger and cold' in all sections of society, and, by some, of the inevitability of dictatorship. All these things attested to the waning of 'moderate rule' and an impending crisis. Public opinion surveys of this period demonstrate that society was split into two opposing camps: those favouring rigid order and a strengthening of state control over the economy, and those favouring market reforms and diverse forms of ownership.[9] In addition, as far as can be established from the available incomplete and fragmentary information, there was a gradual shift in the direction of more radical views. This process is illustrated by the data in Table 5.2. In 1991, 64 per cent of the population generally supported the transition to a market economy, and 37 per cent favoured the dissolution of the CPSU (Nikitina 1997c: 49). At the same time, over 40 per cent of the population agreed that a strong, authoritative leader, to whom the people could entrust their future, was more important than laws.

Thus, in the Russia of 1989–91 all the preconditions for 'dual power' considered in the previous chapter were present: the fragmentation and polarization

[9] A public opinion survey conducted in October 1989 produced the following results: those for and against permitting unemployment were split more or less equally: 42% and 40% respectively. Although the majority of those polled considered the existing income distribution inequitable, 27% regarded income differentials as excessive, while 38% regarded this level of inequality as insufficient. Fifty per cent of respondents thought it necessary to preserve some kind of ceiling on incomes, while 39% opposed such restrictions. When asked how to raise the interest of workers in the results of their labour, one section of respondents chose answers which gravitated towards the establishment of strict order: arrange equitable distribution of incomes (35%), strengthen work discipline and measures to keep order (32%). Another section chose answers in keeping with the logic of the market: sharply increase wage differentials (31%); transfer enterprises into the collective ownership of the employees (24%). Once again respondents were split almost exactly in half (Rutgayzer et al. 1990).

of social forces, a deteriorating economic situation, and a radicalization of the masses. As in other revolutions, at first glance it seemed that the struggle was between 'moderates' and 'radicals', especially since the conflict was personified in the stand-off between Gorbachev and Yeltsin. However, in fact, the social base of the centre, represented by Gorbachev, was continually being eroded, while the real power struggle became that between the radicals and the conservatives. As polarization increased, pressure on the centre mounted not only from Yeltsin's democrats, but also from the opponents of further reforms. Thus in April 1989, in Gorbachev's absence, conservatives organized a show of force in Tbilisi, and twenty people were killed. Later, force was used in other recalcitrant republics. It seems that it was the conservatives who forced the abandonment of the '500 Days' programme.

Throughout 1990–1, conservatives mode repeated attempts to constitute themselves officially as an alternative power centre, although they were not as successful as the radicals, whose efforts resulted in the election of Yeltsin to the position of Chairman of the Russian Supreme Soviet in May 1990, and in his election in a nationwide vote as first President of Russia in June 1991. According to some accounts, a military coup was attempted as early as September 1990 (Galeotti 1997: 107–8). According to Gorbachev, a number of top party leaders discussed the possibility of his removal from power at a meeting of 'hero cities' in Smolensk at the beginning of 1991. In April, the conservatives attempted to remove Gorbachev from the post of General Secretary at the Plenum of the Central Committee of the CPSU, but some of those taking part in the Plenum supported Gorbachev and the conservatives backed down.[10] In June, Prime Minister Valentin Pavlov proposed to the Supreme Soviet that it transfer a significant portion of presidential powers to himself. This proposal had not even been agreed with Gorbachev. The August putsch was merely the last in a series of such attempts.

As is always the case in conditions of fragmentation at the initials stage of the revolution, the authorities started to vacillate. Gorbachev's complaints about developments during this period are almost a verbatim repeat of Kerenskii's comment concerning 'the Bolsheviks of the left and the Bolsheviks of the right' quoted in the previous chapter:

The state *nomenklatura* saw that its days were numbered, and so did the party *nomenklatura*. And they closed ranks. And that is when the most difficult and terrible period began . . . After the 1989 elections pressure was applied from both sides, one was continually between Scylla and Charybdis. The reactionaries and opponents of reform were angry people, and well organized; their pressure was open and brazen. And on the other side, the radicals were spurring us on, and this played into the hands of the former.

---

[10] Yakovlev, in his interview, noted that 'when we got to 1991, when the question of his resignation was raised, 72 members of the Central Committee submitted their resignations. It was a schism.'

The end of 1990 and 1991 witnessed constant zigzags, manœuvring, and shifts in position. Initially Gorbachev tried to build bridges to the conservatives, sacrificing many of the achievements of *perestroyka*. This provoked a turbulent reaction. Eduard Shevardnadze resigned as Minister of Foreign Affairs, warning of the danger of impending dictatorship. Democratic forces in the capital organized mass demonstrations in March 1991 in support of Yeltsin and demonstrated under anti-Gorbachev banners during the May Day parade. Gorbachev then made a U-turn, abandoning his alliance with the conservatives and moving towards the radicals. Active discussion began over the new Union Treaty, which proposed the almost total devolution of power and authority from the centre to the republics. Gorbachev's partners were the new democratic leaders of the Union republics, first and foremost Yeltsin. However, as in other revolutions, the split had already gone so far that the 'rule of the moderates' was doomed. The open confrontation between conservatives and radicals during the August putsch left no room on the political stage for either the Union centre or the political centre. The radicals' victory meant that the revolution had entered its next phase.

5.4. The radical phase: general and specific features

The analysis in the previous chapter showed that in maintaining social unity in the radical phase, as the revolution gathers momentum and opposition from internal and external enemies increases, three types of method are used. These are: the imposition of a single ideology; terror; and the formation of pro-revolutionary coalitions by means of active manœuvring between various social forces. Moreover, the greater the danger to the revolution's achievements, the greater the extent to which the authorities rely on violent methods, although they never limit themselves to such methods alone. During the radical phase of the recent Russian revolution, the political priorities were clearly different: there was relatively little violence and a much greater reliance on manœuvring. Several reasons for these specific features of this revolution can be identified.

First, a real threat to the achievements of the revolution arose only twice over the whole period: during the August putsch in 1991, which effectively brought the radicals to power, and in September–October 1993, at the height of the confrontation between Yeltsin and the Russian Supreme Soviet. These two periods saw the greatest amount of violence on the part of the authorities against their opponents, although this violence never turned into terror.[11] For

---

[11] None the less, the events of autumn 1993 led supporters of the Supreme Soviet, who are inclined to exaggerate the scale of the violence, to draw direct parallels with revolutionary

the most part, the revolution developed fairly peacefully and did not require emergency measures in order for the radicals to retain power.

Secondly, the country's population, affected by post-modernization trends, had fundamentally changed. High levels of education, a significant portion of second-generation (or earlier) urban population—both these factors exercised a stabilizing influence and staved off excesses. In addition, in contrast to other revolutions, by the beginning of the radical phase, hopes for a swift and painless solution to the problems had already been more or less exhausted. According to public opinion surveys, 80 per cent of Russians by the end of 1991 anticipated almost insurmountable material difficulties, and disruption in the supply of food staples, energy, heat, and transport. Two out of three citizens believed that the crisis could not be overcome without 'a temporary fall in people's living standards'.[12]

Thirdly, during the post-war period there had been a radical change in perceptions with regard to human values, the permissible limits of politics, and the role of humanitarian values in the development of society. Certainly, these factors *per se* could not prevent large-scale violence, as the experience of the former Yugoslavia and a number of former Soviet republics has shown. None the less, this factor influenced the formation of the general 'rules of the game' during the recent revolution, and in particular during the radical phase. The reaction of Russians to the events of October 1993 can be cited as an example. As Table 5.3 shows, in answer to the question whether the government's response to the disturbances was adequate, those responding that the measures were too harsh were almost double the number that considered the measures insufficiently harsh in 1993. In 1997 the ratio had grown to more than three to one. The fear of uncontrolled use of nuclear weapons also exercised a restraining influence.

Fourthly and finally, the experience of national and world history convinced Russian revolutionaries that they should try to implement radical reforms while avoiding large-scale social conflict. Whereas the Bolsheviks, following the Jacobin example, consciously accepted terror as one of the effective instruments for realizing their goals, in the recent Russian revolution the avoidance of violence was an equally conscious political line. In the final analysis, it was a deliberate decision of the leaders of the radical phase. Egor Gaidar returned to this topic repeatedly throughout his interview:

cataclysms of the past. Let us cite one example: 'The bloody violence, culminating in the bombardment of the parliament and the death of many hundreds of innocent people, will cover our "tank democrats" with ignominy forever. They have lost all moral and political right to accuse Bolsheviks of adherence to violence and terror in the years of the revolution and civil war' (Volobuev 1995: 288).

[12] For more detailed analysis of the causes of relative social stability during the radical phase, see Mau (1996*b*: 85–92).

TABLE 5.3. *Responses to the question 'Do you think the government's actions in response to the mass disturbances in Moscow on 3 and 4 October [1993] were ——?', 1993 and 1997 (%)*

	1993	1997
Appropriate	31	21
Excessively harsh	28	38
Insufficiently harsh	15	12
Hard to say	26	29

Source: Otsenka (1997: 44).

'We could have radicalized the radical phase further. We could have tried, for example, a law on lustration, a mass assault on the Red *nomenklatura*, the sacking of directors rather than compromise, and heads rolling among the chairmen of local soviets. We could, perhaps, have exacerbated the situation further. But I am not sure I understand how this could have been done technically: who, how, by what mechanisms, and relying on what? And I don't know what the result would have been. But in any case, they would definitely have been fraught with greater risk. I always feared sliding into full-fledged civil war, at least in pockets across the country, with an absolutely unpredictable outcome. And this always acted as a brake on me. My policy was to dampen down the radical phase in order to prevent it from escalating into civil war, which seemed to me to be a real danger. I consciously preferred to buy power from them, rather than to declare a crusade against them.

None the less, the limited application of violence and the striving to make the greatest possible use of compromise and manoeuvre does not alter the fact that during this phase truly radical transformations of society took place. They preclude the possibility of a return to the previous system under any circumstances, even in the event of the communists returning to power. The period of radicalization in Russia is characterized by three very striking episodes: the removal of the CPSU from power; the collapse of the USSR; and accelerated market reforms by means of 'shock therapy'. The political, ideological, and economic base of the *ancien régime* collapsed, and the old élite was deprived once and for all of its traditional levers for controlling society. The state, as the principal bulwark of the former social system, ceased to exist. Despite the absence of terror so typical of the radical phase, some contemporaries considered the policies pursued in Russia to be violent. A well-known Soviet economist, for example, described the developments as follows: '1992 plunged Russia into shock, and for some time paralysed her ability to resist direct historical violence' (Rakitsky 1993: 83). Some foreign researchers echo these words: 'The shock therapy strategy of independent Russia . . . is not at all a strategy of reform in the usual sense of that term. It is a strategy of revolution' (Kotz with Weir 1997: 163).

As is the case with most other revolutions, many researchers find the explanation of radicals' actions in their ideologies. Thus, the entire interpretation
of the recent Russian revolution in Kotz and Weir (1997) is based on the
premise that Gorbachev was opposed in his attempt at building democratic
socialism by the part of the party-state élite headed by Yeltsin, which preferred
a capitalist society. Successfully seizing the moment, they managed to implement their programme. To this end, they engineered the collapse of the Soviet
Union and the removal of the Communist Party from power, and introduced
radical economic reforms, aimed at an accelerated transition to capitalism,
regardless of the suffering that this would inflict upon ordinary people.

This explanation is far removed from reality. In fact, although they shared
a common ideological base, the radicals reacted above all to the needs of the
moment, which were determined by practical circumstances, as was the case
in past revolutions. They were aimed at: (1) overcoming the crisis situation,
with which the moderates had been unable to cope and which had led to their
downfall; (2) manoeuvring in order to shore up the unstable balance of forces
which provided their social support; (3) finding sources of finance for the
reforms under way. Gennady Burbulis explains this very forcefully in his interview:

The August putsch hit the system like a political Chernobyl. The explosion marked a
collapse which had already taken place. In fact, all subsequent events up to the signing
of the Belovezh agreements were an agonizing realization of the truth of an actual
event in world history: the Soviet Union had collapsed, its economy was bankrupt, its
ideology was corrupt and bankrupt, and the country had no resources whatsoever. It
would be a profound mistake to look for anything radical, transformative, or creative
in our reform strategy. Our reform strategy was based on the dismal fact that the
system had collapsed. And in no way did we as a team possess any kind of exceptional
gift of social foresight or intellectual upheaval. We engaged in a highly pragmatic
search for the answers to rather prosaic questions: how to manage the problems we
had inherited, how to feed the people, what to heat homes with, how to escape total
ruin, famine, and that entire nightmare.

Effectively there was no choice as to policy. As Gaidar noted in his interview:
'the path was extremely narrow. To have any realistic hope of success one
could either have done roughly what we did, with very minor variations; or
one could have done nothing, dressing inaction in any attire from statist to
quasi-democratic, to see what came of it, and how to escape'.

In addition to economic restrictions, there were ideological limitations.
However, they originated not in the régime, but in the social forces which
brought the radicals to power. According to Gaidar, these limitations were
primarily 'non-communist or anti-communist ideas and slogans, many of
which grew out of a simple repudiation of the dogmas of the *ancien régime*.
This collection of not very complex ideas, quite natural in an anti-communist
revolution, in some sense exercised an extremely serious influence on the

development of events in the radical phase. You can only do what falls within public expectations'.[13]

One of the decisions made during the radical phase which is considered to be the most ideologically driven was the Russian authorities' move to dissolve the Soviet Union and win sovereignty for Russia. The arguments usually marshalled in support of preserving the Soviet Union include the high degree of interlinkage between the economies of various republics, and the support voiced by the population for the preservation of a renewed Union in the referendum of 17 March 1991. However, such arguments, which are perfectly acceptable when referring to evolutionary development, completely fail to understand the logic of the revolutionary process. As we have tried to demonstrate, the processes of disintegration in the USSR were closely linked to the struggle by various social forces over the direction and pace of reforms; in this process the interests of the regional élites coincided with nationalistic attitudes widespread amongst the population. In such a situation, the logic of social struggle had much stronger effect in a revolution than rational arguments. By the end of 1991, the disintegration was so far advanced that, by all accounts, it could not have been reversed. As Table 5.4 shows, this was felt not just by politicians but also by the people. According to public opinion surveys, in January 1991 66 per cent of those polled believed that the real power of the President of the USSR was either extremely limited or non-existent.

According to Burbulis, negotiations between the republics without the participation of the centre started as early as autumn 1990. In November, Russia and Kazakhstan concluded a bilateral treaty, after which the conclusion of such inter-republic treaties became fashionable. In the spring of 1991, a quadrilateral treaty between Russia, Kazakhstan, Ukraine, and Belarus was drafted, and only the intervention of the Union centre prevented it from being signed. The Novo-Ogarevo negotiations, in the opinion of Burbulis, amounted to this: 'instead of decisively looking for a framework enabling the transition to a new political and legal set-up, participants spent hours discussing things that they did not believe in either individually or as groups. All of Gorbachev's efforts to do things the old way (albeit not without flair) were senseless, because everyone was waving two fingers at him behind his

---

[13] This assertion, made in his interview, is corroborated by survey data of the period, which shows strong anti-communist attitudes: 'An important feature of public opinion at this time was the strong anti-communist sentiment; being a democrat for many people meant being an anti-communist and rejecting everything that was, one way or another, linked to the former régime, including state regulation of the economy. Therefore 'democracy', 'market', 'private property', and 'privatization' were very much welcomed as 'anti-communist' values, when set against the past. However, when these ideas were filled with concrete, 'positive' content, contradictions emerged. In the public consciousness, 'democracy' easily co-existed with 'emergency measures', and 'market' with 'great power' and messianic ideas' (Koval' 1997: 280).

TABLE 5.4. *Responses to the question: 'Does the President of the USSR wield real power today?', January 1991 (%)*

Yes, on all matters	14
Only on matters of foreign policy	32
No, since the republics act independently of the centre	34
Hard to say	20

Source: Nikitina (1997c: 77–78).

back . . . We did not destroy the Soviet Union, in so far as it had already ceased to exist at that point, but we did seek a less painful collapse. The Belovezh agreement was a necessary and inevitable measure'.

The real relationship between ideology and objective necessity can be clearly traced in the implementation of the accelerated transition to the market in 1992, starting with the liberalization of prices. An analysis of the course of radical economic reforms is particularly interesting because during the revolution, the crisis which brought the radicals to power was not of a military-political nature, but first and foremost economic. The overall logic of the radicals' actions was largely dictated by objectives in that sphere. Kotz with Weir explain the selection of the priorities for economic reform in the following fashion: 'The rationale for immediate price liberalization is based on the economic theory found in any traditional Western economics textbook' (1997: 163). They then adduce a set of standard arguments concerning the advantages of resource allocation through the mechanisms of the free market. However, the arguments in favour of price liberalization were of a much more practical nature. The country was heading towards economic catastrophe. Problems of power supply were accumulating and threatened to bring about a swift collapse in production and shortage of heat for the population as winter approached. The consumer market had been completely destroyed and in cities there were growing problems with food supplies. Until the spring of 1992, the government of Russia was receiving daily reports on trade in the major industrial regions, which bore a strong resemblance to military news bulletins.[14]

[14] By way of example, we include extracts from a report of 29 Nov. 1991, about the situation in two *oblasts* (regions), which more than adequately reflect the situation country-wide: 'Nizhnii Novgorod *oblast*. Meat products are rationed, there are not enough resources for December, milk sold out within an hour. Butter is rationed—200 grammes per person per month. There are not enough resources. There is no vegetable oil on sale, as the suppliers in Krasnodar *krai* and the Ukraine are not shipping it, and it is not imported either. Bread is sold intermittently, there is a shortage of grain to bake bread until the end of the year to the tune of 20,000 tonnes.

'Perm' *oblast*. In December, ration cards for butter were issued at 200 grammes per

TABLE 5.5. *Responses to the question: 'What worried you most during this particular year?', 1990–1992 (From surveys organized annually by VCIOM; % of respondents)*

	1990	1991	1992
Growth in prices, falling living standards of the population	67	67	62
Disappearance of the most essential goods from the shops	51	39	10

Source: Nikitina (1997*b*: 43, 1997*c*: 50, 1998*a*: 58).

In conditions of growing economic chaos, the regions refused to ship food-stuffs and other goods in accordance with established rules; they set up their own customs barriers, and strove to achieve self-sufficiency. The threat of Russia's disintegration was very real. There were no administrative levers capable of ensuring that the country was supplied with even the bare essentials. Even in order to ensure that foreign humanitarian aid reached its intended destination, measures had to be undertaken at government level, as regional authorities detained and redistributed such shipments without authorization. At the same time, the economic reserves of the centralized supply system were exhausted: towards the end of 1991, the gold reserves of the former Soviet Union fell to an unprecedented low of 289.6 tonnes, not even enough to provide for the most essential needs of the country. Foreign currency reserves were almost non-existent. The only remaining option available to the authorities in their efforts to avoid total collapse was to jump-start market mechanisms. As the data in Table 5.5 show, this measure succeeded in halting the catastrophic escalation of disintegration that had been continuing during the preceding years.

The idea of price liberalization followed quite logically from the discussions held on the issue of price reform during Gorbachev's period in office. It was clear that the price system could not remain unchanged, and a single upward price adjustment would not resolve the problem. By the end of the 1980s, the issue of price liberalization was, as it were 'hanging in the air', even if it was not discussed openly. The fundamental problem was finding someone who would take responsibility for such an unpopular measure. There

person, but they are not backed up by sufficient resources. Smolensk, Penza, Orenburg, Tver', and Lipetsk *oblasts*, and the republic of Tatarstan are refusing to ship it. There is no vegetable oil on sale, as suppliers from Volgograd, Kostroma, and Saratov *oblasts*, and Krasnodar *krai* are not shipping it. There is no sugar on sale. Factories in Kursk and Voronezh *oblasts* have broken off shipment. Bread is sold intermittently, and attracts long queues. Fifteen thousand tonnes of flour are needed for baking bread' (quoted in Mau 1996*b*: 63–4).

were two respects in which the decision was a perilous one. On the one hand, it was almost universally recognized that price liberalization was fraught with the risk of serious social upheavals, mass protests, and possibly a change of government. On the other hand, some experts believed that price liberalization would neither result in the reappearance of goods on the shelves, nor overcome shortages, because the trade sector was so criminalized that it was incapable of reacting adequately to market signals. In addition, prevailing opinion held that the system of regulated prices was more beneficial for the mafia of commerce, in so far as, in deficit conditions, it enabled this mafia to reap high profits from the black-market price differential. Both these sets of misgivings proved to be groundless, but in order to put price liberalization into practice, a capacity for resolute action was required, which normally only arises in the radical phase.

Thus, price liberalization was not inspired by ideology: rather it reflected the lack of any alternative and the authorities' readiness to sacrifice their popularity on the altar of radical reforms. However, even in this case the authorities were anxious to avoid risk. The implementation of price liberalization was not as decisive and compromise-free as it might have seemed at first glance. A number of key goods and services were exempt from liberalization, including energy prices and public utility charges. Price regulation by means of a prescribed maximum profit margin was practised extensively: in this way local authorities were able retain control over the price of essential goods. Trade margins were subject to a ceiling; and the prices of so-called monopolistic enterprises, which were registered with the Anti-monopoly Committee, were regulated. The liberalization of energy prices was postponed as a result of firm opposition from a broad range of producers.

The policy of curbing inflation by drastically tightening the money supply and reducing the budget deficit was to a greater extent driven by ideological and conceptual motives. But even here, the 'ideological purity' did not at all last for long. While the price liberalization *per se*, despite the huge leap in inflation in January 1992, did not provoke active social protest,[15] by the spring of 1992 the government's anti-inflationary course had engendered serious opposition from a wide spectrum of political forces. Opposition to the radical reform course drove state enterprise managers from different branches and sectors of the economy to organize themselves politically, even those who in the past had competed implacably for budget allocations. At the same time

---

[15] Opinion surveys show that the population was unenthusiastic about price liberalization. However, in the context of Yeltsin's popularity, a generally favourable attitude to market-oriented economic reforms, and the accumulated fatigue resulting from an inability to obtain even the barest essentials, this measure did not provoke mass protests. Throughout 1992, spontaneous public movements gradually receded, rallies and demonstrations attracted fewer people, and the focus of the strike movement shifted from industry to the social sector.

interaction between organizations representing managerial cadres (mainly the Russian Union of Industrialists and Entrepreneurs) and the old trade unions (left over from the communist system) increased. At tripartite talks, which started in February, they effectively united against the third party—the government. This bloc found its political manifestation in the formation of the Civic Union in the summer of 1992, which included a number of centrist and left-of-centre parties and organizations. The Civic Union advocated strengthening state regulation of the economy, injecting cheap credits into the economy, and measures for the protection of domestic producers. The ranks of opponents to the government's anti-inflation course grew with the addition of new commercial organizations which had made vast profits out of economic instability. Under pressure from a well-organized pro-inflation bloc, which was well-represented by producer interests, amongst legislators, and in the mass media, the government was forced to back down from its initial strategy of stopping inflation in its tracks, a strategy which had been accompanied by the first real bankruptcies and by rising unemployment.

In the spring, the authorities had to shift their position, making concessions in their monetary and foreign trade policies. Control over the money supply was relaxed, and this lead to a new bout of inflation by early autumn, with inflation reaching 5 per cent per week in September/October. In the space of two months, the rouble collapsed to one third of its former value. In order to overcome the crisis of payment arrears, large preferential loans were extended to enterprises. The liberalization of energy prices was shelved indefinitely. The change in policy was also reflected in the changing composition of the government, with the arrival of a number of prominent representatives of the managerial corps who had connections to the military-industrial and fuel-energy complexes (Vlademer Shumeiko, Georgy Khizha, and Viktor Chernomyrdin) and the replacement of the chairman of the central bank. At the same time, measures were undertaken to undermine the unity of the pro-inflationary bloc. The privatization process, commenced at the end of 1992, played a particularly important role in this.

The start of privatization presented the reforming authorities with an important problem. In principle, privatization could be geared to achieving three different objectives: the creation of effective owners; the maximization of budget revenues; or the building of a socio-political base for reform. As in any revolution, the authorities had to find the optimum balance of financial and social, long-term and short-term objectives. Initially, the ideological inclinations of the radicals militated in favour of giving priority to strategic and financial goals. Russia's first document on privatization—'On Key Provisions of the 1992 Privatization Programme for State and Municipal Enterprises in the Russian Federation'—listed amongst the goals of privatization: 'assistance in achieving the general aims of economic stabilization'; 'ensuring through privatization a sharp increase in the effectiveness of enterprise operations by handing them over to the most effective owners'; and 'increasing budget revenues' (Ulyukaev and Kolesnikov 1992: 28–9). The pre-existing law on personal privatization accounts was viewed as an irritating obstacle to privatization, and the transformation of the personal account into a freely transferable voucher was reluctantly accepted as a method of improving the privatization mechanism developed by the legislature. Almost everyone who joined the Russian government at the end of 1991 and witnessed the origins of the voucher scheme has noted their initial fundamental objection to the emphasis on mass free privatization contained in the Russian legislation. In this regard, Gaidar reiterated: 'For the umpteenth time I will reveal the "secret" of the origin of privatization vouchers. Both Gaidar and Chubais were firmly against them. *Firmly!* . . . The Supreme Soviet approved the law on voucher privatization before Gaidar and Chubais joined the government. The mass media were obsessed with this idea. For us this was an unpleasant blow; we wanted to conduct cash privatization' (Gaidar 1998*b*: 2).[16]

By the middle of 1992, however, it became clear that conditions were extremely unfavourable for such a privatization policy. On the one hand, opposition to reforms grew stronger and stronger, and the issue of securing a social basis for the reforms came to the fore. On the other hand, a legacy of the *ancien régime* was a complete lack of clarity in ownership rights, with diverse criss-crossing claims on the same property,[17] which could not be disregarded. As a result, the approach to privatization underwent significant change. This can be traced in the two versions of the state privatization programme—of 11 June 1992, and particularly of 24 December 1993. Despite the obligatory reference in these documents to the importance of 'forming a broad class of private owners as the economic basis of the free market' (*Privatizatsya v Rossii* 1993: 70) in the short term, voucher privatization

---

[16] Similar statements were made by Dmitriy Vasil'ev, then Deputy Chairman of the State Property Committee and responsible for the methodology of voucher privatization: 'At the start, our views on privatization (those of Chubais, me, and most of our advisers) differed substantially from the ideas underlying the model that was eventually implemented . . . Our actual Russian model evolved in the course of heated political clashes, and of rethinking the realities of the Russian economy and society. It was, without doubt, the result of certain compromises, and thus carries with it the well-known costs (minuses) of these compromises' (Vasil'ev 1994: 10–11).

[17] According to Gaidar, as soon as the privatization process began, 'it immediately became clear that several social groups were making serious claims on one and the same piece of property (work collectives of the privatized enterprises; the management; the population that were not employed in the sector undergoing privatization; local authorities, and former pre-socialist owners); moreover they all considered their claims justified and natural. Refusal to recognize the rights of some of these groups would have led to immediate paralysis of the privatization process. This is why the process of large-scale postsocialist privatization is inextricably bound up with the search for social compromise' (Gaidar 1997*a*: 470).

resolved fundamentally different problems. It reconciled a strengthening of the position of the managerial corps in the distribution of property,[18] with a popular 'people's' privatization, which involved the country's entire population in the sharing out of property. In addition, urban residents effectively privatized their apartments gratis, while the rural population received plots of land. The objectives of developing an effective class of owners, and the fiscal objectives of privatization, were relegated at this stage.

In these conditions, the privatization voucher turned out to be the ideal tool for balancing the interests of all forces with a stake in privatization: employees, managers, large and small external investors. In order to facilitate the co-ordination of interests, three schemes were worked out for the privatization of major enterprises, providing insiders and outsiders with a variety of possibilities.[19] At the same time, privatization procedures were simplified as much as possible to facilitate a rapid distribution of property rights.[20] The ideologues of Russian privatization openly admitted that its main advantage lay in being a flexible mechanism for co-ordinating interests.

How could it happen that, despite the initial conceptual focus on the priority of strategic and fiscal objectives, in practice social goals came to be so dominant? In the revolution the radicals were extremely restricted in the means available to them for influencing the interest groups that had emerged in society. Unable to use terror for the purposes of intimidation, lacking external enemies to mobilize the population, with freedom of speech severely limiting the use of official ideology as an instrument for manipulating the masses, they largely had to rely on social manœuvring and the search for devices which could foster pro-revolutionary coalitions. The privatization process provided them with a unique, and probably the only available, opportunity for broad social manoeuvring. If they had not availed themselves of this, focusing instead on theoretically more important tasks, their political

---

[18] Bim provides a similar description of the evolving approaches to privatization, stating that 'accelerated and apparently egalitarian privatization by means of privatization vouchers did not initially enter into the plans of the liberal reformers; however, the political imperative of compensating for the confiscatory actions of price and fiscal reforms in 1992—at least on the level of rhetoric and propaganda—logically led the government to a populist-style privatization ('millions of owners', 'just redistribution of state property', etc.) with very strong emphasis on 'social appeasement' of enterprise managers' (1995: 121).

[19] Only two of them were widely practised. Under the first scheme, 25% of preference shares were transferred to workers, and 10% of ordinary shares were sold at a discount, while managers had an option to buy 5% of ordinary shares. Under the second scheme, 51% of ordinary shares was sold to the work collective. The remaining shares could be acquired by external investors.

[20] Amongst the measures which accelerated the privatization process, it is worth mentioning the abandonment of any attempt at determining the market value of the assets being sold, and the decision to determine starting prices according to the book value of the assets.

fate, in all likelihood, would have been sealed. By changing their approach to privatization, the radicals destroyed the unity of the anti-reform front. Privatization effectively divided the managerial corps in two. According to opinion polls, at the time 42 per cent of managers supported the privatization of large enterprises, while 48 per cent were in favour of state regulation and against privatization (Koval 1997: 288).

However, even in the context of a softer policy and the use of diverse methods of social manoeuvring, opposition to reforms continued to grow. The first steps along the path of economic reform produced a split in the hitherto united Russian political structure. Vice-president Alexander Rutskoi and Supreme Soviet chairman Ruslan Khasbulatov were firmly opposed to price liberalization. Thereafter, the confrontation between the legislature and executive continued to escalate. Effectively, in the absence of terror, events were starting to develop along lines which, during the 'rule of the moderates', led to the emergence of a system of 'dual power'. Remaining true to their general strategy, radicals sought to move ahead by means of manoeuvring and compromises. According to Gaidar, the dissolution of the parliament was mooted in 1992, and discussed at least several dozen times in different crisis situations. But in the final analysis, the reformers did not want to risk straying beyond the bounds of the law and into the realm of unconstitutional decisions with possibly unpredictable outcomes. At the end of 1992, Yeltsin made a far-reaching compromise with the legislature, agreeing to the dismissal of Gaidar in exchange for the Congress of People's Deputies' support for a referendum on confidence in the authorities. The struggle over the referendum continued until the end of March; the outcome was that it was finally scheduled for 25 April 1993. Overall, the results of the referendum demonstrated support for Yeltsin and a sharp drop in the level of confidence in the representative organs of power. Fifty-nine per cent of the population voiced their support for the President, while 53 per cent approved of his social and economic policy. Thirty-two per cent of the population supported early presidential elections, while 43 per cent supported early elections to the Congress of People's Deputies. This balance of forces was also confirmed by public opinion polls at the time.[21] However, the results of the referendum failed to bring a halt to the processes of fragmentation, which by autumn 1993 had reached a critical stage.

The confrontation between the legislature and the executive had a number

---

[21] According to VCIOM data, 44% of Russians expressed complete lack of confidence in the Supreme Soviet, while only 5% expressed full confidence (Koval' 1997: 292). According to the data of the Sociological Institute of the Russian Academy of Sciences, about 76% of the population expressed lack of confidence in the Supreme Soviet to a greater or lesser degree, while for the Congress of People's Deputies and the chairman of the Supreme Soviet, Khasbulatov, the figure was over 80%. Figures for the President and government fluctuated within the bounds of 50–60% (*Zerkalo mneniy* 1993: 14).

of facets. In the area of institutional structures, both branches of power subscribed to conflicting conceptions of the new Russian constitution: Supreme Soviet drafts were based on the principles of a parliamentary democracy with strict control by deputies over the government's activities, while the executive proposed a presidential-style republic with a high degree of executive independence from the parliament. In the economic sphere, deputies were demanding further policy shifts which would have increased the budget deficit by increasing expenditure, and a significant revison of privatization mechanisms in favour of insiders. They also called for direct opposition to the government's economic policy, proposing to regional authorities that they remit no taxes to the centre if they lacked the funds to resolve their own socioeconomic problems. One should not underestimate the importance of the personal aspect of the confrontation, in which, according to Burbulis, 'two types of leader-driven cultures clashed on a very narrow platform of power'. This factor was, however, not decisive, reflecting the acuteness of objective contradictions, rather than being the source of them.

Influenced by the confrontation between branches of power, the general mood in the country grew tense, and the authorities lost control over events. On 1 May, an unsanctioned demonstration resulted in a clash with police, and casualties ensued. In July 1993, on the initiative of the Central Bank, which was subordinate to the Supreme Soviet, an openly provocative currency reform was carried out (the exchange of certain denominations of notes at short notice and with a limit on the quantity that could be exchanged), which aroused popular discontent and adversely affected the popularity of Yeltsin. By June 1993 more than 40 per cent of the population believed that there was a very high probability of complete anarchy in the country,[22] while fewer than 10 per cent thought that this was totally improbable (*Zerkalo mneniy* 1993: 22). The public was clearly tired of political disorder and willing to view decisive actions to resolve the crisis in a wholly favourable light. According to public opinion surveys, almost 40 per cent supported the idea of disbanding the Congress of People's Deputies and the Supreme Soviet, and transferring full power to the President for a transitional period (31 per cent were against). Over 45 per cent believed that dissolving the representative organs of power and introducing direct presidential rule would help to improve the state of affairs in the country (*Zerkalo mnenity* 1993: 11, 21). On 21 September 1993, Yeltsin issued a decree on the dissolution of the representative organs of power. The legislators refused to acquiesce and the conflict ended with a violent confrontation on 3–4 October 1993. During the course of the revolution Russia was probably never closer to civil war than at this point. This

---

[22] For comparison, in November 1994 34% of those polled registered the likelihood of anarchy as high, while 13% considered such a eventuality highly unlikely. The figures for June 1995 were 34% and 17% respectively.

would have meant a transition to the 'classic' version of the radical phase with all its inherent perils and costs.

This scenario was avoided and the clash was limited to a two-day battle in the capital. The activity of the population in support of the revolutionary authorities, at least in major cities, turned out to be sufficiently high for the army, after some hesitation, to support the President and government. Once again, and for the last time during the course of the revolution, the authorities had to rely on direct 'grassroots' mobilization, appealing to the nation to protect the achievements of the revolution. And then, in a way not yet repeated, a fundamentally important political decision—the adoption of Russia's new constitution—was effected not on the basis of established legal procedures, but through a direct appeal to public opinion, through a referendum.

The epithets 'authoritarian' and even 'dictatorial' are often used to describe the political régime established after 4 October 1993. It is often said that a coup occurred between 21 September and 4 October, which brought an end to the democratic revolution begun in 1985 (Volobuev 1995: 287). However, there is another view of the crisis, put forward, for example, by Igor Kyiamkin. It associates the events of 21 September—4 October 1993 with the weakness of the state, rather than its excessive strength: 'The dissolution of the Supreme Soviet was simply an attempt by the weak federal executive to break out of the crisis, to free itself by an act of will-power from the contradictions that were tearing it asunder. However, there was no consolidation of élite groups for any strategic purpose worth mentioning: it was simply that other centres of economic and political power turned out to be even weaker than the almost impotent central authorities' (Klyamkin 1993a: 53). This interpretation sees the weakness of the state as being central feature of the revolutionary process (the resort to force confirms rather than refutes this thesis), and regards the absence of consolidation among élite groups as the source of this weakness. Be this as it may, the difference between the events of August 1991 and October 1993 clearly demonstrates the difference between moderates and radicals in conditions of political confrontation: when trapped, a radical régime is prepared to act more toughly, rejecting compromise, and in the final analysis is ready to resort to violence in order to retain power and continue its programme of reforms.

The events of September–December 1993 represented a turning point. Thereafter, conditions gradually emerged for greater calm and stability in the country. The apocalyptic forecasts of increased political instability and social upheaval, in connection with the dramatic redistribution of power in favour of the President after 4 October, proved to be incorrect. On the contrary, political life gradually began to stabilize. Conflicts between branches of power were now resolved according to the 'rules of the game' as established by the constitution. The political régime, with its system of checks and balances, gradually grew in strength. The new constitution clearly laid down the separation of

powers and relations with the regions; over the following years it has demonstrated its ability to ensure stable democratic procedures. Even such explosive
events as the war in Chechnya have not led to sharp political shifts.

By the end of 1993, other characteristic trends could be observed which
manifestly pointed to a gradual stabilization. Despite the fall in industrial
output and continuing inflation, the crisis that had brought the radicals to
power had subsided. Over 1992–3, the devastated consumer market revived.
According to public opinion surveys, in April 1993 70–90 per cent of those
polled noted that all staple food products were freely available (Gaidar 1998*a*:
975). With the development of a market economy and the introduction of a
convertible currency, the threat of Russia's disintegration practically disappeared. Gradually, ideas of an impending catastrophe receded in the public
consciousness.[23] The authorities re-established their control over public life.
Having endured the initial period of chaos associated with the collapse of the
Soviet Union, Russia acquired all the trappings of statehood: borders, an
army, a tax system, its own currency. National gold and hard currency reserves
increased, and it became possible to pursue a sensible macroeconomic policy.
Over two years of market reforms, hyperinflation was successfully averted and
a system of market institutions was built up, making the economic situation
more stable.

The behaviour of the population also changed. Describing the forces which
supported the radical reforms, Gaidar noted that at that time they represented
a rather broad unstructured democratic mass, whose 'main weakness resided
in the fact that it was weakly structured, it did not yet reflect any established
interests, and thus it was somewhat difficult to rely on for support'. By the end
of 1993, attitudes started to change. On the basis of opinion survey data,
Klyamkin described the evolution in this area as follows:

For a long time the behaviour of the population . . . bore only a weak correlation to its
socio-economic interests and values: many, for instance, voted for Yeltsin, despite
being dissatisfied with his reform course. . . . Yeltsin was an anti-communist symbol,
a symbol of the victory over communism. Thus, as long as people seriously believed
that communism could make a comeback, those who feared this supported the President regardless of their attitude to the reforms. But after the storming of the White
House and the dissolution of the soviets, and after the anti-communists themselves
had split into several electoral blocs, society ceased to believe in the danger of a
communist 'revanche'. Political behaviour began to fall into line with socio-economic
interests and values. (Klyamkin 1993*b*: 41)

---

[23] However, this did not happen immediately. Even among professional economists,
rather pessimistic forecasts for 1993 were widespread, for example: 'Winter 1992–1993 will
be much harder than the previous one: lack of electricity (above all in the trans-Baikal and
North Caucasus), unstable prices for oil and petroleum products, increased incidence of
accidents on urban heating grids, acute shortages of fodder in most regions, and possible
food shortages' (Yavlinsky 1993: 113).

The normalization of popular behaviour was accompanied by a change in the priorities that determined people's actions in everyday life. Between 1991 and 1993 sociologists distinguished two main trends. People became more focused on their personal, family, and local problems; private life came to be valued more and more highly. People also became more and more self-reliant, gradually ceasing to expect everything from the authorities. As a result, growing discontent with the reform course was not accompanied by political activity, and was an insignificant factor in the political decision-making process.[24] There was now an upsurge of nostalgia for the old times and increasing idealization of the Soviet past. The Soviet past was principally prized for its stability, certainty, and to some extent its social justice (Koval' 1997: 297). Compared with 1992, by the end of 1993 the number of supporters of the command economy had grown one and a half times, while free market supporters had almost halved in number. In October the figures had been about equal—33 per cent in each category (Sedov 1995: 24). In general, the proportion of those preferring pre-*perestroyka* times remained relatively stable in 1992–3 (42–6 per cent), and started to grow in 1994, reaching 54 per cent in April and 58 per cent in September (ibid. 23). Even so, the overwhelming majority of the population understood that there could be no return to the past, and that the old days were gone for ever (see Table 5.6).

Finally, 1993 was marked by the emergence of a new élite; its interests and the struggle between the various groups within it started to be much more important in political life than public sentiment. Throughout the recent Russian revolution élite groups played a leading role in the formation of the revolutionary government's policies. During the radical phase, in order to defend their interests, they had to mobilize the support of the sections of the population that stood behind them: it was important for enterprise directors to enlist the support, or at least the loyalty, of their work collectives; the political leadership relied at critical moments on the support of the democratically minded

---

[24] VCIOM, in its *Information Bulletin* for 1994, published the results of an expert survey under the heading: 'From revolution "from above" to destabilization "from below" '. Based on the fact that the number of experts considering the change in popular political consciousness to be a destabilizing factor had grown sixfold, the conclusion was drawn that 'the struggle for power in the top echelons of the country's political leadership, hitherto the leading destabilizing factor, had, in the opinion of the experts, been replaced by a new one: the dissatisfaction of various strata and groups of the population with their position. . . . The relative political calm observed recently in Russia, it seems, is only temporary' (Kosals, Ryvkina, and Shuvalova 1994: 16, 17). This conclusion turned out to be completely wrong, as it was made on the basis of the experience of previous years, which was characterized by rather a high level of popular political activity. However, the situation had changed fundamentally: accumulated fatigue, the difficulties of adapting to new market conditions, the preoccupation with problems of everyday life—all this meant that growing discontent did not have serious political consequences.

TABLE 5.6. *Responses to the question: 'Is it possible to go back to the way things were before 1985?', 1993 and 1994 (%)*

	1993	1994
Yes, it is possible	8	15
No, the changes are irreversible	74	70
Hard to say	18	15

Sources: Nikitina (1998*b*: 57, 1998*c*: 54).

populations of major cities; etc. By early 1994, this had tapered off, as the new élite found its feet and became capable of defending its own interests.

All the above-mentioned features unequivocally pointed to the fact that by the end of 1993 the radical phase was coming to an end. The relative failure and subsequent departure of the radical government headed by Gaidar reflected the process of 'decline of the revolutionary curve', marking the beginning of a new phase in the revolution's development—the Thermidor. The interaction and struggle between new élite groups, which had been formed during the preceding stages of the revolution, occupied centre stage in this phase. In order to understand the policy of this period, it is essential to consider the origin and evolution of these groups, as well as the nature of their interests.

5.5. New élites and the Thermidor

The formation of the new élite has attracted the attention of students of the transformation in Russia. Several major studies have been undertaken. For example, in 1993 VCIOM interviewed 1,812 representatives of the old and new élites in 19 Russian regions. Olga Kryshtanovskaya has conducted wide-ranging research in this area.[25] The main body of published data relates to 1993–4. Several attempts have been made at a purely theoretical analysis. But only the first steps of this have been achieved, and many profound processes have so far failed to attract researchers' attention.

The basic features of the new Russian élite may be described as follows.

First, the party and state *nomenklaturas* succeeded in preserving their leading positions during the process of property distribution and consolidated

[25] The findings of the VCIOM opinion survey have been published in a number of works, including Golovachev and Kosova (1996: 45–51) and Ershova (1994: 151–5). Olga Kryshtanovskaya's findings are presented in her articles, in particular Kryshtanovskaya (1995: 51–65).

their position in the new élite. According to a VCIOM survey, 60 per cent of members of the former *nomenklatura* still occupied élite positions in 1993 comparable with the *nomenklatura* positions during the Soviet period. One third of the party *nomenklatura* was in the upper echelons of the government, while one third held top positions in the economy. More than one third of the Soviet state élite continued to occupy leading positions in the state apparatus (Ershova 1994: 154). Available data on 100 top Russian businessmen in 1992–3 showed that 62 per cent of them were directly connected to the former élite. Of these 17 per cent had emerged from the Komsomol apparatus; 23 per cent had been former top managers of industrial enterprises; 14 per cent had held top posts in the Soviet banking system; and 8 per cent were members of *nomenklatura* families (Kotz with Weir 1997: 118, citing the unpublished results of research by Kryshtanovskaya). Table 5.7 provides a general picture of the continuity between the old and new élites.

Secondly, most major fortunes had been made in the 1988–91 period (Gaidar 1997c: 126). These derived from selectively granted opportunities to engage in entrepreneurial activity and privatize property in the *perestroyka* period. It was the *nomenklatura* which had privileged access: to joint ventures; to credits at preferential terms; to import–export operations; and to converting non-cash money into cash. 'Nomenklatura privatization' involved the most promising enterprises and ministries, the material-technical supply system, the banking sector, and real estate (Kryshtanovskaya 1995). The best opportunities for enrichment were open to a section of the bureaucracy, to the managerial corps, to heads of 'selected' co-operatives who received large quantities of state money for one reason or another, and to 'Komsomol businesses'. These groups were from the start relatively closed (Gaidar 1997c: 126–7). Certainly, there were exceptions to this rule (for example, one of the largest Russian banks, ONEKSIMbank, was founded in 1993); however, the foundations of the business élite were laid during the *perestroyka* period.

Thirdly, the élite underwent a significant degree of renewal. On the one hand, changes occurred in the status and rank of members of the old *nomenklatura*.[26] As Table 5.7 shows, recruitment to the élite from the top echelons of the former *nomenklatura* was much lower than from the *nomenklatura* in general. According to VCIOM data, about half the 'newcomers' to the Russian ruling élite joined from the 'second tier' of the old élite (Ershova 1994: 155). On the other hand, it is important not to underestimate the actual process of

---

[26] This issue was discussed in detail in the interview with Gaidar, who underlined the fact that even Chernomyrdin, though an important figure in the old élite, did not make it into the top 100 people of the Soviet system in terms of power and influence; not to mention the so-called group of seven bankers—heads of the seven largest banks, whose names were unknown under the old system. In his opinion, if one were to review lists of the 100 most influential people in 1988 and now, no more than one or two names would figure on both lists.

TABLE 5.7. *Recruitment of Yeltsin's cohort from the old* nomenklatura *(%)*

	Top leadership	Leadership of political parties	Regional élite	Govern-ment	Business élite	Overall
Total from the *nomenklatura*	75.0	57.1	82.3	74.3	61.0	69.9
Proportion of preceding from top *nomenklatura* positions	24.2	35.0	8.9	15.4	5.0	17.7

Source: Kryshtanovskaya (1995: p. 65, table 11).

change in the élite. Half of all party leaders, 59 per cent of new businessmen, one third of deputies, and a quarter of the presidential team and the government were never members of the *nomenklatura*. The regional élite has been recruited in the most traditional fashion, with only 17 per cent free of a *nomenklatura* past (Kryshtanovskaya 1995: 64).[27] According to a VCIOM survey, 22 per cent of the Russian élite are newcomers. Members of Russia's business class demonstrate the greatest upward mobility: two thirds of this group were not amongst those in authority at the end of the 1980s (Ershova 1994: 155). Data on 100 top businessmen reveal that 38 per cent of them were not connected to the previous élite, but came from the most diverse backgrounds, and included academics, the unemployed and criminals. (Kotz with Weir 1997: 118). Table 5.8 shows the sharp acceleration in the change of the élite under Gorbachev and particularly under Yeltsin.

There was also a significant change in the qualitative characteristics of the élite. It became younger: in 1993 more than half of the élite was under 50, and one in five was under 40 (Ershova 1994: 153). The élite became better educated: two thirds of the presidential team hold doctorates, and there is also a high percentage of government members and party leaders with advanced degrees. Moreover, in comparison with the preceding period the educational

---

[27] Admittedly, public opinion polls are not the most reliable source of information on this matter. However, the processes by which local and regional élites are formed are further illustrated by the responses to the question: 'Who now holds real power in your town or region?'

People from the old party leadership	22%
New people from among the democrats and reformers	10
Directors and other economic leaders	14
Mafia and criminal leaders	29
Others	2
Hard to say	23

Source: Nikitina (1998c: 54).

TABLE 5.8. *Representation in élite groups of persons not previously members of the nomenklatura (% of total in each category)*

	Top leader- ship	Party élite	Parlia- mentary élite	Govern- ment	Regional élite	Business élite	Overall
Brezhnev cohort	0	6.0	51.3	0	0	—	11.4
Gorbachev cohort	8.5	28.8	40.6	n/a	0	—	19.5
Yeltsin cohort	25.0	42.8	39.8	25.7	17.7	59.0	35.0

Source: Kryshtanovskaya (1995: 64).
n/a: not available

profile has changed: while two thirds of the Brezhnevite cohort graduated from provincial polytechnics, in the 1990s there has been a decline in the proportion of technocrats and a rise in the proportion of those with human- ities degrees, on degrees in economics and law. And finally, the élite has become more urban: the number of people of rural origin has dropped by a 60 per cent in the last ten years, and in Yeltsin's entourage by 80 per cent (Kryshtanovskaya 1995: 62–4, 61).

At first, most analyses of the élite concentrated on comparing, and exam- ining the relationship between, the old and new élites. Only recently have works appeared which look at the process of formation of new élite groups, rather than merely analysing how individual members of these élites acquired their fortunes.[28] These issues merit special attention. The origins of an élite group very quickly cease to exercise significant influence over its actions. Its new position, interests, and problems are of much greater significance. For example, the fact that new business leaders to a large extent emerged from the ranks of the old *nomenklatura* explains very little *per se* about the policy- making process during the Thermidor period. In order to understand which interest groups actually shaped policy and how, it is essential to examine the complicated process of the evolution of the élite during the radical phase and the first stage of the Thermidor, when new élite group interests crystallized most rapidly. The following complex of problems is the most interesting:

1. the heterogeneity of the élite, and the conflicting interests of different emerging groups;
2. the evolution of the élite's interests during the revolutionary transfor- mation of society;
3. the interrelationship between élite interests and the state of various sectors of the economy;[29]

[28] Zudin (1997: 208–13) and Pappe (1997) are notable in this regard.
[29] An attempt to review some of these issues was made in Mau (1996*b*).

4. the position and instruments of influence of those sections of the old *nomenklatura* which failed to secure a place in the new élite, and their evolution.

The focus of research on the continuity between old and new élites should not blind us to the very real conflicts which had developed between different interest groups by the beginning of the radical phase. In this period it was evident that, at least in the economy, there were two major blocs, whose inter-action was far from harmonious. They were dubbed 'red directors' and 'new businessmen'.[30] In fact the process of 'primary accumulation' took place in both groups, albeit for the most part it took different forms: 'red directors' engaged in syphoning resources from state enterprises to private firms, while 'new businessmen' largely made their fortunes from trade and import–export operations. Moreover, the interests of these two groups often coincided, as mentioned above with reference to the 'pro-inflation bloc'. However, relations between the two groups had been fairly conflictual for a long time. Initially conflict arose in the forming of economic ties. Investigations in 1992 clearly showed that state enterprises were setting advantageous terms on delivery and prices for 'their own' sector, while generally discriminating against the private sector.[31] As the privatization of large enterprises got under way this conflict

[30] 'Russia's entrepreneurial class arose at the intersection of two social streams (the 'managerial corps' and 'new businessmen'), with independent economic bases (the 'old' economy included the majority of the real sector of the economy, and the 'new' economy comprised activities that did not exist within the framework of the administrative system)' (Zudin 1997: 208).

[31] Surveys have helped to identify the stabilizing role played by the 'preservation of tradi-tional ties, reinforced by the personal contacts of directors, business relations, and 'managerial ethics', which dictated tolerance of delayed payments and refusal to make excessive price hikes' (Dolgopyatova 1995: 173). Already by spring 1992, the establishment of a three-tier pricing system for any given product was a part of the pricing strategy of many enterprises: 'Enterprises maintained the lowest prices for their traditional clients. ... Preferential rates were common for a narrow circle of long-term partners. Prices for new or occasional clients among state-owned enterprises were usually set higher than for old clients, but lower than for private structures. The latter paid the highest prices (2.0–2.5 times higher than for traditional partners)' (ibid. 182). Despite the gradual broadening of contacts, state enterprise directors retained a strong bias against the private sector rooted in their traditional approach to business development: 'In particular, some directors thought that commercial structures bought their products not for use in production, but as an investment in order to protect themselves against the devaluation of the rouble. As a result enterprises found themselves working 'to fill another firm's warehouse', while the traditional consumer of the product might have to curtail production owing to a lack of resources, which in the future could result in a permanent contraction of the market' (ibid. 139). Even in the second half of 1993, only 9.3% of about 150 directors polled considered that working with commercial, rather than state, structures offered better prospects, while 10% preferred not to do any business at all with the private sector, and 45.7% did it only out of extreme necessity' (ibid. 142).

reached a new level, in the clash between insiders and outsiders during the redistribution of property, and then in the battle by outsiders for real control over property which they had formally acquired in the process of privatization.

Alongside the antagonistic trends noted, an ever broader area of common interests emerged in the interaction between these groups. State (or privatized) enterprises, facing limited demand and non-payments crisis, started to seek out solvent clients and found them mainly among private firms. As a result, these firms went from being discriminated against to being most attractive clients; and in a number of cases production was specially modified and adjusted in line with their needs.[32] Points of mutual interest were quickly found in the use of 'soft money', received from the state in the form of subsidies and preferential credits, etc. Whereas at the outset of the reforms this money was usually used by state enterprise directors to pay workers' wages, very soon they started passing this money through commercial structures with the aim of the personal enrichment of both parties. In order to gain control of property during the privatization of enterprises, some directors allied themselves with commercial structures in order to obtain the funds necessary for the acquisition of a controlling stake.

The interaction of these two groups can therefore be characterized as 'antagonistic symbiosis': attraction and repulsion, interpenetration and struggle for leadership. Both groups had their 'competitive advantages' in putting pressure on government structures. Major state (or former state) enterprises guaranteed employment for thousands of people (sometimes for whole cities), and provided a wide range of social services to their workers and for the population in general, maintaining a significant portion of the infrastructure of cities and towns where they were located. Naturally, 'red directors' used these social obligations as a weighty argument in favour of state support for those enterprises. At the same time, financial resources, and therefore economic power, became more and more concentrated in the hands of new commercial organizations, which the government could not ignore.

Privatization played a fundamental role in the formation of these new élites. Many students of Russian reforms hold the view that Russian privatization favoured insiders, primarily enterprise managers, while the importance of external parties in the process was minimal. At first sight the available data confirm this proposition. However, it appears that such an unqualified assessment of the privatization process is methodologically unsound. By late 1993 a

---

[32] 'By the second year of reforms the situation had changed and some enterprises' supply and sales links shifted to the private sector. . . . There was a marked trend of establishing solid long-term relations and, more important, there were examples of reorienting sales to the new private sector, which was sometimes attended by restructuring of production. . . . In general, the 1993 survey demonstrated that over 15% of enterprises fully or partly reoriented their sales to cater for new private structures' (Dolgopyatova 1995: 140–1).

prominent Russian entrepreneur was describing the situation as follows: 'Russia has a few very large competitive companies; however, their managements are in such a strong position that they will not let anyone in [As the 1995 loans-for-shares scheme was to demonstrate, he proved wrong on this.] Additionally, there are a number of promising firms which have been privatized by outsiders. All the others are hopelessly uncompetitive, and they have been privatized by insiders' (conversation with the authors). This is not to say that such a categorical assessment is entirely correct, but it neatly reflects the approach of commercial entities on this matter. 1993–4 was a formative period for financial-industrial groups emerging around major financial institutions, via targeted or chaotic acquisitions in the manufacturing sector. At the same time, in a reverse process of sorts, industrial organizations were diversifying into the financial sector.

The formation of financial-industrial groups in the course of privatization undeniably ran counter to the ideological objectives of the organizers of this process. This, yet again, showed the secondary role of ideology in the radical phase when it came into conflict with real interests. It was assumed that Russia would have an American-style stock exchange. As a result there were regulatory restrictions on participation by banks in privatization, and cross-shareholding was prohibited for a long time. However, despite these restrictions, a close fusion of the banking and industrial structures took place. Relevant regulations adopted towards the end of 1993 formalized the existence of these financial-industrial groups and thus merely reflected the reality that had already come into being. Thereafter, restrictions on the formation and operations of such groups became less and less stringent: 'The evolution of the regulatory base governing interaction between the real and the financial sectors of the economy as evident in the course of Russian reforms could be described as a forced drift away from the American to the Japanese–German model of relations between these sectors' (Pappe 1997: 31). This did not mean, however, that the majority of existing groups gained formal status. The largest financial-industrial empires, also known as financial-industrial conglomerates, did not have legal status. Nevertheless, they exerted the greatest influence on the formation of the new élite.

The formation of financial-industrial groups and conglomerates in the course of privatization meant that in terms of various interest groups the distinction between 'red directors' and 'new entrepreneurs' was increasingly losing its relevance. Other criteria were coming to the fore, particularly the wealth and economic prospects of the property acquired. Gradually the following interest groups were formed, and the interactions and contradictions between them have played a very important role in shaping state policy:

1. Owners of internationally competitive export-oriented firms. Domestic prices for the products of these firms are lower than those prevailing on

the world markets. The firms therefore subsidize the rest of the economy. Oil and gas companies, above all, belong to this category.

2. Owners of export-oriented firms, whose competitiveness is maintained
   by artificially low energy prices. A large section of the ferrous and non-
   ferrous metallurgical industry, as well as the chemical industry, belongs
   to this category.

3. Owners of firms operating on the domestic market. These firms make
   import-substituting products and have certain prospects in the event of
   favourable government policy.

4. Owners of firms operating on the domestic market, which, however,
   owing to the nature of their end-product or the structure of demand, do
   not experience foreign competition.

5. Owners of hopelessly inefficient, unviable firms.

Given the widespread criminalization of business, the mafia constitutes a
special interest group, which in many instances is closely linked to political
institutions and is in a position to influence political decisions-making.

It became increasingly apparent that large financial institutions were playing an increasingly important role in the process of the formation of the new
élite, pushing the 'red directors' into the background. All the occasional
attempts by various government departments to save the traditional
economic élites ended in failure. This was particularly evident in the building
of a regulatory base for the activities of financial-industrial groups. Initially,
these regulations were meant mainly to provide financial support to the 'red
directors', and protect them from financial institutions intent upon acquiring
state property in the course of privatization. However, as these regulations
were finalized and implemented, privileges were reduced to a minimum, and
financial assistance became difficult to obtain, while large financial institutions played a leading role in many financial-industrial groups.

The 'red directors' who headed hopelessly uncompetitive, large enterprises
(they nevertheless performed a wide array of social functions) were also losing
their influence over the government. State financial support for them was
steadily declining; lobbying opportunities were dwindling. This appears to
have been a function of two factors. On the one hand, their competitors
gained dramatically in political and financial strength and in the ability to
influence state policy. On the other hand, the authorities themselves, in the
conditions of the Thermidor, were increasingly catering to the needs not of
the mass of the population, but to the interests of élite groups. Therefore,
provision of state resources for them to perform their social functions largely
ceased to be a serious argument. The coal industry and agriculture have been
exceptions to the rule. They have continued to receive substantial subsidies,
above all for political reasons.

The formation of new élite groups had an impact upon the government, which increasingly reflected their interests. The reorientation was gradual, but by 1995–6 it had become visible. This process was particularly evident in the sphere of privatization. The mechanism of voucher privatization described above, although fairly democratic in form, was aimed at harmonizing a wide spectrum of interests and it gave certain opportunities for participation to the most diverse social strata. The vouchers expired in summer 1994, after which, for a variety of economic and political reasons, privatization slowed down sharply. However, in the second half of 1995 the government, while preserving the established methods of privatization, agreed to adopt a completely new approach to property redistribution which served the interests of a restricted circle of influential élite groups. It was decided to transfer large bundles of state shares in the most prestigious companies to certain legal entities in trust, in exchange for loans to the state, so as to acquire crucial additional funds for the budget. In the event that the loan was not repaid, the organizations that were managing the shares were entitled to sell them. In effect, this was privatization—the budget for 1996 did not provide for repayment of the loans to the creditor banks.

The transfer of shares was intended to be carried out on a competitive basis. At the end of 1995, twelve auctions—known as loans-for-shares deals—took place against a backdrop of scandals and irregularities.[33] Conflicts arose as a result of such blatant improprieties as: the organization of the auctions (receipt of bids and pre-payments) by one of the bidders; use of state funds deposited in the banks to compete in the auctions; and the high probability of a pre-arranged carve-up by the participants. Two large Russian banks dominated the roster of winners: ONEKSIMbank and Menatep. In the view of experts, 'these auctions were . . . either a covert buy-out of shares by enterprise management, or, in the majority of cases, a direct non-competitive sale of a block of shares to interested banks (financial-industrial groups)' (IET 1997: 172–3).

It is the interests of the consolidating élite groups that may explain a number of otherwise inexplicable peculiarities of economic policy during the

---

[33] The following examples, typical of the loans-for-shares auctions, can be adduced:

1. In the auction of Lukoil shares, Lukoil bid $35.01 million, and the 'competition', National Reserve Bank, bid $35 million (the starting price); Bank Imperial acted as loan guarantor in both cases.

2. In the auction of Yukos shares, there were two 'contenders': Laguna, a private limited company, and Reagent, another private limited company; both were set up by Menatep Bank (the auction organizer) and had loan guarantees from the bank. Menatep's competitors were disqualified on the pretext that paying part of the deposit in short-term treasury bills (GKOs) was invalid.

3. ONEKSIMbank (winner and organizer of the auction of SIDANKO shares) refused to accept a bid from Rossiiskii Kredit Bank, under the pretext that the deposit was transferred 17 minutes late (Radygin 1997: 245).

Thermidor period. One such mystery was the preservation of a fairly liberal import–export régime at a time when a large part of the economy was uncompetitive and experiencing serious economic difficulties. By the end of 1993 the groups who were interested in increased protectionism (advocated by many academic economists, politicians, and mass media) had consolidated themselves. Representatives of this strand of opinion participated in the government. This situation was reminiscent of the creation of the 'pro-infla-tion bloc', which had pressured the radical government to abandon tight monetary policies. But, the results this time were completely different. Despite occasional changes in the 'rules of the game', the economy remained largely open.

The reasons for this phenomenon are to be found in the dynamics of the influence of various élite groups. The lobbying opportunities for those 'red directors' who had not managed to secure for themselves a place in the new élite had gradually diminished; those social groups whose economic base was tied to export-oriented sectors had increased in importance relative to import-substituting sectoral interests. Those export-oriented sectors inter-ested in a liberal import–export régime had acquired opportunities to exert political influence and engage in lobbying which far outweighed their import-ance in the economy. Liberal policies gained some additional support from below, owing to the large number of people involved in *chelnok* (shuttle) trade—the importing of small consignments of goods on a regular basis. This was not, however, a decisive factor.

Another peculiarity developed in the determination of energy prices. Here the interests of two influential élite groups, associated respectively with poten-tially competitive and potentially uncompetitive exports, were diametrically opposed. Competitive export-oriented sectors, where domestic prices were lower than those prevailing internationally, were interested in the maximum reduction of the differential, and thus in reducing their subsidization of the rest of the economy. Conversely, for those export-oriented sectors whose competitiveness was a function of artificially low input prices, the preserva-tion of the differential between world and domestic prices was a matter of life and death. Here their interests coincided with those of the overwhelming majority of the other economic agents, whom world prices for energy and fuel would render unviable. That is why the struggle surrounding the price of energy turned out to be much greater in intensity, not to say ferocity, than the battles waged over the import–export régime.

Another trend in relation to the formation of the new élite in the course of the revolution was the strengthening of the role of regional élites. Having obtained extensive rights and opportunities to dispose of substantial resources in the radical phase, these élites, in many ways independent of the 'centre', have retained control over the development of business in their regions, the distribution of budgetary funds, and local politics. In relation to their real political weight, they enjoy significant influence in shaping federal policy. Additionally, if decisions counter to their interests are adopted, they can successfully obstruct their implementation. Interaction, contradictions, and conflicts between the élites at the federal and regional levels have been amongst the key factors shaping the process of political decision-making during the Russian Thermidor. Contradictions between various groupings of regional élites, in particular between regions that are net donors to the budget and those that are net recipients, have also played an important role. Thus, in spring 1997 the leaders of several major donor regions came up with an initiative to make housing rents uniform in the regions, claiming that the recipient regions were using federal subsidies to maintain low rents and utility payments.[34]

Processes typical for a Thermidor period in many ways explain the dynamics of the economic situation in 1995–6. During this period the long-promised economic growth did not materialize; rather, by many criteria the economic situation continued to deteriorate: inter-firm arrears continued to build up; the budgetary system was in crisis; massive wage, pension, and benefit payment arrears adversely affected the standards of living. According to public opinion polls, until autumn 1994 the ratio of those who had a positive assessment of the financial situation of their family to those whose assessment was negative generally remained above unity, albeit with considerable fluctuations. From autumn 1994 the ratings deteriorated sharply, and in July 1995 they reached their lowest point—under 0.6. Then they improved somewhat, but on the whole remained below unity, and only occasionally rose above it. Finally, in September 1998 this ratio again fell sharply, to a minimum level of 0.4.

The processes we have reviewed are largely analogous to those trends which obtained in other countries at the first Thermidor stage of development and have much the same causes. The conclusion of Brinton that for the mass of the population the Thermidor is harder than the radical phase is borne out in the experience of contemporary Russia.

5.6 Has the contemporary Russian revolution been completed?

The contemporary Russian revolution is passing into history. Some would argue that it already completed in the mid-1990s. In his interview, Gaidar, for example, maintains that normal post-revolutionary stabilization is already under-way in Russia. In his view, 'the revolutionary period ended in two

---

[34] At the end of 1996, Russians only paid 20–40% of housing and utility costs, and the percentage differed significantly between regions.

stages. The first of these was from 4 October to December 1993, and the second was 3 July 1996' (the day Boris Yeltsin was elected President of Russia for a second term). Yakovlev also claimed in his interview that the current phase is a restoration period, in which many of the old political figures are returning to power.

The fundamental feature of a society in revolution—a weak state—had still not been overcome by the end of 1999. As always happens towards the end of the Thermidor period, this weakness was obvious for all to see. The government's political direction fluctuated wildly and became increasingly unpredictable. Its ideology darted from side to side. The Cabinet was headed by people as diverse as the 'rightist' Kirienko and the 'communist' Primakov. Ministerial leapfrog resulted in five changes of Prime Minister during 1998–9. The decision-making process became increasingly secretive, and was confined to the so-called 'Family'—a group of individual members of Yeltsin's family, together with certain important officials and businessmen. This all attests to a crisis in the system of power created in the course of the revolution. The physical deterioration of the head of state seemed to symbolize the degeneration of Russia's power structures.

To complete the picture we must refer to Russia's chronic economic problems, which manifested themselves most acutely in the financial crisis of August 1998. This crisis led to a threefold devaluation of the rouble (from 6 to 18 roubles to one US dollar), a default on domestic and foreign debt repayments, the collapse of the banking system, and the bankruptcy of several major banks. This gave further impetus to the processes of concentration and redistribution of wealth, and the balance of forces within the business élite changed. The population's incomes were sharply reduced, and savings became worthless.

There have also been unfavourable changes in Russia's position on the world stage. The lack of significant economic improvements, the governmental crisis, the general weakening of Russia's international status and its worsening image—all this has led to a gradual cooling of relations with the West. The refusal to pay foreign debts and the sharp divergence on the question of how to resolve the Balkan crisis greatly accelerated this process. The resumption of military action in Chechnya in 1999 exacerbated relations—the period of 'enthusiasm' for Russia's reforms is over. Previously, Russia had been idealized in the West, and even its most obvious problems and contradictions had been overlooked. By the end of the 1990s, in contrast, its negative features were being grotesquely exaggerated, and any positive aspects were being completely ignored.

All these circumstances, taken together, could create the impression that Russia is becoming increasingly unstable, that the pendulum is swinging more and more violently, that there is no stabilization to speak of, and that more upheavals lie ahead for the country. However, such an impression would be deceptive. In the Thermidor period processes gradually unfold which will strengthen the state and overcome revolutionary instability. We can enumerate these processes as they relate to Russia.

First, there is growing consolidation within the ranks of the élite (Kholodkovsky 1997: 125). The radical, intransigent opposition is being marginalized while most opposition forces are actively entering into dialogue and co-operation with the authorities. The differences between the positive programmes of the various parties are being increasingly eroded, despite their continued formal adherence to diametrically opposed ideological views. Sharp conflicts remain within the business élite, but they are having less and less impact on the overall course of politics.

Secondly, the economic crisis, for all its negative effects on conditions inside Russia, normalized the situation of the budget by bringing expenditure into line with the state's ability to raise revenue. The crisis put an end to the irresponsible policy of large-scale domestic and foreign borrowing, and overall ensured a healthier financial basis for future economic development. Exports became more profitable, and investment in production became more attractive. After the initial shock of the financial collapse, economic growth resumed.

Thirdly, accumulated fatigue within the population meant that the financial crisis did not lead to any sharp social conflicts. Indeed, the fact that wages and pensions now began to be paid more regularly was seen as a positive development, even though their purchasing power had dropped sharply. The absence of active protests 'from below' made it possible to hold to a firm financial policy and to refrain from populist measures despite the presence of communists in the government.

Fourthly, it is clear that all sections of society now require stabilization. They want to avoid further upheavals and to accept the 'gains of the revolution', even if the latter do not fully conform to people's ideas of justice or good sense. Having grown tired of the stresses of the period of revolutionary instability, the public is not prepared to take any active measures 'from below' to achieve any particular end. It is waiting for somebody else to do these things on its behalf. These expectations were clearly reflected in the steep rises in popularity enjoyed by each of the Prime Ministers of 1998–9 immediately after his appointment. In each new political figure the public saw a possible candidate for the role of the 'strong man' who could establish order, overcome the obvious crisis in the system of government, and set things right in Russia.[35]

---

[35] According to calculations based on data from the State Statistical Commission and VCIOM, at the end of 1998 and the beginning of 1999 there was an important shift in the population's social and economic expectations. In the preceding years, people's subjective assessment of what constituted a minimum standard of living had substantially exceeded

If we take all these tendencies into account, then events in Russia at the end of 1999 and beginning of 2000 cease to be a puzzle. Vladimir Putin's popularity first as Prime Minister and then as Acting President rose sharply. There was mass support within Russia for the military action in Chechnya, which reflected a desire to demonstrate the strength of the renascent state. Statist ideas have become mere widespread, ideological differences have become much less important in Russian political life, and a fairly liberal economic policy has been retained. The population has supported parties and movements prepared to recognize the 'gains of the revolution' and to refrain from calling for redistribution of property during the parliamentary elections (Dmitriev 2000). All of this points clearly to the end of the revolutionary cycle and the beginning of a transition to a new, post-revolutionary stage of development. It was not in 1994 or in 1996, but only in 2000, that Russia gradually began to leave the period of revolutionary upheavals behind.

History knows few ways of completing revolutions: only restoration, dictatorship, and restoration after dictatorship. In each case this process is accompanied by a sharp increase in authoritarian tendencies and the overturning of democratic mechanisms. The prerequisites for this concentration of power are also present in Russia in the final stage of its revolutionary cycle. We shall list the basic ones.

First, there is the growing demand for consolidation and strong authority. The destabilization caused by the economic crisis of 1998, the aggravated polit-ical situation in 1999 associated with the military actions in Chechnya and Dagestan, the upsurge in terrorism, and the threat of international isolation all elicited a demand for a strong state authority. Against such a background, the weakening and disintegration of the existing political régime presented a danger that was obvious to any citizen of Russia. In these circumstances, the allure of democratic institutions falls sharply. In 1999, surveys showed that 50 per cent of the population was negatively disposed towards multi-party elections. This proportion had risen from 33 per cent in 1994 (Levada 1999*b*: 7.)

Secondly, the conditions for a concentration of power are coming together. The population is profoundly weary, internal and external threats have led to a partial consolidation of the élite, and the real threat of a communist *revanche* has receded. This produces conditions in which ideological opposition in society becomes less important. A desire for stabiliza-

the official assessment. After the financial collapse of August 1998, this subjective minimum began to lag significantly behind the official minimum. They began to expect stability from the government and, it would seem, nothing more. Consequently, in Russia in 1998–9 a stable inverse relationship could be seen between average per capita income (or real average wages) and trust in the Prime Minister. Surveys of public opinion show that the increase in trust in the Prime Minister coincided with a noticeable fall in the population's living standards (IET 2000: 116, 118).

tion brings together the most diverse strata and groups, irrespective of their political opinions. More intense patriotic and statist rhetoric finds a sympathetic response among the population. It is used by a variety of political forces, thereby creating the impression of social consensus. This change in social attitudes is reflected in the type of leaders who enjoy political support. The 'ideologists' are displaced by 'practical' and 'pragmatic' people. It is perhaps no accident that many of these people have a background not in the intelligentsia or the business world, but in the armed forces. We can get a curious sociological illustration of this change in attitudes by comparing the responses given in 1989, 1994, and 1999 to the question of who have been the most outstanding figures of all time (Levada 1999*b*: 11; Dubin 1999: 22; Sedov 1999: 21). Whereas in 1989 Lenin held a massive lead, this view nowadays is prevalent only among the older generation. Since 1994 Peter the Great has held first position, and, among the foreigners named, Napoleon leads. (In 1989 it was Einstein.) By 1999 the ratings of Peter and Napoleon had increased (from 41 to 46 per cent and from 14 to 19 per cent respectively). Moreover, when compared to 1989, the attractiveness of the figure of Napoleon in the public consciousness has risen from 6 to 19 per cent, and that of Stalin—from 12 to 35 per cent.

Finally, the procedures through which this concentration of power takes place have become clear. The parliamentary elections brought victory to the 'party of power', thus enabling the parliament to be controlled from the Kremlin. Yeltsin vacated the President's post early, and Vladimir Putin was elected President on 26 March 2000 with about 53 per cent of the vote in the first round. All this shows that, most probably, power can be strengthened at the present stage through the existing legal mechanisms envisaged by the current constitution of Russia.[36]

So revolutionary upheavals are now a thing of the past. Russia will gradually embark on a course of gentler, evolutionary change. However, as our analysis demonstrates, this process will be neither easy nor quick. Historical experience shows that the post-revolutionary concentration of power is followed by a new period of political instability, which lasts until a basic

---

[36] In an earlier draft of this book we were much less certain on this matter. To quote from the earlier draft: 'How this concentration of power will take place is another matter. There are various possibilities here. The victory of a strong leader in the presidential elections, able to use fully and to reinforce the authoritarian tendencies in the existing constitution, is one possible scenario. A strong personality may emerge in Russia who does not formally occupy any high state office, but enjoys wide support among the new élite and is able to concentrate real power into his own hands. An unconstitutional seizure of power by force is, unfortunately, yet another possibility. Finally, we should not exclude the disintegration of the country in one way or another, and the emergence of several petty dictators. But, however events unfold, the establishment of authoritarianism seems inevitable.'

post-revolutionary consensus is re-established in society.[37] Only then will the negative consequences of the revolution be completely overcome. Only then will that creative potential contained in any process of revolutionary renewal come fully into effect.

[37] However, this still appears to be a long way off. According to a number of sociological surveys, 43% of the population thinks that people will never become accustomed to the changes which have occurred in Russia (Sedov 1999: 12).

6

The Leaders of the Contemporary Russian Revolution Speak . . .

6.1 The personal factor in the revolution

The role of leaders in a revolution raises important questions for every specialist working on this subject. Some have seen in the personal qualities of individual leaders a key to understanding the essence of revolutionary changes. However, even if we reject the notion that the major figures in a revolutionary epoch can exercise a decisive influence on the course of events (and we, like many other researchers, regard revolution as an objective and mainly spontaneous process), we need not discount their importance as personalities who can capture the spirit of the times to the greatest extent and embody its most characteristic features. Moreover, although we do not believe that the leaders of a revolutionary process can change fundamentally the direction or nature of developments in the revolutionary period, we do think that they can have a substantial influence on the form of that process, and in many cases, on the speed of the transformations. For this reason the natures and features of leaders will, to a considerable extent, determine the particular physiognomy of each revolution. They will lend it the attractive or repugnant aspects which derive from the actions of strong or striking personalities in the historical arena.

The contemporary Russian revolution will not be remembered in the popular imagination as an impersonal process of major changes, but in terms of 'Gorbachev's *perestroyka*', 'Gaidar's liberalization', 'Chubais's privatizations', and 'Yeltsin's constitution'. Without looking at the individual peculiarities, aims, and ideas of the revolutionary leaders, it is impossible to explain such features of the revolutionary process in Russia as the transition from 'reform from above' to 'revolution from above' in the Gorbachev epoch, the limited extent to which violence was used, the search for compromises, and the fact that in the radical phase the authorities were engaged in much more manoeuvring to form pro–revolutionary coalitions than in other revolutions, whereas ideological influences were clearly weak. Also these people had an acute sense of the scale of their historic task and of inexorable nature of the demands raised by the revolutionary epoch. Their view of this period allows us to form a much fuller and more rounded picture of it than would be possible by relying on other sources alone.

In our study, along with generally available materials such as scholarly works and the memoirs of participants in the revolutionary period, we have made use of four interviews we held with key figures in Russian politics of the last decade. These people—Mikhail Gorbachev, Egor Gaidar, Gennady Burbulis, and Alexander Yakovlev—were all directly involved in the most important decisions which determined the fate of Russia at that time. Let us recall briefly the role of these persons in the development of the contemporary Russian revolution.

Mikhail Gorbachev was General Secretary of the CPSU Central Committee from 1985–91 and President of the USSR from 1989–91. He initiated the period of profound transformation of the Soviet system when he launched the policy of *perestroyka* and *glasnost'*.

Alexander Yakovlev was a close associate of Gorbachev and one of the ideologists of *perestroyka*. From 1986–91 he was a Politburo member and Secretary of the CPSU Central Committee (one of the highest positions in the Soviet hierarchy). He was also the head of the special commission for rehabilitating the victims of the repressions of the Stalin period.

Egor Gaidar was Deputy Prime Minister and then Acting Prime Minister of Russia from November 1991 to December 1992. He was the key figure in devising and implementing Russia's radical post-communist economic reforms. He was First Deputy Prime Minister for a short period in 1993. In 1994–5 he led what was then the largest faction in the Duma.

Gennady Burbulis was a close associate of Boris Yeltsin and an important figure in the new Russian establishment in the first year after the collapse of communism. In 1991–2 he held the positions of First Deputy Prime Minister and State Secretary under President Yeltsin. He played an important role in forming Russia's first post-communist government, and in preparing the 'Belovezhye Agreements', which officially marked the disintegration of the USSR.

What distinguishes these interviews is that we asked questions designed to shed light on various aspects of revolutionary theory. We did not attempt to fit all of the interviews into an identical format; rather we tried to ascertain the views of these leaders on a broadly similar range of questions, in order to understand the common features and the differences in their approaches to the revolution. In the preceding chapters we have used these interviews to confirm certain historical events and assess several aspects of the revolutionary process. In this chapter these interviews are used mainly to characterize the leaders themselves and their personalities, and to assess the impact the revolutionary process left upon them.

6.2 The nature of the transformation: modernization and revolution

Our interviewees had differing interpretations of the events in which they were key figures. For Gaidar and Yakovlev these events were primarily a process of social transformation, and therefore such problems as the role of violence, the possibility of civil war, and mechanisms for changing the social system figured prominently in their interviews. Our other two interviewees did not dispute that aspect of the transformation, but they did not regard it as the most significant one. Burbulis referred rather, to the modernizing aspect of the changes, and stressed also that the collapse of an empire of that type and class was unique in world history.

Gorbachev's interpretation of the essence of the transformation is particularly interesting, since he played the principal role in shifting Russian society from a reformist onto a revolutionary trajectory. In his view the changes which began in 1985 were primarily concerned with the need for modernization—'we needed a breakthrough'. He attempted to bring about modernization on various levels. Initially, as Party First Secretary in the Stavropol' region, he supported what were then the most advanced methods of organizing labour and paying workers, and attempted to modernize agricultural production. It quickly became apparent that on this level nothing substantial could be achieved, that many of his efforts were being blocked from Moscow, and that what could be achieved at the regional level would not spread to other regions. Once he had moved to Moscow, Gorbachev discovered that even being a member of the Politburo did not enable him to accomplish very much. In his opinion it was only the position of General Secretary which gave him the possibility to initiate decisive actions. As Gorbachev put it, his first idea was to have new cadres, particularly young and better-educated ones, with a new, effective way of working using a more developed system of incentives, and to go for modernization. At that time politicians were very much attracted by the example of Japan. Gorbachev recalled how even *Pravda* published a few articles by Japanese writers on the role of the state in modernization.

However, almost from the beginning it was evident that this approach could not be applied in Russian circumstances. As Yakovlev put it, as early as 1985 it was clear that even in the military-industrial complex the technological base was becoming outdated, and this was the sector which had been given top priority in the Soviet period: 'This was why we held the Plenum, the very first Plenum under Gorbachev, on scientific and technical progress. We allocated 12 billion roubles for new technology, which in those days was serious money, and it just disappeared. The system spat it out.'

The system, which was geared towards plugging gaps, whatever the cost, and dividing up resources, proved incapable of reorienting itself towards innovative development, even when under political pressure to do so. This incapacity gradually became apparent to the political leaders as well. In his interview Gorbachev somewhat emotionally described the administrative system as 'a voracious, resource-squandering form of economy', in which 'everyone was used to carving things up: the General Secretary carved, the

Prime Minister carved, their deputies carved, Gosplan carved, and so on down to the petty clerk in Gosplan allocating metal here and there. They were all carving, and all living off it.' When asked directly whether the most powerful person in the state, the General Secretary, could have changed the way resources were allocated in the interests of the more advanced sectors, Gorbachev gave an unambiguously negative answer: 'there was no chance of solving that problem fully, that is clear'. Thus, as attempts to solve the problems of modernization within the confines of the existing system and relations failed, it became evident that unless the fundamentals of a system in which 'everyone carves and everyone lives off it' were changed, nothing could be achieved. It followed logically from this that both the political and the economic system had to change, and, according to Gorbachev, this had become clear by 1988. In this respect the social—to a certain extent even the class—character of the transformation was obvious to him: 'They say to me: you should have squared it with the *nomenklatura*. You could not square anything with the *nomenklatura*. Nothing would have come of it.'

In all four interviews the transformations begun in 1985 were understood as a change of system. Both Yakovlev and Burbulis, for example, regarded the process as a change of social system, and Burbulis used such expressions as 'transition to a new quality', 'the beginning of a new era'. Such concepts are commonplace in studies of revolution when efforts are made to describe the specific features of revolutionary events by comparison with other historical periods. But our interviewees were rather guarded in their attitudes to the concept of revolution as such. Some of them were utterly categorical. Yakovlev, for example, said: 'Every revolution—the concept is an absolute blind alley, the outcome is an absolute blind alley, whichever revolution you look at'.

If we examine their responses more carefully, we can see that it is the term 'revolution' that they disliked. It is not that they disputed the radical nature of the changes—in this respect they all almost unreservedly shared the view that the events in Russia were of a revolutionary character. Their doubts were expressed as follows. Yakovlev said, 'In its content, it was, overall, a revolutionary turning-point. But it was not a revolution, as far as its mechanisms were concerned. I would tend to regard revolution as a mechanism—uprisings, barricades, divisions among the masses, general hysteria about nothing in particular, and then, you know, the morning after. It has been like that in all revolutions'. Gorbachev remarked, 'I considered it to be a revolution not in its methods, but in its essential nature, the profundity of the changes', and 'there is no Chinese Wall between revolution and reform'. Burbulis observed, 'When they tell me "You carried out a revolution, when there was another way," I say, "Let's reconstruct the situation which you see as revolutionary activity. You can see it as a revolution if you believe that there were dozens of other, less radical possibilities. But if you grasp the full scale of the crisis and our efforts to salvage at least something out of it to give society some kind of prospect, then it was evolution." ' In other words, they rejected above all the notion of revolutionary action, which they saw as violent and bloody. They also regarded revolution as an artificial product of ideological dogmas, rather than as a response to the demands of the situation.

This is what lies behind these attempts, which at first sight seem entirely scholastic, to reconcile what our interviewees saw as the irreconcilable—a revolutionary essence and evolutionary means. In 1987 there was a polemic between Gorbachev and Yakovlev on how to describe *perestroyka*—as a revolution in evolution or as an evolution in revolution. Gaidar also spoke of the evolutionary nature of the revolution, saying that 'one could have a terminological dispute about whether we had a peaceful, 'velvet revolution', or a radical evolution of the state' (1997c: 116–17).[1] Burbulis, albeit without enthusiasm, finally consented to the formula that they had been as revolutionary as circumstances dictated, and as evolutionary as it was within their power to be.

6.3 The role of historical experience

Strange as it may seem, our interviewees' reluctance to use the word 'revolution' did not prevent them from making considerable use of the experience of previous revolutions in assessing situations and drawing lessons for Russia. However, their preoccupation was not a desire to imitate, but, on the contrary, a wish to learn from the mistakes of others.[2] It would seem that the most important influence in this regard was the revolution of 1917, both the February and October phases, and continuing right up to Stalin's dictatorship. The second most important was the French Revolution. Yakovlev mentioned that when he was still a student he wrote a paper on the February Revolution, and later, when studying abroad, he examined further factual material, including material on Kerenskii and Russian social democracy. During the

---

[1] In his later publications Gaidar expresses his views on this question in a more forthright way. For example, 'The radical political and economic changes which engulfed Eastern Europe and the Soviet Union between 1989 and 1992 were of a revolutionary nature. They were the first full-blown revolution in the modern industrial world' (Gaidar 1997a: 463).

[2] Revolutionaries in other historical epochs were less one-sidedly critical of their predecessors' experience, and often regarded it as a source of inspiration. Thus in 1902 Plekhanov said that every social democrat should be a terrorist 'à la Robespierre', and Lenin, who at the beginning of the 20th century was prepared to accept responsibility for Jacobin methods of revolutionary change—including dictatorship and terror—was regarded by many of his critics as an 'orthodox Jacobin' (see Kondrat↔eva 1993: 38–46).

perestroyka period he set to work on the French Revolution. Gaidar claimed that 'in the process of making decisions I thought about the February Revolution to a very great extent. In the 1991–3 period I often thought about the February and October Revolutions and the gradual transition from one to the other. I thought far less about the French revolution of 1789–93, and less still about the Mexican and Chinese ones. These last two never figured in my decision-making—they were too remote'.

As far as the February Revolution was concerned, the basic lesson was that one should not delay in critical situations. Yakovlev saw an evident similarity between this period and the policies of Gorbachev, and he even referred to this in his report for the celebrations of the seventieth anniversary of the revolution in 1987: 'I drew a parallel with what was happening then. There were the same delays, the same indecisiveness, and the same talking shops'. When asked which politician's mistakes he tried not to repeat, Gaidar without hesitation named Kerenskii.

One effect of the experience of the Bolshevik Revolution and the Stalinist terror was that mass violence had become unacceptable. And yet this experience had also left an abiding sense that major changes are inevitably accompanied by large-scale bloodshed. It would seem that our interviewees had thought long and hard about these problems, and about what would be an acceptable price to pay for a radical transformation. Yakovlev said, 'In general, the revolutions which have taken place hitherto have been bloody. There have not been revolutions without bloodshed and the like, without civil war on some kind of scale. We already understood in 1985 that this would be a possibility. But we more or less vowed that we would carry out our revolution without violence. Fortunately, thank God, Gorbachev is a man of compromise, otherwise it would all have ended in bloodshed'. Gaidar remarked, 'I thought that this was a revolution without civil war. A revolution which was as gentle as possible, non-violent, or at least with minimal violence'.

It is interesting that the analogies with other revolutions were drawn in terms of those negative features which tend to accompany fierce power struggles where there are no firm constraints. As Yakovlev put it, 'What happened in the French Revolution, all that muck, all those underground intrigues—it stank. If you extrapolate from it, apply it to the present, there are many similarities'. Burbulis observed, 'With the collapse of the system and the chance to take part in the creation of a fundamentally new social system, an alarming number of political "favourites" and dilettantes attached themselves to the power structures . . . I am horrified when deep-dyed dilettantes grab the levers of power, at whatever level. We have seen them before in history. The Communist Party *nomenklatura*, with its unique experience of cynical administration, threw itself enthusiastically into that bacchanalia of favouritism, gaining maximum advantage from those five years'. These remarks resemble to a surprising extent the comments Lenin made in his last writings.

Since previous revolutions could not serve as positive examples, the Russian leaders had to look at the experience of radical reforms, particularly in Russia. Gorbachev remarked that he was particularly interested in past periods of reforms. When our interviewees were asked which historical figures they found most interesting from the point of view of applying their experience to the transformation of Russia, the names of Witte, Stolypin, and particularly Speransky cropped up most frequently. But if in relation to revolution the main question is how to avoid bloody excesses, in relation to reform a problem of a different type arises—how to avoid being diverted from the reformist path, how to ensure that things do not simply come full circle. This was particularly well expressed in our interview with Gorbachev: 'How was it that Alexander I began with Speransky, but ended with Arakcheev? This puzzled me, and I had to give it considerable thought. It suggests that there is a course of events which somehow or other sucks you in, and often compels you to do things that go completely against your original idea'.

6.4 Moderates and radicals: different types of leader

On all the questions enumerated above—understanding of the revolutionary nature of the transformation in Russia as a change of social system; rejection of the traditional 'revolutionary' methods of violence and bloodshed in such a transformation; a desire to be only as 'revolutionary' as circumstances dictated, and otherwise as 'evolutionary' as possible; the concern to learn from the mistakes of previous historical figures without idolizing any of them—the positions of our interviewees were broadly similar. However, on several questions there were substantial differences between the leaders of the moderate and radical phases. This can be very clearly seen from the interviews with Gorbachev on the one hand, and with Gaidar and Burbulis on the other.

Gorbachev's view of the tasks, social forces, and mechanisms of change faithfully reflected those specific features of the ideology of the first phase of the revolution examined above. His analytical framework had only two poles—the *nomenklatura* and the people. Moreover, since he regarded the people as a unified whole, and considered that changes were being carried out in the interests of the people, Gorbachev refused to accept that civil war was, and remained, a real possibility, saying that 'the people would not let itself be used'. He admitted that even the scale of the conflicts between nationalities was a surprise to him. He also saw the transformations as being primarily global, general changes, aimed at giving people decent living conditions: 'A market infrastructure, open to the world, a normal, dynamically developing country, giving people the chance to fulfil their potential'. Naturally enough, on this level Gorbachev saw no difference between the positions of different groups of reformers: 'The question was how to get there, how to proceed with the minimum of losses'. He regarded the radicals' contempt for these general objectives, their 'indifference to the fate of human beings', as cynicism and heartlessness, and their concern for the interests of the élite as a sign that the revolution had been blown off course: 'Yeltsin satisfied both the new *nomenklatura*, created by the Gaidar reforms, and the old one. The people were simply driven like cattle.'

As for the radicals, they faced much more cruel choices. Their starting point was not the need to accomplish the long-term, global task of securing a 'radiant future', but 'a situation of real catastrophe, which firmly, even stridently, demanded action' (Burbulis), in which 'famine was not far off' (Gaidar). There was no choice between different variants. It was simply 'impossible not to take certain steps, impossible not to take particular decisions' (Burbulis). The acceptance of the fact that the reforms would have quite a high price ('many would be ruined, many will remain without work'), which Gorbachev regarded as an intolerable indifference to human fate ('You can't talk like that if you are the government!'), was seen by the radicals as a manifestation of courage, an ability to look the truth in the eye: 'Our historical and human role was that we were able not to flinch from certain decisions' (Burbulis).

Though the leaders of the radical phase disagreed with each other on many things, they were virtually unanimous in their rejection of violence. This left them with two political instruments at their disposal: ideological influence and manoeuvring to create and support pro-revolutionary coalitions. Here the priorities of two of our interviewees manifestly did not coincide, and this, in Burbulis's opinion, reflected 'internal, unspoken disagreements and contradictions which cannot be formulated rationally, among the reformers themselves'. Throughout his interview, Burbulis stressed what he considers to be 'the grossest lacuna in our information and propaganda', namely, that they had forgotten that 'the main reformable material is people themselves'. There had been no special propaganda work, not only on economic matters, but also on the wider changes envisaged in the system, particularly in relation to democratic values. There had been an unwillingness consciously to mobilize people in support of the reforms. In Burbulis's view, this was a serious defect of an excessively technocratic approach to reforming society: 'Our wobbling on the referendum, our tacit support for the bombardment [of the Russian Parliament building on 3–4 October 1993] did not, in my opinion, reflect what society really needed. We did not create a layer of support for ourselves'. One of his greatest personal mistakes, he claimed, was that 'I could not persuade Yeltsin to form a political organization to serve as a natural basis and bridge for the reformist programme'. At the same time, like the moderate leaders, Burbulis viewed unfavourably the use of opportunities for manoeuvring, as reflecting an insufficiently defined reform strategy on the one hand, and the personal character traits of Yeltsin on the other: 'The reform of the country's state and politics was undertaken without any distinct strategy, that is, decisions were made from day to day rather than according to a systemic, unified, joint plan of action integrated with economic measures'; 'Yeltsin soon needed his unique talent for self-preservation, using checks and balances and the constant cultivation of rival groups. It had already become clear by the spring of 1992 that the basic element of the reforms—the unity of the team of intellectuals in this new formation—had foundered on the political will of Yeltsin'.

Gaidar clearly stressed different aspects of this question, and frequently underlined, both in his published works and in his interview, the importance of seeking mechanisms for co-ordinating interests, finding compromises, and manœuvring. This is because his conception of reality was vastly more complex. Compared with our other interviewees, he had a fuller grasp of the diversity and divergence of interests of different social forces. For example, while Gorbachev saw an undifferentiated *nomenklatura* as being the enemy of change, for Gaidar the *nomenklatura* had a variety of manifestations 'with all its subdivisions—the military, the KGB, the Ministry of Internal Affairs, the corps of directors, the corps of local chairmen, the regional leaderships, and so on'. In that sort of world, in which social forces are very divided, if the aim is to carry through radical changes, a government can only exist by manœuvring, if it wants to avoid civil war. Unlike Gorbachev and Burbulis, who discounted that danger entirely, and far more than Yakovlev, who mentioned the possibility only in passing, Gaidar claimed that the threat of civil war had been one of the basic determinants of his actions. He admitted that 'I always, constantly live with that threat; I feel it in my bones. I cannot say whether it was a real threat or not. It always seemed to me to be real, and nobody has yet convinced me otherwise'. When radical transformations are under way, this threat can arise from two quarters. The people can take to the streets, or a sharp conflict within the élite can have the same effect, resulting in 'unconstitutional measures, with the direct danger of armed resistance with an unpredictable outcome'. Such a situation, according to Gaidar, poses stark alternatives: 'you either have to start chopping off heads among the élite, or compromise with it'.

It would seem that this choice—between decisive changes using drastic methods, or milder approaches without large-scale violence—played a substantial part in political decision-making at all stages of the revolution. It is noteworthy that both the moderate and radical leaders were quite ready to accept more severe methods at different stages of the revolutionary process, whilst at the same time stressing their fidelity to non-violent, milder variants. Considering a possible alternative to Gorbachev's policies from 1985–91, Gaidar drew the following picture: 'They needed to organize a real internal revolution in the apparatus, and carry it out very firmly, like Ivan the Terrible. They should have chopped off a lot of heads among the élite, and so on, like

Peter the Great'. It should be said that Gorbachev himself appeared to see certain possible advantages in a harder approach, although in his interview he expressed this idea in a highly veiled way: 'You can even take the Stalin period. This was a dictatorial régime, the most terrible. Nonetheless, when Stalin was leader, he carried out a task of civilization by carrying through industrialization. With masses of corpses, millions of victims. But then, Peter the Great built on corpses'. However, in his practical politics he generally preferred non-violent, milder alternatives.

We can only guess how far this moderation derived from the character of Gorbachev himself, whom Yakovlev dubbed 'at first a master, and then a victim, of compromise', and how far it was related to his understanding of the nature of the period. Gorbachev described his time in office as follows: 'The Soviet model had been defeated not only on the economic and social levels, but also on the cultural level. Our society, our people, highly educated and intellectual, rejected this model on the cultural level, because it did not respect people, it oppressed them spiritually, politically, and economically. Therefore what was most important was everything to do with freedom.' Gaidar, facing practically the same dilemma, in an even tenser situation, chose, as we have seen, an absolutely analogous solution: 'We could have radicalized the radical phase further. We could have tried, for example, a law on lustration, a mass assault on the red *nomenklatura*, the sacking of directors instead of compromise, and heads rolling among the chairmen of local soviets. We could, perhaps, have made the situation even sharper. My policy was to dampen down the radical phase, so as not to convert it into a régime of civil war, which seemed to me to be a real danger. I consciously preferred to buy power from them, rather than to declare a crusade against them'.

It was the moderate leaders who expressed dissatisfaction with the degree of radicalism in the transformations, since the old *nomenklatura* has retained important positions in the new system. According to Gorbachev, 'Today the very same directors are sitting in their enterprises, having created a system of co-operatives through which they shuffle money about. They have all signed up to them, and have all they want.' According to Yakovlev,

Not long ago the Agrarian Union had a conference, and demanded that they be given administrative functions. Mister President sent them a message of greetings. That crowd are from the old *kolkhoz* and *sovkhoz* system, what sort of greeting do they deserve? They all need to be thoroughly inspected, if not put in camps! They get trillions of roubles in subsidies, and the people see none of it—it's all stolen. The bureaucrats all take their cut, and there's nothing left! Or there was that appeal, which I wouldn't have anything to do with: 'Reconciliation and Accord'.[3] Reconciliation with

---

[3] In the mid-1990s Boris Yeltsin was inspired by the idea of reconciliation. The date of the Bolshevik Revolution, 7 November, had been kept as a national holiday by the communist majority in the Duma. By presidential decree, Yeltsin declared this day to be a 'Day of

whom? On what basis? On the basis of reforms? They don't give a damn about reforms! They're fighting against them, that's why they exist. If you agree with them, you have to join them—that's the only way.

In his interview, Gaidar gave an extremely interesting analysis of the options that were available to the Provisional Government of 1917 for retaining power and preventing the radicals from taking over. Gaidar, we should not forget, often thought about this when taking concrete political decisions when in office:

To my mind, after the fall of Tsarism there was just one very simple choice: authoritarian modernism or various forms of radical revolution. Was there a chance of getting out of that situation via an authoritarian modernist path? Probably there was, but it would have required a great deal of activity on the part of an élite which understood the dangers. Naturally, there needed to be an immediate separate peace with Germany, at any price, as the minimum necessary condition for the victory of authoritarian modernism. Without a doubt, there needed to be agrarian reform—you cannot separate agrarian reform and peace. There needed to be a consistent and firm assault on the Bolsheviks and any other extremist groups on the grounds of their anti-patriotic nature. In other words, a separate peace with patriotic rhetoric: 'We have been driven to conclude this peace because of these traitors.' It might perhaps have been possible to have stabilized the situation at that point, although that is far from certain. The basic mistakes of the Provisional Government were, first, war to a victorious conclusion, and secondly, its unwillingness to form a decisive bloc with authoritarian forces like Kornilov.

In other words, for Gaidar, the Provisional Government should have acted in many respects as the Bolsheviks did. It should have oriented itself to current requirements without regard to strategy and ideological dogmas; it should have 'played it by ear', using all available means, including looking for 'enemies' to justify their own unpopular actions. Of course, this programme was unacceptable to the moderate leaders in principle. Gaidar's reflections show very well that there are basic common elements to a radical strategy in a variety of revolutions, even if radicals themselves sometimes adopt a variety of widely different methods.

It is thus evident that the logic behind the actions of the moderates and the radicals was based upon quite different presuppositions. Their inability to understand one another, and their rejection of each other's actions, derived not only from the struggle for power, but also from different understandings of the principles, tasks, and mechanisms of revolutionary change. This is why their assessments of the outcome of Russia's radical transformation, in which

Reconciliation and Accord'. In 1994 he also initiated a procedure whereby parties would sign a 'Treaty of Political Accord'. This treaty was signed by a large number of Russia's political parties, including the Communist Party. However, it had little influence on real political life.

they played leading roles, differed substantially. Gaidar thought that 'the Russian revolution was victorious, to the extent that a revolution ever can be victorious'. For Gorbachev 'once again we were knocked off course'.[4] Yakovlev maintained that 'we are now seeing the restoration, the restoration of certain facets of the old, Soviet system'. However, there was a sense in all the interviews that the revolutionary epoch, with its ups and downs, its exalted passions and dirty intrigues, was coming to an end. A period of more ordered, stable, evolutionary development had begun, and revolution was no longer so much a matter of practical activity as a subject for considered analysis.

---

[4] It is interesting that on this matter Gorbachev shared the viewpoint of many students of different revolutions, for whom the radical phase is a deviation from the revolution's normal course.

7

The Economic Cycle of Revolution

7.1 The concept of the revolutionary economic crisis

A process of revolutionary transformation engulfs all aspects of a country's life, and has a profound effect upon its economic system. It affects the economy in two ways. First, it has an immediate impact upon economic life during the revolutionary period. Various economic difficulties arise which have to be tackled by the revolutionary authorities. Secondly, there is the separate problem of the long-term effects of the revolution on the socio-economic development of the country. In this chapter we shall examine only the first aspect, the specific problem of how the economic system operates in a society undergoing revolution.[1]

[1] The socio-political aspects of revolutionary transformation have already been widely studied in some depth. The economic logic of revolution, however, has still only been considered in a very small number of studies. At best the subject is dealt with briefly in general works on the history of individual revolutions, mostly written from a Marxist perspective. It is almost impossible to find works containing a complex comparative analysis of the economic problems of different revolutions.

Strictly speaking, the only book which specially analyses the economic problems of a revolution is Florin Aftalion *The French Revolution: An Economic Interpretation* (Aftalion 1990). It treats the history of the French Revolution primarily as the history of the struggle waged by different governments against an economic crisis which was partly inherited from the *ancien régime*, and partly brought about by the actions of the revolutionary authorities themselves. However, this work has two limitations, which stem from its subject and methodology. On the one hand, it is concerned exclusively with the French revolution of 1789–96 and makes no comparisons with other revolutions. On the other hand, this economic interpretation of the French Revolution is in fact merely an explanation of the course of the revolution in terms of economic policies, in which these policies are presented as an external factor, in practice unrelated to the logic of the revolution.

There are also a number of works devoted to individual problems of economic policy in conditions of revolution, particularly related to the French and Russian-Bolshevik experiences (Fal↔kner 1919; Smirnov 1921; Dobrolyubsky 1930; Harris 1930; Szamuely 1974; Servet 1989; Faccarello and Steiner 1990; Malle 1985; Korotkov 1992). These works examine budgetary, financial, and monetary problems, slumps in production, and the economic doctrines underlying the activities of revolutionary governments.

Finally, one of the few works containing a comparative analysis of the economic problems of a series of revolutions is Dalin's *Infliatsiia v epokhi sotsial'nykh revoliutsii* (Inflation in the Epoch of Social Revolutions, Dalin, 1983). However, Dalin limits himself to just one, albeit exceptionally important, aspect of the problem—the analysis of currency circulation and inflation.

The most obvious and general characteristic of the economy in such a society is that it is in a profound crisis. This crisis continues throughout the revolution. Any revolution may be described as a transition through an economic crisis. The crisis deepens as the revolution spreads and becomes more radical, it provides an impetus to the further development of the revolution, and, finally, is overcome as the potential for social and political struggle is exhausted and the régime stabilizes. In this respect we can speak of an 'economic cycle of revolution', as being the movement of the economic system from a relatively stable state into crisis and then back to a new state of equilibrium. However, at this point we should clarify a few theoretical and methodological aspects of this question.

First and foremost, in this chapter we shall restrict our analysis to full-scale revolutions, those which are characterized as 'great' ones. They share a vitally important feature—an extended period of general socio-political instability, with weak central government and state power. All this has a direct impact on the development of the economic system on both the macro- and micro-levels.

This is the most important feature of a revolutionary economic crisis. It differs from a crisis in the normal business cycle in that the latter is not normally accompanied by a systematic political crisis.[2] In other words, only a revolutionary economic crisis is associated with a crisis of the system, with changes in the constitutional foundations of the economic and political structure. Of course, economic recession often leads to political conflicts and crises, and in extreme cases those may lead to a change of government, either constitutionally in developed democracies, or forcibly in authoritarian systems. However, these crises do not have a systemic character.

A revolutionary crisis is not a phase of those more general cyclical fluctuations, such as Kondrat'iev cycles or Kuznets swings, which take place over a period of decades. A revolutionary economic crisis has a definite relationship both to 'long cycles'[3] and to short-term cycles, inasmuch as a deterioration in the economic situation is a natural catalyst for a revolutionary explosion. However, the socio-political nature of the revolutionary economic cycle[4] is quite specific—it is directly associated with a crisis of power and is to a

---

[2] In this respect the Great Depression of 1929–33 was significantly different from a crisis of the business cycle, in that it actually pushed the developed countries of the West to the brink of revolution. We examine this question in greater detail in Ch. 11.

[3] Nikolai Kondrat↔iev himself advanced the hypothesis that 'periods of ascending waves of long cycles are, as a rule, significantly richer in major social disturbances and upheavals in the life of society (revolutions, wars) than periods of descending waves' (1993: 55).

[4] In this chapter we use the terms 'economic cycle of the revolution' and 'economic crisis of the revolution' interchangeably. What we mean is that revolution is accompanied by economic crisis, which develops in a cyclical form. The economic situation deteriorates as the revolution deepens, and stabilizes as the country emerges from revolution.

considerable extent a product of that crisis. Its duration, therefore, more or less coincides with the beginning and end of the political crisis of the revolution.

Our analysis of the economic cycle of revolution is limited to full-scale, great revolutions. It was only in these revolutions that the crisis of power was endemic. The leaders of 'revolutions from above' succeeded in keeping the socio-political situation under control, preventing the development of a revolutionary economic crisis. In revolutions which ended in political defeat, such as Germany in 1848 and Russia in 1905, the régime only lost control over the course of events for relatively short periods of time, which meant that an economic crisis did not achieve its full political potential. The same can be said about those revolutions which followed on from the great ones, such as the revolution of 1689 in England, and those of 1830 or 1848 in France.

A revolutionary economic crisis should also be distinguished from an economic crisis resulting from the inability of an existing government to ensure economic stability and development. There have been many cases in history where an economic crisis has become chronic. The reasons for this have usually been that the government cannot form a stable coalition of forces with an interest in overcoming the crisis. The longevity of such a crisis, and the absence of a coalition of interest groups in favour of stabilization, makes for a resemblance with revolutionary crisis. The fundamental difference, however, is that a revolutionary crisis develops against a background of, and in the context of, profound, systemic social change.

The key problem for us is the mechanism by which a revolutionary economic crisis develops. There are two underlying factors which together determine all revolutions: a systemic crisis and a weak state.

We can identify three mechanisms through which revolutions will affect the national economy. These are, first, changes in the structure of demand; secondly, the logic of government activity; and thirdly, changes in transaction costs.

Changes in the structure of demand, associated with changes in the political and social structure of a revolutionary society, will clearly alter the structure of economic incentives and, thereby, production. In Chapter 4 we looked at the logic of government activity (particularly that of an early revolutionary government), how it reflects the weakening and subsequent recovery of the power of the state. We also examined the reasons for populism, and for the limited effectiveness of revolutionary administrations.

Transaction costs, which have been much discussed in recent economic literature, are of fundamental importance in a revolutionary economic crisis. Political and social instability, an inevitable feature of any revolution, make economic activity considerably more uncertain. When concluding deals, it is difficult to allow for what might happen in the future, and the predictability of business deals falls sharply. The costs of assessing the firmness of a deal, and the costs of securing property rights, increase, and all this adds to the general cost of transactions.

These costs increase for the following reasons. First, the institutional structure of society breaks down. In other words, the 'rules of the game', to which economic agents have become accustomed, have changed, particularly where there has been a fundamental change in property rights. Secondly, state power is weakened. To a considerable extent the state loses its ability to act as 'a coercive third party', which according to North 'is essential' (1990: 35)—both to guarantee the security of contracts and to protect economic agents from forcible interference in their affairs. All of these problems are aggravated in conditions of civil war, as was the case in all the great revolutions of the past. Consequently, 'firms will tend to have short-time horizons', and 'the most profitable businesses may be in trade, redistributive activities, or the black market operations' (North 1990: 67). Even though trading remains much more advantageous than production, it too suffers significantly from the instability of the 'rules of the game'.

Increased transaction costs were the most important factor in the deterioration of economic conditions even in the English Revolution, during which the revolutionary processes unfolded relatively smoothly and property rights remained more secure than in subsequent revolutions. Naturally, the problem of transaction costs had a much more powerful effect on the course of events in the French and Mexican revolutions, and during the Bolshevik Revolution in Russia.

All of these factors (changes in the demand structure, transaction costs, and government populism) have a broadly similar impact upon the economy—they make the operation of the system less certain. Demand is uncertain, property rights are uncertain, personal and business confidence are lacking, and the course of politics is unstable and subject to constant fluctuations. All of this finds expression in a financial, monetary, and production crisis.

There is a particular methodological problem involved in interpreting economic indices and the information that they provide on a revolutionary economic crisis. Formally, a revolutionary economic crisis displays few differences from any other economic crisis. It might therefore seem at first sight that the economic crisis in a revolution can be described using the standard macroeconomic indicators, particularly production indicators, the condition of the state budget and currency system, and indices of living standards. Ideally, one would like to take a single set of indices and examine changes in them in the course of various revolutions. However, this is impossible. There are two reasons for this, which not only explain the limitations on any analysis of a revolutionary economic crisis, but also allow us to discern certain important features of this crisis.

First, there is no single set of indices we can use to analyse the economic cycle of revolution. The available statistical data are limited and not comparable methodologically. This is particularly true of the earlier revolutions. We can only speak at all of economic statistics for England in the 1640s and 1650s with very great reservations, and even the data for the time of the French Revolution leave much to be desired. Moreover, our analysis requires data to be broken down into very short time-periods, since the relationship between economics and political struggle can only be followed in many cases by using monthly data. Of cause, this is impossible for seventeenth and eighteenth centuries. The closer we get to the twentieth century, the better available statistics become.

Secondly, it is impossible in principle to describe different revolutions using the same indices, and this makes comparisons of economic trends in revolutions exceptionally difficult. For example, paper money inflation became a most important feature of revolutions starting with the French, but was irrelevant to England in the mid-seventeenth century.

Slumps in production are an even more important parameter, but these slumps are specific to certain revolutions. No modern researcher would analyse a socio-political upheaval without looking at the extent of the decline in GNP or in individual branches of the economy. However, although a certain contraction in economic activity took place in all the revolutions of the past, slumps only became a serious feature of the revolutionary economic cycle in the twentieth century. It is not simply that the statistics for the seventeenth and eighteenth centuries are inadequate. So far as we can tell from the historical record, the depth of the slump increases the closer we get to the present day. The extent of the decline was minimal in the English and French Revolutions, and much greater at the beginning of the twentieth century, in Mexico and Russia.

For these reasons, the economic indicators we shall use in our analysis will differ widely from revolution to revolution. We chose them on the basis of two criteria. On the one hand, they had to be as discrete as possible, reflecting changes at least from year to year.[5] On the other hand, we tried as far as possible to use indices which were more or less comparable across different revolutions.

For the English Revolution we shall rely mainly on the currently available data on annual grain production and its price, and on the changes in the wage rates of certain categories of English workers (Rogers 1884; Hoskins 1964; Brown and Hopkins 1981; Clay 1984). We supplement these sources with

---

[5] Since the authors of the book have lived through a full-scale revolution, they know better than most that to describe the economic processes taking place one needs even more detail than is provided by monthly data. The development of social struggle does not coincide with the normal subdivisions of the calendar year. But, alas, when analysing the past, such data are almost non-existent.

diverse, but unsystematic, data on the state of various branches of production and trade, the development of the tax system, the condition of state finances, and so forth.

For eighteenth-century France, we base our analysis primarily on fluctuations in harvest yields, and also on monetary and fiscal data. Data on living standards are fragmentary. However, currency indices are of considerable help in this case. Firstly, they provide a detailed picture, which can be analysed month by month. Secondly, these data are the most important guarantee of the comparability of the French Revolution and the revolutions of the twentieth century, for which analogous statistics exist.

Our analysis of the Russian and Mexican revolutions of the beginning of the twentieth century is based on indices of industrial output, as well as upon monetary statistics. Analogous indices allow us to assess the development of the economic crisis in Russia today, although, we have a much wider statistical base for such an analysis.

We shall analyse in detail below how economic crises have developed in the course of various revolutions. Two main questions naturally arise here. Are there any stable patterns in the development of a revolutionary economic crisis? And what is the relationship between the revolutionary economic crisis and the different phases of the revolutionary process that we discussed in Chapter 4? Let us examine these questions.

7.2 Economic problems at the outset of the revolution

The problem of 'sliding into a revolution' was described in some detail in chapters 1 and 2, in which we pointed to economic growth and the difficulties it gives rise to as the basic process making for pre-revolutionary destabilization. This occurred in all countries in their pre-revolutionary periods, to a greater or lesser extent. The forms and mechanisms by which growth processes influenced the onset of the systemic crisis differed from country to country.

Almost all specialists on the history of early modern England have observed that from the second half of the sixteenth century its economy was developing fairly rapidly, albeit in an unstable, fluctuating way (see e.g. Nef 1940; Kosminsky and Levitsky 1954: vol. i; Coleman 1956a; Supple 1964; Hill 1968; Clarkson 1971, 1985; Snooks 1994). The main developments were in such industries as wool, iron metallurgy, and later coal. There was a corresponding increase in foreign trade. England's pre-revolutionary development was marked by profound structural changes.

Quantitative data for this period are extremely fragmentary. However, even the statistics we do have support this conclusion in general. The output of iron in blast furnaces was 140 tons in 1500, but 10,000 tons in 1600. Coal extraction in Newcastle doubled in the first half of the century (see Pollard and Crossley 1968: 109; Lipson 1931: ii. 114).

There was a sharp increase in the number of trading vessels serving London's food needs. In the first half of the seventeenth century their number increased by almost four times (see Kosminsky and Levitsky 1954: i. 37). These figures can reflect not only the development of navigation and trade, but also the growth of urban population and, consequently, industry. Throughout the first half of the seventeenth century there was a steady increase in the amount of grain brought in, as a consequence of which by 1630 England had become a net grain importer (Clay 1984: i. 103)[6]. This fact can be seen as an indirect indicator of the accelerated development of industry and of the market it creates.

In eighteenth-century France, despite the exceptionally difficult position of state finances, the final decade of the *ancien régime* was distinguished by economic growth which was rapid for the time. Some observers even believe it was more rapid than in England in the same period (Crouzet 1967; O'Brian and Keyder 1978; Mathias and Pollard 1989: 694). From the 1730s onwards French economic development was particularly vigorous and, despite the wars, very stable. This has led certain historians to refer to the France of the time as 'the leading industrial power in the world' (Markovitch 1975, 1976). Although this growth, unlike that of England, was primarily quantitative and was not accompanied by great structural changes in the economy,[7] there can be no doubt about its destabilizing effect on the *ancien régime*.

The two major revolutions of the early twentieth century, in Mexico and Russia, were also preceded by very rapid and quantitatively comparable economic growth, of around 6–8 per cent of GNP per annum. Investments rose rapidly, and a significant proportion of them involved foreign capital.

Between 1877 and 1910 in Mexico GNP tripled and output per capita doubled, while the volume of foreign trade increased nine times. Silver production rose 3.5 times, and copper production rose almost seven times. In the 1890s alone the railway network grew tenfold (see Skidmore and Smith 1984: 231; *Estadisticas Historicas de Mexico* 1985: 311–13; Bethell 1986: 28–9; Maddison 1995: 156, 202).

Russia was also developing exceptionally rapidly, especially in the 1890s and between 1908 and 1913. From 1890 to 1913 GDP increased 2.5 times, and per capita domestic product 1.5 times (see Maddison 1995: 154, 186, 200).

---

[6] See also Thirsk (1967: 524–7, 617–18). However, the figures suggest that from 1670 England became a net exporter of grain (Pollard and Crossley 1968: 126).

[7] 'The growth in output was obtained mainly through the old forms of industry, from a growth in production rather than from a growth in productivity. What needs to be emphasized is that economic growth was taking place at a steady rate' (Mathias and Pollard 1989: 695).

The railway network increased 2.3 times over that period, coal production six times, oil production three times, pig iron five times, sugar 4.2 times, and grain 1.5 times. A positive balance of payments was maintained, with growth in both imports and exports (see Kahan 1989: 11, 69; Mathias and Postan 1978: pt. 2). This sort of growth rate and the qualitative socio-economic shifts which accompanied it were unprecedented in the history of both states, and quite rare in the economic history of any country.

However, although the rapid development which modernized the economies of these countries was quite stable in economic terms, it under-mined their social and political stability, which was, essentially, the stability of pre-modern, traditional societies. If unexpected economic and/or political difficulties were to arise they could very rapidly have a destabilizing political effect upon the régime. The process could then aquire a revolutionary poten-tial, at first politically, and then also economically. It is here that we can see most clearly the connection between the revolutionary economic cycle and short-term economic fluctuations. The 1630s in England saw particularly steep price rises which meant that the incomes of a significant part of the population fell. These incomes had previously been rising, sometimes reach-ing 150 per cent of the level at the start of the 1620s. The bad harvests at the end of the 1630s and the depression in industry and trade made the situation particularly severe (see Figures 7.1 and 7.2.).[8] It was all the more painful because famine as a result of poor harvests had by that time become uncom-mon in England (see Clay 1984: i. 103). Given these circumstances, when a serious financial crisis broke out, it greatly destabilized the position of the authorities and, consequently, their capacity to influence the development of the national economy.

A similar crisis occurred in France at the end of the 1780s. The poor harvests of 1786–8 threatened the population with starvation, since not only urban dwellers, but a significant portion of the poorer peasants, were net grain purchasers. The crisis in state finances became particularly acute—servicing the state debt took up over 40 per cent of budget expenditure and 55 per cent of revenue (see Jones 1983: 230, 284).[9]

After two decades of turbulent growth, at the beginning of the twentieth century both Mexico and Russia came up against an economic crisis, and the development of industry slowed substantially. This was a world crisis, but it

[8] Overall, the 17th century was a century of crisis for the whole of Europe (see Aston 1965; de Vries 1976). However, the crisis in England, according to many authors, began later than it did on the continent—in the mid-1630s (see Supple 1964: 120–4, 139, 266; Lublinskaya 1965: 16–18).

[9] The situation in viticulture was particularly bad; grape harvests fell sharply in 1787–9. Labrousse (1990), in his painstaking statistical econometric study, even concluded that the crisis in viticulture and winemaking was one of the main reasons for the revolution of 1789.

hit those countries particularly hard that were trying to industrialize to catch up. In both countries, industrialization was being carried out at the expense of the peasantry and was accompanied by a deterioration in the position of certain sections of the population.[10] Once the signs of crisis began to appear in the economy, the social consequences were not far behind. The revolution of 1905, which was accompanied by mass peasant uprisings and raised the spectre of the *grande peur* of 1789–90 in the minds of politicians, was, as Lenin put it, a 'dress rehearsal' for the events of 1917. In Mexico a full-scale revolution broke out in 1910. In both cases the government was rejected by the middle strata and the peasantry, both of whom had been hit particularly hard by the economic effects of the crisis and/or war.

Of course, the outbreak of the Russian revolution of 1917 was connected first and foremost with the First World War, which had brought a substantial deterioration in the economic situation. An inflationary monetary policy caused prices to rise rapidly, and military activity led to contraction in the output of certain basic industrial products. Between 1914 and 1917 industrial output fell by one quarter. Iron ore extraction declined by 43 per cent, steel smelting by 28 per cent, and production of cotton fabrics by 47 per cent. The grain harvest fell by a third (see Figure 7.15). At the same time, the quantity of money in circulation increased fivefold, causing prices on average to rise, according to various estimates, by between three and six times over the same period (see Falkner 1924: 138; Dalin 1983: 163, 168). As it turned out, the pre-war economy enjoyed considerable reserves of stability. Although the government resorted to printing money from the first days of the war, it was considerably later that the inflationary processes gathered momentum, and serious difficulties with foodstuffs did not occur until the end of 1916 (see Katsenelenbaum 1924: 70). In other words, the course of events in Russia confirmed the fears of those leading Russian dignitaries, particularly Sergei Witte, Petr Stolypin, and Vladimir Kokovtsov, who, having studied the experience of 1904–5, argued that if peace were maintained for one or two decades, Russia would be transformed, whereas to participate in war would be to risk revolution (see Gerschenkron 1968: 277; Kokovtsov 1992: i. 364).

The experience of these revolutions shows that at the outset there may be an improvement in the economic situation after the first popular government

---

[10] In Mexico certain economic measures taken by the Diaz government were another important destabilizing factor—particularly the move from silver coinage to a gold standard and the sharp increase in the tax burden upon the middle strata of the population. Although the intention was to overcome the financial crisis, to modernize the financial system and bring it into line with the world system, it led to a steep fall in the standard of living and greater social tension (see Bethell 1986: 63–4). In other words, taxation problems played a similar role in the Mexican Revolution to that which they played in England and France.

has assumed power. A number of factors may contribute to this. The establishment of a new, and, so it seems, long-awaited régime may bring about a certain social and psychological stabilization. Diverse social forces temporarily co-operate in order to overthrow the *ancien régime*. The crisis in food supply or in industry which sparked off the social explosion may gradually be overcome, leading to a certain short-term economic improvement.

As far as we can tell from the available data, this was the pattern of events in England in the 1640s, in France from the end of 1789 to the beginning of 1791, and in Mexico in 1910–11. The recovery from the two years of bad harvests in England in 1638–9 led to a fall in consumer prices and a certain rise in the standard of living. The harvests in France in 1789 and 1790 were not bad, which meant that the price of bread fell, and there was a general expectation in French society that things would get better. In Mexico the situation stabilized and output increased in the main branches of industry and agriculture (see Figures 7.1, 7.2, 7.3, and 7.9).

In Russia, embroiled as it was in the First World War, there could be no significant improvement. Negative processes, particularly inflation and a slump in industrial output and grain deliveries, had already gathered momentum and continued to worsen. Between March and November 1917, that is, in the eight months before the radicalization of the revolution, prices increased fourfold—as much as during all the preceding years of the war. The outbreak of the revolution served only to give a new impetus to the inflationary pressures, as the Provisional Government had no source of revenue apart from the printing press, but had to fund both the costs of the war and the costs of the revolution.[11] But even here in 1917, there were positive developments in several economic indicators, including, for example, coal extraction and electricity production. In some sectors which were placed under the special control of the Provisional Government, its intervention was not as destructive as it was in agriculture (see *Itogi desyatiletiya* 1927: 244–7).

7.3 Aggravation of economic crisis, intensification of political struggle

The improvements in the economic situation which have in a number of cases occurred at the outset of a revolution never have been, and never could be, lasting. From the very start of a revolution factors begin to operate which cause the economic crisis to worsen. The conditions for that crisis mature from the very beginning of the revolution, although they may only manifest

---

[11] 'The need for paper money . . . on the contrary, after the February revolution of 1917 became even more pressing . . . The printing press began to work not only for the war effort, but for the revolution too' (Katsenelenbaum 1924: 48).

themselves after a certain time. The reasons for the crisis, even at the early stages of the revolution, are not natural or climatic, but social. Of course harvests may play some role, but they are certainly not the key factor in the development of the crisis. The basic reasons for the crisis are the same as those which determine the crisis of moderate rule. We have examined them above, and so, therefore, shall just discuss them only briefly here.

First, the actions of an early revolutionary government, based as it is on a programme developed under the *ancien régime*, involve numerous mistakes and confusions which have a deleterious effect on the economic situation. Secondly, the early coalition of revolutionary forces collapses and the existing groups become polarized; the struggle between these groups for power reduces economic problems to the status of a hostage in this battle.[12] Thirdly, the socio-political changes which occur in the course of the revolution upset the basic conditions in which economic agents operate—the structure of demand, and the legal and political framework. Naturally, this has negative consequences. This deterioration in the economic situation leads to political crisis resulting in the fall of the early revolutionary government.

The indicators of the deteriorating economic situation and the beginning of the economic crisis differ from revolution to revolution. The mechanisms of the economic crisis also differ. The development of the crisis will depend to a considerable extent, for example, on the country's monetary system and on whether the government has such an instrument as paper money at its disposal. Or it might depend on the stage at which war breaks out, or on how the war is progressing. All these factors can change the form of economic developments, but their general direction remains broadly similar.

In England, although the period of bad harvests was over and consumer prices had fallen somewhat in the first half of the 1640s, problems arose at the very outset of the revolution which caused the economic situation to worsen substantially. From the beginning two factors had a negative effect on the condition of English production and trade. On the one hand, England's development was highly dependent on external trade, and at this time demand for its manufactured goods was tending to fall. On the other hand, the circulation of metal coinage was sensitive to the jittery mood which accompanied the political crisis and the outbreak of the revolution. The population began to hoard money, and entrepreneurs, both English and foreign, withdrew money from domestic circulation. This severe currency crisis greatly complicated commercial transactions. From the very beginning of the revolution in

---

[12] 'Economics has finally given way to politics', as B. E. Supple characterized the course of events in England in 1642 (1964: 131, 146), and this assessment is applicable to the corresponding period in any revolution. Supple also observed that 'the political anxieties which accompanied the preparation to Civil War themselves had serious repercussions for the economy' (ibid. 125).

England the process of increasing transaction costs received a powerful impetus, and this process continued apace during the revolution. This was the background to the non-payment crisis and the contraction of production.[13]

The examination of the English experience allows us to identify an important feature of the revolutionary economic crisis. The political instability of the revolution leads to a contraction of the money supply, that is to say, the national product is demonetized. Where the currency is metallic, it is simply removed from the economy, hoarded and saved 'for better times'.[14] This is yet another consequence of the weakening of the state. It is unable to enforce contracts, which means that there are insufficient guarantees that money will be able to play the role of a universal equivalent.

This means that a crisis in the system of payments and accounting is an important phenomenon inherent in any revolution, not just those which occur where paper money is in circulation. The political crisis itself undermines the monetary system, and this leads to an attendant crisis of production, although not necessarily to high inflation. Where the government does not have the option of printing money, the economic situation deteriorates at an earlier stage, but the revolutionary economic crisis as a whole takes a much milder form, particularly if we compare the English Revolution with the French, Mexican, and Russian.

The preparations for civil war and its outbreak in England caused the economic situation to deteriorate further. This can be seen particularly clearly in the movements in the price of bread and in the cost of living (see Figures 7.1 and 7.2). In the mid-1640s both these indices started to rise rapidly. By 1647 bread prices had reached their highest level for the entire period since 1620, and they settled around that level.

Moreover, the war further complicated the movement of goods around the country. It destroyed traditional economic links,[15] although demand for goods needed by the army increased. The main negative factor here, as in any revolution, was the general political instability, brought about by the inability of the state in conditions of *de facto* dual power to guarantee that contracts are

---

[13] 'In 1642 the "want of money" was seen as "an epidemical disease raging like the sweating sickness of late years over the whole land"; and it is clear that constitutional crisis did have precisely this effect. By directly and indirectly reducing confidence it also increased the liquidity preference of merchants, and this must have manifested itself as a shortage of cash, a restriction of credit, and a reduction in demand' (Supple 1964: 131).

[14] Where paper money is in circulation a standard, self-reproducing mechanism operates, whereby depreciation accelerates in line with the velocity of circulation.

[15] The King and Parliament were literally deluged with petitions complaining of the economic problems of producers as a result of the fall in demand for their produce. For example, the Essex clothiers complained to the King in 1641 about the almost complete cessation of orders from London, their main customer: 'Our cloaths for the most part for the space of this eighteen months remain upon our hands, and flocks lying dead therein, and we can maintain our trading no longer' (cited in James 1930: 59–60).

observed. There was an increase in transaction costs, even in relation to their already high level in the seventeenth century. The state authorities were unable to ensure the necessary conditions for observance of property rights on goods produced and supplied—they could neither protect them from possible confiscation by the local authorities (this happened particularly frequently in London—see James 1930: 60), nor enforce the observance of commercial agreements.[16]

The factors which brought about the economic crisis in the French revolution were also operating from the summer of 1789, although they did not manifest themselves fully until later. At first, developments seemed favourable: the abolition of feudal laws pacified the peasants, the hopes for a better life and cheap bread pacified the workers, and the *de facto* removal of taxes and cautious inflationary financing stimulated a growth of output. But new problems were soon to follow. As a consequence of the sharp reduction in the tax burden, the peasants had less need to sell the products of their labour. Their needs were limited, and now that it was no longer necessary to pay taxes they could be satisfied with much less money. The reduction in demand for luxury goods from the nobility undermined the material well-being of Paris and many other French cities.

The worsening condition of foreign trade destabilized the economy in the port towns. Although the French economy depended less on foreign markets than England's, the social consequences of these developments were still very dangerous. The government, despite the warnings of many deputies of both right and left (particularly Saint-Just), increased the supply of *assignats*, because there was no other source of state revenue. Metal coinage rapidly disappeared from circulation. This increased the need for paper money and at the same time made the currency system vulnerable, as the state no longer had an adequate reserve of precious metals. The destruction of trade followed on inexorably, with disturbances in the movement of foodstuffs, particularly grain, from producer to consumer. Government economic policy, combined with poor harvests from 1791 (Jones 1983: 228–9), and a worsening political situation both at home and abroad, provided the impetus for a sharp and rapid deterioration of the economic situation which continued, with a few fluctuations, until the middle of 1796.

The economic crisis in France was much more severe than it had been in England, both in terms of price rises for consumer goods and in terms of interruptions in the food supply to the towns. The position was made worse by the fact that the French peasants were themselves food purchasers to a significant extent, so their material well-being was also inversely related to food prices. Inflation, which operated as an indirect tax, adversely affected the

---

[16] '[B]oth merchants and chapmen, do now generally refuse to make payment for goods long since sold and delivered' (cited in Supple 1964: 130–1).

entire population as the issue of *assignats* gathered pace, but the politically active urban poor were particularly hard hit. The printing of paper money was also a factor in destabilizing the normal movement of goods from producer to consumer, thus exacerbating the shortage of goods.

In Mexico the intensification of the internal political struggle was accompanied by the destabilization of production and the start of a profound economic crisis. The outbreak of the civil war led to a rapid contraction in output. The shortfall in financial resources drove the government to cover its needs by recourse to the printing press, which led to the rapid depreciation of the national currency from the second half of 1913 onwards (see Figures 7.8 and 7.9). This was soon followed by a sharp deterioration of supply on the goods market and a massive upsurge in speculation (see Bethell 1986: 117).

Finally, the most extreme example of a desperate economic situation was Russia, which had already been fighting for three years in World War I. The breakdown of the transport system, which had already begun under the *ancien régime*, and the ineffectual economic policy of the Provisional Government, led to a serious destabilization of the food supply to the cities, particularly Petrograd and Moscow. Inflation soared, and production contracted. The government rapidly lost control of the food market, which had to a significant extent been centralized under the Tsarist régime in 1915–16. The inconsistent policies of the Provisional Government disoriented the peasants and undermined the incentives for agricultural production. Consequently, the 1917/18 agricultural year saw the worst fall in grain procurements for the entire period of war and revolution—from 323.1 to 47.5 million puds of grain (see Narkomprod 1922: 18).

Against this background there was a rapid deterioration in the macroeconomic situation. As in other revolutions, from the English onwards, the population started to hoard money, which resulted in currency shortages: 'The currency shortage occurs solely because money ceases to circulate. It flows in one direction only, from the state treasury, until it reaches a sock, boot, or chest, into which it disappears for ever' (Lomeyer 1918: 57). This added to the state's need to print more money. The hoarding process continued actively even after the Bolsheviks had taken power. Now it was not only metal coinage that was hoarded, but also the paper money of the *ancien régime* which had officially remained in circulation. This behaviour reflected reasonable political expectations for that time.

7.4 The economy of political radicalism

It is the profound economic crisis which brings a government of radicals to power. This is least applicable to England, although here, too, prices were rising, reaching unprecedented heights in 1648–50 (Brown and Hopkins 1981: 30; Hoskins 1968: 29). Economic problems played a large part in bringing the Jacobin dictatorship to power in France, although here the deteriorating external position of the Republic and the danger of the defeat of the revolution in military conflict with the leading European powers were no less important.[17] The unpreparedness of the Madero government in Mexico to solve its socio-economic problems in a consistent fashion and find a way out of the crisis of the post-Diaz economy did much to exacerbate the political struggle within the Mexican élite and did even more to drive the peasants to rebellion. Events in Russia developed in a similar fashion, where the depth of the economic crisis and the inability of the Provisional Government to cope with it produced a rapid rise in popularity of the Bolsheviks and brought them to power in October 1917. It is clear from this list of examples that the closer we get to our own time, the greater the role of economic problems in exacerbating the political crisis of the revolution and moving it towards its radical phase.

The importance of the economic crisis in bringing the radicals to power becomes clearer when one compares the basic problems being discussed among the political élite and in the revolutionary press of the various countries on the eve of the takeover by the radicals. For all the difficulties in the economic situation brought about by the Civil War, English society at the end of the 1640s was much more concerned with ending the Civil War, the constitutional structure of the country, and the nature of political and civil liberties, especially religious liberties. Almost the only economic theme discussed was the unjust distribution of property, and this was a concern only of the left, the Levellers.

In France at the end of 1792 and the beginning of 1793 the main concerns were the new constitutional structure, and the organization of the defence of the Republic against Foreign intervention and domestic peasant uprising. There was also growing pressure from the urban poor, who demanded an end to the economic crisis and a rise in the people's living standards (see Kunov 1923; Murray 1985; Gough 1988). However, it was only later, under the Jacobins, that economic problems became the central issue of political struggle. The economy was also one of the priorities of the first Thermidorian government.

In Russia between August and October 1917 the question of power was precisely the question of how to overcome the economic collapse. How to achieve this was discussed in sessions of the Pre-parliament, at congresses of political parties, and in newspapers. It was at this time that Riabushinsky

---

[17] Aftalion has argued that it was the economic course of events that brought the Robespierre group to power (1990: Ch. 7).

uttered his famous words about the 'bony hand of hunger'.[18] It is also typical that the most important articles by Lenin of a programmatic nature, 'The Impending Catastrophe and How to Combat it' and 'Can the Bolsheviks Retain State Power?', were devoted to economic questions.[19] Indeed the scale of the slump in Russia between 1918 and 1920 had not been experienced in previous revolutions. The only remotely comparable case is Mexico, but even there the collapse of production was not so all-embracing (see Bethell 1986: 86–8).

The assumption of power by the radicals is no guarantee of an improvement in the economic situation. Chaos in the economy is determined by chaos in politics. The lack of any powerful and legitimate authority, along with a multitude of power centres, deepens the economic crisis in every revolutionary country. It is primarily a result of the continuing political struggle, and this precludes any stable resolution of economic problems. Among the various economic problems of the radical phase of the revolution, the most important are the worsening state budget crisis, rising prices (inflation), and, often, a slump in output.

The main causes of the deteriorating economic situation at this stage are, first, a crisis in the institutional system of the revolutionary society; secondly, a crisis of the economic structure (military destruction and profound changes in the traditional demand structure); and, thirdly, a sharp increase in the role of illegal (black market and speculative) economic activity, despite attempts to ban it by the radical authorities. This all leads to further economic disorganization and to an increase in transaction costs.

The political conflict occurs in a situation where a complete reorganization of power and the economy has already begun, but for understandable reasons has not been completed. This makes it even more difficult to supplement the state budget at a time when government expenditure, continues to increase. The government's struggle to survive necessitates the adoption of a complex of economic and political measures which will be of critical importance in shaping the post-revolutionary society.

Similar economic conditions brought the radicals to power in France and in Russia. In both cases political radicalism and armed struggle coincided, and the practical economic policies of both the Jacobins and the Bolsheviks resembled one another. Consequently, there are also clear analogies in the ways that the economic crisis developed in the radical phases of these revolutions.

---

[18] 'The bony hand of hunger . . . would grasp by the throat the numbers of the different committees and soviets', said Riabushinsky, a well-known businessman and politician of the time (Chamberlin 1935: i. 267–8).
[19] 'Unavoidable catastrophe is threatening Russia. The railways are incredibly disorganized and the disorganization is growing. The railways will come to a standstill. The transport of raw materials and coal to the factories will cease. The transport of grain will cease', wrote Lenin at the end of September 1917 (*PSS* xxxiv. 155).

Although the radicals in France and Russia found themselves in an even more difficult political situation than that of the English radicals, they managed, through exceptional efforts and the widespread use of coercion, to create the illusion for a time that the government could sort out a range of economic problems. The Jacobins were able temporarily to stabilize the value of the *assignat*, although to do this they had to introduce the death penalty for breaking the laws on the Maximum and on the compulsory exchange rate for paper money.[20]

For the Bolsheviks, money was a secondary instrument of economic life which would wither away.[21] Therefore, on the economic front they devoted most of their attention to the supply of foodstuffs to the towns. They achieved a considerable increase in the volume of state grain procurements, which in 1918/19 were double the 1917/18 level. By the end of the civil war procurements had grown almost six times (see Figure 7.13).[22] Bolshevik ideology meant that the financial sphere was of less concern to them. However, in the first year of their rule, there were some, albeit very limited, positive developments in this area too. There was a noticeable reduction in the budget deficit. The deficit for 1918 was 66.2 per cent of expenditure, which was less even than in 1915 (74 per cent). Subsequently, of course, the deficit increased, to 77.3 per cent in 1919 and 86.9 per cent in 1920 (Katsenelenbaum 1924: 66).[23]

The improvement in some areas and in some indicators which may occur when the radicals take power is soon followed by an inexorable worsening of the economic crisis. Military actions exacerbate the economic difficulties, production declines, the standard of living falls, and inflation rises. According to the available data, in England at the end of the 1640s and beginning of the 1650s there was a deterioration in the material condition of a significant part of the population. Food prices rose and the real wages of urban workers fell (see Figures 7.1 and 7.2). In France inflation took off and the real value of the *assignat* fell continually, for all the draconian measures brought in by the

---

[20] The *assignat* was worth 36% of its original value in June 1793, and 34% in July 1794 (see Jones 1983: 237). Admittedly, its value fluctuated wildly from month to month, reaching 22% in August 1793 and 48% in December of that year. This reflected changes in the military-political position of the French Republic, the successes of the revolutionary armies, and the struggle against European intervention.

[21] 'The transition from money to a moneyless exchange of products is indisputable', wrote Lenin to the People's Commissariat of Finance in 1920 (*PSS* lii. 22; see also *PSS* xxxvi. 430, xxxviii. 89).

[22] The actual figures, in millions of puds, are: 1916/17—323.1; 1917/18—47.5; 1918/19—107.9; 1919/20—212.5; 1920/21—283.4 (see Narkomprod 1922: 18).

[23] Of course, the ways in which the budget deficit was covered were quite different in 1915–16 and in 1918–20. During the First World War the deficit was covered to a large extent by foreign loans, and therefore prices rose relatively slowly. During the civil war the budget was replenished mainly by printing money, which expressed itself in galloping inflation.

Jacobin government to maintain price stability (see Figures 7.4 and 7.6). Infla-tion increased and output fell rapidly in Mexico after the fall in 1913 of the moderate Madero government (see Figures 7.8 and 7.9). In Russia the assumption of power by the Bolsheviks was accompanied by a sharp rise in inflation, which by the end of 1917 was completely out of control; the decline in output also worsened rapidly (see Figures 7.10, 7.14 and 7.15).

In a word, for all the radicals' efforts, their *economic* goals are almost never realized. The examples of France and Russia show this particularly clearly. Major fluctuations in the exchange rate of the *assignat* and a rapid deteriora-tion in supply to the cities obliged the Jacobins to mitigate their orthodox economic policy. This did little to stimulate market forces, but did enough to lose them the support of the Parisian *sans-culottes*.[24] The Bolsheviks were also unable to solve any of the economic problems facing them. They could neither ensure the exchange of goods between town and country (the peasants still refused to supply the towns with grain, and hid it), nor secure stable money-less supply to the towns (the workers still had to purchase more than half the bread they consumed on the free market),[25] nor overcome the barterization of the economy, which was beyond the control of the authorities. However, both radical régimes were able to accomplish their main *political* goal, which was to prevent the victory of the counter-revolutionary forces.

7.5 Economic problems of the end of the revolution

Economic conditions change substantially after the fall (or transformation) of the radical régime. There is also a certain duality in the way events develop. On the one hand, the authorities adopt a package of justifiable measures, aimed at stabilizing the economic situation and the prospects for economic development. On the other hand, the immediate result of their policies is an aggravation of the economic crisis, which strikes hard at various strata of the population, particularly the poorest.

The Thermidorian government in France tried to reactivate trade and boost the economy by refraining from offensive forms of state intervention, by removing the price regulations which had become almost all-embracing, and by abolishing the compulsory exchange rate for paper money, allowing metal coins to circulate. The same goals were being pursued by the Bolshevik leadership when it announced the transition to the New Economic Policy (NEP) in the spring of 1921.

---

[24] Many historians see the adoption of the 'Ventôse decrees' as the 'beginning of the end' of the Robespierre dictatorship.

[25] Lenin himself recognized this (see *PSS* xxxix. 275–7, and also Mathias and Pollard 1989: 997).

However, the immediate consequence of such decisions is a deterioration in economic conditions. Moreover, the character of the crisis differs substantially from the crisis of the early phases of the revolution. In addition to the slump in output, which cannot be halted suddenly, there is a noticeable further decline in the standard of living of a significant part of the population, even when compared to the period of wartime radicalism. The deterioration here is both absolute and relative. In contrast to earlier phases of the revolution, this deterioration takes place against a background of growing social polarization, as the position of those who are the first to benefit from the fruits of post-radical economic policy improves. We can identify a number of reasons for this.

First, the contradictions which accumulated in the radical phase and which the radicals either could not solve, or could not bring themselves to solve, are laid bare. A situation of intense struggle against open opponents of the revolution, or a situation of military action, gives the government moral justification for political expediency. This makes it possible, at the cost of enormous effort, to maintain the exchange rate, to supply the towns with food and factories with raw materials. Not infrequently, these goals are achieved at the expense of future productive potential, even in the short term. Now, after the radical phase, the time has come to settle up, just as the radicals in their time paid for the inconsistency and indecisiveness of their moderate predecessors.

Secondly, a post-radical government does not have to pay so much attention to the attitude of the masses. Fatigue, accumulated over the years of revolution, makes itself felt more and more. The revolutionary wave recedes, and the benefits of the political and military successes of the radicals, as well as the strengthened apparatus of coercion, accrue to their successors. Spontaneous disturbances still occur, but they are no longer successful. As Tocqueville observed, the people in this period already want to be betrayed.

These negative developments can be seen even in England in the mid-1650s. The most intense phase of the political struggle had taken place in the pre-radical period, and few of the ideas of the radicals (the Small Parliament in 1653 and the Levellers) had been realized in practice. In England, there were no sharp changes in the political and legal foundations of the economy. However, here too, as the Protectorate régime consolidated itself, there were negative movements in the indices of living standards. Consumer prices started to rise, and real wages fell substantially (see Figures 7.1 and 7.2). The government experienced serious problems in filling the state coffers, even though it succeeded not only in collecting taxes, but even in increasing them. Indeed, the almost continual increase in the tax burden during the years of the revolution in England ultimately weakened the government. And this happened in a situation where the government could allow itself to be unpopular, but could not allow itself to be weak, or else a political crisis would become inevitable. Such a crisis did indeed occur in England after the death of Cromwell.[26]

The situation was much more acute in France in 1794–5 and in Russia in 1921–2.

The immediate macroeconomic result of the post-Jacobin liberalization of the economic régime in France was a catastrophic fall in the value of the *assignat* (owing to the abandonment of state price regulation) and, as a result, a rapid destabilization of urban–rural relations. In the autumn of 1794 the rate of paper currency issue accelerated noticeably, and from the middle of 1795 it took off in leaps and bounds (see Figures 7.4–7.7). The state remained weak, and appeared to be even weaker because spontaneous processes, including economic ones, were no longer being held in check by Jacobin coercion. As Georges Lefebvre described the situation: '[The] insurmountable obstacles raised by the premature reestablishment of economic freedom reduced the government to a state of extreme weakness. Lacking resources, it became almost incapable of administration, and the crisis generated troubles that nearly brought it to collapse' (1964: 143).

The Government printed money and prices started rising rapidly. In July 1794 the real value of the *assignat* was 33 per cent of its nominal value; a year later that figure was 3 per cent. The technical difficulties involved in restoring the circulation of metallic currency led to a rapid naturalization of commodity exchange. In 1795 Paris was hit by the worst famine of the revolutionary years.[27] The situation which had arisen was summed up strikingly by one of the deputies to the French Convention of 1795: 'If you destroy the Maximum, everything, that is true, will be dear; but if you keep it, there will be nothing left to be bought' (cited in Aftalion 1990: 167).

This catastrophic development was influenced both by the legacy of the

---

[26] Margaret James illustrated this well: 'It was natural for men to turn against the Government which had promised so much in the way of reconstruction, and performed so little. A writer of 1658, describing the ruin of trade, asked: 'Is it probable you can subsist much longer by imposed taxes without the people's affection...?'. Charles II was welcomed back as a saviour of trade no less than of the constitution' (1930: 76–7). For all the differences in their positions, both Margaret James and Maurice Ashley see the financial and budget crisis as the main reason for the fall of the Protectorate and the restoration of Charles II. The central chapter of Ashley's book, *Financial and Commercial Policy under the Cromwellian Protectorate*, is entitled 'The Public Debt and its Influence on the Fall of the Protectorate' (1962: 97–110).

[27] 'The Famine of Year III took place because dirigisme, requisitions, war, the Maximum and, above all, inflation had reduced agricultural production to chaos' (Aftalion 1990: 170; see also Dobrolyubsky 1930: 111–12, 117; Lefebvre 1965: 29). Another important factor here was that the peasants, deprived of any incentive by the Maximum, did not sow enough in the autumn of 1794 to satisfy the country's grain requirements. The Maximum was not abolished in time to affect the producers' behaviour, and this had its effect on the food supply in France.

Jacobin régime, and by changes in the social conjuncture, which reduced the dependence of the new leadership on the mood of the crowd. The policy of maintaining stable bread prices had undermined all incentives for peasant households to produce grain, but the decision of the Thermidorian government to induce producers to sell grain by raising the price for it in November 1794 came too late. In a situation in which the exchange of goods between town and country had broken down, the price rise had the opposite effect. A politician in the government wrote: 'the farmer, expecting higher prices or even the abolition of the Maximum, refused to sell grain for a low price, which in many places hardly covered the costs of labour, seed and harvesting' (cited in Dobrolyubsky 1930: 97).[28]

The unprecedented rise in inflation under the Thermidorian régime was brought about by the preceding compulsory maintenance of the exchange rate of the *assignat*, as well as by the Jacobin practice of allocating land for which payment was deferred to the long term. This measure bolstered the social base of the Jacobins, but in the medium term it deprived the government of a substantial source of revenue, and thereby further stimilated the uncontrolled price rises of 1794–5.[29] However, the ability of the government to pay less heed to the popularity of its policies allowed it to introduce a series of measures which were essential for economic recovery. At the end of 1794 and the beginning of 1795 the government abolished the Maximum, reverted to selling land at auction rather than distributing it among smallholders, and later felt itself secure enough to default on the major part of its debt and restore a normal tax system (see Dobrolyubsky 1930: ch. 2; Lefebvre 1965: 139–40).

The 'self-Thermidorizing' Bolshevik government began from the spring of 1921 to take measures to secure the economic and financial recovery of Soviet Russia. These measures were not based on ideology or doctrine, but on a sober assessment of the economic and political capabilities of the state. Food requisitioning was replaced by a tax in kind, which meant a repudiation of attempts to realize the communist principle of centralized allocation of all resources. The 'exchange of products' which was at first announced gave way in a matter of weeks to a real exchange of commodities through the medium of money.[30]

---

[28] So far as we can tell, this was one of the first cases of an erroneous understanding of how to influence a peasant economy through the price mechanism, in which an increase in procurement prices proves to be an economic disincentive. A similiar situation recurred with surprising regularity in both Russian revolutions, in the summer of 1917 and the autumn of 1990. In Russia, however, these analogous measures were taken in the pre-radical stage of the transformation.

[29] '[T]he leasing system, which delayed payments, proved catastrophic in the post-Thermidorian inflation' (Bouloiseau 1983: 185–6).

[30] 'Nothing came of exchange of commodities, the private market proved to be stronger than us, and instead of the exchange of commodities we got ordinary buying and selling, trade', remarked Lenin in autumn 1921 (*PSS* xliv. 208).

The government, as it became aware of its inability to ensure the restoration and stable functioning of industrial enterprises, not only denationalized small enterprises, but also distanced itself from the remaining state-owned enterprises. It introduced a legal principle that the state and state-owned self-financing enterprises were not responsible for each other's debts.[31] In 1922–3 the government successfully stabilized the monetary system using a parallel currency. This allowed the government for a time to print money to finance the post-war economy, whilst at the same time strengthening the position of the hard *chervonets*.

However, it was precisely in this phase that the socio-economic situation drastically deteriorated. First, to a much greater extent than before, the government met its needs by printing money, and in 1922 the average monthly supply of paper money tripled (see Figure 7.12). In 1920, while the civil war was still continuing, 87 per cent of state expenditure was covered by the printing press. In 1921, with no war, the figure was still 84 per cent. This was considerably worse than in 1918 and 1919 (67 per cent and 73 per cent respectively) (see Katsenelenbaum 1924: 66). Bearing in mind the time-lag involved, inflation in Russia reached its peak in 1922.[32]

Secondly, in 1921–2 large swathes of Russia were struck by a famine of appalling magnitude.[33] It was caused by a severe drought. However, as in France in 1795, the shortage of food came on top of not only the economic collapse, but also the removal of incentives in the radical phase. This could not fail to have an additional effect on food supply in the revolutionary country.

These two features of economic development—accelerating inflation and famine—in the post-radical, Thermidorian phase were practically identical for both France and Russia. This can easily be seen by comparing Figures 7.4, 7.5, and 7.6 with 7.10, 7.11, and 7.12, which show very similar patterns.

Finally, a common feature of the post-radical period is a severe budget crisis.[34]

The social and psychological dimension of the worsening economic crisis in this phase is an upsurge of nostalgia for the 'good old days' before the revolution. Rumours begin to circulate about the restoration of the old order,

---

[31] This position was laid down in the Soviet Decree on Trusts of 10 April 1923 (see Ginzburg 1926: 4).

[32] According to Dalin, the inflation of 1922 in Russia was at the time the highest level ever recorded. However, the following year the record was lost to Germany (see Dalin 1983: 228).

[33] The harvest failure covered 34 *gubernias* with a population of 30 million. The grain harvest for the entire country was just 40% of the annual average for the five years before the war, and in the famine-stricken regions that figure was considerably lower. The figures available suggest that nine million people starved, and two million children were orphaned (see *Ekonomicheskaya zhizn' SSSR*: 82, 108).

[34] The problems of budget crises and their place in a revolutionary economy is analysed in Ch. 9.

particularly since the policies of the government to a certain extent tend to encourage such ideas.

Documents with this sort of content began to appear with increasing frequency in London from the mid-1650s. For example, one petition circulating in London declared, '[Since] these seven years last past have almost devoured the Wealth and Credit that the City had for seven hundred years before ... [t]here is only one expedient to recover our Religion, Laws, Trade, that is a returning to the condition and State of Affairs where we began' (cited in James 1930: 75).[35]

Many similar statements were being made in France in the second half of the 1790s. Demands for the liberalization of prices at the end of 1794 became increasingly urgent, as people tired of the lack of the most essential commodities and of the need to queue for hours for foodstuffs. At the same time, there was increasing concern and even alarm among the urban population about the prospect of even higher inflation. As it turned out, these fears were well founded. The *Gazette Française* wrote as follows about the abolition of the Maximum: 'A part of the population, unfortunately, a large part, having become used to thinking about how to exist from day to day, cannot see the beneficial and absolutely essential reasons for abolishing this absurd law. Women in particular, most of whom cannot remember yesterday and cannot conceive of tomorrow, are beginning to express dissatisfaction' (15 Dec. 1794; cited in Dobrolyubsky 1930: 164).[36] Moreover, many ordinary citizens believed that the new economic realities merely allowed speculators to get rich and obliged everyone to engage in speculative trade—'if you want to live, you have to be a thief or a speculator'. From this flowed a more general conclusion, containing both political and economic aspects: 'until they curtail freedom, we shall never be happy' (see Dobrolyubsky 1930: 164, 166). Such a situation should encourage the growth of monarchist attitudes and, just as in England, there was much talk in France in 1795–6 of the need to restore Louis XVII as a precondition of general economic and political stabilization.

The political régime of Russia during the NEP did not change very much from that of 'war communism', and it is not possible to judge public attitudes to that régime from published sources. However, even the polemics in the press of the time about the future development of the NEP and the policies of 1918–20 allow us to conclude that similar attitudes were to be found. The degeneration of the régime was expected, and even within the ranks of the Bolsheviks themselves there were calls to abandon their monopoly of power (see Mau 1993: 122–3).

---

[35] According to Margaret James, such petitions and remonstrances were circulating widely in England in the latter half of the 1650s (1930: 75).

[36] It was observed at the time that women would often openly declare: 'Let them bring the King back, so long as we have bread!' (see Dobrolyubsky 1930: 25).

Thus, in the post-radical phase, the dominant sentiment is discontent with the economic situation, and interest in constitutional, legal, and political problems declines. People are prepared to accept any government that will bring more stability and order rather than democracy and freedom. Public opinion becomes relatively less important for the authorities—fatigue and disillusionment make spontaneous disturbances ineffectual and increasingly uncommon. From now on the main threats to the authorities are to be found within the ruling élite itself.

In addition, the economic situation gradually improves. This is the result, on the one hand, of the positive effects of the longer-term aspects of the new, post-radical economic policy, and, on the other hand, of the political changes that are under way. The government consolidates itself, and gains greater control of society, including the economy. At this point it is able to rely fully on the support of the new political élites. In France, Mexico, and Russia, the budget system stabilized and output began to increase.[37] Further economic advantages accrue from the political and military successes of the new régime. (This was particularly important in England and France.) The consolidation of power leads, albeit with a certain time-lag, to improvements in the economic situation. In this way, the revolutionary economic cycle reaches its conclusion. The subsequent development of the economy may be rapid or slow, smooth or crisis-ridden, but it is no longer determined by other political and social factors.

7.6 The revolutionary economic cycle: general trend and national peculiarities

Our analysis of the economic practice of the great revolutions of the past allows us to formulate a kind of general model of the revolutionary economic cycle. Like any generalization, this model simplifies the real course of events, and lacks the richness of real life. However, it helps us formulate clearly the most important characteristics of economic processes in a revolution, which in other approaches risk being concealed by specifics and petty details.

Figure 7.16 presents a generalized economic trend for a revolution. This graph shows the development of economic processes of revolution. In a generalized form these processes follow the curve *e*. Where *e* rises, this represents an improvement in the economic situation; a fall represents a deterioration.

---

[37] For example, after 1796 France experienced a deflationary crisis, but this was a sign of the recovery of the economy. The USSR experienced deflation in the spring of 1924, and by 1926 it had more or less reattained the economic level of 1913.

It is clear that the terms 'improvement' and 'deterioration' should be used with some care. The vertical axis of our graph is highly circumstancial, and there is no point in talking about a common scale for that axis. For the reasons we explained at the beginning of this chapter, it is impossible to make direct quantitative comparisons and describe the economic trends of different revolutions using the same (or even a quantitatively comparable) set of indices. In addition, improvements in some indicators may be accompanied by deterioration in others. This makes a formal comparative analysis even more difficult—but not impossible.

The horizontal axis on the figure represents the passage of time. For understandable reasons we have not measured time in months or years, but in logical stages in the development of socio-political and economic processes in a revolution. The specific points (R_1, R_2, R_3) denote stages in the revolutionary process, as they were set out in Chapter 4. The projections of points A to H show phases in the revolutionary economic cycle. In this way we can easily follow the relationship between the stages of the revolutionary process and the phases of the revolutionary economic cycle or crisis.

Figure 7.16 shows the following basic phases which together form the economic cycle of a revolution.

The *preparatory phase* (interval AB) is the run-up to a revolution. It is characterized by fairly rapid economic growth (over a period of 30–50 years), distinguished by substantial differences in the way the positions of existing socio-political groups and classes change. This growth destabilizes the traditional socio-political equilibrium, making the situation vulnerable to all kinds of external shocks, such as economic and political crises, reforms, and wars.

The *first phase* (interval BC) involves a rapid deterioration of the situation and the outbreak of the revolution (point R_1 on the horizontal axis). A government of moderates comes to power. The most striking features of this phase are a more or less serious financial crisis and a deterioration in the well-being of substantial sections of the population. The latter can have a variety of causes—poor harvests and the threat of famine, the disorganization of economic life in wartime, and so forth. In some cases there may be the beginnings of a decline in production in particular sectors of the economy, such as agriculture in the earlier revolutions, or industry in the revolutions of the twentieth century.

The *second phase* (interval CD) shows a certain improvement in the economic situation. There is social stabilization, linked to factors both political (hopes for a popular government) and economic. Both the financial situation and production trends improve. These temporary positive economic changes in the early stages of the work of the moderate government are a feature of many revolutions. The exception is Russia in 1917, which had already been embroiled in a world war for three years. The broken line between C and E shows the alternative, 'Russian' development pattern.

In the *third phase* (interval *DE*) the crisis intensifies sharply, and so does the socio-political struggle. There is an almost complete loss of government control over economic and financial processes. Production contracts, the standard of living continues to fall, the threat of hunger and cold (in northern countries and regions) becomes more real than ever before. This is almost invariably linked to the radicalization of the political régime (point R_2 on the horizontal axis).

In the *fourth phase* (interval *EF*) the economic situation continues to worsen under a radical political régime. The slump in production reaches its lowest point, and inflation remains on a high level. However, this stage in the deterioration of the economy has two important features.

First, in certain cases the assumption of power by the radicals can lead to improvements in certain aspects of economic life. For a short time, a firm mobilization régime can ensure stabilization, for example, in the financial sphere, or in certain branches of production, and it can organize and support an emergency system for supplying the population with basic foodstuffs. In other words, it can solve individual economic problems, and this allows us to speak of a short-term upward trend, after which the full-blown crisis reasserts itself. On Figure 7.16 this alternative, less likely course of events is shown by a broken line, and the point at which this trend comes to an end is designated E_1.

Secondly, the deterioration of the economic situation in the radical phase does not take the form of a complete collapse. The economic slump is already approaching its nadir, and the decisiveness and activity of the government means that these negative trends can at least be slowed somewhat, if not actually softened. However, the crisis continues to develop, and against this background the radical régime falls (point R_3).

The *fifth phase* (interval *FG*) is a new twist to the economic crisis which follows the fall of the radical régime. It is common at this stage for the living standards of a significant portion of the population to take a sharp turn for the worse, up to and including widespread famine. The crisis of state revenue also worsens, and this leads to a protracted budget crisis.

In the *sixth phase* (interval *GH*) there is gradual stabilization, and the country moves to a calmer, evolutionary path of economic development. Of course, not everything happens smoothly, but the currency stabilizes, finances gradually become more healthy, and production beings to rise. However, the pre-revolutionary level of economic development is only attained much later, and not in all areas at once.

We shall now trace this process with reference to the experience of the great revolutions of particular countries.

In *England in the mid-seventeenth century* rapid economic growth gave way to crisis, made worse by the poor harvests of the 1630s. The outbreak of war with Scotland made matters worse. The convocation of the Long Parliament, despite the conflict with the King which soon ensued, stabilized the situation for a certain amount of time. The legitimacy of Parliament allowed its government to pursue a responsible financial policy, which ensured a certain financial stability even in the Civil War years. However, in the second half of the 1640s, as the Civil War became more intense, the economic position of the country and its population deteriorated. Later, in the first half of the 1650s, economic life became more active, although conditions remained very unstable. Then the situation deteriorated rapidly, and against this background the Restoration took place. It was not until the mid-1660s that the economy was clearly emerging from the crisis.

In *France at the end of the eighteenth century* the economy had grown rapidly between 1770 and 1786. Then a severe economic crisis ensued, which expressed itself in a slump in agricultural output (especially in grain and viticulture), and in a crisis of state finances. 1790 and 1791 were marked by stabilization and a certain improvement in the situation of the people, although Parisian industry showed all the signs of stagnation. Then from the end of 1791 the country slid into a profound economic crisis. During 1793 and 1794 the situation continued to deteriorate, and by mid-1794 the Jacobin régime had fallen. At the end of 1794 the food crisis broke out, which turned into a widespread famine. Inflation accelerated, and in 1795–6 it reached a record level for the whole revolutionary period. Thereafter the situation gradually stabilized, although the budget crisis persisted in France throughout the first decade of the nineteenth century.

Mexico at the beginning of the twentieth century had experienced rapid growth from the 1870s. In 1908–10 there was a crisis, accompanied by widespread famine. In 1910–12 the revolution broke out, and economic conditions stabilized in this period—production increased and the value of the currency remained stable. Thereafter, there was a profound slump in production, and inflation began and accelerated in 1912–14. The crisis continued in 1915–16, with inflation reaching its highest level, but growing military demand brought on by the First World War led to growth in some sectors of the economy. The end of the war and the reduction of military demand gave a new twist to the crisis, which was overcome as the political situation stabilized and the post-revolutionary régime was consolidated in the course of the 1920s.

In *Russia at the beginning of the twentieth century* the rapid economic growth of the periods from the 1870s to the 1890s and from 1908 to 1914 gave way to an economic crisis brought on by the war. Production was gradually becoming disorganized, and inflation was developing. The outbreak of revolution was not accompanied by any temporary economic stabilization, and as a result a radical government came to power eight months later. The civil war of 1918–20 precluded any improvement in the economic situation. The abandonment of the radicalism of 'war communism' at the beginning of 1921 created the preconditions for overcoming the crisis. However, it was in 1921–2 that the country experienced the most terrible famine and a sharp rise in paper currency inflation. Against this background economic growth began.

The analysis in this chapter would be incomplete if we did not pay attention to economies operating for long periods in conditions of crisis. There are several examples of this in world economic history (especially twentieth-century history), involving crises which resemble revolutionary crises, but which develop in different economic and political circumstances. Such crises occur under a weak state, which lacks a mechanism for solving problems in a way generally acceptable to leading socio-economic groups, and in which the political authorities are unable to realize their aims in a consistent fashion. In such circumstances, events can develop in the following way.

To begin with, a country descends into a state of permanent economic crisis, with an unstable currency and financial system, budget crises, and stagnant or declining production. This course of events (apart from cases of war and long-term armed hostility such as in the Middle East) is generally linked to profound political change accompanied by attempts to overcome the country's socio-economic problems decisively and quickly. These are situations either close to revolution, or actual cases of 'revolution from above'. This was the nature of the most significant political changes in Brazil (the *coup d'état* of Vargas in 1930), Argentina (Peron), and Chile (the Popular Unity victory in 1970). In all these cases the new governments, which had come to power on a wave of economic and political crisis, found themselves obliged not only to introduce reforms, but to demonstrate positive results quickly.[38]

The processes of change that they began were sufficient to lay claim to the epithet 'revolutionary', and their populist nature and the way they were implemented are also very similar to the actions of the 'early revolutionary government'. The consequences were also similar. In the initial stage the transformations had a positive socio-economic effect (wages and employment levels rose, although reserves of precious metals were exhausted), but before long these positive trends were replaced by an acute economic crisis. (See Dornbusch and Edwards 1991: 11–12. The applicability of this model to present-day Russia will be examined in the next chapter.) The subsequent course of events can proceed along one of two lines.

The first scenario is a victory for the counter-revolution, or at least for a régime which is 'counter-revolutionary' in relation to the revolutionaries of the preceding, populist government. The new régime restores political order, and strengthens the mechanisms for exercising political power. On that basis it can then carry out more cautious reforms, for which the time is ripe and which, albeit within a different political and ideological setting, the previous, overthrown régime had been trying to bring about. This was the scenario that

---

[38] The need to show quick results arises either because the régime lacks legitimacy, as in Brazil, or because it is not sufficiently politically stable, as in Chile.

developed in Chile. In its most important aspects it differs little from that of the interrupted revolutions in Germany in 1848 or Russia in 1905.

The other scenario is that the first régime can degenerate into a military dictatorship, abandon the aim of reforming the system, stop or reverse its own reforms, and then operate solely with a view to its own survival. The social problems which brought about the original change of government remain unsolved, and the unwillingness of the authorities to deal with them makes the crisis permanent. The firmness of the political régime and/or its support from outside (for example, for geopolitical considerations) allows it to remain in power for a long time, despite all the pressing problems of that society. This variant differs little from an extreme case of the long-term survival of an inefficient dictatorship which is strong enough to prevent serious economic and political change, but too weak to take consistent measures to pull the economy out of crisis.[39] Obviously, these sorts of cases have nothing to do with the economic crisis of a revolution.

These final considerations lead us to draw yet another general conclusion: the characteristics and tendencies of the revolutionary economic cycle do not in themselves add up to a revolution. The existence of similar trends in other circumstances and historical epochs did not necessarily denote the existence or maturity of revolutionary processes. It is, rather, the other way round—profound revolutionary changes, if they take place in a certain country, will be accompanied by economic processes resembling those discussed in this chapter.

---

[39] The course of events in such cases is determined by the balance of forces between group interests and their ability to influence the government. In recent works on political economy this situation is described as the problem of the 'weak dictator'. These works analyse the mechanisms which can prevent for a long time any solution to the problems of macroeconomic stabilization and the achievement of sociopolitical stability in a given country. For more detail, see Alesina (1992).

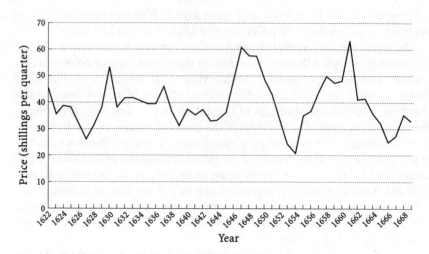

Figure 7.1 Annual harvests classified by quality, England, 1620–1669

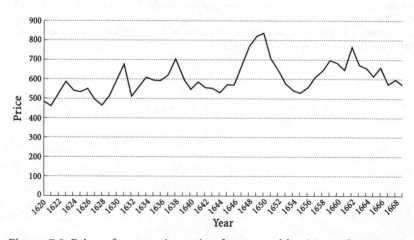

Figure 7.2 Price of composite unit of consumables in southern England, 1620–1669

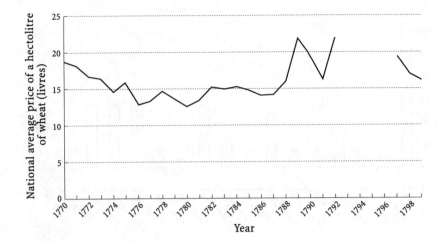

Figure 7.3 Price of wheat, France, 1770–1779

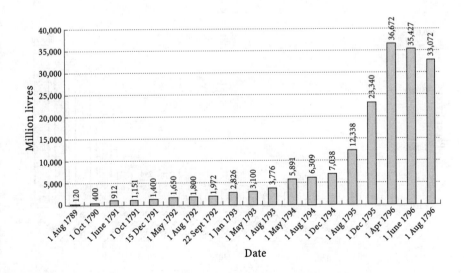

Figure 7.4 Quantity of paper money in circulation, France, 1789–1796

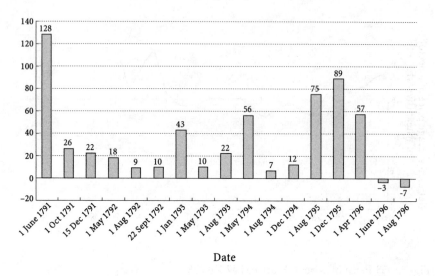

Figure 7.5 Change of quantity of paper money in circulation, France, 1789–1796

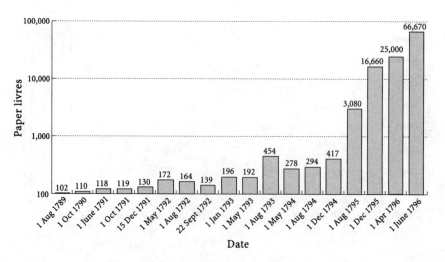

Figure 7.6 Rate for 100 silver livres in paper livres, 1789–1796

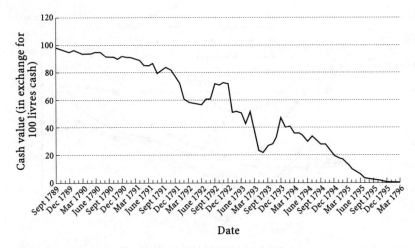

Figure 7.7 Cash value of the *assignat*, France, 1789–1796

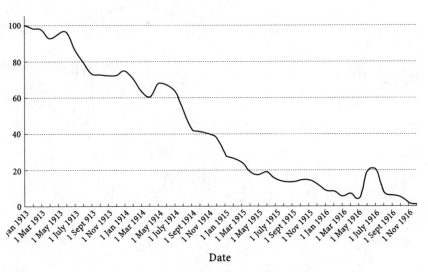

Figure 7.8 Value of Mexican banknotes against US dollar, 1913–1916

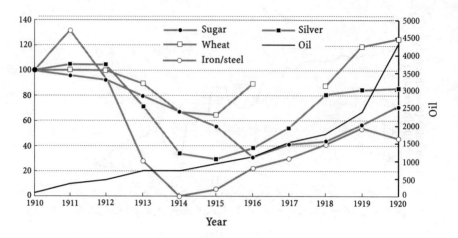

Figure 7.9 Output of various products, Mexico, 1910–1920

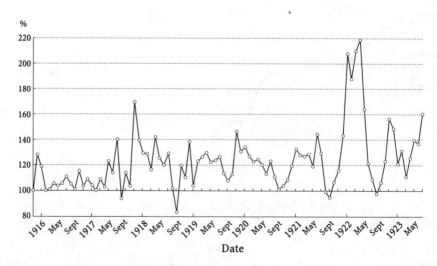

Figure 7.10 Price index, Russia, 1913–1922

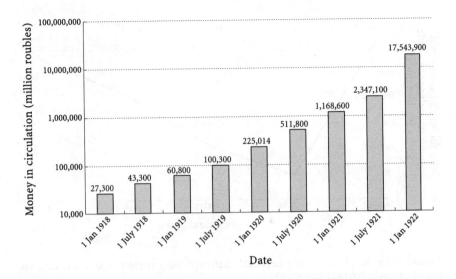

Figure 7.11 Quantity of paper money in circulation, Russia, 1918–1922

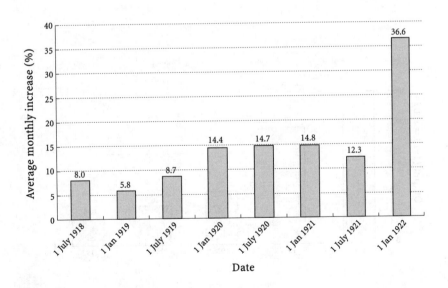

Figure 7.12 Average monthly increase in the quantity of paper money in circulation, Russia, 1918–1922

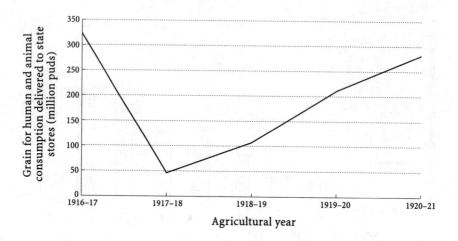

Figure 7.13 Total state procurement through requisition and exchange of goods, Russia, 1916/17–1920/21

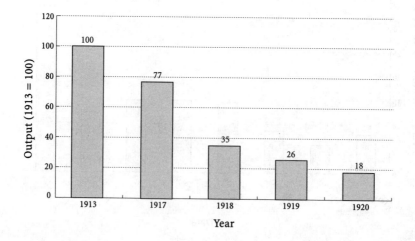

Figure 7.14 Decline in industrial output during First World War and civil war, Russia, 1913–1920

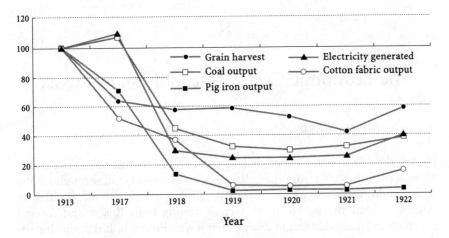

Figure 7.15 Output of various products, Russia, 1913–1922

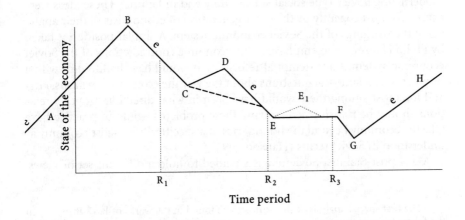

Figure 7.16 The development of economic processes during a revolution

8

The Economic Cycle of Revolution in Russia

8.1 The USSR: economic reform and economic crisis

During the 1990s Russia experienced a profound economic crisis. The country inherited the crisis from the collapsing Soviet Union, and throughout the 1990s could not manage to overcome it. Although there are many differing opinions about the nature of this crisis among both Russia and foreign experts, almost nobody would dispute that it was directly linked to the destabilization of the Soviet economy in the second half of the 1980s.

Various explanations have been advanced in recent economic literature for the failure of the reform efforts of the Gorbachev administration and the outbreak of economic crisis in the USSR.

First, there is the interpretation to be found in the works of the older critics of the Soviet system, the 'hard-liners' of Sovietology. Their views are based on the fundamental premise that any attempt to improve socialism (or, more accurately, Soviet communism)—particularly in the direction of 'market socialism'—is fanciful and unrealistic. Only a normal capitalist market economy can be an efficient economy, and any reforms aimed at improving or modernizing Soviet-type socialism can only end in failure.[1] These ideas were expressed most cogently by the older generation of economists in their analyses of the workings of the Soviet economic system. A similar position is taken by Philip Hanson, who emphasizes the economic contradictions of the Soviet economic system. Any attempt at reforming it would have had to deal with a number of fundamental questions about the way the economy functions. First and foremost among these would have been in what direction property relations should be transformed. Solving these problems would in practice have take the economy beyond the boundaries of a specifically socialist economy as understood in Soviet terms (Hanson 1992).[2]

Many post-Stalinist Sovietologists tended to hold a different set of views.

---

[1] The first special analysis of this sort is to be found in the works of B. D. Brutskus. In the following generation of economists a similar system of arguments was developed in detail by A. Bergson. See Brutskus (1922); Bergson (1966, 1967: 663–75).

[2] It should be noted that the works of Hanson were always quite distinct from those of the 'Sovietological mainstream', in that he took a more right-wing and 'economics-oriented' position than was usual among Sovietologists.

They believed that a reform of the Soviet economy was feasible, although this would be a difficult task. Reforms would require the solution of a series of complex problems, which in part contradicted each other. A temporary deterioration in the situation would be inevitable during a reform process. For the changes to be carried through successfully, they would need to be implemented in a controlled and gradual way.[3] If either the political élite or the population were unwilling to exercise restraint, then crisis and political struggle could only intensify.

Some of the proponents of this school of thought subsequently modified their positions. They stressed the mistakes of Gorbachev and his colleagues, and blamed them for the fact that the outcome of *perestroyka* was considerably worse than they had anticipated (see e.g. Goldman 1991)[4]. Naturally enough, this argument became particularly popular after the collapse of the USSR and the removal of Gorbachev. Similar interpretations are to be found in most of the Soviet and post-Soviet analytical works and memoirs of participants in the events between 1985 and 1991.

The interpretation of Egor Gaidar is substantially different. He has shown that the Gorbachev–Ryzhkov government was from the very outset severely restricted by the legacy of the economic policies pursued between 1973 and 1984. The economic crisis at the end of the 1980s was not so much the result of their mistakes as a consequence of the flow of petrodollars which had pulled the Soviet system out of its condition of stagnating equilibrium (Gaidar 1997*a*: 450)[5]. Gaidar does not deny that the Gorbachev leadership made mistakes, but he argues that they were not the prime cause of the crisis which struck the Soviet economy in the course of *perestroyka*.

A number of other writers have taken a similar position. They see the crisis which broke out at the end of the 1980s as the result of an unsuccessful attempt by the Soviet leadership to effect a transition to a higher technological level, to adapt the socialist socio-economic system to the challenges of the post-industrial age (see e.g. Rosser and Rosser 1997). The economy was incapable of adjusting to these new challenges (particularly to new technology),

---

[3] 'To change everything at once is impossible, but partial change creates contradictions and inconsistencies', wrote Alec Nove at the time (quoted in Hosking 1990: 133–4).

[4] It is noteworthy that these sorts of views were to a considerable extent intended to excuse the predictions of the 'Sovietological mainstream', the erroneous nature of which had become obvious to everyone by the end of 1991.

[5] In summing up the results of his analysis, Gaidar stresses that 'an objective assessment of the factors we have set out, and of the very nature of the economic growth which took place in the 1970s and early 1980s, obliges us to admit that the economic mistakes of Gorbachev and Ryzhkov did not play as large a part in the collapse of socialism as is generally believed . . . These mistakes determined only the duration and the specific mechanisms of the crisis, but not its nature or scale. *The crisis itself was inevitable*' (Gaidar 1997*a*: 450, our emphasis).

while the state for the last time attempted to use its diminishing mobilization potential, rooted in the industrial age, to break away from industrialism.

Finally, there has been speculation about the social nature of the crisis in its initial phase. It is argued that the direction of the economic reforms of 1985–8 was correct, but that there was a change in the balance of social forces when the majority of the élite opted for the market rather than for democratic socialism. This proved fatal, in that it led to the collapse of the reform effort and initiated a profound economic crisis (Kotz with Weir 1997: 73–80).

There are elements of truth in all of these explanations. The reforms were indeed very complex, and many mistakes were made. The very idea of 'market socialism' at the end of the twentieth century was unrealistic. However, the unreality of the goal does not account for the speed of the collapse, and the complexity of the problem does not fully explain the large number of mistakes made. The *ancien régime* was too stable to collapse quickly simply on account of the incompetence of its new leadership.

In our opinion, the fullest picture emerges when we are able to see the specific features of a revolutionary economic crisis amongst the mass of peculiarities and problems of the late Soviet and Russian transformation. Even a superficial glance at the economic developments of 1985–2000 reveals the characteristic tendencies of economic life in a revolutionary period, and the usual range of economic problems which face society and the state at such times. For this reason we shall analyse the economic crisis in the Russia of the 1990s in terms of our findings in the preceding chapter. We shall make particular use of our general model of the economic cycle of revolution (see Figure 7.16).

The economic development of the USSR and Russia in the 1980s and '90s can be regarded as a crisis which progressed inexorably as the state weakened, whilst the first signs that the trend was reversing became apparent as state power began to strengthen. The lengthy duration of the economic crisis, which certain politicians and economists have claimed to be unprecedented in peacetime, is in fact not unusual for periods of revolutionary upheaval. In other words, the nature of the economic processes in Russia is determined not by a state of war or by short-term market fluctuations, but by social and political developments.

Indeed, economic processes in Russia between 1985 and 2000 in general resemble the specific pattern of economic dynamics that we examined in Chapter 7 (see Figures 8.1, 8.2, 8.4, 8.5, 8.6, and 8.8).

The impetus to initiate fundamental changes was provided by growing economic difficulties. These quickly acquired a revolutionary character (see interval *BC* in Figure 7.16). The new government's initial measures were accompanied by some positive developments in the economy between 1986 and 1988 (interval *CD* in Figure 7.16). However, mistakes of the new authorities meant that from 1989 the overall economic situation deteriorated, and this was followed by a further weakening of state power (interval *DE*). The collapse of production gathered pace, inflation accelerated, and the system of state finances broke down.

The transition of the revolution to its radical phase was marked by a certain, short-lived improvement in the economic situation (interval EE_1). More accurately, the situation improved (stabilized) in some respects, but in other respects the crisis continued and worsened. In particular, the radicalization of economic policy at the end of 1991 and beginning of 1992 meant that the intractable shortage of goods, the most typical feature of the communist system, was overcome. The prospect of cold and hunger which threatened the country, particularly its major industrial centres, at the onset of winter 1991/2 receded (interval E_1E). However, it was followed by a long period of overt high inflation and a deepening decline in production (interval E_1F). Moreover, at the end of 1994 and beginning of 1995 there was a sharp deterioration in the state of the economy, and the country faced a situation which in many respects resembled that of the end of 1991 (interval *FG*).

Finally, we observe the slowing down of the rate of inflation and economic decline, followed by signs of a shift to economic growth in 1996–7 and again in 1999–2000. This coincided naturally in time (and logically) with the strengthening of state power (interval *GH*).

8.2 The final attempt at reforming the Soviet economy and the beginning of the revolutionary economic cycle

In Chapter 3 we examined the symptoms of crisis which impelled Mikhail Gorbachev to initiate reforms. The first years of the reform process, *perestroyka*, showed a certain improvement, as may be seen from the indices for production and consumption (see Figures 8.1–8.4). According to both Western and Soviet figures, between 1986 and 1988 the rates of growth of GNP, national income, and consumption increased. Whereas in 1981–5 the average annual rate of GNP growth was 1.8 per cent, in 1986 GNP rose by 4.1 per cent, and by 2.1 per cent in 1988. From 1984 onwards investment increased by 6–8 per cent per annum. In 1987 wages began to increase more rapidly, and the annual rate of increase of private incomes approached 10 per cent in money terms. It was at this time, according to the official statistics, that per capita consumption of basic foodstuffs reached its highest level. In any case, it would seem that despite all the experiments and populism of the 'government of moderates', up to 1989 growth rates remained positive (see Joint Economic Committee 1990: 58, 1993: 14, 17; IMF 1992: 41, 43, 49).

This positive trend covers the period of the mobilization campaign to reform the Soviet economy under the slogan of 'acceleration' (*uskoreniye*) and the first few years of democratization and *glasnost'*. The crisis in its overt form developed later—in 1989 and 1990. This pattern of economic development initially raised the hopes of some Sovietologists for a gradual, successful transformation of the Soviet system. It also subsequently led certain Western economists to conclude that the last Soviet leadership had indeed set the country on course for genuine democratic socialism, a development that was blocked by an unexpected political conflict, in the course of which a significant section of the party and state élite opted for capitalism.[6] However, this line of argument cannot account for the economic decline—if it is the élite which takes over, it has the chance to control socio-economic processes rather than play with fire and bring about a twofold decline in output.

Moreover, the way in which this crisis developed is not unprecedented in economic history. It can be explained without recourse to 'social conspiracies' or forces with an interest in the destruction of socialism. In reality, the explanation is both simpler and more complicated. In purely economic terms this was a crisis of populist economic policy, which many countries have undergone during the twentieth century. At the same time it was a typical crisis for the early stage of a revolutionary process. The peculiarities of that stage also greatly affected the USSR's economic development in the second half of the 1980s. There were therefore two groups of factors which determined the specific features of the Soviet economy in that period. We shall examine them further.

A populist economic policy is an attempt at a quick solution of fundamental economic problems, such as a need for industrial growth or higher living standards, by means which involve the mobilization of the population. Dictatorial régimes usually concentrate on solving the growth problem, while improvements in living standards are—at best—postponed. Stalinist industrialization followed this pattern. In democratic societies both problems have to be tackled simultaneously, and this almost invariably leads to an economic and political crisis. The most striking example of this sort of development is Chile in the early 1970s.

As Dornbusch and Edwards have shown (1991: 11–12), populist policies generally pass through four consecutive phases.

In the *first* phase, the government tries to accelerate industrial growth by transferring resources from export sectors to import substitution, often into heavy industry. It also tries to boost demand by decreeing wage increases. The economy does indeed begin to grow, and living standards rise. The impression is created that the government has achieved major successes, and that the

---

[6] These views are set out in their most consistent form in Kotz with Weir (1997). Similar positions are taken by Michael Ellman and Vladimir Kontorovich, although in their analysis they do not go so far as to conclude that there was a '*nomenklatura* revolution' in the USSR. See Ellman and Kontorovich (1992: 19–30).

country is on the verge of an economic miracle. The popularity of the government rises considerably.

In the *second* phase, the economy runs into bottlenecks, and imbalances begin to manifest themselves. It turns out that the growth of production and of living standards are accompanied by a deterioration across a range of macroeconomic indices—the deficits in the balance of trade and in the balance of payments increase, currency reserves fall, foreign debt rises. For a time, however, these negative changes are visible only to professional economists (and not to all of them, if the country has been divorced from real market economics for long enough). Difficulties arise with the state budget, but few pay any attention to these 'short-term minor problems', given the acceleration in the rates of industrial growth.

In the *third* phase there is a rapidly growing shortage of goods, extreme acceleration of inflation, capital flight, and demonetization of the economy. Attempts to freeze prices aggravate the goods shortage, and the inevitable devaluation of the national currency gives a further impetus to inflation. Taxes become more difficult to collect, and the state budget collapses. Whatever measures the government recourse to, living standards decline and production contracts.

In the *fourth* phase the government falls, and the new authorities, often a military or emergency government, take radical measures to stabilize the situation.

This model is wholly applicable to the development of the USSR during the second half of the 1980s. Soviet statistics were fairly scanty, and were intended more to conceal than to reveal real tendencies. However, the data that we do have for the development of the budget deficit, external debts, and the trade balance allow us to describe the development of the Soviet economy as, characteristically, a movement towards a profound economic crisis of the populist type. The attempt at a socio-economic breakthrough led to a considerable increase in demand for both producer and consumer goods, a significant proportion of which had to be imported. The volume of imports rose rapidly, while exports, by contrast, fell. In 1989, for the first time in many years, the USSR had a negative trade balance.[7] External debt in 1989 was double, and in 1991 three times, the level of 1985 (see Figures 8.5, 8.6, and 8.7).

Thus, macroeconomic developments were heading steadily towards a crisis, and this trend could be observed from the very outset of the project of

---

[7] It is understandable that to a certain extent the decline in exports would be the result of the fall in the world price for oil. At first, between 1986 and 1988, attempts were made to make up the losses from falling prices by increasing the volume of energy resources exported. Even under these conditions, foreign currency earnings nonetheless declined. By the time that the price of oil on the world market began to rise again after 1989, the USSR's oil output had already begun to decline, and the physical volume exported also began to fall.

socialist renewal. This course of events was not entirely without precedent in the economic history of the USSR. The development of the Soviet economic system had also been characterized by a certain cyclical trend, which had been dubbed the 'socialist investment cycle'. This cycle typically contained the following phases: (1) the realization of an investment programme; (2) a slowing of growth rates; (3) liberalization measures; (4) faster growth rates; (5) greater macroeconomic imbalances; (6) rejection of liberal reforms and the start of a new investment programme (see Bajt 1971: 53–63; Bauer 1978: 243–60; Ickes 1986: 36–52). This raises a question which is vitally important in order to understand Soviet economic development under *perestroyka*: what happens if the conservative reaction does not take place?

The particular way in which economic policy was formulated and implemented in the initial stages of the revolution was in many respects determined by specific economic developments. It was a two-sided process, in which the relaxation of state control (or decentralization of economic administration) made the symptoms of the crisis worse, and this in its turn contributed to a further weakening of state power.

The main components of the economic reform package adopted by the Gorbachev administration were as follows: (1) greater independence for socialist enterprises (which were to become fully separate, self-financing entities, with partial administrative autonomy); (2) the development of individual and co-operative forms of property; and (3) capital investment from abroad in the form of joint ventures (see *O korennoy perestroyke* 1987). The contradictions in this programme have been described in some detail in the economic literature (see e.g. Joyce *et al.* 1989; Golman 1991; Boettke 1993), and we need not dwell on them here. We shall merely look at certain aspects of them which are particularly important for our analysis.

First and foremost, the microeconomic limitations of this plan came to light. As soon as enterprises were granted greater freedom, they tended to orient themselves towards consumption at the expense of investment. Moreover, the weakening of central control was accompanied by a set of measures to increase the role of labour collectives at the expense of management. The introduction of elections for managers was a typical reflection of the mode of thinking of the moderate government. It was trying to implement new, non-standard ways of rapidly improving socio-economic conditions. Instead this measure had negative consequences[8], both economically and socially. On the one hand, it exacerbated the economic crisis, because the increased indepen-

---

[8] The Bolsheviks tried something similar immediately after they seized power. However, they were also able to change track very speedily, as soon as it became clear how politically and economically damaging this policy was. But they were able to do this because they were already in the radical phase of the revolution, in which they were no longer concerned with popularity but with immediate political expediency. For more detail, see Mau (1993: 63–4).

dence of enterprises was not underpinned by measures to make them more accountable for the outcome of their activities. On the other hand, it undermined the position of the director as *de facto* 'owner' of the enterprise, a position which had become quite evident by the mid-1980s. This exacerbated the problem which arises in all revolutions of bringing the *de jure* and *de facto* status of property owners into line.

The result was a rather paradoxical situation in which the directors of enterprises were effectively freed from the control of the state bureaucracy, but did not come under the control of either a real owner, or the market. The temptation to act in a populist and/or criminal manner in these circumstances was extraordinarily strong. Directors were pushed towards populism by their unaccustomed dependence on the labour collectives, who were interested in rapid wage increase and a greater consumption fund. How far in reality directors were dependent on these collectives was at first not entirely clear.[9] They were also pushed towards criminality by the new opportunities for private entrepreneurial activity. For a long time the question of reforming property rights was not even raised—until 1990 or thereabouts.[10]

This half-hearted approach to reforming the traditional sectors and forms of property was combined with a readiness on the part of the authorities to resort to exceptionally stringent and inadequately thought-out measures in the new areas of economic activity. The *de facto* recognition of the co-operatives as real private enterprises was not accompanied by the establishment of suitable legal mechanisms to prevent criminal collaboration between co-operative and fully self-financing state enterprises. What is more, the traditional Soviet values even encouraged the creation of 'co-operatives' attached to state enterprises. At a later stage an analogous situation arose with the commercial banks, which were able to spring up in the USSR much more easily than in countries with a developed market economy.

Another key factor which affected the economic trend was democratization. Some people have argued that in 1989 Gorbachev could have continued with the policy of democratization whilst tightening the economic regime and implementing various unpopular measures, particularly on price and fiscal matters (Kotz with Weir 1997: 86). However, things were not so simple. At this particular juncture the development of democracy was incompatible with

[9] The proportion of enterprise profits which went to develop production fell from 57.5 to 35.9 %, whereas the proportion which went on consumption rose from 21.4 to 38.1%. (Sinel'nikov 1995: 60).

[10] This indifference to the transformation of property relations was shared by many Western Sovietologists. It would seem that they, too, had been 'hypnotized'—first, by the political impossibility of privatization in the USSR, and then by the internal logic of the Soviet reformers' programme, which seemed quite comprehensive even in the absence of any transformation of property rights. The works of Hanson stand out as one of the few cases where this problem was understood in the West (see e.g. Hanson 1988).

carrying out any responsible macroeconomic policy. In the first half of 1989 the government came under the firm control of the people's deputies, amongst whom populist attitudes predominated.[11] The Soviet leadership, though it was partially aware of the destructive nature of populist politics,[12] was unable to reduce budget expenditure while remaining within the constitutional boundaries it had itself proclaimed.

The government's weakness was most apparent in the area of price reform. This showed itself in two ways. On the one hand, the ill-conceived expansion of the rights of enterprises led to a rapid growth of wages followed by the collapse of the consumer market, requiring immediate measures to balance supply and demand. The government of Nikolai Ryzhkov took no such measures. Not only did it reject full price liberalization (there had never been any question of that), it did not even increase prices to the level of market equilibrium.

On the other hand, as the government weakened, it attempted to make use of the price mechanism to strengthen its position. In order to raise its standing among influential economic agents, the USSR government, from the autumn of 1990, started taking measures gradually to raise enterprises' wholesale prices, even by effectively releasing them from state control. This was done in competition with the Russian Federation leadership, which had been preparing to take similar measures itself. Retail prices remained untouched. Consequently, not only did the goods shortages worsen, but state revenue decreased (its main source was a turnover tax as the difference between fixed wholesale and retail prices) while state expenditure increased (from subsidizing retail prices).

A similar situation was developing in agriculture. In the autumn of 1990 the USSR Council of Ministers increased prices for foodstuffs procurements, which was remarkable for at least two reasons. First, given the shortages of almost all goods, the increase clearly undermined the incentive of agricultural producers to sell their produce, as they now needed to sell less to cover their cash needs for purchases and taxes. Secondly, this measure almost exactly repeated the actions of the Provisional Government in a similar situation in

[11] Ryzhkov and many members of his 1989–90 administration also complained about this. For example, the USSR Minister of Energy and Electrification at the time, Yuri Semenov, wrote: 'The Ryzhkov government lacked the will and backbone to take a firm line and not give way to the Supreme Soviet or the President' (see Nenashev 1993: 184). In fact, the problem was not only that the ministers were insufficiently decisive or courageous, but also that the constitutional and legal status of the different branches of the cabinet was very hazy.

[12] In December 1988 the CPSU Politburo discussed a memorandum produced by Otto Latsis and Egor Gaidar which dealt with the growing financial crisis in the USSR. The leadership was inclined towards adopting restrictive financial measures. However, once the new, democratically elected Congress of Deputies started work in May 1989, it was able to hinder such measures indefinitely. For more detail, see Mau (1996b: 49–51).

1917. To a significant degree, it also mirrored the situation in France in the autumn of 1794 (see Chapters 5 and 7). As in the earlier revolutions, the government's actions served only to worsen the shortage of agricultural produce.

The government lost its ability to collect taxes. First, these functions were increasingly taken over by the constituent Union republics, which were demanding the introduction of a single-channel tax system and a say in determining how much was needed to finance the federal centre. By acceding to this demand, the USSR government fell directly and entirely into dependence upon attitudes within the Union republics.

Secondly, the government of the USSR was unable to introduce its own tax policies, even though it could have done so quite constitutionally, and would have had the support of the legislature. The most striking example of this situation was the attempt to introduce a sales tax. This tax was similar to VAT, and would in some measure have reflected the new economic realities—price stability had gone, and so, therefore, had the stability of turnover tax revenues. The attempt to introduce the sales tax at the end of 1990 and the beginning of 1991 failed completely. A significant proportion of economic agents, and subsequently regions, gained exemptions from this tax, and the number of 'exceptions to the rule' soon made the tax itself pointless.

Thirdly, both the federal and the republican governments were compelled by the pressure of circumstances from the autumn of 1990 onwards to reduce tax rates in an attempt to win over influential pressure groups. Governments at various levels began to compete over who would reduce taxes further and faster, because the governments hoped in this way to bring enterprises under their jurisdiction. This race to reduce tax rates was taking place at a time when the deficit in the USSR state budget was approaching 10 per cent of GNP.

Finally, there was a developing 'war' of economic programmes. Various power centres and groups of economists working for them were all busily devising programmes for overcoming the crisis and further reforming the Soviet economic system. This 'war of the programmes' clearly exemplified processes which typify this phase of the revolution. The position of the political centre was being eroded, while the position of forces proposing solutions based on a more consistent logic was getting stronger.

The official programme of the USSR government was prepared under the direction of Leonid Abalkin, the deputy Prime Minister responsible for economic reform. This was a typical document for a 'government of moderates' at the stage when its political power is being eroded. Its authors, recognizing that there were three main variants being proposed for bringing in anti-crisis measures and market reforms—the radical-liberal, the moderate, and the conservative—naturally declared their adhesion to the second way (see Gorbachev 1995: 566–7; Ryzhkov 1995: 414–28). The moderate variant did indeed seem to be the most sensible and justifiable. It rejected both a rapid move to a market economy through liberalization and privatization, and the conservation of existing economic relations with a greater use of administrative principles in running the economy (which would have meant rejecting the recent democratic advances). This moderate route avoided extremes, and promised the 'smoothest' and 'most painless' transition to a market economy. However, this plan had one serious defect—there were no longer any social forces (interest groups) prepared to support it, and the 'moderate government' had exhausted its credibility.

Alongside the 'Abalkin programme', two fundamentally different approaches to overcoming the crisis were developing in the USSR. These were essentially packages of measures proposed for immediate adoption which were being discussed in Soviet society. They did not take the form of a concrete, published document, although some of them were also produced as formal programmes.

By the beginning of the 1990s the liberal-market proposals for action had in practice been developed and put forward. Their basic elements were an open recognition of the need for privatization and price liberalization. The most succinct expositions of these positions were to be found in the '*500 Days* programme', produced in autumn 1990 under the guidance of Sergei Shatalin and Grigori Yavlinsky, and in the programme of market reforms put forward in autumn 1991 by Egor Gaidar and his colleagues. The political conflict between these leaders created the popular impression that these two documents represented alternatives, that they somehow presented opposite roads to stabilization and the market. In fact, the differences between the programmes were a product solely of the different times during which they were devised. When *500 Days* was written, there was little expectation that it would be implemented straight away. It was seen more as a political manifesto in the conflict between the institutions of power of the Soviet Union and the Russian Federation, at a time when the latter were inclined to demonstrate their more 'market-democratic' nature. This document bore many of the hallmarks of the early phase of the revolution, in that it was populist and all-embracing. It promised to carry out reforms 'without lowering living standards', so that all social groups would benefit. Gaidar's programme, on the other hand, was produced in a situation in which the Union centre had already collapsed, and the entire burden of political responsibility for the subsequent course of events lay with the Russian authorities. They were now obliged to act, to undertake practical measures to implement an anti-crisis programme. Consequently, the document they adopted had a more practical, technocratic character.[13]

---

[13] A typical example, which illustrates the differences in approach between these two documents, can be seen in their attitude to privatization and price liberalization. Yavlinsky proposed starting with privatization. This was in accordance with his theory, and was

At the same time another model was coming into being, which we can describe as the 'administrative stabilization' model. It attracted those social and economic groups who saw that too rapid a transition to the market threatened the stability of their position. This approach was to halt the processes of political democratization, to increase the role of administrative organs in the Soviet economy, to restore order (including macroeconomic order) and on this basis implement measures to strengthen the Soviet economy. In a certain sense this approach was reminiscent of the Chinese path to modernization in the 1980s.

The market and administrative programmes had two features in common. First, their authors clearly understood the political basis of the economic crisis and the need to reinforce political authority as a precondition for overcoming the crisis. Secondly, the political groups which stood behind these programmes were prepared to take responsibility for implementing them. The danger this presented for political reputations was quite clear. However, the recognition of the need to choose between the alternatives and the existence of fairly solid social support for each of them strengthened the positions of their leading advocates and pushed them onto the offensive.

This is a fairly common situation in a revolution, but it was modified in Russia by two circumstances. From the end of 1990 a typical 'war of attrition' was waged (Alesina and Drazen 1994: 389–93), in which the representatives of each of the two opposing doctrines looked to the other side to make the first move, that is, to take the first, painful measures necessary for either variant (primarily, balancing or liberalizing prices) and thereby discrediting themselves, to leave the political scene.[14]

The first attempt at implementing a more or less consistent anti-crisis programme was undertaken in 1991 when Nikolai Ryzhkov resigned and a new cabinet was formed under Valentin Pavlov. Formally, in keeping with the amendments to the USSR Constitution introduced in December 1990, this was a presidential cabinet, directly responsible to Gorbachev. However, its socio-political make-up ensured that it was this cabinet which was most independent of the President. Its support base was primarily found among conservative forces in the military-industrial complex and security services.

---

intended to alleviate the shock of liberalization. Gaidar based his approach on the experience of other countries, including a number of post-communist states, and for that reason he proposed starting with liberalization. (On this debate, see also Fischer and Sahay 2000: 12).

[14] For example, among politicians of the democratic (market) persuasion there were hopes that a conservative government, having implemented a long overdue price reform, would be at the same time the last communist government, thereafter giving way to democrats. In other words, they hoped for a repetition of the Polish scenario, in which the government of Mieczyslaw Rakowski ceded power to the anti-communist government of Tadeusz Mazowiecki, having first of all brought in a package of preliminary reforms.

The Cabinet of Ministers of the USSR formed in January 1991 grasped the essence of the problem quite correctly—the vital need to strengthen state power. The government immediately set about demonstrating its will to restore order. It took a range of pointless but politically forceful measures, from breaking up demonstrations in Vilnius and Riga to withdrawing high-denomination banknotes. It was officially announced that support would be given to the military-industrial sectors of the economy and to Soviet heavy industry in general. Some xenophobic rhetoric was thrown in for good measure, such as the accusation that a number of Western banks had been buying up Soviet currency. This was followed by the long-awaited decision to raise prices, which could have been the first step towards stabilizing the goods market. The legislature was presented with a corresponding series of draft laws which expressed the intention to move towards a 'regulated market economy'. Finally, an attempt was made at political consolidation in the *coup d'état* of 19 August 1991. The defeat of the coup was also the defeat of 'administrative stabilization' in the economic sphere.

However, the economic situation was deteriorating from day to day. The only model which had not been tried in practice and which fitted the radical mood of the moment was the liberal-market model. It had not been discredited, and could count on fairly widespread political support. The personal popularity of Boris Yeltsin was an additional factor which lent political credibility to the programme of liberal reforms.[15]

8.3 The radical nature of the post-communist economic reforms

The radicalization of the process of change as the country embarked on the post-communist phase of its development at the beginning of 1992 did not produce immediate positive results—at least, not in the economic sphere. Over the next few years the country continued to experience high inflation, falling output, and a decline in the most important indices of the quality of life (see Figures 8.1, 8.8, and 8.9).

The new cabinet formed in November 1991, which became the first government of post-Soviet and post-communist Russia, immediately set about implementing economic measures which came to be known as 'shock therapy'. The essence of the programme was to deregulate the economy, particularly prices, production, and foreign trade. The government soon set about introducing a programme of mass privatization on an unprecedented scale. The results of these measures were somewhat contradictory.

---

[15] Here we have in mind a willingness to accept a temporary deterioration in conditions, as well as a mixture of support for private property and the market and an unwillingness to accept free prices. See *Zerkalo mneniy* (1993: 7–9, 24).

For all the costs and difficulties, the initial phase of the government's work achieved positive results. In the first half of 1992 the goods shortage was overcome, and the consumer market, destroyed between 1989 and 1991, was restored. The extent to which the state budget depended on the printing press was sharply reduced. The tax system was radically overhauled, so that it began to correspond to the conditions of a market economy with unregulated prices. Decisive steps were taken towards making the rouble convertible in current accounts, and its exchange rate strengthened somewhat (from 213 roubles to the US dollar in December 1991 to 120.5 roubles/dollar in May 1992). Right up to the end of summer 1992 the monthly inflation rate fell, from 296 per cent in January to 7.1 per cent in July. The disintegration of Russia as a state was halted. A precipitate rise in unemployment was avoided.

All of this was achieved in the course of those seven months, at the very beginning of the radical economic and political reforms. Opinion polls showed that these results were received positively: in the first half of 1992 the popularity of the government and of Egor Gaidar personally was rising.[16]

Soon thereafter, however, this policy experienced a crisis which reflected the real weakness of the radical government and its need to manoeuvre between social groups. On the one hand, the government was unable to carry through its measures of 'shock therapy' consistently. As early as April 1992 it became necessary to make concessions to the industrial and agrarian lobbies. The extent to which the state budget was financed by the printing press increased, and this added to the inflationary pressures. By August 1992 the crisis had come out into the open—the exchange rate of the rouble was falling precipitously, and inflation was rising rapidly. People's real incomes were declining noticeably. The country had fallen into a long and persistent economic crisis, in which high inflation was combined with a profound decline in output.

The economic crisis continued to worsen from 1993 to 1995, and this was expressed in high rates of inflation and large reductions in the volume of production. The post-communist development of the Russian economy can be divided into the following periods and can be briefly described as follows.

1993. A new attempt at stabilization had been undertaken by Gaidar in autumn 1992, and this led to a noticeable decline in the rate of inflation in spring 1993. However, following the replacement of Gaidar in December 1992, the new Prime Minister, Viktor Chernomyrdin, announced a policy of a 'gentle' transition to the market, which resulted in a sharp deterioration of the macroeconomic situation in the summer and autumn of 1993. On his return

---

[16] According to the Moscow opinion pollsters *Mnenie*, support for Gaidar at the head of government was 39% in February 1992 (monthly inflation 27.3%), 49% in July (monthly inflation 7.1%), and 31% in September (monthly inflation 15.2%). The findings of the VCIOM agency were similar. See Mau (1996*b*: 125–8, 135).

to the government in September, Gaidar took a series of measures to tighten budgetary and monetary policy. This caused the inflation rate to decline, but its political result was the defeat of the reformers in the State Duma elections of December 1993. The departure of Gaidar and of Boris Fedorov from the government in January 1994 was followed by another round in the inflationary spiral.

1994. Reacting to the strengthening position of the left and of the nationalists in the State Duma, Chernomyrdin again declared it necessary to follow a 'moderately firm' course and reject 'monetarist methods' of macroeconomic stabilization. Throughout 1994, under the influence of political lobbying and blackmailing of the government by the pro-inflationary majority in the legislature, there was a gradual increase in the rate of growth of the money supply, and this led to a deep currency and financial crisis in the autumn and winter of 1994/5.

1995. The fall in the exchange rate of the rouble and a sharp surge of inflation obliged the executive to return to a firm macroeconomic policy. During 1995 monthly inflation fell from 17 per cent in January to a record low of 4 per cent in December, foreign exchange reserves grew many times over, and basic macroeconomic parameters became more predictable. However, this adoption of stabilization measures just one year before elections were due led to the defeat of the pro-government forces at the polls in December 1995.

It is not hard to discern a cyclical pattern in the development of the economy between 1993 and 1995 (see Mau 1996a). Overall, however, this was a period in which social and economic conditions continued to deteriorate. An enfeebled state could not implement anti-inflationary policies in a consistent way. Consequently, macroeconomic situation that was not at all conducive to arresting the decline and initiating structural reforms and economic growth constantly reasserted itself. The periodic alternation of firm and loose budgetary and financial policies between 1992 and 1994 led to general economic instability and to the degradation of the financial system.

Certain short-term cyclical trends, or fluctuations in economic conditions relating to the political situation in the period of revolutionary radicalism, can be discerned in some of the earlier revolutions we have examined. For example, they can be observed in the dynamics of the exchange rate of the French *assignat* between 1793 and 1795, which varied according to military and political circumstances. At that time, however, these cycles had no regular, stable form, did not play any important role, and did not determine the development of the revolution. The lack of any legal opposition to the revolutionary radical government made the existence of a durable mechanism for economic and political fluctuations impossible. In Russia in the 1990s these fluctuations were determined by the political process of post-communist transformation and by the balance between the diverse socio-political forces operating legally within it.

The crisis reached its peak at the end of 1994 and the beginning of 1995. In October 1994 the rouble's exchange rate fell sharply, and the government's attempts to stabilize the macroeconomic situation led to the almost complete exhaustion of Russia's foreign currency reserves. Against this background, the return to macroeconomic stabilization policies had a doubly negative effect: the crisis in production intensified sharply (GDP fell by 14 per cent in 1995), and living standards fell. In the first quarter of 1995 more than 30 per cent of the population were classified as 'poor'. Social polarization reached its highest point—the Gini coefficient exceeded 40 per cent (see Figures 8.1, 8.4, 8.8, 8.9, and 8.10). This situation was reflected in public opinion polls—in the first half of 1995 all the indices of the public mood in relation to the situation in Russia and the economic reforms were worse than they had ever been since polling on such questions began.[17]

Despite all its serious political problems—the victory of the left and of the nationalists in the parliamentary elections, and the approach of presidential elections, which had an important bearing on the reforms—the executive decided against weakening its monetary policy. Such a step had been expected, and would have been entirely normal for an executive in such a position. But, for a number of reasons, the government did not take the traditional approach of increasing the money supply.[18] As it turned out, in 1996 the government changed its 'economic reaction' to the political struggle. Instead of weakening its monetary policy the government opted to relax its tax demands. This led to the severe budget crisis of 1996–8.

Nonetheless, solving the problem of macroeconomic stabilization was in

---

[17] See VCIOM (1997: 3–5). One can see that over the 1994–7 period support for the continuation of reforms reached its lowest point in March 1995. People's assessments of the situation in Russia and in their own families were at their lowest point (over the 1993–7 period) in May–June 1995; indices of political and economic optimism reached their nadir (over the 1994–7 period) in January 1995; and so forth.

[18]   Here we can discern both economic and political causes. Among the former is the fact that by 1996 a financial market was formed in Russia and a certain experience had been acquired of helping to finance the state budget through domestic borrowing. Amongst the latter is the specific political situation in which, on the eve of the elections, low inflation was virtually the only obvious economic achievement the government had to its credit. It was quite plain that if the government started another wave of inflation, even if it paid off all its debts and obligations, it would not be forgiven by the electorate.

To a certain extent the correctness of that political conclusion has been confirmed by various studies that were conducted after the elections. One example is a poll conducted by the Institute of Sociological Analysis on 5 December 1996. Over 60% of respondents declared their unwillingness to support a government which paid off the arrears of wages and pensions at the cost of increasing inflation. Another example is the result of a correlational analysis of the influence of various economic and political parameters on the results of the presidential elections. It found that electors' political preferences formed long before those elections were a stable and far more significant factor than economic indices. See Gambarian and Mau (1997); Kochetkova (1999).

effect a turning point in the economic development of post-communist Russia. Following the slowing down of the inflation rate to 21 per cent in 1996 and 11 per cent in 1997, positive trends began to appear in a number of other indices of economic and social development. The decline in production stopped in 1997, and the first signs of economic growth appeared. The number of people living below the poverty line began to fall. Various socio-political indices began to improve, such as life expectancy, the extent of income differentials, and the crime level.[19]

However, in 1998, the financial and budgetary crisis took a sharp turn for the worse.[20] There were two main aspects to this new turn in the economic crisis. On the one hand, it should be seen as a manifestation of a global economic crisis, which began in 1997 in Asia and has embraced the majority of emerging markets. On the other hand, the Russian crisis must be understood in terms of the logic of a revolutionary economic crisis.

This crisis has a clearly defined socio-political nature, and was above all a result of the weakness of state power. It was this weakness which left Russia vulnerable to the effects of the world economic crisis. The key factors in this were as follows. The authorities were unable to collect taxes, and this was the reason why the budgetary crisis became acute. This in turn led to the need to increase domestic and foreign debt. Certain interest groups also wielded exceptional influence, and as the danger of a financial explosion approached, they were able to hinder the implementation of those government decisions which went against their interests. Finally, both in society as a whole and in political institutions there was a lack of consensus concerning the most basic interests of social development. This meant that constant struggle between the government and part of the legislature was unavoidable at a time when the greatest possible unity between the various institutions and political groups was needed. This last factor was particularly important: a variety of political forces hoped to make political capital out of the crisis, and democratic procedures were unable to secure united, or even co-ordinated, action to counteract the looming danger.

The result of this crisis, which broke out in full force in August 1998, was another round of the inflationary spiral, a sharp fall in the rouble's exchange rate, a further decline in production, and another precipitous fall in living standards. But the crisis had political consequences typical of the final stages of revolution. The processes of economic, social, and political consolidation had been launched.

The new and characteristic features of the economic situation of 1999 were rather typical for that phase of revolution: a reduction of the government's financial commitments (depreciated by high inflation), the consolidation of

---

[19] For more detail see WCER (1998).
[20] This question will be considered in greater detail in Ch. 9.

fiscal policy (the federal budget for 1999 was at last adopted, with a primary surplus), an increase in tax collection. Despite the collapse of 1998, the Russian élite (even the left-wing cabinet of Yevgeny Primakov) did not turn inwards and continued the policy of macroeconomic stabilization. And as a result economic growth resumed in 1999.

People were exhausted. The crisis decreased public expectations and increased positive attitudes towards the government. In 1998–9 sharp falls in real wages were followed by growing popular support for the government and Prime Minister, no matter who (the left-wing Primakov, the right-wing Sergei Stepashin, or Vladimir Putin). All of them easily obtained support in the Duma.

This reflected the process of consolidation of the Russian élite, particularly on economic matters. Political debates and the elections (to the Duma in December 1999 and of the President in March 2000) demonstrated an emerging consensus among the leading political parties. Certainly, their views did not and could not coincide, but no one still doubted that the very foundations of the market economy–private property, setting of prices by the free market and market competition—were vitally important for Russia. The newly elected Duma easily formed a common alliance with the executive, which had never happened in the 1990s. The main political parties and interest groups agreed that political consolidation and the strengthening of the state were of crucial importance for sustainable economic growth and social development (see IET 2000: 9–18, 109–18, 313–19).

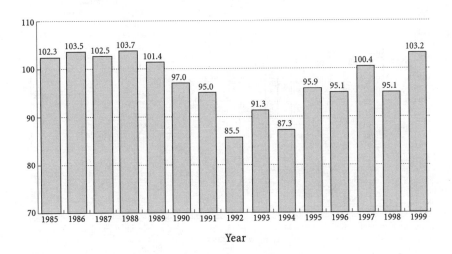

Figure 8.1 Changes in GDP, Russia, 1985–1999

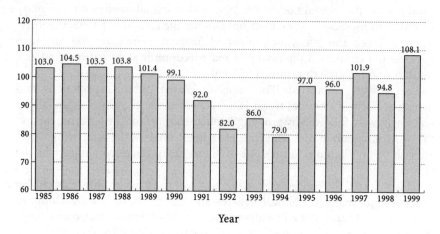

Figure 8.2 Changes in industrial output, Russia, 1985–1999

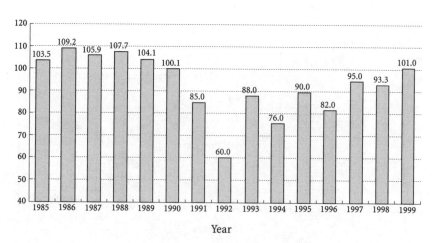

Figure 8.3 Investment in fixed capital, Russia, 1985–1999

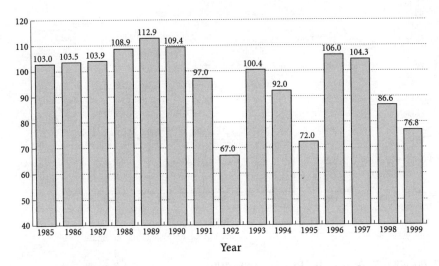

Figure 8.4 Average monthly real wages, Russia, 1985–1999

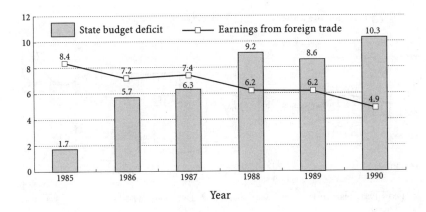

Figure 8.5 State budget deficit and earnings from foreign trade, Russia, 1985–1990

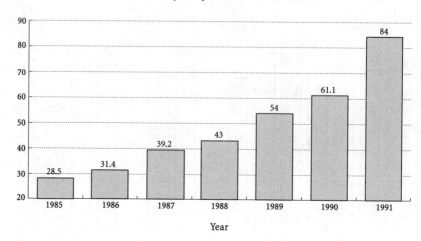

Figure 8.6 Foreign debt, Russia, 1985–1991

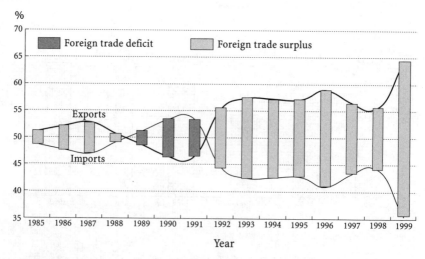

Figure 8.7 Balance of foreign trade [nation], 1985–1999

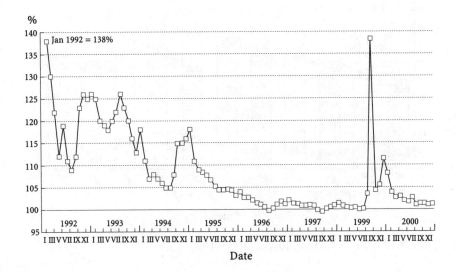

Figure 8.8 Consumer price index, Russia, 1992–1999

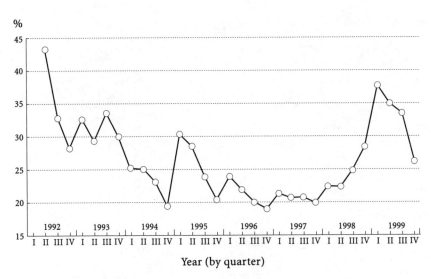

Figure 8.9 Proportion of the population classified as poor, Russia, 1992-1999

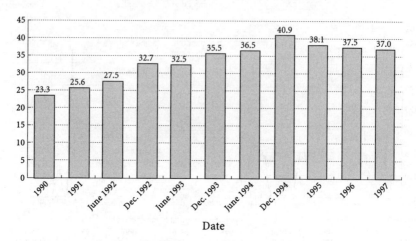

Figure 8.10 Gini coefficient, Russia, 1990–1997

9

Economic Problems of Revolution

The revolutionary economic crisis cannot be reduced to a particular direction of economic development. A number of special economic problems also arise in any revolution. It is well worth while analysing them, as this will provide important information about the nature and patterns of revolutions, and about the peculiarities of post-revolutionary development.

The main economic problems faced by a country in revolution are financial instability, particularly budgetary and taxation crises; changes in property relations; and a depression, possibly followed by a slump in production. However, the relationship between these crises, and their roles, have varied greatly in different revolutions. The financial crisis may precede the revolution, but may remain latent, developing fully only as the revolution proceeds. A budget crisis and a transformation of property rights are integral to the revolutionary process, and they become particularly acute during the radical and post-radical phases. Finally, a major slump in production has featured particularly strongly in the revolutions of the twentieth century, as we showed in Chapter 7.

9.1. The role of finance and the budget in a revolution

Financial crisis plays a central role among the economic problems of revolution. It persists throughout the entire process, at all phases and stages, appearing in different guises in each of them. Many other economic problems of revolution are in one way or another concentrated in the financial crisis. It is very closely linked to the crisis of state power.

During a revolution, the financial crisis expresses itself primarily as a crisis of the state budget, that is, as the inability of the state to cover its expenditure through normal and legitimate channels.

How to supplement state revenue is always a central problem for the last pre-revolutionary government, for all the revolutionary governments, and for the post-revolutionary régime. The question of how to finance the revolution will underlie the most serious and severe clashes in domestic and foreign policy. The search for money for the revolutionary authorities largely determines not only reparations, requisitions, and new taxes, but also the measures taken to redistribute property rights (nationalization, privatization, and various types of confiscation). Finally, the two great revolutions of the eighteenth century—the American and the French—discovered the large-scale printing of money as an inflationary method of financing the state budget.

Most revolutions have begun with the country descending into a financial crisis. The government is particularly affected, as it loses its ability to collect taxes. As the revolution develops, the financial crisis worsens. In the twentieth century this has led to the complete collapse of the financial systems of countries in revolution. Eventually the crisis is overcome and the revolutionary economic cycle ends, once the authorities have re-established their ability to cover budget expenditures through normal taxation, without having to resort to extraordinary measures.

The growth in economic activity in the years and decades preceding the revolution is in sharp contrast to the state of government revenues at this stage of the country's development. This budget crisis is particularly significant for the outbreak and progress of the revolution. The development and eventual overcoming of the budget crisis expresses in a concentrated form the central conflict of the revolution—the state authorities' loss of control over the situation in the country and the gradual reassertion of that control. Both economic and political processes are focused in the budget, and therefore the budget crisis of the revolution deserves separate consideration.

There has been an underlying budget crisis at the outbreak of many revolutions, although this does not mean that it is an essential precondition for the outbreak of all revolutions. The starting points of both the English and French Revolutions had many external similarities: in both cases the authorities were unable to resolve their financial problems by themselves, and the assemblies of 'people's representatives' that convened took decisive steps to assert their own control over the movement of financial resources. Other revolutions have begun differently—the fall of the *ancien régime* was initially linked to purely political problems, such as the mechanisms for forming governments or the constitutional structure of the country. But, however the revolution begins, financial and budgetary problems appear in the very first phase,[1] and very soon tackling the budget crisis becomes one

---

[1] The reasons for this are many and varied, but essentially they coincide with the reasons for the outbreak of a revolutionary economic crisis, which is itself, in part, a crisis of the financial and budget system. There are two main factors here. Firstly, the pre-revolutionary system as a rule is fairly fragile and vulnerable to any unusual economic and political pressures. Budget instability is already present in a latent form, and the political crisis of the revolution may sometimes simply break out before the budget crisis has developed sufficiently to become apparent. Secondly, the actions of the early revolutionary government which, as we have seen, are invariably populist and often doctrinaire in their nature, make a substantial contribution of their own to the deterioration of the budget situation.

of the authorities' main tasks. The weakening of state power becomes synonymous with the loss of state revenue.

We can distinguish two basic types of financial crisis which are characteristic of the beginning of a revolution.

One involves a sharp rise in the financial needs of the existing authorities where the sources of finance for this expenditure are limited. A typical example of this sort of development is provided by England in the second half of the year 1640, when worsening domestic and foreign conflicts necessitated a substantial rise in state revenue. This proved impossible in the existing political conditions of non-parliamentary rule and arbitrary introduction of taxes. The financial crisis appeared at first to be temporary, but the options for overcoming it were limited by the political régime's lack of legitimacy and authority.

The other type occurs where the *ancien régime* gradually slips into a financial crisis, which even before the outbreak of revolution has acquired a chronic, persistent character. The crisis, related to the inefficiency of the existing political and economic system, leads to a paralysis of government. As in the first case, the authorities then try to locate and activate new sources of legitimacy, which turn out to be independent and competing centres of power. Events then unfold as in the first scenario. A typical example of this course of events can be found in late eighteenth-century France.

Judging from the available historical experience, the first type is more common. Not only in pre-revolutionary England, but also in Russia and Mexico at the beginning of the twentieth century, financial problems were accumulating under the surface. Certainly, the finances of Diaz's Mexico, and even more so those of Russia during the First World War, were not in ideal shape, but neither country was suffering a financial crisis of the French type, which clearly demonstrated the crisis of the *ancien régime*. The situation which developed in the USSR in the mid-1980s was in many respects similar: the crisis in state finances was already beginning to show, but had not reached a critical point.

In such situations the authorities have two main ways of supplementing their financial resources—the sale of any property accessible to the state, and the printing press. There are also other possible sources of revenue, including, of course, the tax system, domestic and foreign loans, indemnities, wars, and even piracy, although only the Protectorate government in England employed this last method (see Ashley 1962: 17). The combination of instruments used to supplement the state budget has varied substantially from revolution to revolution, although there are many similarities between them.

9.2. Traditional methods of supplementing the state budget during a revolution: taxes and loans

In almost all revolutions scope for supplementing the state budget through the tax system is extremely limited. As we have seen, neither the moderates nor the radicals can allow themselves to increase the tax burden. The moderates are in principle unable to adopt unpopular measures, even when political conditions would permit them. The radicals are faced with an economy which has all but slipped out of government control, and are therefore in no position to make serious use of tax revenues to finance their policies. This source of revenue is also limited for the post-radical government, because here the authorities must square their actions with the élite, with those social forces which are increasing in strength, who are not going to agree to an excessive tax burden.

A notable exception to this is provided by England. The state budget, which by 1640 was already in deep crisis, was finally destroyed by the outbreak of the Civil War and the division of the country into two hostile camps.[2] However, the Long Parliament was able to restore the financial system, basing the budget upon taxes (including excise duties, never before imposed in England), loans from the City, and fines ('compositions') levied against royalist landowners on territory held by Parliament. This was a situation which was never to be repeated in the history of full-scale revolutions.

The crucial factor in England was the introduction of excise duties on a wide range of consumer goods. This measure had hitherto been categorically rejected by the House of Commons, but they assented to it when faced with the threat of financial collapse at the start of the Civil War. This was a timely but risky step, adopted by John Pym under force of circumstance. On the one hand, the introduction of excise duties corresponded to the level of England's economic development, in that they were unlikely to have (and, as it turned out, did not have) too deleterious an effect on the economy.[3] On the other hand, these duties led to a storm of public protest for being 'unjust, scandalous, and destructive' (see Hexter 1941: 25; Wilson 1965: 129). Despite the circumstances of war and revolution, these customs duties and the single direct tax, the 'monthly assessment', were collected quite successfully. However, in England, too, budget problems became more severe once the country passed through the radical phase and established the Protectorate.

---

[2] 'When the civil war broke out the system of the King's exchequer was naturally completely dislocated and the whole fiscal machinery of the country fell to pieces' (Ashley 1962: 39).

[3] 'All parties instinctively perceived that the economic development of the nation had reached a point at which internal taxation of commodities was both feasible and productive. Excise duties were steadily developed and became one of the chief heads of revenue' (Meredith 1933: 216; see also Kennedy 1913: 52; Wilson 1965: 129–30).

The French tax revenue system at the beginning of the revolution was not so much destroyed as abolished altogether. Even the recognition that taxes were 'unlawful' in June 1789, although they were to be retained for the time being, caused ferment in the country and agitation for their immediate abolition, which was formally declared by the legislature in 1791. At the time such innovations in taxation were inspired not only, or even mainly, by theory, but rather by concrete economic and political circumstances. Taxes were in any case hardly ever collected, and such a measure, popular with the people, could serve as an additional social and political prop for a moderate government which was rapidly losing support.[4]

Thereafter, the proportion of tax revenue in government expenditure in revolutionary France in 1789–95 fluctuated between 0.7 and 5 per cent (see Harris 1930: 51).[5] This proportion reached its lowest point in 1793, during the crisis of the moderate government, and the radicalization of the régime led at first to a certain, albeit insignificant, increase in state receipts. In the same way the budget crisis of the French Revolution was reflected in changes in the proportion of tax receipts in total state revenue—over the same period it fluctuated between 8 and 48 per cent (ibid.).[6] If we compare these figures, it is not hard to see that they have a common pattern of fluctuation. We can thus assess the importance of the inflationary factor in financing state expenditure.[7]

The situation with regard to indemnities and loans in both countries was analogous. The French 'voluntary donations' produced from 8 to 20 per cent of the expected amount (see Smirnov 1921: 8; Korotkov 1988.) Since France was engaged in conflict with almost all the European monarchies, there could be no question of foreign loans. The inability to collect taxes, not to mention their abolition, could only serve to undermine the possibility of getting credit in France itself. The government's creditors, not unreasonably, doubted its ability not only to repay any new debts, but even to service the old ones. Even the passing of a special law recognizing the state debts of the *ancien régime* and placing the government under an obligation to repay them did not alleviate this problem. As Dalin put it, 'in France the problem of financing the revolution was complicated not only by the abolition of taxes and the impossibility of getting new loans, but also by the need to discharge the old indebtedness' (1983: 57–8).

---

[4] 'The revolution had swept away the unfair system of taxation of the *ancien régime*, but no new satisfactory system had been devised to take its place' (Henderson 1961: 77).

[5] More specifically, this proportion comprised, in 1789, 5%; in 1790, 2.4%; in 1791, 1.2%; in 1792, 2.1%; in 1793, 0.8%; in 1794, 1.3%; and in 1795, 0.7%.

[6] The corresponding series of figures here looks like this: 48% (1789), 30% (1790), 16% (1791), 25% (1792), 9.5% (1793), 15% (1794), and 8% (1795).

[7] 'The issues of paper money stemmed from the state's need for funds. The printing press was used to provide what could not be acquired from the population either through taxes or through loans' (Katsenelenbaum 1924: 65).

In Russia between 1917 and 1920 any significant addition to the state budget through taxation was also quite out of the question, since during this period the country was ruined first by World War I, then by the civil war.[8] As early as 24 November 1917, following the natural logic of its struggle for power, Sovnarkom (the Bolshevik government) abolished land taxes and indirect taxes, and a significant part of the population (the workers and poor peasants) were relieved of the obligation to pay the remaining direct taxes. Both indirect taxes and excise duties, exceptionally important components of Russian state revenue, were abolished as 'socially unjust'. Customs duties brought in no money, because foreign trade had dwindled to almost nothing. Although a 5 per cent surcharge on all goods was soon introduced, the rapid development of the practice of state price-fixing had within months nullified the usefulness of this surcharge.

The peasantry, 80 per cent of the population, was formally relieved of any tax obligations at all. It is true that the peasants were expected to make grain deliveries to the state, but the Bolsheviks regarded this obligation not so much as a tax, but rather as a 'loan' to the proletarian state, which would in return free the peasants from the yoke of the landowners.[9] The forced nature of this 'loan' only enhanced its resemblance to those compulsory loans which are levied in almost all revolutions.

As in France, so in Russia, ideological dogma and practical policy considerations were intermingled. The expectation that the monetary system as a whole would wither away meant that no serious work was done to establish and enforce a tax system. Along with money, the Ministry of Finance, finances as such, and, consequently, all traditional means of supplementing the budget were expected to disappear. However, there was an additional argument which was no less important—a weak government was simply unable to collect taxes. This was fully recognized by Lenin, who said in the spring of 1918, 'If we were to try to carry out any kind of taxation, we would immediately come up against the fact that at present individual regions impose taxation according as someone takes it into his head to do so, as he has occasion to do so, and as local conditions allow him' (*PSS* xxxv. 226).

Attempts were made to assert firm control over the cash holdings of the population with a view to normalizing the currency situation and obtaining

---

[8] It should in fairness be mentioned that the Bolsheviks initially tried to increase the rate of tax collection, and for a time they had some successes. This was reflected in a reduction (of about one third) in the issue of currency in the second half of 1918 (see Matthias and Pollard 1989: 996). However, the attempt in the winter of 1918/19 to levy an 'extraordinary revenue tax' on property owners failed completely (see ibid. 999).

[9] Lenin posed the question: 'Will the peasants trust the workers' state sufficiently to loan their surplus grain to it?' His answer was that 'the peasants have no alternative—either they trust the worker or they trust the capitalist: they give their confidence and a loan either to the workers' state or to the capitalist state' (*PSS* xxxix. 154).

additional financial resources for the state. A social rationale was given for these measures, namely that the money was to be found primarily in the hands of the bourgeoisie. The nationalization of the banking system was intended primarily as a means to gain control over currency circulation. As early as December 1917 a decree was passed obliging people to keep their money in current bank accounts or in the savings bank. Money was only to be spent for purposes of production with written permission from organs of workers' control, and expenditure for personal needs was limited to a certain sum. The inviolability of accounts was guaranteed. However, for all the serious penalties that were threatened, observance of this decree was minimal (see Dalin 1983: 190–1).

It is well known that the Bolshevik government, unlike the French, repudiated the debts of the *ancien régime*. This closed off any possible avenues for obtaining credits from abroad. Moreover, given both their messianic conception of their role, and the historical precedent of the French revolutionaries, the Bolsheviks probably realized that external sources of finance would not be available to them, and that in such a situation the old bourgeois debts would be an unnecessary burden. The situation was further complicated by the large indemnities that Russia was supposed to pay Germany under the conditions of the Brest-Litovsk Peace Treaty.

The Bolsheviks were not constrained by any links to the propertied classes, and therefore they actively tried to extract indemnities from groups within the bourgeoisie. However, as in the case of France, indemnities from the bourgeoisie, a demand entirely in keeping with the spirit and experience of the Jacobins, could not be a stable source of finance. As in France, these indemnities raised less than 10 per cent of the sum planned (see Al'sky 1925: 69; Dalin 1983: 195). Moreover, the weakness of the government was demonstrated in its inability to centralize financial resources—the job of collecting these indemnities was left entirely in the hands of the local soviets, which were disinclined to share their takings with the Sovnarkom (see Gladkov 1956: 241).

In the final analysis, the state budget of Bolshevik Russia in the critical years of the revolution was covered by tax receipts to more or less the same extent as that of France in the same period in its history: about 10–15 per cent—or even less than 5 per cent by some estimates—of total expenditure (see Henderson 1961: 77; Dalin 1983: 56).

Under such circumstances the printing of money was an attempt to take control of the economic situation by similar and, it seemed, the only feasible and 'historically advanced' means. The repudiation of Tsarist debts, both state and private, to foreign creditors was aimed at the same goal: overcoming the budget crisis and stabilizing general socio-economic conditions.

When the Mexican Revolution broke out, the country possessed a fairly stable financial system. It had not been destroyed, either by the pre-revolutionary government, as in France, or by war, as in Russia. Thus in Mexico, at first, the government should have been able to count on both tax receipts and loans. However, these options soon evaporated. As the political struggle intensified and the authority of the government evaporated, the possibility of supplementing state revenue by taxation became increasingly illusory and eventually disappeared altogether. In the initial stages any increase in the tax burden was resisted by powerful economic players, including American oil companies, and these players were responsible for the failure of the attempts by Presidents Madero and Huerta to widen the tax base of the revolutionary governments in 1912–14. As the revolutionary governments started to print more money, they further reduced the efficacy of the taxes they were able to collect. A vicious circle developed: 'As the peso depreciated new taxes were imposed and the rates on old taxes were repeatedly raised. Taxes in general, however, did not advance anything like as rapidly as the peso depreciated ... Of course, the Mexican Revolution, like the American of nearly a century and a half before, was financed chiefly by paper-money inflation and not by taxes' (Kemmerer 1940: 62).

The attempts by the Mexican government to raise domestic and foreign loans also failed to bring lasting results. Within eighteen months of the outbreak of revolution, the domestic efforts had already openly taken the form of forced loans, and, as the revolution radicalized, they were imposed upon the Church and upon merchants. As in France, the contribution to the state budget made by these loans was not great (see Bethell 1986: 91–100, 114).

Russia's abandonment of communism was also accompanied by the collapse of the tax system and the system of domestic debt. We can identify two groups of factors which worked against the possibility of supplementing the budget through taxation.

On the one hand, there was the crisis and the destruction of the existing tax system. The Soviet system of taxation was based upon the almost complete state regulation of prices. The most important taxes for the budget, such as the turnover tax, were laid down as a fixed quantity in the price of goods. The loss of revenue from alcohol sales, which generated a significant proportion of the turnover tax, was just one episode in the crisis of the Soviet tax system. The main element was the *de facto* breakdown of state price formation at the end of the 1980s and the beginning of the 1990s. This led to the rapid disappearance of a substantial portion of state income (for more detail, see Sinel′nikov *et al.* 1998: 5–11.)

On the other hand, the crisis in the tax system was the inevitable consequence of the crisis of the state. The stages of development of the crisis of the state coincided neatly with the stages in the crisis of the tax system. They expressed themselves in the destruction of the revenue base of the USSR state budget, in the failure of a series of attempts to reform the tax system, and in the contraction in the revenues of the federal budget of post-communist Russia during the mid-1990s.

We showed in Chapter 8 that the Soviet government in its final years lost tax revenue not only through the 'natural' cause of the collapse of state price formation, but also because of political developments. First, in 1990–1 the Union republics attempted to take control of USSR revenue and began to move towards a *de facto* single-channel system of tax collection, at the same time limiting the transfer of money to the Union government. Secondly, the attempt by the USSR authorities to reform the tax system ended in failure, even though they partially adapted it to a situation of market price formation by introducing a 5 per cent sales tax. The centre was incapable of ensuring that this tax was collected, even though it was, technically, a fairly simple tax to administer.[10]

The actions of Russia's post-communist governments to secure tax revenue have been contradictory. On the wave of the economic and political radicalism of 1991–2, the government was able to reform the tax system fundamentally, and to introduce a value-added tax (VAT) as the major source of revenue for the Russian federal budget. However, its inability to overcome the weakness of revolutionary government meant this success was short-lived. Subsequently the government had to retreat, and federal income declined. First, it had to try to find a compromise with the regional authorities, many of whom (particularly the resource-rich national republics such as Tataria, Bashkiria, and Yakutia) secured special rights in the domain of taxation. Secondly, the development of the political crisis during the years 1992–6 entailed the loss to the federal centre of a certain part of its tax revenue and increasing losses to the budget, both through tax evasion and an increase in the level of arrears.[11]

As for internal debt, the Soviet government had been making use of this source of income mainly through borrowing on the population's savings in the Savings Bank (*Sberbank*) and the state insurance system (*Gosstrakh*). The collapse of the system of state price-fixing and the change from hidden to open inflation meant that the government lost this source of revenue, in addition to enduring the harsh socio-political consequences of the depreciation of

---

[10] In a similar situation in 1918 the Bolshevik government attempted to introduce an almost identical tax, with similar results.

[11] It has been shown that the most severe crisis of the central authorities coincided with the largest increases of arrears to the Russian federal budget. Tax arrears, which were on a fairly low level during the first year of radical reform, began to rise consistently in 1993. They reached their peak in August/September—that is, when the conflict between the President and the legislature called the continued existence of one or the other branch of power into question. The other peak in arrears came at the end of 1995 and the beginning of 1996, when the communists enjoyed a resounding victory in the elections to the State Duma and there was a very strong chance that they might win in the presidential elections in June 1996. For more detail, see IET (1997: 22); Mau (1997: 65).

savings. In fact, this became a form of forced loan imposed in 1989–91 and legalized in 1992. A new growth in domestic debt, this time in the form of bonds, began to develop in Russia after 1993. Up to 1998 it was the most important way of financing the budget deficit once the government had renounced the unsecured printing of money.

There have been at least two revolutions in which foreign loans have played an important part—in Mexico, and in contemporary Russia. From the outset the French Revolution was received with hostility by the foreign powers, and for that reason it could not count on support from abroad. The Provisional Government of February–October 1917 was able to count on the support of its Entente allies, but the radicalization of the revolution, in addition to the Bolsheviks' refusal to recognize the debts of the *ancien régime*, closed off this source of finance for the Soviet state.

The Mexican Revolution had been in a somewhat more favourable position. Its government was able to exploit the struggle between the leading world powers (especially Great Britain, the USA, and Germany) for influence over that country. This meant that it was not only the first revolutionary government of Madero, which enjoyed respect and a fund of goodwill, that could obtain foreign loans without particular difficulty. This source of income remained available in the later phases of the revolution, even when civil war was raging across the country and its political outcome was far from certain. What is more, these loans continued to be granted at a time when the main lenders were engaged in the First World War.

The USSR during *perestroyka* was a recipient of large financial resources. The USSR was regarded as an exceptionally reliable partner with an excellent credit history. The era of Bolshevik maximalism was long past, and for decades the Soviet Union had honoured its external financial obligations. Once the Gorbachev reforms had removed the threat posed by communism and made the USSR more open and, it was believed, predictable, financial support for these reforms seemed to the Western powers to be a contribution to stabilizing international relations. Consequently, between 1985 and 1991 the external debt of the USSR trebled, and continued to grow rapidly throughout the 1990s (see Sinel'nikov 1995: 35).

However, foreign loans have never been crucial in solving the financial problems of a revolution. In the case of Mexico and in post-communist Russia, the revolution was mainly financed by the printing press.

Financial assistance from abroad can be an important stabilizing factor once a revolutionary government becomes strong enough to embark upon financial recovery and overcome the economic crisis of revolution. This can be seen in the experience of Mexico, which, thanks to a sound financial policy and the availability of foreign loans, rapidly restored its economy and moved back into growth in 1921–5. The recent experience of Russia also bears this out. Inflation was brought under control, with the state budget receiving support in the form of loans from such international financial institutions as the World Bank and the IMF. Additionally, from the second half of 1996 (following the defeat of the communists in the presidential elections), Russia's credit was restored on the international financial markets. Admittedly, the financial crisis of 1998 and the recourse to the printing press to shore up the budget has again raised the question of the role of currency emission in the revolution and the overriding importance of finding domestic resources to overcome the budget crisis. This means not only economic resources, but also factors for political stabilization, particularly since the precipitate devaluation of the rouble and Russia's default has undermined its creditworthiness.

Thus, where the state is greatly weakened and has lost its ability to collect taxes and raise loans on the market, the redistribution of property and the printing of paper money become the main sources of state income.[12] We shall examine these two economic mechanisms of revolution below. They are not alternatives—indeed, they have tended to complement each other. As the experience of the French Revolution shows, the redistribution of (landed) property was originally the way in which paper money was to be secured.[13]

On the face of things, the experiences of England, France, Mexico, and Russia look entirely different. The English Revolution, unlike the others, did not experience paper currency inflation. The English and French Revolutions strengthened the system of private property, whereas the goal of the Bolsheviks was nationalization. The list of differences can be extended. But it is much more important to explain the interconnection between the problems of property, finance, and money. This question is important for understanding the socio-economic crises of revolutions, and for this reason deserves to be examined more closely.

[12] 'The Treasury guaranteed regular services and supported the war only by the *assignats* and the sale of national property; and it is not without reason that these are credited with saving the Revolution', wrote Lefebvre about France, and these words can be applied to all subsequent full-scale revolutions (See Lefebvre 1964: 286).

[13] Edmund Burke was the first to point out this connection. In his biting criticism of the French *assignats*, he drew attention first and foremost to their redistributive aspect, seeing them as a 'scandalous violation of property and liberty', a source of future crises ensuring that the French Revolution could not succeed, unlike the English: 'So violent an outrage upon credit, property and liberty, as this compulsory paper currency, has seldom been exhibited by the alliance of bankruptcy and tyranny, at any time, or in any nation' (see Burke 1982: 205, 226, 239–45). Burke also wrote: 'We entertain an high opinion of the legislative authority; but we have never dreamt that parliaments had any right whatever to violate property, to overrule prescription, or to force a currency of their own faction in the place of that which is real, and recognised by the law of nations' (see ibid. 261). However, Burke failed to notice that analogous processes, albeit on a smaller scale, had taken place in England during the Civil War and Protectorate.

9.3. The printing press and its role in revolution

Increasing the issue of paper currency (or the inflationary tax) has been a feature of almost all revolutions since the American War of Independence and, particularly, the French Revolution. The subject has been well covered in the economic literature,[14] so we shall consider it only briefly here.

This particular mechanism for supplementing budget income arose at a later historical stage than the redistribution of property, although it has become the dominant method in most of the more recent revolutions. As the twentieth century approaches, the redistribution of property as a source of income is increasingly displaced by the issue of paper currency. In the French Revolution, which resorted to the printing press to solve its financial problems, property was used more as an argument in the political struggle without regard to the budgetary efficacy of the measures proposed.[15] This was even more characteristic of Mexico and Russia, where the financial needs of the revolutionary governments were almost entirely covered by the inflation tax.[16]

The logic underlying the actions of governments that resort to the printing press is quite obvious. The revolution is in a financial blind alley: the revenue base of the budget has been destroyed, whilst the expenses of the revolutionary government are rising rapidly. The government resorts to printing money, which becomes increasingly divorced from its backing by gold (or foreign currency reserves). Money depreciates, and this impels the revolutionary government to adopt a standard range of forcible measures: it enforces the acceptance of banknotes at their face value; it bans the use of metal coinage, including the use of metallic currency as a measure of value or a price index; and it bans trade in basic consumer goods at market prices. The reactions of economic agents to these measures are no less standard. Even when faced with the threat of the death penalty, as in Jacobin France, they refuse to accept these 'rules of the game'. During the Mexican Revolution, 'A great many different devices were adopted by the various military authorities to check the depreci-

[14] See e.g. Fal'kner 1919, 1924; Katsenelenbaum 1924; Sterrett and Davis 1928; Dobrolyubsky 1930; Harris 1930; Kemmerrer 1940; Mathiez 1963–4; Dalin 1983; Aftalion 1990.

[15] A declaration by Cambon in the Convention in September 1793 is typical in this regard: 'There is no longer any source of revenue other than the *assignat*; all taxes are exhausted, the government is in no condition either to collect them or levy them. We have to resort to *assignats* and, to back them, we must speed up the sale of state land' (quoted in Dalin 1983: 60).

[16] This was particularly the case in Mexico, where for much of the revolution numerous centres of power existed, and almost no property deals could be relied upon at all, even in the short term. For this reason the authorities were inclined to finance their expenditure by printing money. This also happened in Russia during the civil war, but there the amount of paper money issued by the Bolshevik government undoubtedly played the decisive role.

ation of their own respective kinds of money, and all sorts of excuses or "alibis" were advanced to explain away the depreciation or to shift the blame for it . . . The chronicle of the efforts to check depreciation reads like the story of the *assignats* of the time of the French Revolution . . . Declaring the money to be unlimited legal tender and forced currency at its par value, and imposing of severe penalties for counterfeiting were not sufficient' (Kemmerer 1940: 63). It should be added that the logic and consequences of inflationary financing of the budget and the actions of the authorities in this regard are fairly universal, and are certainly not limited to governments in revolutionary times.

The consequence of accelerating inflation is that the printing of money gradually becomes less effective as a means of covering budget needs. Although it is the scarcity of other sources of finance, particularly tax revenue, which impels the government to print worthless money, this policy undermines the tax base still further. Consequently, the proportion of non-inflationary revenue in the state budget continually diminishes as inflation gathers momentum. The quantity of paper money in circulation grows at an increasing rate, and the depreciation of its value likewise accelerates.

The effectiveness of the printing of money as a source of revenue diminishes in all countries which have high inflation for a long time. Revolutionary economies are no exception to this rule. In France, by the time the Directory had come to power it was no longer possible to use the *assignat* as a convenient and effective way of supplementing the state budget. As Jean-Mortini Comby put it, 'the daily needs of the state exceeded the available means of fabrication of the notes' (quoted in Aftalion 1990: 172). The same processes were at work in Russia at the beginning of the 1920s. As the issue of currency accelerated, state revenue from the issue diminished at an increasing rate. According to Katsenelenbaum, 'in 1921 the printing press produced 17 times less income than in 1917, and 2.5 times less even than in 1919' (1924: 67). Almost all writers on the financial problems of revolutions have drawn attention to the similarity of these processes in different countries (see e.g. Katsenelenbaum 1924: 67; Kemmerer 1940: 62–3; Dalin 1983; Aftalion 1990: 172).

In the political sphere such developments may give rise to scandal. For example, the deputies to the National Assembly in France voted to peg their own remuneration to the market price for gold, even though the sale of gold on the market was strictly prohibited by law. Legally, no real rate for gold existed.

9.4. Financial crisis and redistribution of property

We shall now discuss the redistribution of property as a key factor in solving the financial and socio-political problems of revolutionary governments. The general tendency here takes the following form.

In the first stage the revolutionary government decides to resort to the sale of property belonging to the state or Crown, the Church, or opponents of the revolution. This is seen as a source of finance for the revolution and at the same time as a way of solving major social and political problems.

Since the cash demand for property available for sale proves to be inadequate, the government decides to use this property as security in the issue of bonds, which, it hopes, will broaden the social base of the revolution and serve as a means for paying off its own debts. In other words, these bonds begin to function as credit notes.

A budget crisis—a lack of revenue to cover the state's financial obligations—impels the authorities to issue too many of these bonds, and this hastens their depreciation. And since the government generally implements its programme of transferring property into private hands at prices agreed in advance (related to the nominal value of the bonds), it turns out that the property is sold off at artificially low prices.

This was exactly how events developed in England, and in France, albeit to a different degree in each case. The initial decisions taken in both revolutions were similar—the moderate revolutionaries of the end of the eighteenth century took note of the experience of their predecessors a century and a half earlier. In both cases it was decided to cover the extra costs incurred by the revolution primarily at the expense of those who made this expenditure necessary. The experiments in redistributing property in England during the Civil War and the Protectorate are of the greatest interest, because they were a forerunner of, and perhaps even a model for, the French revolutionaries 150 years later.

In its efforts to solve their financial problems, the Long Parliament turned its attention to the lands owned by the Crown, the bishops, the royalists, and finally the Irish rebels. As we have seen, at the start of the Civil War, Parliament decided that it should be paid for by the guilty parties. This decision applied to the royalists and also to the Irish rebels. The methods used in each case, and their consequences, were in many respects identical.

During the 1640s, that is, in the period of the Civil War when considerable political uncertainty remained, the practical implementation of this decision mainly took the form of levying fines, or 'compositions', on royalists. For all the severe financial problems experienced by the government in wartime, hardly anybody considered confiscating royalist lands. It was only after the execution of the King and the proclamation of the Commonwealth that the new government, finding itself still in the midst of a desperate financial crisis, began seriously to tackle this crisis by redistributing property. In 1651 the sale of royalist and other property began in earnest, and it was around this time that similar operations began with the lands of the Irish rebels.

The contradictory nature of the fiscal and social tasks tackled by the revolutionary government had a negative impact on the extent to which these property deals could supplement the Commonwealth treasury. Let us examine two mechanisms which tended to reduce the fiscal (or budget) efficacy of these property deals.

First, there was a political component to the pricing of property. A substantial number of the initial purchasers of royalist property consisted of Members of Parliament, generals in the Commonwealth army, entrepreneurs associated with the Commonwealth, and government creditors, who received parcels of land in repayment of loans they had granted to Parliament earlier. Some estimates put this proportion as high as 50 per cent or more (see Arkhangel'sky 1933: 376; Thirsk 1952: 207). Naturally enough, these people regarded the receipt of royalist lands not as a mere property transaction, but as a reward for the loyalty they had shown in one form or another, or simply for their close connections to the victorious side. They were therefore disinclined to pay the full price for it.

Secondly, socio-political uncertainty persisted, and this considerably increased transaction costs to secure property rights. This persistent uncertainty about future developments, even after the end of the Civil War, caused many of the initial purchasers to resell their land.[17] The secondary market in confiscated land developed very rapidly, and this also tended to depress land prices and the fiscal efficacy of sales of confiscated land.

The same problems arose with the decision to use Irish lands for fiscal purposes. In 1642, shortly after the beginning of the Irish rising, the idea arose of financing the costs of its suppression by selling bonds secured against Irish lands to be confiscated from the rebels after the restoration of order in that country. A joint stock company was formed whose members put their capital together for a specific task (in this case, military-political) in the expectation of dividends if their enterprise succeeded. Later, from 1647, the practice was introduced of paying soldiers of the parliamentary army with state obligations secured against Crown lands.

The fall of the monarchy complicated the problem of the state debt. The resources originally collected for restoring order in Ireland were spent by Parliament almost immediately on waging the Civil War even before the 'Irish problem' was solved. Not only did the government have no other financial resources, it was also heavily in debt to the army, as well as other recipients of state funds. Under these circumstances, Cromwell took a step which was to become common in future revolutions. He increased the issue of liabilities secured against land, and used them to pay the soldiers and officers of the expeditionary force sent to Ireland.

---

[17] As Douglas North wrote, 'the greater the uncertainty of the buyer, the lower the value of the asset' (1990: 63). Of course, this is related to the problem of increased transaction costs in a revolution, which we discussed in Ch. 7.

This meant that there were considerably more state securities issued than there were resources to secure them. The successful prosecution of the Irish campaign presented the government with a new dilemma—how to distribute the limited quantity of land available between investors, soldiers, and foreign Protestant creditors. This last category was, in the event, soon excluded from the agreement, since the claims of the army and City were far more pressing upon the government, and an increasingly authoritarian régime was able to allow itself such financial improprieties. To an extent, this measure pre-figured the so-called 'bankruptcy of the two thirds' of the Directory government in France, which we discuss below.

An additional complication was that, for reasons related to the war and the limited interest among soldiers in receiving parcels of land, the price of land fell substantially, and this, in its turn, led to the depreciation of government bonds. However, the government's need to pay off its debts required even more active selling of land. This depressed land prices still further and much land was now sold at speculatively low prices. This led to complaints that the land was not going to those who worked it or needed it, but to speculators at well below its market price (see Bottigheimer 1971: 119).

A generally similar method for overcoming the budget crisis was used in France. At first, *assignats* were intended as government interest-bearing bonds, which could be exchanged for state landholdings. However, the French treasury was receiving much less real revenue (i.e. revenue not obtained from the printing press), and this, along with other factors, turned these state bonds into fully fledged paper money, which soon became the main source of finance for state expenditure.

The logic by which this system developed was in many respects similar to that of the English Revolution: too many bonds were issued; they became detached from their material basis and depreciated. A peculiarity of the French case was that the radical government, seeking social support, significantly extended the period allowed before land was to be paid for, which greatly reduced the budget efficiency of such operations. In addition, the price of privatized land fell sharply, and this later led to accusations that the authors of the idea of large-scale property sales were conniving with speculators to the detriment of the 'common people', who, it would seem, still lacked the wherewithal to buy land. Dobrolyubsky quotes a contemporary comment: 'It is terrible to see that while the emigration of the traitors and the execution of the conspirators broke up the massive holdings and turned them over to the cause of liberty, bankers, speculators and army suppliers appear and try to restore these enormous holdings' (1930: 129). Land, in view of the depreciation of paper money and the significant time-lags between the conclusion of a deal and the need to settle accounts, was becoming the cheapest of commodities. Moreover, its abnormally low real price fell still further in 1795, when the currency began to depreciate much more quickly.[18]

The budget crisis, which worsened rapidly after the fall of the Jacobins, drove the government to speed up its sale of the remaining state property in exchange for depreciating paper currency—the *mandats territoriaux*, which had replaced the *assignats*. Property was again sold for exceptionally low prices, first and foremost to speculators who bought up the *mandats territoriaux* at depreciating market prices and used them to buy property while the nominal value of these government tokens was maintained at a higher level. The newspapers in 1796–8 were full of details of such deals, where houses and estates in the provinces were sold for *mandats territoriaux* at prices tens of times lower than their real value—their pre-revolutionary value expressed in metal coinage or related to the rent they could bring in. Here considerations of social expediency were intermingled with the personal interests of representatives of the revolutionary government, especially the deputies. The personal interests of deputies and officials in these deals were frequently pointed out.[19]

The analogy between the problems of England and France, arising from the budget crisis and the attempts by the revolutionary government to solve it by issuing state bonds, is fairly obvious. Bottegheimer, drawing attention to 'a common economic phenomenon, the classic example of which is the behaviour of the *assignat* during the French Revolution', writes: 'Like the revolutionary government in France, that in England possessed an important asset in confiscated land. The problem was to make maximum use of it. In France it was done by issuing currency backed by the value of the land, in England by making certain forms of government indebtedness dischargeable in land at fixed rates' (Bottigheimer 1971: 118–19).

In Mexico, too, the redistribution of property as a means of strengthening the position of the authorities was important, although less so than in other revolutions. Land reform in the years of revolution was only implemented when this was necessary to calm peasant risings, and even then only in regions where the risings were particularly serious. Additionally, the redistribution of land was used to strengthen the position of the post-revolutionary élite, especially the generals and the new political leaders.[20]

---

[18] S. E. Harris estimated that between 1790 and 1795 the nominal price of land increased 4.4 times, whereas the *assignat* lost 93% of its value (1930: 118).

[19] Dupont de Nemours wrote of a special 'redeemers' faction' among the French deputies—those members who were particularly actively involved in speculative land deals (see Aftalion 1990: 174–5).

[20] Moreover, in the interests of the generals of the revolutionary army, the government was obliged to consent to their *de facto* control over the nationalized railways. It was not possible to change this position until the mid-1920s, when the now-strengthened state was able to renationalize the railways (see Bethell 1986: 125, 192).

The situation was somewhat different in Bolshevik Russia, where the redistribution of property took the form of nationalization, and of a partial redistribution of nationalized lands.[21] But here, too, we can trace the connection between financial problems and the problem of property. Immediate nationalization did not even formally stem from the pre-revolutionary policies of the Bolsheviks. Rather, it was a consequence of the worsening economic crisis and the loss of control over flows of finance—there was no revenue coming in, and the tax system had been destroyed.

Gorbachev's reforms of the 1980s, unlike most previous revolutions, but in many ways like the English Revolution of the mid-seventeenth century, did not initially envisage transforming property relations. The conceptual basis for economic reform worked out during the 1970s and 1980s had carefully avoided the question of property, and the Soviet leadership gave this matter its serious attention only at the end of the 1980s. Even at the end of the 1990s, the creation of effective owners was still not central to the policy of privatization, for all the declarations made on this count.

The first (late Soviet period) documents produced by the Russian Federation on privatization were dominated by socio-political and fiscal considerations.[22] They were concerned to strengthen the social base of the Russian leadership against the USSR authorities. This can be seen both in the flirtation of the Russian leadership with directors who were in fact already privatizing their own enterprises, and in the various benefits offered to workers' collectives in the event of their enterprises being privatized. New rules were introduced which reinforced the rights of directors over enterprises. These included such measures as granting state and municipal property to enterprises 'with full economic rights', which in fact legalized the uncontrolled use of state property in pursuit of private interests, and granting the right to buy outright enterprises that were currently under lease. This was in fact a way for the heads of enterprises and associated 'co-operative' businessmen to acquire their enterprise legally. It was expected that such measures would help reinforce the political position of the Russian authorities, both directly and by encouraging enterprises to subordinate themselves to the Russian Federation rather than to the USSR.

The mass privatization of 1992–5 had an even more openly social and

---

[21] 'The first bourgeois revolutions resorted to donations, to the sale of lands confiscated from the church and the feudal nobility and then, after a certain time, to taxes. The poor had nothing to donate, the land had become common property and could not be sold, the old tax apparatus had broken down and a new one had not been created' (Dalin 1983: 195). Ideological jargon aside, Dalin's conclusion here is quite correct.

[22] See the Russian Federation laws 'On Property in the RSFSR' (24 Dec. 1990) and 'On the Privatization of State and Municipal Property in the RSFSR' (3 July 1991) (*Privatizatsiya v Rossii* 1993: 5–22, 11–68).

political character.[23] This we demonstrated in Chapter 5.[24] On the one hand, high inflation remained an important supplementary source of state revenue, and for a time this made budget problems less onerous. On the other hand, political instability meant that the government could not expect any influx of capital or, therefore, substantial state revenue from privatization.[25]

The government's efforts ensured that by 1996 its socio-political aims had largely been achieved. Enterprise directors had, as early as 1993, showed signs of splitting into supporters and opponents of continued market reforms. A significant part of the population, it is true, considered itself to have been betrayed, and this was expressed in the results of the parliamentary elections of 1993 and 1995, but the presidential elections, of key importance for the country's development, were won by the supporters of market reforms.

For these reasons, by 1997 the conjuncture had changed. With the end of the period of high inflation the government was faced with a severe budget crisis, and privatization began to be seen as an important way of topping up the state treasury. The government resorted to selling stakes in a number of commercially highly attractive enterprises. We can trace the increasing importance of privatization in the state budget in Table 9.1. However, this measure met with firm opposition from business leaders—active participants in privatization who had an interest in lower prices for those objects being privatized.

[23] Incidentally, in the first document of post-communist Russia specially concerned with privatization, the emphasis was somewhat different. In 'Basic Principles of the Programme for Privatizing State and Municipal Enterprises in the Russian Federation in 1992' (29 Dec. 1991), the aims of privatization are stated as: 'assisting the general goals of the policy of economic stabilization', 'ensuring in the course of privatization a sharp rise in enterprises' 'operational efficiency by transferring them to the most effective owners', and an 'increase in state revenue' (Ulyukaev and Kolesnikov 1992: 28–9). The declamatory nature of this document, adopted at a time when the economic and political crisis was becoming particularly intense, hardly requires explanation.

[24] This can be traced in detail in the first two versions of the State Privatization Programme, of 11 June 1992 and especially 24 December 1993. The predominance of the social goals of privatization at the expense of fiscal ones has been noted by many reformers, particularly Egor Gaidar: 'We needed to create a critical mass of private ownership as quickly as possible. Given the trade-off between the speed and the quality of privatization, we consciously opted for speed' (Gaidar 1997d).

[25] This would explain the low returns to the budget of the auctions of securities at the end of 1995 (loans-for-shares-deals) which we discussed in Ch. 5. This was the result not only of the desire of the authorities to win the support of financial circles on the eve of the elections, but also of the genuinely low demand for such assets, given that the presidential elections could have been won by the communists, who rejected privatization.

Several economists have noted the contradictions between the social and the financial and economic aspects of Russian privatization. They characterize the situation which arises here as a problem of transaction costs. For example, Silvana Malle has written that the socio-political struggle around privatization in Russia 'has a negative effect on the level of transaction costs. They become greater than they would have been had the transfer of property rights taken place on economic criteria alone' (Malle 1994: 55).

TABLE 9.1. *Financial results of privatization, Russia, 1992–1998*

Year	Federal budget revenue from privatization		
	Billion roubles	% of all federal budget revenue	% of GDP
1992	19	0.6	0.1
1993	66	0.3	0.04
1994	116	0.15	0.02
1995	3,408	1.5	0.2
1996	831	0.3	0.04
1997	18,781.3	5.8	0.7
1998	14,978	5.0	0.6

Source: Institute for the Economy in Transition.

The serious political conflicts which ensued led to political losses for both sides in the struggle, both business and government.

1998 saw yet another turn of events. The financial crisis led on the one hand to an acute worsening of the budget crisis and, therefore, to greater government interest in the fiscal results of privatization. On the other hand, it led to a fall in demand for the objects being privatized, and to a consequent fall in prices. Those who were speculating on further price falls seemed to have a much firmer basis for their expectations. Throughout that year the government was torn between these contradictions, without being able to find an effective solution. The new burst of high inflation, the banking crisis, and the collapse of Russia's credit rating subsequently postponed any possibility of the treasury obtaining any significant fiscal returns from privatization.

9.5. The budget crisis and the end of revolution

An important feature of almost all revolutions is that the budget crisis becomes particularly severe in the post-radical stage. This is quite explicable. Firstly, the redistribution of property can only be a short-term source of finance, as it cannot provide the state budget with continuous revenue. Secondly, the financial efficacy of such measures turns out to be much lower than expected; this is related partly to the government's need to manoeuvre between social groups, and partly to the fact that in conditions of political instability the value of the assets offered for sale will naturally be depressed. Thirdly, as the immediate threat to the gains of the revolution recedes, the social groups which support it become less inclined to tolerate those extraordinary methods of solving financial problems which characterize the radical phase. As a result, the final stage of the revolution is when the financial crisis becomes most severe. It is at this time that the state budget deficit rises sharply, and arrears in state payments become an important factor in political life.

The government's normal means of supplementing its revenue are significantly reduced, and it has to look constantly for new ways to cover its expenses. Even in England, where the revenue system emerged from the Civil War in fairly good shape, and had even been reorganized in line with the requirements of the time, budget problems worsened after the end of the radical phase and the establishment of the Protectorate. The City businessmen, who had energetically supported the Presbyterian leaders of the Long Parliament with loans and donations during the Civil War, did not show much readiness to collaborate with Cromwell and his administration in the 1650s. Their hopes for repayment of their loans soon evaporated, and the political and religious views of the Independent generals did not find much sympathy in the City. Consequently, most of Cromwell's approaches to the City Chamber for loans met with refusal, accompanied by requests to repay the debts from the 1640s (see Ashley 1962: 98–9). In France under the Directory the state budget crisis took on a chronic form, owing to the inability of the government to create a new, stable revenue system.[26]

Taxes also prove to be of very limited use as a source of revenue. For Cromwell, increasing the tax burden was undesirable, as taxes had already risen substantially during the Civil War, and had caused dissatisfaction among the gentry and merchants. The attempts of the Directory to solve its financial problems by restoring a normal tax system had a very limited effect given France's degraded system of tax levying, which could not be revived quickly. Moreover, in both cases the response to attempts to widen the tax base was an increase in arrears. In England in the mid-1650s one of the basic economic problems was 'why the arrears of assessments are not paid' (Ashley 1962: 98). In France, the question was what new taxes could be introduced to cover the losses from non-payment of the already existing taxes.[27] For all the efforts made over a long period of time, the French budget remained chronically in debt and unable to fulfil its obligations: 'The budget was reduced by more than 160 millions, and was relieved of payments in arrears' (Lefebvre 1964: 209).

As tax arrears grow, so do the government's debts to recipients of state funds. In socio-political terms this is a more serious problem. Many more people were dependent on state spending in France than in England. As

---

[26] 'The Directory, instituted late in 1795, was both unwilling and unable to introduce the semblance of a budgetary system' (Harris 1930: 45; see also Henderson 1961: 81).

[27] 'In spite of the reform of fiscal administration, and in spite of the tracking down of tax-payers who were in arrears, tax returns were lower then ever. Being unable to fill its coffers with the returns from already established taxes, the government proceeded to invent some new ones . . . Yet all these measures proved wholly ineffectual' (Aftalion 1990: 177).

H. A. L. Fisher described, the situation: 'If we could revisit any great provincial town of France as it stood in any year from 1808 to 1815 we should find the school-masters and clergy starving upon miserable pittances, the schools empty of scholars, the public hospitals short of nurses and appliances, industry at a standstill, and the government of the town listless, incurious and sapped of all initiative' (cited in Henderson 1961: 81). We should note that the period described here was somewhat later, and therefore more prosperous, than the end of the 1790s.

Gradually, however, as the political régime consolidates itself, measures of financial and economic stabilization begin to bear fruit. The advantages of this are not usually enjoyed by those who introduced these measures, but by subsequent governments. The innovations in taxation introduced by the Long Parliament and the Protectorate were retained in full by the Restoration government (see Kennedy 1913: 54–5; Meredith 1933: 216–17). The results of the Directory's stabilization measures became fully apparent only under Napoleon Bonaparte.[28] Having acquired enough strength to pursue a responsible financial policy, Bonaparte devoted particular attention to achieving financial stability, regardless of possible social costs: 'Financial recovery was the first concern of the Consulate, and with the power of the state, Bonaparte's popularity drew great strength from it' (Lefebvre 1964: 286).

An aggressive foreign policy was one of the most important means which enabled the governments of England and France to survive the post-radical budget crisis. These governments did not have many of the domestic problems of their predecessors, in that the main forces of counter-revolution had already been suppressed. But, the non-payment of outstanding debts to the army created a politically explosive situation. For this reason 'revolutionary wars' became almost unavoidable for both countries. The army became almost self-financing, and the income from its foreign adventures was of real value for the budget.

Some authors have seen this as the explanation for Cromwell's aggressive foreign policy, which, from a twentieth-century standpoint, looks very strange for a financially impoverished government: 'Yet an army and navy regularly in arrears was as dangerous as a dissatisfied squire or merchant. The only solution which Cromwell seems to have conceived in face of this dilemma was that his vigorous foreign policy . . . might itself be made a source of revenue' (Ashley 1962: 17).[29] We should also note here that this sort of political logic

---

[28] 'In this matter, the directory did not receive any revenue from its profound financial reforms. Nevertheless, its important positive development was the liquidation of the *assignat*, and the formation of a coherent tax system, which existed for more than 100 years. However, Bonaparte was the one to truly gain from this development' (Godechot 1951: 440).

[29] To this we might also add the attempt by the Protectorate administration to use the army and navy to collect various types of state revenue, particularly from fishermen operating in English waters, which Ashley called a 'method of using the armed forces . . . as collectors as well as consumers of revenue' (1962: 17).

went against the general attitudes of Parliament in the first half of the seventeenth century (see Russell 1979; Hughes 1991: 21) and could only be implemented under the essentially authoritarian Protectorate government. MPs preferred to economize on war, whereas the Cromwell leadership proposed to profit from it.

France's 'revolutionary wars' were even more significant. For many years they provided an important source of state income, and the only way of restoring the country's gold reserves—from August 1796 hundreds of millions of gold francs began pouring into the country from abroad. At the same time, despite the beginning of an economic upturn and a flow of capital into the country, the government was able to carry out a financial and political operation known as the 'bankruptcy of the two thirds', which meant that the state defaulted on two thirds of its domestic debt (see Godechot 1951: 435–6). Following this, the budget, particularly the tax system, very gradually began to recover. Although the system was unpopular, it remained fairly stable (Lefebvre 1964: 283–5).

Paying the army became the major concern of the Mexican government at the end of the 1910s and the beginning of the 1920s. At that time it took up more than 60–65 per cent of the federal budget, whereas at the start of the revolution it took up only 20–25 per cent. Serious problems arose with financing other items of state expenditure. In a search for financial stability, and without the option of substantially economizing on the army, the Mexican government at the beginning of the 1920s opted to slash many other items of state expenditure. It cut the wages of state employees drastically, reduced the administrative apparatus, and introduced draconian measures to economize in other areas of the budget. Taxes were raised and many important items of state property were transferred into private hands, including the railways (see Bethell 1986: 90, 137, 135, 173). These measures notwithstanding, in the 1920s the state got into arrears in its payments not only to state officials, but even to the army (see Sterrett and Davis 1928: 124; Shrewell 1929: 70). This package of measures allowed the government to start repaying the debts of previous administrations. This restored trust in Mexico, and enabled the government to resume borrowing from foreign states.

In Bolshevik Russia too, it was in the concluding phase of the revolution, with the transition to the NEP, that the budget crisis emerged as a separate, severe economic problem requiring serious attention. During their first few years in power, it had seemed quite natural to the Bolsheviks to solve their budgetary and financial problems by printing money, since they expected the money economy as such to disappear. Even at a later stage, Bolshevik economists continued to believe that the victory of the proletariat meant that the narrow bounds of 'economic rationality', particularly 'budget rationality', had been overcome (see e.g. Stepanov 1918: 113–14). The winding-up of the People's Commissariat of Finance, *Narkomfin*, was expected to take place in the near future. In such circumstances, the crisis of the state budget during the civil war was seen purely as a technical problem of the limited capacity of the state banknote printing house, *Gosznak*, and the continuing political instability of the régime in wartime. The plans produce at that time for the large-scale reconstruction of the country on a new technological basis, notably the electrification plan, GOELRO, were based on purely technocratic principles, with no attention paid to the financial side of things.[30]

The NEP, with its partial privatization, not to mention the separation of the financial responsibilities of the trusts and the state, represented an attempt to reduce the financial burden and overcome the budget crisis in keeping with the logic of market economics. However, this was just one side of the process of restoring financial and economic stability.

The other side was the gradual recognition of the vital importance of restoring the budget and particularly the tax system. Tax problems once again became crucial. Lenin gave them priority when considering the question of devising a realistic (that is, balanced) budget. In a note to Finance Commissar Grigory Sokol′nikov, Lenin indicated that the main tasks were 'raising trade, *increasing* and *collecting taxes*' (*PSS* liv. 132–3, Lenin's emphasis). Moreover, in constructing their new tax system, the Bolsheviks laid special emphasis on the introduction of indirect taxes, whose proportion of state revenue rose consistently in the first half of the 1920s (see Dalin 1983: 267, 271–2). This was the instrument which had always been rejected not only by the Bolsheviks, but by all socialists, since the general opinion was that the main burden of these taxes falls on the poorest strata. However, by now, at the end of the revolution, the main argument in policy formation was budgetary expediency, rather than conformity to the party programme or considerations of social justice.

It was at precisely this stage that the budget crisis took the form of an acute socio-political conflict. The conflict between financial stability and social justice could be easily resolved in favour of the former. However, the conflict between financial stability and industrial expansion proved much more dramatic, and this was not so much an economic as a social and political

---

[30] There was a very revealing polemic on this question between Petr Osadchii, a well-known engineer and one of the key members on the GOELRO commission, and Nikolai Shaposhnikov, the well-known early twentieth-century Russian economist. 'Among the circumstances which favour innovation in the field of electrification is the abolition of budget constraints in our country, which in the past had prevented the introduction of many useful innovations', claimed Osadchii in 1921 (Osadchii 1921: 12). In response, Shaposhnikov wrote: 'In normal circumstances the income of any economy determines its expenditure, but in conditions of uncontrolled currency issue there is no such limit. Here, our economic options are limited solely by the productivity of the printing press. Given that productivity, anything is possible, at least from the budgetary point of view—a university in every provincial town, or the immediate electrification of the whole of Russia. But here we can never make ends meet, we do not have and cannot have a normal budget' (Shaposhnikov 1922: 51–2).

conflict. The new élite, concentrated mainly in the 'commanding heights' of the economy (large-scale state industry), demanded financial resources. And it was precisely the political resolution of this conflict which destroyed the NEP system. It is typical, though, that this took place only after the revolutionary cycle had been completed, once a new government had consolidated itself and a new élite had been formed. These later developments took place in a fundamentally different political framework—that of stable and firm government, which was able to risk 'economic experiments'.

It is still more typical that the undermining of the financial system which took place at the end of the 1920s and the beginning of the 1930s was the final demonstration by the new élite of its political power. This new élite consisted primarily of the party *nomenklatura*. It had concentrated the management of large-scale nationalized industry in its hands, and was vitally interested in a policy of unrestrained industrial expansion, for which it was prepared to sacrifice financial stability. This was the policy pursued by the leadership during the First Five-Year Plan (1929–33), which led to a rapid growth of industry, a financial catastrophe, and the complete consolidation of the personal rule of Joseph Stalin. It soon became clear, however, that the Bolshevik régime could only risk deviating from the path of budget stability for a very short time. For Stalin's dictatorship the re-emergence of financial instability was politically destabilizing. Soon there was a literally forcible return to a balanced state budget, and this position was maintained throughout the entire period of Russia's communist development—right up to the mid-1980s.

The budget crisis in Russia in the 1990s has received a great deal of attention in recent literature (Sinel'nikov 1995; Illarionov 1996; Gaidar 1997*b*; IET 1997). It is one of the most important features of revolutionary development in Russia today. Although its roots are to be found in the second half of the 1980s, it became particularly acute in the mid-1990s.

This was a typical crisis of the end of a revolution. The gradual strengthening of the state gave the government the chance at last to secure, after a few false starts, monetary stabilization. However, tackling this problem led to a noticeable aggravation of the state budget crisis. The tax system, eroded by years of high inflation, could not bring in enough revenue, while the other normal source of income, printing money, had been cut off. The government had been strong enough to secure this basic condition for macroeconomic stabilization, but it was not strong enough to balance its revenue and expenditure. The government was repeatedly in arrears to recipients from the state budget—medicine, science, education, the military. The state pension system was also engulfed by the crisis.

The essence of the budget crisis can be traced to changes in the government's share of gross domestic product. Its share fell consistently during the 1990s, reaching a minimum figure of 34.4 per cent in 1996 (34.9 per cent in

1997) compared with 40.4 per cent in 1992. The corresponding figures for state budget expenditure were 42.0 per cent (43.5 per cent) against 51.3 per cent (see Gaidar 1998*b*: 197–8, 321–3, 353–5; Sinel′nikov *et al.* 1998: 45–7). The reduction in the budget deficit from 25 per cent to 7–8 per cent of GDP did not mean that the budget crisis was alleviated, given that in 1996–7 the government gave up supplementing its revenue by printing money. This showed itself particularly sharply during the severe financial crisis which began in 1998.

The attempt to resolve the problem by issuing state bonds only temporarily relieved the situation, in 1995–6, after which the crisis took another turn. Increasing the rate of tax collection is impossible in practice without strengthening the state, and the state cannot strengthen itself unless it collects taxes. This problem we have observed in previous revolutions: the government, finding itself unable to collect taxes, tries to solve the problem by introducing new taxes. This vicious circle can, in theory, be broken in two ways. One can either balance the budget at a level which corresponds to the status quo budget commitments through tax collection, or one can reduce taxes to make them more collectable, thereby raising the volume of tax revenue later. The governments of Viktor Chernomyrdin and Anatolii Chubais in 1997, and of Sergei Kirienko in 1998, tried the first method. The government of Evegenii Primakov chose the second route from the autumn of 1998. Experience shows, however, that both approaches required the state to reduce its expenditure commitments.

This development was entirely justified. At a given level of per capita GNP it was difficult (if not impossible) to raise significantly the level of tax revenue in real terms, while preserving a democratic political régime (see World Bank 1996: 114). On the one hand, future successful *economic* development necessitated a balanced budget at the existing level of revenue. On the other hand, balancing the budget came up against obstacles of a *social* character, because it was necessary to cut social expenditure in real terms. In such circumstances sharp political conflict can develop, leading to authoritarian tendencies in the political system.

However, this is only one part of the story. Experience of revolutions clearly demonstrates that growing financial stability brings political benefits. Authorities can achieve higher popularity when they are able to stabilize the economy, as happened in Russia in 1999–2000: frightened by the financial crisis, people were ready to support a consistent financial policy which would bring economic and political stability. This explains why the decrease in real wages during that period was followed by an increase in the popularity of the government (see IET 2000: 109–18). And, as in France, default contributed to financial and political stabilization: since the government failed to continue paying a substantial part of its debt, it was able to improve payments of nominal wages and pensions as well as of other budget commitments.

Strengthening of political power had, in its turn, an important impact upon the development of the financial system. A number of Russian regions had obtained important privileges during the period when the federal government had been extremely weak, but in 2000 they had to give up these privileges.

Finally, stabilization made it possible for President Putin to announce sweeping tax and budgetary reforms, intended to decrease radically both the level of taxes and the government's financial commitments. These reforms were publicized as a means of stimulating economic growth, but their socio-political context was clear enough—the reforms primarily met the expectations of the new economic and political élite.

9.6. Slumps in production during revolutions

So far we have paid most attention to the budgetary and monetary aspects of the economy of a revolutionary society, as well as to their relationship to the process of property redistribution. These are fundamental issues, which have permeated all revolutions past and present. Let us now consider changes in production levels. In Chapter 7 we pointed out that the problem of slump and growth does not occur in all revolutions, or that, at least, its significance varies substantially from revolution to revolution. It has only been in the revolutions of the twentieth century that fluctuations in production have begun to play a key role.

Slumps in production are not a key feature of all revolutions, even in their radical phases. Declines in productive activity have, of course, taken place, but their political and economic significance has varied. In England and France, for example, the slump primarily took the form of smaller harvests (partly as a result of the weather), and of a deterioration in conditions for distributing goods (largely as a result of military activity). In France the slump in production was also influenced by the policies of the radical authorities: the Law of the Maximum and the controls on imports and exports removed incentives for peasant producers and merchants, and led to a decline in sowing and trade. In other words, the economic system was notably disorganized, but this should not be equated with a large slump in production in the strict sense of the term.

Deep slumps in production were a feature of the Russian and Mexican Revolutions. They started before the radical phase, and thereafter accelerated noticeably. This acceleration was associated with the widespread civil wars and foreign intervention. If we compare these slumps with the slump in postcommunist Russia, we see that the difference lies in the greater complexity of the current economic system, which is less dependent on natural factors and more dependent on social ones.

Indeed, a society dominated by a primitive agrarian economy depends to a lesser extent on the general economic conjuncture, on changes in demand, or on the stability of the technical basis of production. The key factors here are weather conditions, and whether military actions are taking place in agricultural regions. Urban economies are more sensitive to political instability, which is why they suffered more than agriculture in the revolutionary upheavals of the seventeenth and eighteenth centuries, both from the breakdown of economic links during the civil war, and from changes in demand for the goods of artisans. However, the urban economy was only a small part of the total national economy, and therefore did not much affect the overall situation in the country.[31]

The revolutions of the early twentieth century took place in more developed economies. This meant that a complex technological process could be brought to a halt if some of the conditions for production were not met. If certain components or inputs were in short supply, the level of output would plummet. Consequently the civil wars caused a substantial slump in production, particularly industrial production, which suffered greatly from the military actions and the breakdown of economic links. When the revolutions and civil wars in Russia and Mexico were at their height, production declined in some sectors by as much as 50–80 per cent. However, once military action had ceased and political power had become consolidated, the pre-revolutionary level of production was quickly restored in those areas where it was just a question of recovery—the reactivation of old productive potential, which required not so much investment as political stability and demand.

Here we should draw attention to two specific features of the revolutions of the early twentieth century. We can characterize them as patterns of slump and recovery in economic systems attempting to tackle the problems of industrial modernization.

First, in the much more primitive agrarian sector production declined much less than in industry. This confirms and illustrates our conclusion as to the increasing importance of production slumps as we get closer to modern society.

Secondly, the structure of industry directly influenced the nature of the slump in general, and in particular sectors. Decline in production was smallest in those sectors with a relatively simple technological base, which did not need complex equipment or complex patterns of co-operation. The same can

---

[31] For this reason, if there is any sense at all in asking what impact the early revolutions had on production levels, the question needs to be put differently: Did the revolution lead to a slowing of economic growth compared to the rates achieved on the eve of the revolution? This is the sort of influence on economic development which economic historians have discussed in relation to the English and French Revolutions (see Nef 1950: 149; Crouzet 1967). These works discuss not only the slowdown of growth in the course of the revolutions themselves, but also the negative effect of the revolution on post-revolutionary economic development.

be said about sectors serving the most important human needs, such as food. These also proved more resistant to decline. At the beginning of the twentieth century these two groups of sectors coincided—the sectors which satisfied the most basic requirements were as a rule the ones which used the most traditional, primitive technology. The more complex, modern sectors were in a more difficult position, as they were much more vulnerable to the disorganization of economic life. This particularly affected engineering.[32] Finally, as can be seen from the experience of the Mexican Revolution, output levels remained virtually unchanged in sectors which worked to demand from abroad, such as the Mexican oil industry (see Bethell 1986: 86; *Itogi desyatiletiya* 1927: 244–7).

An even more complicated situation arises when a country is faced with the task of fundamentally restructuring a fairly developed economy—when the revolutionary crisis coincides with a structural one. This was not typical for revolutions in earlier periods. It only becomes an issue where society is in its industrial or post-industrial stages of development. Here the slump in production is not associated with the destruction of productive forces, but with the need for their radical renewal, and by contrast with the more stable agrarian societies, renewal particularly affects industry (see Chapter 3).

In other words, the most important feature of the current Russian transformation, which distinguishes it fundamentally from earlier full-scale revolutions, is that socio-political renewal of the system is combined with a rupture in the economic structures established in the industrial stage of development. The transformation of the system involves not only a fundamental change in the institutional and political structure, but also in the structure of production.

The structural crisis in Russia led to the emergence of corresponding groups of interests. There was a conflict between those who were ready to adjust their enterprises to the new challenges and demands, and those who preferred to carry on as before. These groups were attached to the specific features and prospects of their particular industries in Russia's new environment. This contributed to a diversification of the social structure of revolutionary society and to a further weakening of the state.

The conquest of high inflation is a basic macroeconomic precondition of growth.[33] However, the experience of 1997 showed that stable prices and low

---

[32] The logic behind these distinctions between sectors of production was set out by Soviet economists in the 1920s, in analysing the 'patterns of post-war economic restoration' (see Bazarov 1925; Groman 1925). They showed how and why the most damaged sectors recover more quickly, and how at the end of a certain period the pre-revolutionary equilibrium is restored in the economy.

[33] It was expected that Russia would follow the pattern of most other post-communist countries, which moved into rapid growth shortly after inflation was curbed (see Fischer *et al.* 1996).

interest rates create only a general basis for economic growth: the indebted-ness of the state budget triggered macroeconomic instability and tied down financial resources which could have gone into production; as a result, invest-ment continued to fall (see Gaidar 1998*b*: 785, 789). But the most important factor was that the state failed to create institutional, political, and legal condi-tions necessary for investment. The problem of transaction costs—notably the security of property rights and law enforcement—became particularly acute.

It has been widely noted that in the Russia of the late 1990s property rights were not secure. Privatization has only partially overcome the 'erosion of property rights' as a factor which increases transaction costs.[34] The absence of developed legislation and of a developed state means that the institutional environment is not conducive to growth. Small and medium-sized businesses are under constant threat of extortion by criminal organizations and of unwarranted interference in their activities by government (particularly regional) authorities. Investors who have acquired shares on the secondary market cannot be sure that their property rights will be observed in practice. The rights of minor shareholders *vis à vis* large ones are inadequately guaran-teed. Strategic investors have no protection against arbitrary amendments to the law and adverse changes in business conditions. The rights of benign shareholders are not guaranteed if it emerges that an earlier deal in those shares, or a long-established privatization, was carried out in contravention of the law. Finally, the banking system is rather weak and unreliable.

The creation of incentives which would promote economic restructuring is another problem of post-communist development, since the ability of enter-prises to react to changes in demand is noticeably weak. The behaviour of economic agents differs substantially from that of corporations formed in market conditions. The leadership of former state enterprises is inclined to maintain the employment levels and production profile of the firm for a long time, and to put off adapting production to new parameters of demand. This raises a special question about the mechanisms of economic growth which was widely debated at the end of the 1990s.

Amongst the diversity of viewpoints in Russia, we can identify two main approaches to solving the problem of economic growth and the role of the state in this process. These approaches are backed by different groups of inter-ests, that is, by different political forces.[35]

---

[34] Kokorev has drawn attention to a phenomenon which on first sight appears paradox-ical: 'institutional changes aimed at liberalizing the market and defining property rights, contrary to theoretical expectations, not only do not decrease transaction costs, but cause them to rise substantially'. He explains this by saying that 'in reality, during the initial stages of reforms the hidden costs of inefficient resource distribution and absence of incentives to work are transformed into visible transaction costs' (1996: 66, 68).

[35] For more detail see Mau, Sinel'nikov-Murylev, and Trofimov (1996).

One approach proposes more direct government interference in the investment and economic activities of corporations—the creation of an indicative plan with certain industries prioritized. The state should concentrate maximum financial resources in its own hands, and redistribute them to the priority sectors. In essence this would mean distributing export earnings to Russian engineering, emphatic protectionism, and the limiting of competition from foreign producers.

The other approach is mainly concerned with developing the legal and incentive-creating functions of the state. It concentrates on maintaining stability (legal, political, and macroeconomic) for entrepreneurial activity, and ensuring that legal norms operate, including bankruptcy for those who cannot demonstrate their efficiency in competition. That is, for sustainable economic growth the government must ensure a favourable entrepreneurial climate, which, in turn, would stimulate the structural reconstruction of the economy.

But any variant of economic policy requires the consolidation of the government and of the political élite. That is why the beginning of sustainable economic growth would be a sign of the completion of the revolutionary economic crisis, a criterion of the end of the revolution.

The economic problems we have discussed in this chapter do not occur only in revolutions. All of them may arise in other circumstances, and their presence is not in itself sufficient to demonstrate the existence or absence of a revolutionary economic crisis.

Furthermore, we have not considered here all of the economic problems of revolutions. We have analysed only the most typical and universal ones, that is, those that have appeared in all of the full-scale revolutions.

A general characteristic of these problems which we have examined, and of the revolutionary economic crisis as a whole, is their causal relationship with the phenomenon of the weak state. It is during revolutions, as well as in other situations where the state is significantly weakened, that these problems arise. The most obvious sign of the state's political and economic weakness is its inability to collect taxes. This is directly reflected both in the state's fulfilment, or rather non-fulfilment, of its budget commitments, and in its inability to pursue an economic policy necessary to ensure stability and growth.

10

The Russian Experience: Theoretical Interpretations

10.1 Defining revolution: the role of violence

The theory of revolution has been elaborated within the social sciences for many years, but many basic questions (for example, what constitutes a revolution, how we should classify the various types of revolution, what are the various forms of revolutionary action) remain imprecise. In this chapter we will consider how the theory of revolution might develop further in the light of recent events in Russia. The recent Russian experience can be assessed in two ways. Either we could treat what we consider to have been a revolution as a case-study within existing theory, in which case our task would be to point out peculiar traits possessed by that revolution when compared with the 'classic' revolutions of the past. Alternatively, we could combine our analysis of the recent Russian events with what we consider to be a necessary revision of the general theory of revolution. We take the view that the second approach is more productive and this is the one we have adopted. If it emerges that revolution is not solely a phenomenon of pre-industrial, underdeveloped countries, then the peculiar features of revolutionary processes in societies at earlier stages of development, with low levels of literacy and overall culture, cannot be regarded as universal features of revolutionary change in a theory of revolution.

The most important problem in this regard concerns the place of violence in the definition of revolution. The vast majority of definitions of revolution have included violence as a distinguishing feature,[1] and researchers see violence as a criterion, if not the essential criterion, which distinguishes revo-

---

[1] We can cite a number of examples. In his definition of revolution, which has become the classic one, Huntington describes it as 'rapid, fundamental, and violent domestic change in the dominant values and myths of a society, in its political institutions, social structure, leadership, and government activity and policies' (1968: 264). Dunn defines revolution as 'a form of massive, violent and rapid social change' (1972: 12). Gurr regarded it as a subspecies of a group of phenomena 'a common property of which is the actual or threatened use of violence' (1970: 3–4). Johnson defines revolution as 'a special kind of social change, one that involves the intrusion of violence into civil social relations' (1982: 1).

lution from evolutionary change. However, as we have seen, one of the peculiarities of the recent Russian events has been a lack of mass violence involving significant sections of the population and exercising a decisive influence on the speed and direction of change. Whilst it would be wrong to imagine that violence has been completely absent throughout the course of the recent Russian revolution, its scale has been so limited that it cannot be regarded as an integral or decisive feature of Russia's retreat from communism. Writers on contemporary Russia deal with this paradox in different ways. In order to reconcile the widely held view of revolution as an act of violence with his firm conviction that the recent events in Russia were of a revolutionary character, Michael McFaul has proposed a special category of revolution, the 'peaceful revolution', and suggests that the Russian events should be regarded as an example of that new category (McFaul 1996: 170). However, the very possibility of 'peaceful revolutions' obliges us once again to return to a more basic question—is violence a necessary feature of revolution, or is it merely a peculiarity of some revolutions that has been assumed to be common to all?

Long before the recent events in Russia some writers began to doubt whether violence should be counted among the integral features of revolution. This problem has been best analysed in a work of A. S. Cohan, *Theories of Revolution: An Introduction*. Cohan draws attention to the internal contradiction of definitions of revolution which single out both large-scale violence and social change as criteria or distinguishing features of revolution. For Cohan, 'revolution is at the end of a continuum of social change, and it is possible to place it on a continuum of violent behavior. But violence and social change may be mutually exclusive phenomena. The degree of social change does not necessarily increase in proportion to the degree of violence that is present. Either can occur in the absence of the other' (Cohan 1975: 27). Although he does not argue his case at great length, Cohan's approach contains some important ideas which deserve to be considered in more detail.

First, Cohan stresses the importance of the 'system of co-ordinates' used to examine the phenomenon of revolution. If revolution is regarded as a type of violent action, and is lumped together in that general category with peasant and urban uprisings, putsches, wars of independence, and other forms of active resistance to the authorities, then violence is a criterion of primary importance. However, if revolution is placed in a different 'system of co-ordinates', based on some form or other of radical transformation of social relations, not only may violence not be of primary importance—it may be altogether unimportant. There are no serious reasons why revolution should not be considered from this point of view. In this work, for example, revolution 'from below' is regarded as one of the mechanisms by which constraints on social development can be removed, and is analysed alongside other such mechanisms, such as reforms, revolution 'from above', and foreign occupation.

Secondly, Cohan stresses that the diminishing role of violence in the revolutions of the twentieth century is historically conditioned, in that it is linked to the rise of the philosophy of non-violence. The examples he cites (the winning of independence by India under the leadership of Gandhi, and the US civil rights movement led by Martin Luther King) cannot indisputably be categorized as revolutions, and the reasons for a change in the role of violence cannot simply be reduced to the emergence of the philosophy of non-violence. Even so, Cohan's analysis of the influence of the historical and cultural context upon the mechanisms by which revolutions are carried out is an important methodological point that is forgotten in theories of revolution.

A peculiar kind of 'philosophy of non-violence' was a feature of the recent Russian revolution. Although it had never been elaborated as a special political doctrine, in practice it was shared by the overwhelming majority of the population. What is more, this attitude was prevalent at a time when, according to the traditional analysis of such events, the likelihood of violence was very high. Gorbachev's reforms brought about a massive surge of positive expectations in society, but the hopes of the first years of *perestroyka* were not realized. Assessing the evolution of public opinion towards *perestroyka*, sociologists noticed a growing gulf between the actual state of affairs and the notion of how things ought to be (Koval. 1997: 276). Table 10.1 shows that even among those social groups who came out most strongly in favour of *perestroyka*, the workers and intellectuals in major cities, disenchantment was growing. Subsequently the situation got even worse: those social strata which had been the keenest supporters of the changes at the outset and had pinned the greatest hopes upon them were the ones who suffered most from the economic crisis and the decline in their social status. Writers on the theory of violence apply to this process the concept of 'relative deprivation', the intensity of which is determined by the extent of the gap between expectations and real possibilities. This process provides a foundation for violent actions. The potential for violence should increase still further when there is growing social and economic differentiation, especially, in the Russian case, in view of the powerful demonstration effect when society is opened up and information about living standards in the West is made available (Gurr 1970).

In present-day Russia, however, there are powerful countervailing tendencies which work against the use of violent methods in tackling social problems. First and foremost, there is the overall nature of the Russian population, which is almost entirely literate, urbanized to a fairly high degree, and educated to reject the bloody experience of the past. This means that, even though the economic and social position of many people has deteriorated substantially, they are much less predisposed to violence than the masses that played the major role in earlier revolutions, who were primarily agrarian, illiterate, and living at the level of physical subsistence. In his analysis of the reasons for the predominantly peaceful nature of the Russian events, Egor

TABLE 10.1. *Responses to the question: 'Is perestroyka meeting your expectations?',*
1989 (%)

Region	Social group	Yes (in full or in part)	No	Hard to say
Moscow	Workers	50	36	11
	Engineers/ technicians	50	46	4
	Non-industrial intelligentsia	63	37	—
Leningrad	Workers	28	59	13
	Engineers/ technicians	52	43	5
	Non-industrial intelligentsia	46	54	—
Tomsk	Workers	38	55	7
	Engineers/ technicians	52	37	11
	Non-industrial intelligentsia	72	22	6
Irkutsk	Workers	42	50	8
	Engineers/ technicians	44	52	4
	Non-industrial intelligentsia	60	37	3

Note: Unfortunately, not all the data are accurate. For example certain rows add up to less than 100%.
Source: Intelligentsiya o sotsial′no-politicheskoy situatsii v strane (1990: 30).

Gaidar argues that the most important factor which prevented full-scale civil war in Russia was 'the very maturity of urbanized, educated, late-socialist society, which differed sharply from those early industrial countries which underwent peasant revolutions' (Gaidar 1997*a*: 463).

Thirdly and lastly, Cohan quite correctly notes that the concept of violence is ambiguous, in that different writers use it to denote quite different phenomena. He concludes that 'a clear, concise and widely accepted definition of violence does not appear to have been derived' (1975: 26). Indeed, violence in revolutions can be considered from many different angles, and can involve different combinations of phenomena. It is useful to examine various types of violent action during a revolution, in order to determine in each case whether the form of violence in question is an integral aspect of revolution, or a particular instance of other, more general processes which could take place in a non-violent form.

Several authors consider a certain type of violent action, such as an illegal seizure of power, to be a necessary distinguishing feature of a revolution.

Trimberger (1978), for example, defines revolution as a kind of extra-legal takeover of the state apparatus. However, a legal assumption of power and an extra-legal one can be easily distinguished without ambiguity only in societies with relatively simple mechanisms for changing the holders of power. As soon as it is a matter of societies with more complicated state structures and mechanisms, the number of 'borderline' cases increases sharply. How should one assess leaders or parties which come to power in elections involving large-scale pressure on the electorate? How widespread do abuses in the course of elections have to be before the victor can be considered to have taken power unlawfully? The manner in which various dictatorial and fascist régimes have come to power illustrates this question very clearly. The recent Russian revolution raises similarly complex problems. Can Yeltsin's rule as leader of an independent Russian state in 1991 be regarded as legal? On the one hand, he was the popularly elected President of Russia; on the other hand, at the time of his election Russia was not an independent state. On the one hand, the Union Treaty did envisage in principle that constituent republics could secede from the USSR; on the other hand, the mechanisms for secession had not been defined, and it remains unclear whether the manner in which the Union Treaty was repudiated can be regarded as having been constitutional.

Also, how should we assess those cases where sharp changes in the social basis and in the mechanisms through which power is exercised occur without any overall change of political régime? There have been numerous examples of this in world history, which tended to be regarded as 'revolutions from above'. They have been particularly prevalent in German history. As examples of this sort of revolution, Barrington Moore has cited Stein-Hardenberg's reforms in Prussia between 1807 and 1814, and the unification of Germany under Bismarck in the 1860s (Moore 1966). Other writers on the subject would only apply that description to the Prussian reforms of the early nineteenth century, whilst not rejecting in principle the possibility of similar phenomena in other periods (Skocpol 1994*a*). Gorbachev's sharp change of direction around 1987–8, when the course of the Soviet democratization process under *perestroyka* fundamentally changed the social basis of the régime, could be put into this category.

Although revolution necessarily involves some kind of 'interruption in the gradualness' of the political process, it can take many forms. And, although a violent seizure of power is the most clear-cut form of this interruption, it is not always possible to draw a firm boundary between legal and illegal ways of coming to power in countries with a relatively complex form of state structure and which lack stable democratic traditions. What is more, the definition of revolution as a forcible seizure of power cannot encompass a whole series of phenomena traditionally regarded as 'revolutions from above', but which take place within the established legal framework.

The second type of violent action that is typical of revolutionary periods is violence on the part of the authorities against a movement from below. This type of violence is not usually included in definitions of revolution. On the contrary, many researchers consider that one of the conditions for the outbreak of revolution is that the *ancien régime* is insufficiently decisive in its use of force to defend its power. Violent actions by the authorities in the course of the revolutionary process may be aimed at forestalling any escalation of the revolution, or entail a struggle against counter-revolution. Either way, the use of violence is not in itself a necessary indicator of the revolutionary nature of the changes. In many cases the use of terror is a specific feature of the most radical phase of the revolution but, as we have shown above, this has not been typical of all revolutions. Moreover, mass terror may be employed not only during revolutionary processes, but by any dictatorial régime, including those not connected with any kind of revolutionary change. For these reasons, violence 'from above' on the part of the authorities cannot be regarded, and in practice has not been regarded, as a distinguishing feature of revolution.

It is the third form of violence, violence 'from below' in the form of popular movements, uprising, riots, and so on, that has attracted the most attention from specialists on the theory of revolution. For Theda Skocpol an essential feature of revolution is that a rapid systemic change in the class and state structure of society 'is accompanied and in part carried through by class-based revolts from below' (1979: 33). Moreover, in her schema, peasant revolts are an absolutely necessary attribute. Other authors stress the importance of urban uprisings in the course of revolutionary development.

In order to understand whether violence 'from below' is a necessary attribute of revolution, it is essential to establish what role this violence plays in the interactions of various social forces with the authorities, and with each other. It would seem that overall it has two functions. First, it creates an exchange of information, a 'feedback mechanism' with the authorities, aimed at improving the position of these groups when other methods of attaining this goal have proven to be ineffective. Secondly, violence puts pressure on the authorities to change their policies in line with the more general, primarily political demands of these social groups, or it may be used in support of the programmatic demands of other social groups. The first function can be observed in the French Revolution, when the peasants demanded that the Estates General revoke seigniorial obligations and then, having realized that this method of communication was ineffectual, moved on to more active, violent ways of achieving this end. The second function has been more prevalent in urban uprisings. There are numerous instances when the most import-ant political questions, crucial to the fate of the revolution, have been decided under pressure from a populace in revolt, starting with the popular movement in London in May 1641 which brought forward the decision to execute Strafford.[2] In practice, both functions are closely interwoven, as may be seen in the slogan of the Parisian poor: 'Bread and Constitution!'

Obviously, uprisings and riots are extreme methods of attaining these ends, and they are used when all other methods have proved to be ineffectual. This raises the question of how one should characterize events in which radical systemic changes are accompanied by actions 'from below' of a non-violent character. This problem will be examined in greater detail in our analysis of the relationship between the concepts of 'social revolution', 'political revolution', and 'revolution from above'. For the moment it is important to note that violence 'from below' is not an end in itself. It is rather a way in which definite functions can be exercised and definite problems solved, things which could, in principle, be done no less effectively through other, non-violent methods.

Our short discussion of the role of violence allows us to draw the following conclusions. Revolution may be characterized in two ways – as a mode of bringing about changes or in terms of the essence of those changes. As far as the mode is concerned, stress is usually laid on the violent, non-judicial character of the processes. As for the essence, emphasis tends to be upon the profound, rapid, and systemic nature of the changes. There is, however, no necessary connection between the depth of the changes and their violent character. In each of the cases we have examined, violence has been an instrument used to solve certain tasks in a specific historical situation, particularly where the state structure has been fairly inflexible, and literacy levels low, and there has been no institutional structure permitting interactions between the authorities and different social strata and groups. There is no theoretical reason why the same tasks could not have been solved by other, non-violent or less violent methods. The recent Russian revolution has demonstrated that changes of a radical and systemic nature are not necessarily accompanied by large-scale violence. It would seem, therefore, that there are insufficient grounds for preserving this dualism in the definition of revolution. If the essence of revolution is deemed to consist in a rapid, profound, and systemic social transformation (one might sometimes add the word 'unexpected' to that list), then violence as such need not be regarded as an integral feature of the revolutionary process.

10.2 Defining revolution: spontaneous development and the weakness of the state

The analysis undertaken in the preceding section leaves open the question of what, if not violence, distinguishes revolutionary from evolutionary

---

[2] For greater detail on this question see Kosminsky and Levitsky (1954: i. 152–4).

development. It seems to us that the criterion consists in the spontaneous character of the revolutionary process: it is not controlled either by the authorities or by any particular political group. Skocpol describes the distinguishing features of revolution as follows: 'In fact, in historical revolutions, differently situated and motivated groups have become participants in a complex unfolding of multiple conflicts. . . . The logic of these conflicts has not been controlled by any one class or group, no matter how seemingly central in the revolutionary process. And the revolutionary conflicts have invariably given rise to outcomes neither fully foreseen nor intended by—nor perfectly serving the interests of—any of the particular groups involved' (1979: 17–18).

It is precisely this spontaneous, uncontrolled nature of the revolutionary process which makes possible the general patterns of revolutionary development examined above, and which determines the surprising similarity in the logic of development of revolutionary processes which have occurred at different times and in dissimilar circumstances. This peculiarity of revolutions has been well understood by the revolutionary leaders themselves. They have been aware of the impossibility of controlling the course of events even when they have not had to contend with mass violence 'from below'. As Gaidar put it in his interview with the authors: 'our experience shows that it is in revolutionary periods that we see the operation of very powerful social forces, very powerful processes, which can hardly be directed at all. There are certain turning points, certain forks in the road, when these processes can go in quite different directions', and, in his opinion, it is at these turning points that the actions of the authorities can be of fundamental importance. For the rest of the time the process remains mainly spontaneous.

The reasons why social processes slip out of the control of the authorities are to be found in the specific conditions and developments of the pre-revolutionary period. The spontaneous nature of the revolutionary process is a consequence of the fragmentation of society and the weakness of the state on the eve of, and in the course of, the revolution. We have already considered various aspects of this phenomenon, and we can now draw certain conclusions.

The concept of a 'weak state' can be interpreted in a variety of ways, so it is necessary to define more precisely what is meant here. The weakness of the state in a revolution is not the same as the kind of limited role for the state envisaged in liberal ideology, where the state minimizes its interference in the economy and social life overall, giving free rein to private initiative. This liberal state should be cheap to run, should not be over-bureaucratized, and should carry out its minimal set of necessary functions efficiently. It is clear that any revolutionary régime has little in common with that sort of state.

We see the weakness of the state in revolution first and foremost in the régime's inability to control the speed or direction of the changes under way, or to implement coherent or stable policies to achieve certain ends. This is why a large part of the population perceives the situation in a country in revolution in terms of a 'lack of order, powerlessness, anarchy'. According to the public opinion polls in Russia, about 50 per cent of respondents regarded the political situation in the country as 'anarchy, powerless, lack of order'. This figure did not change much in the 1990s: 58 per cent in November 1990, 52 in July 1994, and 48 in March 1998 (Levada 1998: 10). This weakness has nothing to do with the personalities of individual leaders—in any revolution the political stage is filled with a galaxy of striking and quite extraordinary political figures. There are deep, settled social reasons for this weakness.

The most important of these is the destruction of the general social consensus around the norms, values, and principles of the country's development. New processes and phenomena in social and economic development are incompatible with the traditional system of values, and in the pre-revolutionary period this causes society to fragment. The structure of society becomes markedly more complex, as the boundaries between traditional classes and groups dissolve, interests within those groups diverge, and new social forces emerge which were not represented in the old system. Society now collapses into a multitude of groups possessing a complex mosaic of interests, which converge in certain areas, and conflict in others. A feature of this sort of system is that not one of the development paths open to the country is capable of gaining widespread support amongst either the élite or the masses. The coalitions of interests 'against' are usually stronger than the coalitions of interests 'for'. Both government action and government inaction lead to growing dissatisfaction. Sensing a lack of social support, the authorities start to waver, and this weakens their position still further. This equivocation ultimately leads to the collapse of the existing régime and the start of the revolutionary process.

In the course of the revolution society remains fragmented, and the structure of interests is in constant motion. The position of different groups in the course of revolution can change very sharply and uncontrollably, from substantial improvement to catastrophic deterioration. For this reason, throughout the entire course of the revolution, the government has no stable social support. It is obliged to balance constantly between different social forces, to look for all possible means of uniting their interests if only briefly, and to prop up pro-revolutionary coalitions as they head for collapse. The opportunities for manoeuvre are very limited, and the costs of mistakes are very high—one wrong step can mean the loss of power. This characteristic process, in which the groups holding power alternate in chaotic fashion, will only come to an end once a redistribution of power and wealth has resulted in the emergence of a new élite that is powerful enough to provide the basis of a relatively stable régime. However, even this does not mean that the situation has finally stabilized. It can be several more decades after the immediate completion of the revolutionary process before society acquires a post-revolutionary consensus and the élite becomes fully structured, achieving a balance between its new and its remaining pre-revolutionary elements. During these decades there can be sharp changes in domestic and foreign policy, coups, 'secondary revolutions', and other such manifestations of instability.

Another factor which weakens both pre-revolutionary and revolutionary régimes is chronic financial crisis. This arises when governments are either deprived of their traditional sources of revenue and cannot find new ones, or cannot cope with some sharp increase in budgetary expenditure. The financial crisis greatly limits the authorities' ability to work towards strategic, long-term goals and to pursue coherent policies. All the acts of the ruling régime are then mainly determined by the need to reduce the pressure of this financial shortfall, to plug the holes in the budget. To try to do this the government may attempt to undertake radical reforms and to resurrect the customs and habits of the distant past, to support the most advanced ideas and to rely on the most reactionary forces, all at the same time. This political inconsistency intensifies the conflict between government and society. It turns the most diverse social strata and groups, whatever their views, against the régime.

The authorities are dogged by financial crisis throughout the entire course of the revolution. It is exacerbated by the emergence of a wider spectrum of economic difficulties. These limit still further the already insignificant freedom of manoeuvre available to revolutionary governments, compelling them to shape their policies not only to ensure social support, but also to cope with the permanent threat of financial disaster. The financial crisis is normally overcome only in the final stages of the revolution, by means of extraordinary and painful measures.

The weakness of the state in the revolutionary period has many manifestations, of which the following are the most important.

First, the government's political course wavers continually. The authorities are subject to unremitting pressure from various quarters, and, in order to survive, they have to manœuvre constantly between different groups and forces. Consequently, their actions are inconsistent and often unpredictable, and the bases on which decisions are taken are far from clear.

Secondly, the number of centres of power multiplies. A revolutionary régime is never able completely to concentrate power in its hands, and there are always various alternative power centres with which it has to reckon. They may exist within the framework of the existing political system, or outside it, as counter-revolutionary movements. The most clear-cut manifestation of this tendency, although certainly not the only one, is the situation of dual power which arises at a certain stage in any revolution. However, there may be even more centres of power, and their interaction and confrontation may take many forms, up to and including civil war.

Thirdly, there are no established and generally accepted 'rules of the game' in any sphere of public life. The procedures for decision-taking are not firmly laid down. Decisions which are taken are not always implemented, and even those that are put into effect are often interpreted highly subjectively. The supremacy of the law is not regarded as an immutable rule. Robespierre's statement that the actions of a revolutionary government are based on the most indisputable of foundations—necessity—and that the constitution can only be effective after the revolution has triumphed over its enemies is an excellent illustration of the conditions in which a revolutionary government is obliged to operate.[3]

Therefore, an essential distinguishing feature of a revolutionary period is a weak state which not only cannot control or direct powerful social processes, but is itself a plaything of those processes. Revolution itself can be defined as a spontaneous process of abrupt social transformation, not under the control of the authorities, with unpredictable consequences.

10.3 The classification of revolutions: the role of mass movements

The diversity of the revolutionary process and the combinations of different forms of revolutionary change is reflected in the different classes of revolution that have been identified. The most radical, full-scale form, marked by the depth of the changes involved, is usually considered to be the social revolution. Social revolution has traditionally been distinguished from other, less global revolutionary upheavals in two basic respects. On the one hand, it involves a widespread popular mass movement 'from below'. On the other hand, it leads to radical changes in property rights, as a result of which the formerly dominant class loses its leading position. Skocpol has described this type of revolution as follows: 'Social revolutions are set apart from other sorts of conflicts and transformative processes above all by the combination of two coincidences: the coincidence of societal structural change with class upheaval; and the coincidence of political with social transformation' (1979: 4). In cases where the mass movement 'from below' is absent, and the socio-economic transformations do not lead to a substantial change in the class structure of society, the revolution is generally regarded as 'political'. However, if in spite of the subsidiary role of mass actions, the social transformations are of a radical nature, such a phenomenon is sometimes regarded as a 'revolution

---

[3] 'A revolution is a war between liberty and its enemies; a constitution is a régime of victory already secured and a world of liberty'; 'Revolutionary government bases its actions on the most sacred law of social salvation and on its most indisputable foundation—necessity' (Robespierre 1967: 274, 275).

from above', in contrast to a 'revolution from below', where the masses play a decisive role. At first glance, this sort of classification system appears quite tidy. In practice, however, there are several cases which cannot be categorized unambiguously. The most important of these are the English Revolution of the seventeenth century, and the recent Russian events.

Skocpol has argued in detail that the English events were a political revolution. Her main arguments in support of this thesis are basically as follows. First, the revolution was accomplished not through the mechanism of class struggle, but in the course of a civil war between different segments of the dominant class. There were no widespread peasant uprisings against the landlords in England. Secondly, the English Revolution did not lead to a substantial transformation in the class and social structure. It did not place a new class at the summit of society. Its main achievements were in the political sphere: the power of the monarch to intervene in political, economic, and religious matters was circumscribed, and there was a fundamental change in the role of Parliament in the political system (Skocpol 1979: 140–4). Similarly, some researchers have described the recent events in Russia as a 'revolution from above', arguing that 'the ultimate explanation for the surprisingly sudden and peaceful demise of the Soviet system was that it was abandoned by most of its own élite, whose material and ideological ties to any form of socialism had grown weaker and weaker as the Soviet system evolved' (Kotz with Weir 1997: 6).

There are very clear similarities in the arguments which are deployed against the idea that the English and the recent Russian revolutions were social revolutions. This is no accident. Although they are very far apart in time, they have quite a lot in common in terms of the mechanisms which brought them about. In both the English and the recent Russian revolutions the role of spontaneous risings 'from below' was quite limited, violence in the radical phase did not take the form of full-scale terror, there was no radical change of élites, and a 'social utopia' did not play an important role in the ideology of the revolutionary forces. At the same time, both the form of the movement 'from below' and the nature of the changes in property in these two revolutions have a specific feature which has usually escaped the attention of their students.

It is usually assumed that during a revolution the masses can either participate in spontaneous revolts (such as the peasant uprisings in France), or be indifferent and apathetic (such as in the Meiji Revolution in Japan, seen as a typical example of 'revolution from above'). However, both the English and the recent Russian revolutions demonstrate that there are other possible patterns. There can be institutionalized forms of pressure 'from below', which, while they are not spontaneous or uncontrollable, none the less represent the active involvement of the masses in the revolutionary process. Indeed, all revolutions have involved a certain relationship between spontaneous and institutionalized forms of action 'from below'. The greatest degree of spontaneity has tended to be shown by peasant movements. The English Revolution was not without these movements. There were peasant actions against enclosures during those years, such as the struggle in East Anglia against the draining of the Fens, and the uprisings in South-west England, as well as specific forms of movement 'from below' brought about by the Civil War, such as the Clubmen. On the other hand, the scale of these actions was much more modest than in most of the other great revolutions. It is also important that the tendency for the interactions between different social forces to be institutionalized has been manifested mainly in the cities. For example, it was the Commune of Paris which to the greatest extent expressed the demands of the *sans-culottes* in the course of the French Revolution.

The institutional mechanisms for applying pressure 'from below' were vastly more important in the English and recent Russian revolutions than in the other great revolutions. In England this institutionalization took a fairly simple form: pressure 'from below' was exercised primarily through the New Model Army. As various studies have shown, this army embraced a significant part of the politically active population, including peasants who had been thrown off the land as a result of enclosures. The army provided the social base for the activities of radical political forces in the English Revolution, especially the Levellers. Indeed, pamphlets by the Leveller leader Lilburne were regarded by some soldiers as articles of law (see Kosminsky and Levitsky 1954: i. 209). It was pressure from the army which radicalized the aims of part of the élite, giving the revolution as a whole a more radical nature. This fact has been used by some researchers to argue that there were two revolutions within the English Revolution, one of which was political, while the other can be seen as a social revolution (Russell 1973). In this sense the role of the army in the English Revolution can be likened to that of the *sans-culottes* in France, who radicalized the originally much more moderate politics of the Jacobins.

The events of the recent Russian revolution are rather more ambiguous. It began as a 'revolution from above', although this has been true of all the great revolutions. It is quite possible that in the initial phases, changes 'from above' were more important in that revolution than in any other. Alexander Yakovlev observes in his interview that in 1985 he was 'already absolutely convinced that nothing would happen in our country through the dissident movement. A totalitarian system can only be overthrown through the totalitarian party.' He sees the introduction of *glasnost* into the totalitarian system, which 'at a certain stage began to play its own tune and acquire its own logic', as the only 'forcible' act in the attempt at a non-violent transition to a new social system. However, this phase did not last long. As Gaidar puts it, 'the revolution, unleashed from above, was seized upon by those below, and taken up with anti-*nomenklatura*, egalitarian slogans' (1997c: 116). The institutionalization of pressure 'from below' in this revolution was far more complex and diverse than in any previous revolution.

First, Russian society was more developed, and the revolution proceeded through democratic mechanisms. This meant that expressions of popular will, such as elections and referendums, played an important part in providing 'feedback' between the government and various social groups. The support given to the President and the reform programme at the referendum of April 1993 was of vital importance in determining the fate of the radical régime, and the referendum also approved the new Russian constitution. Conversely, the results of the elections in December 1993 showed a decline in support for the radical reformers, and this was immediately reflected in the government's political course. The head of the government was replaced by a more moderate figure, and the rate of change was slowed. These sorts of feedback mechanisms existed in embryonic form in other revolutions (mandates, petitions, elections of delegates to representative bodies), but played a much more modest, subsidiary role.

Secondly, the most active, politically advanced sections of the population did not confine themselves to spontaneous uprisings. They strove to have their interests represented in organized institutions, and to use these institutions to exert constant pressure upon the authorities. Only in especially critical situations did they supplement these methods with direct action 'from below'. An example of this is provided by the miners, who were the most active cohort of the working class in the recent Russian revolution. During the wave of miners' strikes in the summer of 1989, which were a form of direct political pressure on the authorities, the miners created their own trade union, the Independent Union of Mineworkers, which went on to represent their interests in an institutional form. The same can be said about the movement of the politically active groups of the population, particularly in the major towns. These groups became institutionalized at first in individual towns and cities, and then, in 1990, organized themselves at the all-Russia level, initiating the 'Democratic Russia' movement. Even those who argue that the revolution was a revolution 'from above' are obliged to admit that 'Democratic Russia was a real movement from below' (Kotz with Weir 1997: 135).

However, institutionalization could not completely overcome the instability, nebulousness, and changeability of interests which are a feature of any revolution. This made the institutionalization itself unstable; the institutions lacked any clear programme of action, and their positions changed constantly or even ceased altogether to represent the views of those social groups that had originally backed them. The difficulties this caused were fully appreciated by the leaders of the revolutionary movement, particularly in its radical phase. As Gaidar puts it, the revolutionary changes were supported by 'a fairly broad, unstructured, democratic mass, which was at that time still revolutionary. It was opposed to the communists, and could be mobilized in critical situations. However, its main weakness was that it was not very structured, it still did not reflect any stable interests, and for that reason one could not rely upon it'.

Gennady Burbulis, describing the same phenomenon, argued that the transformations 'did not have a social base, but a socio-psychological one. A social
base is one which is rooted in the interests of organized groups'.

10.4 The classification of revolutions: changes in forms of property, classes, and élites

The question of transforming property is one which deserves particular attention. In the literature on revolution, the degree of radicalism in changing the
character of *property* is often equated with the degree of radicalism in changing the *property owners*. The logic behind this is essentially as follows: in
England the landowners were not dispossessed, therefore there was no
substantial change in the nature of property, whereas in France there was a
significant redistribution of property in the interests of the peasantry, therefore in this case there were radical changes in property relations. However, on
closer examination we find serious problems with such a simplistic schema.

It is quite true that the English Revolution did not involve any large-scale
change of property owners, although the resale of the confiscated property of
the counter-revolutionary aristocracy did increase opportunities for the
urban bourgeoisie and army officers to acquire land. Even in these cases,
however, the land was often bought back by its former owners through inter-
mediaries. However, although landholdings remained the same physically, the
economic content of this property altered significantly. It was no longer held
by grace and favour of the monarch, with limitations on its use and with
conflicting rights for different economic agents to use that property in its various functions. It had become fully private property, over which the holder
could exercise in full the functions of ownership, use, and disposal. The
English Revolution produced major changes in the nature of property. It abolished Tenures by Knights Service,[4] thereby taking a major step towards establishing fully fledged private property in land and equalizing the property

---

[4] Tenure by Knights Service was originally a military tenure, which subsequently
retained many feudal features: numerous payments to the lord, restrictions on inheritance
and forms of usage, etc. When a non-adult noble inherited a tenure the lord became his
warder and could administer the property of the person under wardship. This gave rise to
considerable protest. To ensure that the obligations connected with Tenure by Knights
Service were observed in practice, a Court of Wards was established in 1541, and lasted
until 1646. Tenure by Knights Service, along with the system of wardship and the Court of
Wards, were abolished by an Ordinance of the Long Parliament of 24 Feb. 1646. This was
later confirmed by a special Act of Cromwell on 27 Nov. 1656, and finally reaffirmed in the
course of the Restoration in 1660.

rights of all landholders.[5] The abolition during the revolution of those institutions which, on behalf of the Crown, had prevented the enclosure of common land and the eviction of peasants, also served to clarify land relationships in the English countryside and to regularize the private property rights of the landlords. Overall, the English Revolution meant that although the landlord class retained its ownership of the land, the nature of that ownership changed substantially, becoming much more capitalistic in character.

The changes in property which took place during the French Revolution are also susceptible to an interpretation different from the traditional one. The French peasants were, in reality, already owners of the land before the revolution. They could use it as they thought fit, buy it, sell it, and leave it in their wills, even though they did not have formal title to it. Only one quarter of the land belonged to the aristocracy (Furet 1996: 11). The revolution did not so much change the character of landholding as bring its real status and formal status into line with each other. At the same time, the French Revolution reinforced certain forms of common landholding of a typically feudal, medieval nature. It would of course be an inadmissible oversimplification to infer from this that the French Revolution did not have a substantial impact on property relations in land, or that the resale of confiscated land on terms acceptable to small owners did not greatly strengthen the position of peasant landholding. The interpretation of events outlined above is intended, instead, to show that the transformations of property relations in both the English and the French Revolutions were not so vastly different in scope. Both took an important step in establishing full-blown private property rights, essential for further social development. And in both cases certain features of feudal, medieval landholding were preserved. The difference was that in the first case the land question was resolved mainly in the interest of large-scale private property, and in the second case, mainly in the interest of small-scale private property. In this respect the question of whether there was a change of ruling class in the English Revolution becomes a legal and economic question rather than a question of sociology. One can claim that the landed aristocracy was transformed by the revolution into a class of private landowners, and in that respect the form of class domination changed.

The real difference between the English and French Revolutions was that in England there was almost no change in the political élite, whereas in France it was to a significant degree replaced. This is not, however, of paramount importance in determining whether the revolution was a social one. The relative stability of the political élite during the English Revolution does not prevent us from regarding it as a successful political revolution, because the mechanisms of political power were substantially altered as a result. On the

---

[5] An exception was made for copyhold, which was preserved as common tenure, a medieval form, in which property rights were not clearly laid down.

other hand, we are not prevented from seeing it as a social revolution, because social relations, particularly property relations, were substantially transformed. This transformation permitted a sharp increase in the rate of enclosures in the eighteenth century, which led to major changes in the English agrarian sector. To a great extent this determined not only the features of English agriculture, but also the subsequent development of the country's economy as a whole.

The transformation of property during the recent Russian revolution has features in common with both the English and the French variants. As in France, although property rights have ostensibly undergone a sharp and radical change, in fact to a large extent they have merely been granted formally to those persons who had in practice already long been the owners and controllers of that property, namely, the managements of enterprises. At the same time, in the course of the recent Russian revolution, as in the English one, it has been necessary to resolve the problem of conflicting claims to the same property, where the contenders have been the enterprise director, the workforce, the local authorities, and others. In analogous cases in England the property was usually divided up between all the various claimants who were able to substantiate their demands. Instead of having the right of partial use of all the property, they each got full private ownership rights over part of the property. In some respects the approach in Russia has been similar. As we have seen, the mechanism of voucher privatization, which in theory allowed every citizen of the country to take part, combined with certain privileges for particular categories of voucher holders, allowed differing interests to be harmonized. In practice, this solved the same problem: partial claims to one and the same item of property were replaced by full ownership rights, in the form of shares, over part of that property.

Our comparison of the nature and extent of the transformations brought about by the English, French, and recent Russian revolutions has allowed us to conclude that there are grounds for regarding all three as social revolutions. This comparison also allows us to make another, more universal observation, drawing together the conclusions of the preceding paragraphs. In the earlier periods, the form and content of the revolutionary changes were more closely and unambiguously interlinked. In the present period the same processes have assumed more varied forms. In many cases this can confuse researchers, in that they are observing a familiar and comprehensible process developing in a form which differs from the hitherto typical pattern. In fact, those manifestations of the revolutionary process which we can observe in present-day Russia existed in the experience of preceding revolutions, in an embryonic, or sometimes even in a well-developed, form. It was just that writers on this problem had not paid them sufficient attention.

11

Marx's Theory of Revolution and the Revolutions of the Twentieth Century

11.1 The inevitability of revolution: theory

It is held by many Russian authors that the origins of the crisis which led to the recent Russian revolution can be explained perfectly well in terms of Marxist theory. This has been argued by writers with very different ideas about the nature of the crisis and the course of Russian development over the last decade. Egor Gaidar recently put it this way:

The post-socialist revolution, in fact, fits Marx's analytical schema of revolutionary processes better than any other: it occurs at a stage when the possibility of developing productive forces within the existing (socialist) mode of production is exhausted. Their further progress requires the use of other (market) productive relations. In the pre-revolutionary period this exhaustion of the options for stable economic growth leads to an ideological crisis, in which the official ideology loses its attractiveness, and to a crisis of legitimacy and stability of political institutions. As they lose confidence in their own viability, the late-socialist authorities find themselves in a situation similar to that which faced the traditional monarchies in the early industrial period: whatever they do, whether they flirt with the masses, attempt to democratize, or use force—everything merely destabilizes the situation. (Gaidar 1997*a*: 463–4)

The same idea has been put forward by critics of Gaidar and of his analysis of Russia's transformation. The article by Krasil'shchikov mentioned earlier has a section entitled: 'The collapse of the Soviet system—confirmation of the correctness of Marx's theories'. He writes: 'Indeed, the very fact that the Soviet system collapsed provides the best possible confirmation of one of the basic precepts of Marx's theory: however important political events, wars, or the actions of leaders might be, in the final analysis, the movement of history is based upon the development of productive forces. Moreover, again as Marx saw it, this development of productive forces resembles the development of a person, his knowledge, habits, abilities, and social relations' (Krasil'shchikov 1996: 72).

Such unanimity may surprise those Western students of revolution who believe that 'Marxism as a theory, a coherent body of doctrine, is false. . . . The history of twentieth-century revolution . . . is still a commentary on the falsity of Marxism' (Dunn 1972: 19). Even those specialists who accept that Marx's theory of revolution has great theoretical significance, and regard it as 'perhaps the most significant of any of the schools of revolutionary thought' (Cohan 1975: 54), nonetheless stress that 'as a way of predicting outcomes it has not been validated with reference to industrial societies' (ibid. 68).

Even some of the Russian politicians who were directly involved in overthrowing a régime which formally claimed to be based on Marxist ideology still consider the Marxist analysis of revolution to be far-sighted. Although this may appear to be illogical at first sight, it in fact reflects a different interpretation of Marx's views on revolution. Western authors have tended to see the Marxist theory of revolution as a theory of social conflict, class struggle, and revolutionary violence: 'In short, Marx sees revolutions as emerging out of class-divided modes of production, and transforming one mode of production into another through class conflict' (Skocpol 1979: 8).

Less attention has been paid to another of the preconditions for revolution, the consequences of the development of productive forces which, as Marx put it, at a certain stage 'come into conflict with the existing relations of production', necessitating a revolutionary change in the social structure. Although Marx's famous dictum, 'A social order never perishes before all the productive forces for which it is broadly sufficient have been developed, and new superior relations of production never replace older ones before the material conditions for their existence have matured within the womb of the old society', is often cited, its connection with the theory of class struggle remains obscure. Moreover, some specialists consider the lack of clarity with regard to this linkage to be one of Marxism's principal theoretical defects:

> Marx was not at all clear about when the revolutionary change might happen. He did say, as we suggested earlier, that the revolution could not occur in society before 'all the productive forces for which there is room in it have developed'. This stage of development implies that the revolution could occur only when the subjective readiness of the proletariat meets the objective conditions. . . . What Marx was saying was that the revolution may succeed because the stage of development is right. If it fails it failed because the stage of development was not right. . . . It is not based on infallible powers of analysis. (Cohan 1975: 72)

This sort of criticism of Marxism is groundless. Marx not only formulated the thesis that 'At a certain stage of development, the material productive forces of society come into conflict with the existing relations of production' (Marx 1987: 263), he analysed in detail the forms taken by this conflict in capitalist society. In particular, a large part of his major work, *Capital*, is devoted to this question. *Capital*, however, tends to be largely overlooked in examinations of the Marxist legacy in the theory of revolution. We will therefore cite at length a passage from volume 1 of *Capital*, which is devoted to this problem. In his analysis of the processes of capitalist accumulation, Marx regarded the evolution of the capitalist mode of production as follows:

The transformation of the individualised and scattered means of production into socially concentrated ones, of the pigmy property of the many into the huge property of the few, the expropriation of the great mass of the people from the soil, from the means of subsistence, and from the means of labour, this fearful and painful expropriation of the mass of the people forms the prelude to the history of capital. It comprises a series of forcible methods, of which we have passed in review only those that have been epoch-making as methods of the primitive accumulation of capital. The expropriation of the immediate producers was accomplished with merciless vandalism, and under the stimulus of passions the most infamous, the most sordid, the pettiest, the most meanly odious. Self-earned private property, that is based, so to say, on the fusing together of the isolated, independent labouring-individual with the conditions of his labour, is supplanted by capitalistic private property, which rests on exploitation of the nominally free labour of others, i.e., on wage-labour.

As soon as this process of transformation has sufficiently decomposed the old society from top to bottom, as soon as the labourers are turned into proletarians, their means of labour into capital, as soon as the capitalist mode of production stands on its own feet, then the further socialisation of labour and further transformation of the land and other means of production into socially exploited and, therefore, common means of production, as well as the further expropriation of private proprietors, takes a new form. That which is now to be expropriated is no longer the labourer working for himself, but the capitalist exploiting many labourers. This expropriation is accomplished by the action of the immanent laws of capitalistic production itself, by the centralisation of capital. One capitalist always kills many. Hand in hand with this centralisation, or this expropriation of many capitalists by few, develop, on an ever extending scale, the co-operative form of the labour-process, the conscious technical application of science, the methodical cultivation of the soil, the transformation of the instruments of labour into instruments of labour only usable in common, the economising of all means of production by their use as the means of production of combined, socialised labour, the entanglement of all peoples in the net of the world-market, and with this, the international character of the capitalistic régime. Along with the constantly diminishing number of the magnates of capital, who usurp and monopolise all advantages of this process of transformation, grows the mass of misery, oppression, slavery, degradation, exploitation; but with this too grows the revolt of the working-class, a class always increasing in numbers, and disciplined, united, organised by the very mechanism of the process of capitalist production itself. The monopoly of capital becomes a fetter upon the mode of production, which has sprung up and flourished along with, and under it. Centralisation of the means of production and socialisation of labour at last reach a point where they become incompatible with their capitalist integument. This integument is burst asunder. The knell of capitalist private property sounds. The expropriators are expropriated. (Marx and Engels, *CW* xxxv. 749–50)[1]

It is clear that Marx did not conclude that socialist revolution was inevitable simply on the grounds that the worker was alienated from the fruits

---

[1] As Schumpeter put it, 'to predict the advent of big business was, considering the conditions of Marx's day, an achievement in itself' (1970: 34).

of his labour, the masses were becoming impoverished, and the class consciousness of the proletariat was growing. Marx noted another aspect of this trend. The growing division of labour and extent of co-operation meant that workers were increasingly making only a small part of a product, while at the same time there was growing socialization of the productive process, expressed in the concentration and centralization of capital. In other words, Marx saw increasing monopolization and the consequent need for social control over the economy as a natural outcome of the process of capitalist accumulation. This in its turn would necessitate a social system in which the organization of production and the appropriation of the fruits of labour could be organized collectively.[2] The individual organization of production and individual appropriation in circumstances where the need for social control is constantly growing would exacerbate the contradictions within the capitalist system. For Marx, this was an essential condition for the greater activity and class consciousness among the proletariat which would culminate eventually in a socialist revolution. In Marx's schema the objective exhaustion of possibilities for developing productive forces within the capitalist system was directly linked to the preparation of the subjective preconditions for proletarian revolution.

Before we examine how a Marxist approach might be applied to an analysis of recent events in Russia, let us examine the respects in which Marx's prognosis for the capitalist system has been borne out, and the respects in which it has not. A more complete picture of Marx's theory of revolution shows that not all of his predictions for capitalism have proven to be wrong. Marx was right to state that increasing monopolization of production and the economic and social processes it causes would lead to sharper contradictions with the mechanism of free competition and thereby necessitate stronger regulation and control. The First World War and the Great Depression of 1929–33 fully demonstrated that capitalist society in its monopolistic phase was unstable and unable to regulate itself. Many people viewed the crisis of the late 1920s and early 1930s as the inevitable end of capitalism.[3]

---

[2] This idea was expressed succinctly by Friedrich Engels, who argued in *Anti-Dühring* that the solution to the contradictions of capitalist society 'can only consist in the practical recognition of the social nature of the modern forces of production, and therefore in the harmonising of the modes of production, appropriation and exchange with the socialised character of the means of production. And this can only come about by society openly and directly taking possession of the productive forces which have outgrown all control except that of society as a whole' (Engels 1987: 266).

[3] Abraham Barkai, for example, states that the deepening of the economic crisis 'was widely interpreted as a sign of the end of capitalism', and this strengthened the tendency to idealize rural life in Germany (1990: 98). Many authors have noted that the idea that the economic crisis meant the death of capitalism was also widespread in the USA at this time (see e.g. Ekirch 1969). The vitality of such views can be gauged from a comment made by Schumpeter in 1949: 'Socialism has ceased to be resisted with moral passion. It has become

At that time it was generally accepted in economic theory that the mechanisms of free competition and capitalist entrepreneurship were unable to guarantee the survival and normal development of society. This idea was certainly not unique to Marxism. Many prominent academics warned of the dangers of monopolistic regulation of production, including such an irreconcilable opponent of Marxism as F. A. Hayek. In his celebrated work *The Road to Serfdom*, Hayek observed that

all the changes we are observing tend in the direction of a comprehensive central direction of economic activity; the universal struggle against competition promises to produce in the first instance something in many respects even worse, a state of affairs which can satisfy neither planners nor liberals: a sort of syndicalist or 'corporative' organisation of industry, in which competition is more or less suppressed but planning is left in the hands of the independent monopolies of the separate industries. . . . Once this stage is reached the only alternative to a return to competition is the control of the monopolies by the state, a control which, if it is to be made effective, must become progressively more complete and more detailed. (Hayek 1991: 30)

It is true that, unlike the Marxists, Hayek did not believe that monopoly was an objective consequence of the development of capitalist society, but rather that it had been artificially appended to it for ideological reasons. However, this did not prevent him from recognizing the transitional nature, the internal instability of monopolistic regulation and its inherent tendency to transfer regulation to the state. This tendency manifested itself in practice in all of the developed industrial states. The idea of economic planning enjoyed enormous popularity in the USA in the 1930s, where it reflected a growing disenchantment with individualism as the dominant idea of American society (see Ekirch 1969; Lawson 1971). In Britain, as a writer in *The Spectator* remarked in 1939, there were 'many signs that British leaders are growing accustomed to thinking in terms of national development by controlled monopolies' (cited in Hayek 1991: 31). This ideology, which affected even the most democratic states, developed to the greatest extent under fascist régimes, where anti-liberalism was one of the basic ideological doctrines. 'What matters is to emphasize the fundamental idea in my party's economic programme clearly—the idea of authority', remarked Hitler even before his accession to power; 'the Third Reich will always retain its right to control the owners of property' (quoted in Barkai 1990: 26–7).

These characteristic facts and tendencies of capitalist development in the 1920s and 1930s are well known, and were considered in our analysis of the crisis of mature industrialism in Chapter 2. It is important to stress the

---

a matter to be discussed in terms of utilitarian arguments. There are individualist diehards, of course, but they do not seem to evoke sufficient support to count politically. And *this* is the writing on the wall—proof that the ethos of capitalism is gone' (Schumpeter 1970: 410).

connection between these real processes and those inherent features of capitalist development that Marx discussed in *Capital*. We can see that the diagnosis Marx made of bourgeois society was in many respects correct. However, he was fundamentally mistaken about how the disease would be treated. His prognosis was wrong in two respects. First, many countries were able to adapt to the new circumstances without political upheavals, and substantially alter the relationship between the state, business, and workers by means of complex and far-reaching reforms. Secondly, where the process *was* accompanied by drastic changes in the state's political and social structure, these changes did not result from socialist revolutions carried out by the proletariat. Instead, in country after country totalitarian régimes came to power to implement 'revolution from above', with varying degrees of success. This raises three questions. Why, after predicting quite accurately how contradictions would develop in capitalist society, did Marx advance a quite erroneous hypothesis as to how these contradictions would be overcome? Why were certain countries able in practice to adapt their social system to these new conditions in an evolutionary way, while in other countries this process was accompanied by political upheaval, with catastrophic consequences not only for these countries, but for the entire civilized world? And finally, why, instead of proletarian revolutions 'from below', did the world witness attempts at fascist and other authoritarian revolutions 'from above'?

Other writers on this question have already analysed in some detail the reasons for the inadequacy of Marx's prognoses. In our view, there are two basic factors here.

First, Marx definitely overestimated the factors which caused instability in capitalist society, and did not pay due attention to those processes which could increase its stability. Marx noted the tendencies of early capitalism to impoverish the working class, and to increase inequality and exploitation, and inferred that these would apply to the whole of capitalist development. However, mass industrial production requires a mass consumer. It therefore needs to ensure that the bulk of the population has an income substantially above subsistence level. Marx completely ignored this as a factor which could enable the contradictions of capitalism to be overcome. Moreover, as production becomes more concentrated and centralized, the competitive pressure to reduce costs by all possible means is reduced, while the need for stable consumer markets becomes ever more pressing. As Joseph Schumpeter, for example, observed, 'the capitalist engine is first and last an engine of mass production which unavoidably also means production for the masses' (1970: 67). He drew from this the logical inference that 'the capitalist process, not by coincidence but by virtue of its mechanism, progressively raises the standard of life of the masses' (ibid. 68). In these conditions internal stabilizing mechanisms begin to operate within the system, and in the final analysis they prevent the class struggle from escalating to the point where it becomes an uncontrollable force, destroying the foundations of the social order.

Secondly, and probably more importantly, Marx's theory of the state has proved to be quite inadequate. In their earlier works Marx and Engels sometimes regarded the state as an independent entity, referring to it as the private property of the bureaucracy, and recognizing its capacity to acquire an autonomous role and to manœuvre between the interests of different social forces. In their later works they finally settled on an interpretation of the state as a 'machine of class despotism'.[4] This meant that the Marxist theory of socialization necessarily contained an internal contradiction. The need for nationwide control over economic activity, a consequence of the processes of monopolization, naturally required a single centre for such control. This centre had to have both the right to change the 'rules of the game', even to interfere administratively in the activities of economic subjects and other social institutions, and an effective ability to regulate processes over the whole of society. It is obvious that the only institution capable of exercising these functions in modern society is the state. Thus the development of socialization processes must inevitably lead to an increased role for the state, particularly in the economic sphere. However, Marx, seeing the state primarily as an apparatus of class domination and violence, deprived himself of the chance to be consistent on this question. The idea of social property and social control of production, or, as Lenin put it, of turning the entire economy into 'a single office and a single factory', was combined with a paradoxical insistence that the state will wither away under communism.

However, this inadequate theory of the state not only meant that Marx's conception of the new social order was contradictory. It also meant that later Marxists found difficulty in appreciating the independent role the state could play in solving the contradictions of capitalist society and overcoming the negative consequences of its spontaneous mode of development. If the state is merely 'a committee for managing the common affairs of the whole bourgeoisie' (Marx and Engels 1976: 486) or 'the ideal personification of the total national capital' (Engels 1987: 266), then when the contradictions of the capitalist system become more acute, it must inevitably take the part of the capitalists against the workers, thereby making the class struggle more confrontational. By this argument, there is no way out of these contradictions, until the 'machine of repression and violence' is broken or placed at the service of the workers against the capitalists. In other words, there is a transition from

---

[4] 'At the same pace at which the progress of modern industry developed, widened, intensified the class antagonism between capital and labour, the State power assumed more and more the character of the national power of capital over labour, of a public force organized for social enslavement, of an engine of class despotism. After every revolution marking a progressive phase in the class struggle, the purely repressive character of the State power stands out in bolder and bolder relief' (Marx 1986: 329).

the dictatorship of the bourgeoisie to the dictatorship of the proletariat. Marx and Engels's simplistic conception of the role and function of the state made it impossible to envisage, even on a theoretical level, any way of resolving the contradictions of capitalism arising from the socialization of production, other than by a proletarian revolution.

In fact, processes were at work in quite the opposite direction, increasingly strengthening the role of the state as an arbiter in social conflicts and as a guarantor of economic and social stability. Two sets of circumstances impelled the state to develop in that direction from the beginning of the twentieth century. First, many developed countries were adopting universal suffrage, so that political power came to depend not merely on certain privileged groups of the population, but also upon other social strata. Secondly, it was becoming increasingly obvious that economic and social relations were incapable of regulating themselves, and that the state needed to intervene in these areas. This came about first in wartime, and then in the inter-war period. There was now a decisive increase in the state's dependence upon society, and in its role in regulating social conflicts. This new role for the state had a fundamental effect upon the way society adapted to changes in the course of its development. These changes were particularly manifest during the inter-war period.

11.2 Reforms and revolutions in the period between the two world wars

Although Marx's predictions as to the inevitability of socialist revolution in Europe were not borne out, the period between the First and Second World Wars was marked by a high level of political and social instability in most developed countries. At this stage, as in the earlier 'crisis of early modernization', and the subsequent 'crisis of early post-modernization', the capacity of society and the state to adapt to fundamentally new development requirements became crucially important. Where inbuilt constraints hindered appropriate reactions to new challenges, the difficulties this caused were exacerbated. Whether or not a state proved able to adapt in an evolutionary way to the new realities depended on how fully these constraints had been removed in previous historical periods. The most striking example of evolutionary adaptation through the mechanism of radical reforms was Roosevelt's New Deal in the USA. Conversely, the most extreme demonstration of an inability to adapt in an evolutionary fashion was presented by Germany, where the democratic mechanisms of the Weimar Republic gave way to a totalitarian régime.

Numerous theories have been advanced to explain the rise of Nazism. Some of them see the cause in the peculiarities of the German cultural legacy, which set Germany apart fundamentally from the rest of Western Europe. It is true that certain specific features of German philosophy and culture were compatible with the victory of Nazism. We should, however, recognize that in many countries the Great Depression gave a boost to ideological currents resembling certain traditional German ideas. The typical German idealization of the countryside was not unknown in the USA. The American farmer was no less attractive an object for sentimental national feelings than the German peasant. Both Roosevelt and Hitler 'tended to romanticize rural life and the virtues of an agricultural existence. They hoped to check the trend of population movement to the cities and to disperse urban-centered industries' (Garraty 1973: 919–20; see also Ekirch 1969: 82–3, 108–14). The movement for distributism in the USA was based on the assumption that large-scale production has no advantages over small-scale, and that therefore industry should be decentralized, which would mean that many people would return to agriculture. As in Germany, these ideas were linked to a desire for autarky— in this case, for a self-sufficient Western Hemisphere. For instance, Alain Lawson notes, that 'the emphasis of Distributism on anticapitalist self-sufficiency resting on an agrarian base was reminiscent of European Fascism's praise for similar agrarian values' (Lawson 1971: 138).

The Great Depression in the USA led to a growing disenchantment with individualism, and demands for economic planning and government intervention in the economy became more widespread (Ekirch 1969: 49–70).[5] Of course, the USA, unlike Germany, did not have a deep-rooted cultural tradition of the subordination of the individual to the state or a philosophy of state service as the highest virtue. However, some very similar ideas and proposals emerged in the USA, not as a result of traditionalism but, on the contrary, of modernism. They arose from a belief in the unlimited capabilities of science. Élitist ideas gained currency in the USA in this period, particularly the idea of a society administered by engineers who understood the requirements of technology, with government in the hands of a responsible minority (see Ekirch 1969: 63, 68–9; Lawson 1971: 47–50, 70–3, 80–3).[6]

Thus, in the intellectual history of other countries and peoples at this time,

---

[5] 'While some Americans sought relief in communism and flight to Moscow, others toyed with the idea of fascism and authoritarian type of society at home. Characteristic of almost all levels of social and political thought was the conviction that drastic changes had to be made in the American economic and business system. For the first time since the Populism of the 1890s, radical fiscal and political theories enjoyed widespread support. Significantly, no important economic interest group or social class appeared willing to let natural forces take their way. In contrast to the state of affairs in the nineteenth century, when the business cycle was allowed to run its course, there was now a general demand for some form of economic planning and government action' (Ekirch 1969: 37).

[6] Analogous arguments in favour of authoritarian and totalitarian forms of administration were used not only in the USA, but also in Germany and other countries at that time: 'It was not just in Germany in the inter-war years that many members of intelligentsia and scientific professions believed that the technocracy of the future was incompatible with democracy. It was time for rule by the experts' (Roseman 1996: 206).

ideas can be found in embryonic form that resemble German conceptions. In the USA these ideas remained fairly moderate. The more extreme versions of these ideas did not gain much support, let alone become the basis of state policy. In Germany, however, the most extreme manifestations became the dominant political ideology. This requires an explanation which looks beyond the cultural traditions of the two countries.

Another explanation of the advent of Nazism stresses the peculiar nature of Germany's development, which was a process of 'catching up'. Its modernization was belated and incomplete, and many elements of the old, patriarchal society survived in its social structure and social relations. This meant that in the wake of Germany's military and economic dislocation, forces which rejected social progress and the values of modern society were able to take power and use barbaric methods in their assault on the achievements of modern civilization. This interpretation sees Nazism as a kind of counter-revolution, a total rejection of the ideas of the French Revolution—liberty, equality, and fraternity.

However, the more detailed analyses of Nazi policy and ideology cast doubt on this interpretation. They argue that the Nazis' policies were a response to the needs of a mature industrial society and were aimed at solving its problems. Hitler prioritized the development of modern branches of production, and actively encouraged the adoption of new technologies. Even before they seized power, the Nazis used the most up-to-date methods of transport and communications for their propaganda, and made special efforts to gain a dominant position within Lufthansa (Newman 1970: 298–9). They paid much attention to making consumer durables more widely available. They made efforts to produce and sell cheap, mass-produced radios, and popularized the use of refrigerators to store perishable foodstuffs. They had plans for a cheap popular car (see Barkai 1990: 232–3).[7] By 1939, 70 per cent of German homes had radios, the highest proportion in the world (Eatwell 1996: 118). It has been observed that by the end of the 1930s 'there were clear signs of the emergence of a consumer society' (ibid. 125). In Nazi ideology traditional, archaic ideas co-existed alongside promises of a dynamic new society of full employment, of an industrial and military renaissance.[8]

If we compare the main problems tackled by Roosevelt's New Deal and by the Nazi régime, and the methods used, we find that here, too, they had much in common. Both governments had to deal with the economic consequences of the Great Depression and devise means of regulating the economy counter-cyclically while retaining intact the institution of private property. They

[7] Roger Eatwell has observed that 'Hitler had taken a strong personal interest in the design details of the car that was meant to bring motoring to the masses' (1996: 126).

[8] For a detailed analysis of differing conceptions of the relationship between modernizing and anti-modernizing features in Nazi ideology and policies see Roseman (1996).

adopted approaches that were similar in many respects—indeed, the Nazis have often been called 'Keynesians before Keynes', in that they anticipated his ideas of stimulating production by boosting demand. Although direct administrative interference in the economy went much further in Nazi Germany, there are many parallels between German and American policies in this area as well: 'Production controls, limitation of entry, and price and wage manipulation were common characteristics of government policy in both countries' (Garraty 1973: 913–14). In both cases, although they basically relied on private property, the authorities did not shrink from organizing their own, government projects when they felt that private business would not or could not realize their policies adequately.[9] The similarity extends to the measures adopted against unemployment. Both governments took steps to alleviate the hardship of the neediest sections of the population through social assistance combined with programmes of public works. As Garraty observes, 'there was, furthermore, little difference in appearance or intent between the Nazi work camps and those set up in America under the Civilian Conservation Corps' (1973: 910). In both instances the aim was to remove combustible material— young people—from the cities and keep them apart from an already oversaturated labour market. As for work relationships in general, here too it has been recognized that the Nazi approach was 'less a return to feudal conditions than a National Socialist variant of the human relations approach being adopted in the USA' (Roseman 1996: 211).

Social problems in this period were closely intertwined with economic ones, and the overall question facing both régimes was 'how to integrate the working class into the nation' (Eatwell 1996: 98),[10] thereby securing class reconciliation. In their search for ways to achieve this, both countries undertook a series of corporatist experiments. However, in neither case did corporatism become the dominant model, nor were these experiments taken as far as they were in fascist Italy. In the USA from the mid–1930s the industrial trade unions were becoming increasingly influential, and their support became increasingly important. As a result, some writers have argued, a system was established in which competition was replaced by the financial and organizational control of giant corporations, the government, and the orga-

---

[9] Ekirch has described the creation of the Tennessee Valley Authority as one of the most socialistic measures of the New Deal. In this venture the government became directly involved in business and entered into direct competition with private enterprise. In Germany, as Ian Kershaw has noted, 'the foundation of the Reichswerke-Hermann-Göring in 1937, if marking no long-term threat to private industry, did register the fact, as Petzina pointed out, "that private industrial interests were not automatically identical with the interests of the régime, and that in case of conflict the régime would not shy away from effecting its aims against the resistance of sections of heavy industry" ' (1993: 52).

[10] It is interesting that the author uses this expression in describing the sphere of interests of Goebbels, one of the leading ideologists of Nazism.

nized labour movement over almost every aspect of the economy (see Davis 1970).

These questions could not be resolved in Germany as they were in the USA. The German trade unions had taken an anti-Nazi position, and Hitler completely destroyed them. Corporatist approaches evolved in a different direction in Germany, where they took the form of direct state intervention in the economy.[11] No representatives of the workers or their organizations were allowed any influence over the setting of wage rates or working conditions. Other methods had to be used to blur the divide between workers and other strata of the population. In their propaganda the Nazis used phrases like 'the nobility of labour'. They devoted a lot of effort towards organizing the retraining of workers, as well as controlling their leisure time, for example through mass tourism. They supplemented their propaganda with practical measures to remove status barriers within the working class,[12] and between the working class and other social groups. Describing the lot of the worker under Nazism, Schoenbaum observes that if this was indeed slavery, it was a 'slavery which he shared with his former masters and thus a form of equality or even liberation' (1967: 98). Whatever the case, it is generally recognized that there was significant support for the Nazis within the German working class, despite the limitations on the economic and political rights and freedoms of workers (especially during the early stages of Nazi rule).

Another vital social task for both régimes was to determine policies towards the 'middle class', the position of which was increasingly threatened by the concentration of production and the economic crisis. Both the initiators of the New Deal and the Nazis were sensitive to pressure from this quarter, and took certain steps to improve its position, although in both cases the interests of economic progress were given priority.

As we have seen, the latest interpretations of Nazism differ fundamentally from earlier conceptions: 'Nazi social policy often embodied innovative responses to problems of industrial society, that sometimes paralleled, sometimes preceded analogous efforts in other advanced industrial nations and which in any case often proved themselves consistent with the smooth functioning of that society. Nazi societal policy was not dysfunctional' (Roseman 1996: 216). But if we reject the notions that Nazism was a product of a peculiarly German ideology and culture, or that it was simply a matter of barbarians coming to power in the civilized era; if we recognize that there was much in common in the problems tackled by the Nazis in Germany and by demo-

---

[11] For more detail on the evolution of the institutional structure of the Nazi economy, see Barkai (1990: 116–38).

[12] 'In terms of wages, social policy, informal gratification, and collective organization the differences between manual and white-collar workers were being eroded on all sides' (Roseman 1996: 210).

cratic governments in other countries in the same period, and even that there were similarities in the way these problems were dealt with, the question remains: why were the political mechanisms used so different?

This question can be put another way. In many countries it was well understood at the time that mechanisms for state control of the economy, direct government intervention in economic life, and the regulation of relations between classes had an anti-democratic potential. Critics of the New Deal in the USA noted fascist tendencies in certain measures adopted by the Roosevelt administration. During the Second World War, when regulation of the national economy was intensified, there was widespread alarm that centralized planning and totalitarianism were necessarily closely associated. The USA was often portrayed at that time as a country either moving towards fascism or returning to slavery. However, this anxiety proved to be groundless. During the war the President was granted special powers to deal with the economic crisis, but the USA was able thereafter to return to the normal procedures of democratic society. In Germany democratic mechanisms were quite unable to prevent the rise of totalitarianism, and the anti-democratic potential of economic centralization was fully realized in the political sphere as well.

The roots of this difference lie in the peculiarities of Germany's modernization, although not in the sense in which some have tried to portray Nazism as an anti-modernization movement. The German road to modernization meant that the country still had a mass of inbuilt constraints as it entered the inter-war crisis period. These constraints prevented Germany from adapting adequately to new circumstances. Some of these constraints were left over from the pre-industrial period, others were a consequence of the effort to 'catch up'. The resultant system was excessively rigid and resistant to change. This manifested itself in various ways in different areas of social relations.

The German economy was greatly affected by the fact that it had industrialized to 'catch up'. From the outset enterprises were large-scale. Finance capital was highly influential and becoming more concentrated. All this created the conditions for an unprecedentedly high level of cartelization and monopolization in German industry. According to some estimates, at the beginning of the twentieth century up to 25 per cent of German industry was subject to various forms of monopolistic regulation (Tilly 1996: 113). This included 23 per cent of rail freight, 48 per cent of cement production, 50 per cent of steel smelting, 74 per cent of coal production, and 90 per cent of the output of paper (Borchardt 1973: 138). Monopolization was actively encouraged and supported by the state. In the USA the dangers of monopolization were recognized fairly early, and the first anti-trust laws were passed at the end of the nineteenth century. At around the same time in Germany, the legality of forming cartels was confirmed. This sort of policy approach had led by the inter-war period to a system of economic relations which some researchers have characterized as an 'over- and ill-organized form of capitalism': 'This form of 'organized capitalism' . . . reinforced the rigidity of the German economy in the post-war period, encouraged bureaucratic mechanisms of resource allocation and made for a concentration of the power of cartels and vested interests. In general, it was not conducive to innovation and was poorly suited to dealing with the new conditions on post-war international markets' (Peukert 1991: 114). It is also widely recognized that the uncontrolled domination of monopolies and the contradictions between different monopolistic groups were very important in exacerbating conflicts between industrialists' organizations and the trade unions. This contributed considerably to the collapse of the political institutions of the Weimar Republic.

In many respects the social structure retained the rigid caste divisions of the pre-industrial epoch. This was not the only source of division in German society, but 'regional and confessional divides were ultimately of less consequence than the rigid horizontal segmentation inherited from the *ancien régime*, the divisions between estates or *Stände*. Despite industrialisation and the lifting in 1918 of the last laws that enshrined social distinctions, the divisions between *Stände*—especially those frozen into the educational system— retained much of their force' (Knox 1996: 116). The army officer corps was particularly marked by rigid caste distinctions, but they were also to be found among other social groups like the bureaucracy. The November 1918 revolution failed to overcome the obstacles to greater social mobility, and the crisis of 1929–33 placed further constraints on opportunities for advancement.

In addition, the country was in the throes of major economic and social change. New branches of industry, such as chemicals and electrical technology, were growing in importance. These spheres, represented by monopoly capital, were increasingly able to compete politically with the traditionally dominant groups. The Bismarck régime had been founded on a compromise between these traditional groups—the monopolists of heavy industry and the Prussian Junkers. The economic and political status of the Junkers, whose position had been undermined by the November revolution and the loss of their export markets, continued to decline in the inter-war period. Although there was relative economic stagnation during the Weimar period, there were considerable advances in industrial technology, and these led to changes in the structure of the workforce and the prospects of the middle classes.[13] The period of hyperinflation between 1921 and 1923 increased this differentiation further, promoting more stratification in formerly united social groups.

The superimposition of technological, economic, and social changes upon the rigid German structure of social relations caused the social structure to fragment, as had happened in the pre-revolutionary societies considered

---

[13] For details of the technological and economic changes which took place in inter-war Germany, see Peukert (1991: 112–24).

above. Society disintegrated into individual interest groups, unable to form sufficiently large, stable social agglomerations. This picture of social fragmentation, disunity within various classes and groups, has been noted by various researchers as one of the most characteristic features of the Weimar Republic. They have stressed the 'polycratic character of the state', which expressed itself in the tendency towards fragmentation within the establishment (Knox 1996: 117); 'social and regional ghettoisation which characterised German parties' (Eatwell 1996: 91); 'growing segmentation and deadlock among the groups which had established the Republic' (Peukert 1991: 41); 'pronounced segmentation of the labour force' (ibid. 117); 'contradictions and conflicts within various monopoly capitalist "groupings" ' (Kershaw 1993: 41), as a result of which 'no united political action could be agreed upon' (Barkai 1990: p. xi). Overall, in the Weimar Republic the entire population 'remained divided by innumerable rigid subdivisions' (Roseman 1996: 200). Moreover, the old divisions were supplemented by 'new social divisions, which in turn caused new socio-political groupings to split off from the old' (Peukert 1991: 148).[14]

Such a situation, as in other countries, led to the weakening of the state and prepared the way for the fall of the *ancien régime*. Had it followed the pattern we outlined above, this should have initiated a revolution, which would then have passed through various phases in accordance with a continual realignment of social forces. Only once the revolutionary process had produced a new élite which was sufficiently strong and united would state power have been re-established and the revolution brought to an end. However, events in Germany developed along quite different lines. We can identify a number of factors which explain this difference.

The assumption of power by the Nazis was the end of the political cycle initiated by the November revolution of 1918. This period bears all the hallmarks of the trajectory of revolution. However, the 1918 revolution had only succeeded in bringing about *political* changes. It had been defeated as a *social* revolution, and this greatly influenced the composition of the groups of interests and aspirations that were connected with Nazism. The November revolution had passed through its 'honeymoon' phase, and social forces had become differentiated and polarized to a considerable degree. Society was ready to be

---

[14] Peukert describes the various forms of fragmentation as follows: 'These new forms of segmentation did not run in one single direction: tensions arose between, for example, gainers and losers from inflation; between different groups vying more fiercely than before for a greater share in the stagnating national income; between the younger and the older generations; between men and women competing for jobs, between white- and blue-collar workers, between the skilled and the unskilled; between those whose qualifications enabled them to profit from modernization and those whom modernization left deskilled; and between the employed and unemployed' (1991: 148–9).

radicalized, but that radicalization did not take place. This meant that any régime that came to power could count on neither the potential of general, albeit short-lived unity and enthusiasm, nor a desire in society for freedom and democracy. In such circumstances a régime has to resort to those methods which typify the radical phase of any revolution: terror, an 'external ideology' imposed on different social strata and groups, and active manœuvring between different interests. From this point of view it is quite legitimate to regard Nazism as a modern form of Jacobinism.

If we approach Nazism from this perspective, we can make sense of some of the peculiarities which would otherwise seem inexplicable. The illogicality and internally contradictory nature of Nazi ideology has often been noted. Its medieval features and its idealization of patriarchal relationships were combined with the most modern and advanced scientific ideas. However, in so far as the real function of that ideology was to co-ordinate and combine the aims of various groups with objectively different and even contradictory interests, such ambiguity and opacity was highly appropriate. This was particularly important under German conditions. Large sections of the population— the small landowners, artisans, and petty entrepreneurs—were still employed in so-called 'pre-capitalist' sectors, and were hostile to the process of modernization. At the same time the country possessed the enormous potential of modern industry, and was striving for industrial hegemony. The pragmatic nature of Nazi ideology can be seen, for example, in relation to the role of women in society. When the labour market was saturated, the idea that women should return to the family, and concern themselves with bearing and bringing up children, was actively propagated and even elevated to the level of state policy. However, as soon as the economy was put on a war footing, the 'increased need for female labour forced concessions to the point of ultimate reversal of ideological prerogatives by the middle of the war' (Kershaw 1993: 144).

The same can be said of the practical measures taken by the Nazis in order to manœuvre between the interests of different social groups. All of these groups were obliged to make concessions in certain areas, in return for substantial benefits in others. Big business lost a lot of its decision-making freedom, including freedom in economic matters, but gained opportunities for making large profits on state military orders, enrichment through the 'Aryanization' of Jewish property, and for exploiting the labour of prisoners of war at almost no cost. Nazi policies were able to satisfy both 'old' and 'new' branches of industry. The rearmament programme facilitated their development. Hitler's expansionist plans were also in keeping with the interests of both monopolistic groups, one of which looked to expansion westwards, while the other sought expansion to the east. The workers lost their rights to defend their economic and political interests through their trade unions, and also suffered from the freezing of wages, but gained an almost guaranteed right to work, since the problem of unemployment was solved fairly quickly. When the Nazis took power, one third of the labour force had no work; by the end of 1936 full employment had been reached (see Barkai 1990: 1). Although the Nazis abandoned their most radical proposals concerning the interests of the lower middle class, and preparations for war made other matters more urgent, even so the régime did not neglect the interests of this stratum. Measures were taken to protect small-scale retail trade from the competition of large trading centres. Interest rates were reduced. In branches of the economy in which competition was particularly fierce, compulsory cartelization measures were introduced, directed mainly at protecting small and medium-sized producers. Special protection was given to agriculture, and its interests were prioritized even to the detriment of other sectors of the economy. Hitler demanded that consumers 'make sacrifices for the sake of the peasant class' (quoted in Barkai 1990: 46).

Thus we can, in fact, find much in common in the approaches of the Nazis and of political régimes in the radical phase of a revolution. In one respect, however, there was a very substantial difference between Jacobinism and Nazism. For all their inclination towards radicalism and terror, the Jacobins' power was relatively weak and unstable. The Nazis, on the other hand, were able to create a powerful state which enjoyed fairly broad mass support. In this case those tendencies we examined above for the role of the state to increase were vitally important. It was these tendencies which allowed state intervention in different spheres of life to become so wide-ranging. They enabled contradictory interests to be reconciled by the centre so effectively, and the individual to be subordinated to the state so completely. Totalitarianism, the result of the confluence of these processes, was a product of a mature, highly organized society. It could not have been established by the radical régimes of previous revolutions.

One reason why the Nazis were able to build a strong state was that they were able to take those factors which can temporarily unite different strata of the population and allow the radicals to remain in power for a certain time, and make them operate continually. There were two particularly important factors—the constant invocations of a common enemy and of a common aim. In previous historical periods the need to defend the gains of the revolution made it possible to unite diverse forces against a common enemy, and for a time this could smooth over the conflicts of interests which caused social divisions. However, as soon as the immediate threat receded, social fragmentation resumed and the consequences for the radicals were fatal. When the Nazis came to power, although social contradictions were extremely acute, there was no immediate threat of military opposition to their policies within the country, nor of any external intervention. An image of the enemy was artificially manufactured and assiduously cultivated throughout the life of the Nazi régime. At first the forces of the left were cast in this role, and thereafter the

Jews and other 'non-Aryans'.[15] This propaganda played on the basest of chau-vinist instincts, and the Nazis skilfully deployed it to maintain the illusion of a united 'Aryan race', obliged to struggle for a dominant position in a hostile world.

However, the Nazis not only used the technique typical of other revolu-tions, of uniting people 'against'; they were able to a far greater extent than their predecessors to provide a positive basis for unity. The acquisition of more *Lebensraum* appeared to be the way to overcome those internal contra-dictions that were tearing German society apart. For a time this goal suited almost all strata of the population, and this made it possible to co-ordinate their efforts. Industrial circles expected that the conquests would give them abundant sources of raw materials, a cheap workforce, and unlimited markets for their goods. Small-scale producers hoped that under such circumstances 'everyone would find their place in the sun', and the threat of competition from large-scale capital would be reduced. The peasants, and everyone who wished to be involved in agriculture, were given the prospect of acquiring new fertile land. War increased the prestige and influence of the army. The prospect was held out to workers that they would all be engaged in skilled, creative work, since hard unskilled labour was to be carried out by 'non-Aryans'. The nation as a whole was to succeed and prosper through dominat-ing other nations. Thus the overall goal was not merely the achievement of some elevated ideal, but also a series of highly 'earthly' advantages for various strata of the élite and for the population as a whole. This was why it proved so effective in helping to unite society.

The fact that the Nazis and radical revolutionaries in previous historical epochs used similar methods to mould society tells us little about the depth of the real changes brought about by the régime. Was there, in fact, any such thing as a Nazi, or more generally a fascist, revolution? Students of the subject continue to debate this issue. Some have spoken of a Nazi 'revolution of destruction', a social revolution which broke with those remnants of patriar-chal relations characteristic of German society, liberating an 'arrested bour-geois-industrial society' (Schoenbaum 1966: 287), and thereby bringing about, albeit involuntarily, 'a strong push toward modernity' (Dahrendorf 1968: 403). Others, conversely, have stressed the conservative and reactionary aspects of Nazism, regarding it as a reactionary stabilization of German soci-ety or even as a counter-revolution. Some have attempted to explain the phenomenon as an interaction between the initially revolutionary impulse of the movement and the conservative influence of the existing establishment:

---

[15] The following episode clearly shows how Hitler regarded this question: 'During the 1930s Hitler is said to have been asked whether he thought that the Jew had to be destroyed. "No," he said. "We should have then to invent him. It is essential to have a tangible enemy, not merely an abstract one" ' (Rauschning 1940: 234, cited in Gurr 1970: 207).

'Though the authentic core of fascism contains a truly revolutionary dynamic, in the majority of cases it was neutralized or suspended through the strength of traditional conservatism either in the global society or in the movement itself. . . . Everywhere compromises were made, and only in Germany, Hungary, and Romania did fascism conserve a substantial share of its revolutionary élan' (Hagopian 1974: 355–6). Naturally, these assessments depend greatly on how profound the changes, and how substantial the break with the past, have to be before the writer in question is prepared to apply the term 'revolution'. Most recent authors reject the idea that Nazism represented a social revolution, although they accept that the Nazis brought many new elements of both a modernizing and an anti-modernizing character into the German system.[16]

Let us try to analyse how the policies of the Nazi régime affected the inbuilt constraints upon German society's capacity to adapt. It is generally accepted that the Nazis made great strides towards abolishing social barriers. The régime's most important social task was to 'overcome the rigid immobility and sterility of the old social order by offering mobility and advancement through merit and achievement, not through inherited social rank and birthright' (Kershaw 1973: 141). Under Nazism, the power of the feudal, pre-industrial élites was broken. They lost their positions in the army and the diplomatic service, and they were completely defeated after the failure of the conspiracy against Hitler in 1944. As a political force, the Prussian Junkers ceased to exist.[17] The procedures for promotion through the ranks of the army were substantially democratized, and by the middle of the war it was at last recognized that only personal qualities and achievements could serve as a basis for promotion. The corporate exclusiveness of the traditional bureaucracy was undermined by the informal, unbureaucratic mechanisms for decision-making in the Third Reich, and by the creation of, and conflict between, alternative structures which fulfilled analogous functions. We have already seen how the Nazis tried to destroy the status divisions within the working class. Some writers would also claim that the Nazis substantially undermined the regional divisions which led to the localism of such areas as the Saarland, the Ruhr, and Bavaria (see Roseman 1996: 223). Moreover, the very ideology of totalitarianism tended to level everyone, regardless of status or calling, before the all-embracing power of the totalitarian state. In this way, the Nazis were able to carry out a kind of 'status revolution'. This 'status revolution' fundamentally altered the mechanisms for upward social mobility, and

---

[16] For a more detailed analysis of the different positions on this question, see e.g. Kershaw (1973: 131–49).

[17] Barkai has linked the decline in the political role of the Junkers not only with the failure of the 1944 plot, but with the whole system of change in agriculture introduced by the Nazis, and has observed that if 'one can speak at all of a 'National Socialist Revolution', it occurred primarily in agriculture' (1990: 155).

removed significant constraints. This allowed the Nazis to integrate heterogeneous social groups into a single nation with considerable success.

Nazism also influenced substantially the mythology and value system of
German society, particularly through its influence on German youth. It is
generally accepted that the Nazis had their most impressive ideological
successes in the socialization of the younger generation. Although historians
have differing assessments of the depth and longevity of this influence, they
none the less accept that the efforts of the Nazis made 'the transmission of
older traditions and values very difficult in the postwar period' (Roseman
1996: 224).

In economic matters, the Nazi record is more ambiguous. The Nazis tried
to resolve the contradictions of a highly monopolized economy through state
interventionism. They placed severe limitations on the rights of private property owners to take decisions about their property, but did not change,
formally at least, the form of ownership. The only large-scale redistribution of
property took place in the 'Aryanization' of Jewish capital, and did not result
in major social changes. This suggests that in this area the goals of the Nazis
were profoundly conservative. There are, however, two crucial questions
which arise in regard to the Nazis' economic policies.

First, if restrictions are placed upon owners' rights over the use of private
property, at what point does that property cease to be private, becoming
instead a new, transitional form, concerning which, as Hitler put it, 'each
property owner should consider himself appointed by the state'?[18] As was
observed at the time, 'the German employer of 1939 was 'free' only with regard
to the internal organization of his enterprise and the choice of managers. All
his other activities—the level of wages and prices, joining cartels, distribution
of profits, the use of credit, the choice of markets and the manner of competition and advertising, investment, and development of new products—were
fettered or at least directed by state agencies'.[19] Some authors consider that the
scale of these changes represented a break with capitalist society. They argue
that the fascist régimes 'changed the rules of the game so that a new system
was emerging' (Milward 1979: 435). Fascism, in this interpretation can be
reduced neither to capitalism nor to socialism; rather it represents a 'third
way'.

Secondly, in what directions could the Nazi economic system have developed further? The Nazis' initial economic policies did not produce a viable
system, and the régime found itself increasingly beset by economic difficulties—'chronic shortages of foreign exchange, raw materials, and labour,

---

[18] Quoted in Barkai (1990: 27). In accordance with the regulations established by the
Nazis, the owner of each concern was appointed as an industrial leader: 'As the owner he
was a state official and a private capitalist in one person' (Newman 1970: 304).

[19] Related by Barkai from a German newspaper of 1940 (1970: 3 n. 5).

strains, blockages, over-heating, balance of payments difficulties, inflationary tendencies' (Kershaw 1993: 52). Some see this as proof of the self-destructive nature of the Nazi system, which was profoundly dysfunctional. Others have argued that the Nazi revolution was never completed, and that war was not only a means of conquering foreign territory, but also a mechanism for radicalizing internal politics.[20]

The extent to which the Nazi régime was really 'revolutionary' therefore remains controversial. We think that it can be regarded as a 'revolution from above', albeit perhaps an incomplete one. However, its effect on German society was in many respects analogous to that of the so called 'Stalin revolution' on the USSR at the end of the 1920s and the beginning of the 1930s. The Nazis overcame certain contradictions which hindered development in the shorter term, and removed certain constraints left over from the past, but the system of social relations they tried to create would have placed serious constraints on longer-term social progress. In the event, these potential constraints were removed as a result of Germany's defeat in the Second World War and the fall of the Nazis. The post-war régime forcibly transformed the mechanisms by which society functioned, putting West Germany, at least, onto an evolutionary path of development.

It was not only in Germany that the state in the inter-war years determined how society adapted to inevitable changes. The state affected the mechanisms for transforming the social system in almost every country which could not adapt through evolution. Two features of this process can be identified. First, most of the radical transformations that were implemented can be seen as belonging somewhere between reforms 'from above' and revolutions 'from above', in that the authorities retained their control over the course of events and played the leading role in effecting change. The fascist régime in Italy and the dictatorships in Spain and Portugal provide typical examples of this, as do many of those military régimes in Latin America which substantially transformed their countries. Secondly, even those revolutions which started as movements 'from below' proved incapable of resolving the contradictions within society, and ended up as revolutions 'from above', using totalitarian methods of integrating society. Along with the Nazi revolution the most striking example of this kind of development is the 'Stalin revolution' The Nazi and the Stalinist régimes have been compared and contrasted for many years, and specialists in the field continue to disagree as to whether they should both be categorized as 'totalitarian' or regarded as quite distinct phenomena.

These comparisons are of great interest for the theory of revolution. They help us understand better the characteristic features of the revolutionary process in the inter-war years. It is clear that in both Germany and the USSR,

---

[20] 'The wars of Fascism and Nazism, far from aiming to avert revolution, were designed to make it' (MacGregor 1996: 114).

the state assumed the task of resolving those social contradictions which had not been resolved through mechanisms of self-regulation and self-adaptation. At that particular time the problems both countries were facing greatly increased their potential for internal integration and united action. In both cases, however, conflicts arose not over the redistribution of property, but over how to overcome the system's own internal contradictions and bring about an essential unity of interests. The mechanisms for regulating conflict by means of normal legal procedures proved ineffective in both countries, and social and political relations became more tense and potentially explosive. The problems that were tackled in these 'revolutions from above' had many similarities, and this determined the régimes' common features. However, there were also profound differences.

The most important type of contradiction which made a 'revolution from above' necessary was, in both cases, social fragmentation. Stalin had to deal with a very specific kind of economic fragmentation, stemming not so much from the contradictions of mature industrial society as from the fact that the Bolsheviks had undermined the basis of private property relations. The pursuit of any forward-looking policy based on real economic interests and mechanisms was precluded by the Soviet economic structure. There were two basic elements to this structure. First, there was the peasantry. The tendency for peasants to become 'middle peasants' after 1917 had reduced the extent to which agriculture produced for the market. This rendered it less susceptible to external economic stimuli. Secondly, there was large-scale industry, the 'commanding heights' of which were controlled by the bureaucracy. Here the system of interests was more complex and contradictory. If the bureaucratic élite was to retain power, it needed to repress the peasantry and maintain high rates of industrialization. But in the absence of private property this general political interest could not be transformed into the direct economic interest of every member of the élite, which would have ensured that they acted in unison to achieve their common goals. As Moshe Lewin has observed, by its very nature the bureaucracy 'tended to split into powerful, difficult-to-coor-dinate bureaucratic fiefdoms, each aiming at full control over its respective domain and tending, if unopposed, to tear apart the state system' (1997: 56). Within the system, therefore, there were rigid constraints, which prevented it from adapting to the demands of industrialization. The goal of industrializa-tion expressed the general political interests of the ruling élite, but not neces-sarily the real economic interests of each of its members.

For this reason the Stalin régime, like the Nazis, had to use totalitarian mechanisms to integrate a profoundly fragmented society into a unified whole. It did so, but in quite different circumstances. Its actions were aimed at suppressing contradictions by force, both within the élite itself and in other strata of the population, and at strengthening the position of this élite rather than weakening or infringing its interests. This determined the Soviet author-ities' choice of methods. Here, too, we can see features in common with the

Nazi régime. The full range of instruments typical for the radical phase of a revolution was brought into play, complemented by the creation of a common enemy ('enemies of the people') and a common goal ('to catch up and overtake') to help stabilize this radical policy. In the USSR manœuvring by the régime was less important, since in this Thermidorian phase political struggles took place exclusively within the new élite. Moreover, the primary contradiction, arising from the fact that members of the ruling élite did not have the motivations which stem from ownership of property, could not be overcome within the confines of the Soviet system. This meant that the negative mechanisms for uniting society ('unity against') proved much more effective than the positive ones ('unity for'). This helps account for the continual renewal of internal terror during the Stalin régime, and for the fact that the terror was on a greater scale than in Nazi Germany. The slogans of industrialization, modernization, and military strength fulfilled the functions of a common goal under Stalin, but they operated more on the ideological level. They were not so obviously directed towards the immediate interests of certain social strata as the idea of *Lebensraum* was under the Nazis.

This analysis of the common features of radical changes in the inter-war period raises a question: do we need to create a special class for these revolutions, since they display certain specific characteristics not found in comparable earlier revolutions? This type of revolution can be distinguished by the following features.

First, the central conflict in this kind of revolution does not revolve around the redistribution of property or establishment of property rights as such. Instead, it revolves around how to regulate contradictions between existing social strata and groups that cannot be resolved through normal, traditional, juridically established procedures.

Secondly, in this process political institutions do not directly express the interests of individual social strata. On the contrary, their function is one of mass mobilization, integrating local, group, and private interests into a single system for achieving common goals.

Thirdly, the state takes on the task of combining diverse interests into a single whole, using forcible, totalitarian methods. These are the methods that are typical of the radical phase of any revolution, but in this case they incorporate internal stabilizing mechanisms which permit these policies to be pursued for a fairly long period.

Fourthly, although such revolutions can produce positive results in the short term, their longer-term consequences are usually destructive. The constraints on longer-term development that they create are unusually durable and rigid. They prevent an evolutionary development path from being followed subsequently.

One can argue about whether such phenomena should be labelled 'revolutions', although their essential similarity to revolutions in the classic sense of the term is clear. Whether they should be described as totalitarian revolutions, fascist revolutions, or whatever is a matter for debate. We shall label them 'mobilization revolutions', as distinct from 'liberalization revolutions' of the more traditional type. All the revolutions of the first half of the twentieth century have possessed strong mobilization features, and in the inter-war period this type of revolution was undoubtedly predominant.

11.3 Marxism and the recent Russian revolution

Our analysis of the real revolutionary processes in the first half of the twentieth century, particularly in the inter-war period, enables us to determine which of Marx's prognoses for the future were correct, and which were erroneous. Marx's predictions as to the type of contradictions that would lead to the revolutionary cataclysm were quite correct. He demonstrated the link between the technological structure, the predominant type of worker of the time, and the sharpening of the contradictions which characterized industrial society. However, the classical Marxists were quite wrong in identifying the manner in which these contradictions would be overcome. The utopia of a classless society of general equality and fraternity, in which the free development of each is the condition for the free development of all, was not realized. Dystopias were established instead.[21] The world depicted by the dystopian novelists of the first half of the twentieth century was of a standardized people with only the most basic needs, living under a rigid system of rules and constraints, having neither the opportunity nor the desire for individual development, with this whole undifferentiated mass dominated by an octopus-like state, whose tentacles penetrated every aspect of social life.[22] This vision proved to be much closer to the reality of totalitarian régimes than the societies dreamt up by Fourier and Owen.

In the industrial society the role of the worker was reduced to that of a cog in a machine performing monotonous, repetitive tasks; the system of mass production created standardized output of a single type within gigantic, rigidly centralized concerns. If we use Marx's conceptions of the relationship between productive forces and productive relations, and of the fundamental role of economic relations in the structure of society, we can see that all this

---

[21] Peter Drucker has argued that totalitarianism was born of the collapse of the belief that freedom and equality could be attained by implementing Marxist doctrine. He expressed this idea in the following aphoristic way: 'Fascism is the stage reached after communism has proved an illusion. And it has been proved as much of an illusion in Stalinist Russia as it was proved an illusion in pre-Hitler Germany' (1939: 230–1).

[22] It was in this period that the dystopian genre in literature flourished, as reflected in the works of E. Zamiatin, A. Huxley, and G. Orwell.

gave little scope for the development of free, creative labour.[23] It was far more likely to lead, and in practice did lead, to the emergence of societies in which, as Foucault put it, 'prisons resemble factories, schools, barracks, hospitals, which all resemble prisons' (1979: 228), and in which scientific predictions about their future cannot be distinguished from the worst nightmares of the creators of dystopias. A noted Russian specialist on labour organization, Aleksei Gastev, waxed lyrical about tendencies in industrial society which we would now consider dystopian:

Purely human standardization of labour was a faint foretaste of firm machine-based standardization of labour, in which all subjectivism will be submerged, and in which the naked principle of technology will triumph, transforming itself little by little from a purely technical problem into a social one . . . As they gradually extend their reach, standardizing tendencies will take root in the way people are fed, housed, and, ultimately, even in their private lives, embracing the aesthetic, mental and intellectual inquiries of the proletariat . . . We are moving towards an unprecedentedly objective demonstration of things, of mechanized crowds and of tremendous overt grandeur, knowing nothing of intimacy or lyricism. (Gastev 1919: 43, 45)

Such tendencies really did manifest themselves in all spheres of social life, affecting science, art, politics, and ideology. Describing the peculiarities of the inter-war period in Germany, Detlev Peukert observed the same processes: 'It was a period of mass marching columns, huge rallies, great sporting events and mass spectacles in the theatre, as well as of mass production in industry and mass construction in the new architecture. The organizing principle underlying this generally more regimented public sphere was the standardization of the individual unit: uniform behaviour on the part of the people involved, and the reduction of the basic component elements to highly simplified, often cubist, forms' (Peukert 1991: 161).[24]

---

[23] The ideas of Marx and Engels on these interconnections were succinctly expressed as follows: 'In the social production of their existence, men inevitably enter into definite relations, which are independent of their will, namely relations of production appropriate to a given stage in the development of their material forces of production. The totality of these relations of production constitutes the economic structure of society, the real foundation, upon which arises a legal and political superstructure and to which correspond definite forms of social consciousness. The mode of production of material life conditions the general process of social, political and intellectual life' (Marx 1987: 263). From this followed the logical conclusion that 'the final causes of all social changes and political revolutions are to be sought, not in men's brains, not in men's better insight into eternal truth and justice, but in changes in the modes of production and exchange. They are to be sought, not in the *philosophy*, but in the *economics* of each particular epoch' (Engels 1987: 254, emphasis his).

[24] Continuing this line of reasoning, Peukert comments that 'mass production and mass consumption helped give this large-scale form of public activity an image of attractiveness and modernity', seeing also 'the transition to a mass culture' as 'a final stage in the process of the mechanization of the world' (1991: 162, 167). The fascists were very sensitive to these

However, in the post-war period technology and social relations gradually change. We described this process in Chapter 2 in our analysis of the preconditions for the crisis of early post-modernization. The type of technology in use has changed, and the scientific and technological revolution has given greater scope for creativity and innovation. The role of the worker in the productive process has become more important, and the outcome of productive activity now depends increasingly on initiative and responsibility at all levels of the organization of production. Vertical links, between those who give orders and those who carry them out, have become less important, while horizontal co-ordination and the participation of subordinates in the decision-making process become more important. Taken together, these processes mean that both the sort of division of labour which condemned workers to performing just one small part of the productive process, and the system of socialization described by Marx with all of its contradictions, are gradually receding into the past. So, too, is the threat of totalitarian régimes as a means of overcoming these contradictions.

This does not mean that the methodological principle on which Marx's prognoses was based has lost its relevance. If the technology which developed towards the end of the nineteenth century demanded ever greater centralization, the latest technologies in many respects are pushing the structure of social relationships in the opposite direction. Moreover, many authors recognize that the Marxist approach can be of use in analysing these new developments; to quote just one example:

This may be explicable from a classical Marxian perspective, and an example of the contradiction between the forces of production and the relations of production. Marx and Engels [in the *Communist Manifesto*] argued that the collective nature of large-scale industrial production conflicted with the individualistic nature of capitalist relations of production. Stalinist success with centrally planned heavy industrialisation may reflect that observation. But using information technology is an individualistic and freely flowing process. The centralized relations of production inherent in the socialist planned system contradicted the forces of freely flowing information networks (Rosser and Rosser 1997: 220)

The changes in the way production becomes socialized mean that the mobilization type of revolution is also becoming a thing of the past. The recent events in the USSR and Eastern Europe demonstrate that liberalization revolutions have once again become the predominant type, removing those constraints and proscriptions which fetter social development. In this respect it is more useful to compare the recent Russian events with the much earlier

tendencies, and used them to achieve their ends: 'Hitler admitted that he adopted the techniques of the mass rally, marches and processions, press campaigns and his usual methods of political propaganda from the Social Democrats and simply applied and developed them to their logical conclusion' (Newman 1970: 298).

revolutions in England, France, and Germany than with the events of the inter-war years, despite the fact that inter-war events are historically closer.

The aspects of the theory of Marx and Engels which we find to be applicable to the analysis of the recent Russian revolution are not those which have do with class struggle or with their vision of the future. Rather we have made use of their ideas concerning the mechanisms of social development, the role of various elements in that process, and the type of contradictions which denote the exhaustion of the capacity of a society to develop technology or production as a whole. At those stages of development when society is undergoing a period of radical change in the structure and organization of productive forces, 'economic materialism remains a powerful tool of analysis and prediction, and this is in no way altered by the collapse of the earthly religion and socialist experiment linked to the name of its founder' (Gaidar 1997a: 295). [25]

[25] Gaidar argues that there are two historical periods for which the Marxian conception of history has real analytical value: the Neolithic revolution and modern economic growth (1997a: 293–5).

Conclusion

Knowledge of the past should inoculate against hysteria but should not instill complacency. History walks on a knife edge.

(Schlesinger 1986: p. xii)

In the Preface to this book we set ourselves two tasks: to examine the implications of recent events in Russia for the theory of revolution, and to consider how the theory of revolution can help us understand what is taking place on in Russia. The time has come to draw our conclusions.

1. The Theory of Revolution through the Contemporary Experience of Russia

Most modern theories of revolution have been designed to explain events in the period of early modernization, and this seriously limits their heuristic value. Unless the conceptual approaches to the study of revolution are substantially revised, this paradigm cannot be used to analyse events in Russia. The ideas we have developed and employed in this book on the theory of revolution can be expressed as follows.

1. Revolutions do not occur in stable societies where there is no dynamic change. They are invariably associated with the phenomenon of economic growth. Moreover, the preconditions of revolution come into existence only at certain crucial periods in history, which we have called 'crises of economic growth'. There have been three such crises in history:

- *the crisis of early modernization,* which encompasses the period in which the prerequisites for a transition to economic growth are being formed, and also the first, most painful stages of that growth;
- *the crisis of mature industrialism,* in which the contradictions of mass industrial production become manifest;
- *the crisis of early post-modernization,* which marks the beginning of the transition to a post-industrial, information society.

The crisis of early modernization occurred at various times in different countries. The preconditions for this crisis had already developed in England in the seventeenth century, whereas in Russia they did not appear until the latter half of the nineteenth century, and in China not until the latter half of the twentieth century. By contrast, the crisis of mature industrialism, which began in the developed countries at the end of the nineteenth century and reached its peak in the Great Depression, was artificially extended to countries where a mature industrial society had yet to be established. It was thereby internationalized and synchronized. The crisis was particularly acute in those states where the first and second crises coincided in time. Russia at the beginning of the twentieth century can be included among those countries. The crisis of early post-modernization, which occurred in conditions of economic globalization, has been partially synchronized: the first wave of this crisis came in the 1970s and 1980s, whereas the second wave, so far as we can tell, broke in the second half of the 1990s.

The onset of each of these crises presents society with fundamentally new challenges, which, if they are to be met, will require substantial changes to the institutional structure. The crisis of early modernization requires adaptation to the new circumstances of rapid population growth, international competition, and dynamic economic change. The crisis of mature industrialism takes the form of a crisis of the self-regulating mechanisms of a market economy, and requires changes in the nature and degree of state intervention in the economy and the life of society as a whole. Finally, the crisis of early post-modernization obliges societies to respond to the challenges of globalization and destruction of the environment, and to ensure conditions for the free flow of information.

If the established institutional relations of a society are able to adapt to these new demands, the crisis can be overcome by evolutionary means. However, if the institutional structure is rigid and unable to adapt, if it contains inbuilt constraints—institutional relations which prevent a flexible response to changing conditions—then the likelihood of revolution increases. During the first crisis, these constraints usually consist of methods of regulating production and trade carried over from traditional society, a rigid caste system, and absolutist forms of government. Adaptation to the challenges of the second crisis may be hindered by a very high degree of monopolization, and a lack of political democracy and of political mechanisms for achieving social compromise. Overcoming the third crisis can be hindered by authoritarian or totalitarian régimes, excessive state involvement in and regulation of social, particularly economic, life, and by artificial barriers between states.

The specific nature of each of these crises determines the basic direction of the changes which take place in the course of the revolution. The revolutions of the first and third crises are generally of a liberalizing type. Their overall direction is towards strengthening civil liberties, deregulation, and greater autonomy of society with respect to the state. Revolutions of the second crisis, by contrast, are of a mobilizing type. They increase state intervention in the economy and in social life in general, make for a proliferation of rules and regulations, and limit individual freedoms.

2. Even if a society contains inbuilt constraints which prevent its adaptation

to new conditions, it does not necessarily require a social revolution to remove them. There are other means by which the institutional structure can be rendered more flexible, such as reforms, revolutions 'from above', and conquest by more developed states.

There have been numerous examples in history when established régimes have carried out successful reforms which have made it possible to adapt to the demands of the time and to postpone, if not avert, a social revolution. Russia and Germany in the nineteenth century provide typical examples of this. We need only mention Alexander II's abolition of serfdom and his other modernizing efforts, or the unification of Germany and concomitant reforms undertaken by Otto von Bismarck. The Meiji Revolution in Japan is often regarded as a classic example of a revolution 'from above', in which the most radical representatives of the ruling élite took power and carried out profound economic and social changes, thereby ensuring the rapid modernization of the country. The most important examples of constraints being removed by foreign conquest are provided by the Napoleonic Wars, and by the occupation by the Western powers of the states of the fascist bloc at the end of the Second World War.

For all the differences between these various methods of overcoming inbuilt constraints, they share one common feature: the constraints are overcome on the initiative of state authorities powerful enough to retain control of the course and outcome of events. These authorities may be legitimate or illegitimate, formed by a process of historical development or imposed from outside, but they are a real power and are able to take consciously directed action in their own interests.

By contrast, in a social revolution the changes occur uncontrollably and spontaneously. Revolution may be defined as a transformation of society which occurs spontaneously, with an enfeebled state that is unable to control the events and changes taking place. It is not, as most authors think, violence, but the weakness of the state which distinguishes social revolution from other methods of social change. A severe weakening of state power in the pre-revolutionary period makes revolution inevitable; the restoration of a state which is strong enough to be able to implement consciously directed policies marks the end of the revolutionary cataclysm. Between these two points in time lies the period of revolutionary upheavals, which usually last ten to fifteen years.

3. In pointing to the causal link between revolution and a weak state we are saying nothing new in the theory of revolution. However, the origins of this weakness have not hitherto been adequately explained. As we have shown, the weakening of the state in the pre-revolutionary period derives from the interaction of certain economic and social processes. Above all, this weakness stems from the fragmentation of society—a sharp increase in the complexity of its social structure. This results from a breakdown in the boundaries between, and a divergence of interests within, traditional classes and groups,

and from the emergence of new social forces not catered for by the old system.

Pre-revolutionary periods are always marked by the appearance of new forms of economic activity, new sources of income, an active redistribution of wealth, and the emergence of new economically significant groups and strata. If this occurs where the structure of society is fairly rigid, incapable of adapting to new economic processes and of bringing the social status of different forces into line with their real economic position, then conditions develop for pre-revolutionary social fragmentation. This is the inevitable consequence of the pressure of dynamic economic change upon the inbuilt constraints in the social structure.

This fragmentation particularly affects the élite, which gradually changes from being a relatively united stratum into a diverse and divergent mosaic of forces and interests. There are economically powerful social groups excluded from the official élite and 'parvenus' who have entered the highest stratum by fair means or foul, but are still not fully accepted there. There is the flourishing section of the traditional élite, which has found a place in the new economic order; there is a section of the traditional élite that has been ruined by the new economic relations; and so forth. The fragmentation process is not confined to the élite. Stimulated by growing economic stratification and the emergence of new ways of making a living which coexist alongside the traditional ways, this fragmentation spreads throughout pre-revolutionary society. Consensus as to basic norms and values breaks down. The more extensive the fragmentation, the more difficult it becomes for any programme of action by the state authorities to find social support. As the crisis escalates, society is driven ever more insistently along the path of change.

Dynamic economic change, and the social fragmentation it gives rise to, severely weaken the power of the state and revolution becomes inevitable. Whatever approach the existing régime tries to take—whether it resurrects old traditions or implements reforms, whether it tries to find compromises or shows firmness—it will not find social support. Dissatisfaction grows, and revolution approaches.

Fragmentation persists throughout the entire course of the revolution, and the structure of social interests remains in a constant state of flux. This has to do with the profound and unpredictable way in which the revolutionary process can affect the economic and social position of different strata. Throughout the revolution the state lacks a stable base of social support and remains weak. Conditions for the strengthening of the state and the completion of the revolution will be present only when new social forces, particularly among the élite, who possess stable interests rooted in the new structure of property ownership created by the revolution, have emerged.

4. A grasp of the spontaneous nature of change in revolutionary conditions, and an analysis based on the concept of social fragmentation, help explain the similarities in the courses taken by revolutions in very different

circumstances and epochs. The course of a revolution is determined by the processes in which unstable pro-revolutionary coalitions are formed and are subsequently disbanded. These coalitions are not bound together by any internal identity of interests; they unite only in response to external, and changing, circumstances. The disintegration of these coalitions is associated with a change of government. The process of revolution can be represented schematically as follows.

(*a*) There is a crisis of *the ancien régime*. Attempts at reform fail for lack of social support owing to the fragmentation of the élite. The economic situation deteriorates drastically, partly owing to the crisis of the state, and partly owing to external factors such as war or the failure of a harvest. A revolutionary coalition is formed, which is directed against the *ancien régime*. There is an illusion of general unity. The revolution breaks out.

(*b*) The moderates come to power, relying on a coalition of forces opposed to the *ancien régime*. An attempt is made to implement a programme of measures devised under the *ancien régime*, and which tries to unite all that is best in the old and new systems. The programme is largely utopian, remote from current problems and the real relationship between interest groups. The government tries to rely on an illusory unity of social forces and upon revolutionary enthusiasm, and is unwilling to take firm, consistent measures. It is excessively ideological, and makes crude mistakes in practical politics.

(*c*) This is a crisis of the rule of the moderates. The first pro-revolutionary coalition breaks up as the tasks which brought it together are completed. The interests of divergent social forces become structured, better defined and articulated. Economic and social conditions deteriorate, given that the economic problems created by the revolution remain unsolved. The moderates make mistakes, the political struggle intensifies, and transaction costs increase. The gains of the revolution come under threat, from war, counter-revolution, or economic disaster. Social forces become polarized. A new pro-revolutionary coalition arises, united around the need to defend the gains of the revolution. At the other extreme, the conservatives consolidate. A situation of dual power emerges, in which the moderates, having lost their basis of social support, vacillate between the two poles. There are clashes between radicals and conservatives.

(*d*) The radicals come to power, on the basis of a coalition committed to defending the gains of the revolution. They implement a policy of uniting society by coercion, by imposing an ideology, by the suppression of dissent, and by terror. At the same time they display greater pragmatism than the moderates. They are prepared to engage in social manœuvring, even where this runs counter to their own dogmas. There is an active redistribution (through sales and transfers) of the property of opponents of the revolution in an effort to solve financial problems and ensure social support for the régime. There is a temporary stabilization of the economy through the use of new instruments of economic policy and the mobilization of resources.

(*e*) There is a crisis of the rule of the radicals. Their pro-revolutionary coalition disintegrates once the immediate threat to the gains of the revolution has passed. The economic crisis worsens in response to their shock methods of dealing with the economy, particularly where these methods are administrative. The emerging élite groups do not accept harsh, dictatorial measures, and the radicals fall from power.

(*f*) A Thermidor ensues, in which new élite groups actively form, accompanied by further redistribution of property. The population is by now exhausted, and unwilling to be involved in further political activity. The government continues its policy of manœuvre, but this manœuvring is increasingly between different élite groups—the interests of wider social strata are taken into account less and less. The economic crisis continues to deepen, and the living conditions of the population deteriorate. There is a profound state budget crisis. Gradually the conditions develop for a strengthening of the state and for the solution of the most severe economic problems.

(*g*) A post-revolutionary dictatorship comes to power, which is based on the new élites and which facilitates the temporary consolidation of the élites.

5. The formation of the post-revolutionary dictatorship represents a most important step in the strengthening of state power, but it does not bring about the final stabilization of the régime. The strength of the post-revolutionary dictatorship does not derive from any link with basic social values, but from its ability for a time to overcome the conflicts between the interests of the main groups within the new élite and to subordinate these groups to itself. It exists in a situation in which society is profoundly fatigued in the aftermath of the revolution. Such a social base cannot be stable. The revolution is necessarily followed by a period of political instability, which generally lasts several decades. The social conditions for this instability derive from the new type of social fragmentation created during the Thermidor.

During this period society remains divided. This is because the aims of different strata and groups have not been satisfied to the same extent by the outcome of the revolution, and because there is a deep conflict between the pre-revolutionary system of values and the basic norms and principles created by the revolution. For this reason the fragmentation persists, but it is now of a fundamentally different character. The interests which the authorities have to contend with are rooted in the new economic structure, in the new property relations. These interests are defined and predictable, even though they are frequently a source of conflict. They are first and foremost the interests of the new élite. In cases where the revolution is followed by a restoration, things are even more complicated. The contradictions which already exist are compounded by those which arise from the return of part of the old élite, with its claims on its former property.

This new type of fragmentation is also associated with a change in the nature of the state. On the one hand, it is strengthened in that it is less dependent on day-to-day fluctuations in public opinion. It can maintain order, collect taxes, and in general carry out basic state functions. On the other hand, given the absence of a social consensus, and the profoundly conflicting and even mutually exclusive interests of different élite groups, the régime remains exceedingly unstable. Several decades after the revolution there can still be chaotic changes of political régime or sharp fluctuations in the policy of existing régimes, a lack of firm guarantees of property rights, and irreconcilable contradictions within the élite and society as a whole.

Only once the period of post-revolutionary instability is at an end, and a basic social consensus has been restored upon a post-revolutionary system of values, can the consequences of the revolutionary cataclysm be regarded as overcome. It is from this moment that it at least becomes clear what the long-term results of the revolution are. Has it opened up new prospects for economic development, or has it placed additional constraints in the way? Has it made possible the effective co-ordination of interests, or do these interests remain irreconcilable? Has the new society turned out to be more just and inclusive than the *ancien régime*?

6. The outcome of the revolution is virtually impossible to predict. This is because the shape of the post-revolutionary system is influenced by the redistribution of property which takes place during the radical phase, and this is a largely aleatoric process aimed at solving immediate problems. This redistribution of property serves two main purposes: the acquisition of additional resources to finance the revolution, and the consolidation of support through the retention of old allies and the attraction of new ones. Consequently, the property may be sold to or redistributed among supporters of the radicals. These processes of redistributing property create the conditions for the formation of a new élite, which in many respects determines the physiognomy of the post-revolutionary society.

The continuity between the post-revolutionary system and the *ancien régime* is rooted in the need, when redistributing property and making overall changes, to take account of the aims and interests of strata and groups which formed under the *ancien régime* and which bear its indelible imprint. The extent to which it is possible to break with the past is determined by the extent to which the economic role and social significance of these groups and strata have been altered. Here the redistribution of property plays a central role.

The outcome of a revolution can be evaluated in various ways. In this work the criterion has been how fully it succeeds in removing the inbuilt constraints upon a society's adaptation to the new challenges of the age. At least three variants are possible here.

(*a*) Constraints can be removed in ways which increase the flexibility of the system as a whole, and its ability to adapt to changes, whatever their nature.

In this case the conditions are created for that system to develop in an evolutionary way in the future. Overcoming subsequent crises of economic growth may involve serious conflicts and stresses, but it will take place in a non-revolutionary fashion. Such an outcome to a revolution is not particularly likely. It is possible in liberalizing revolutions, if the initial contradictions of the pre-revolutionary society are not too profound, and if the period of post-revolutionary instability results either in a democratic political régime, or in one which creates the possibility of greater democracy.

(*b*) The only constraints removed are those which have been preventing society from adapting to the new challenges placed upon it by a particular crisis of economic growth. The system nonetheless remains inflexible, and when fundamentally new challenges arise its capacity to adapt remains inadequate. A society in such a condition can show great stability and a capacity for dynamic development in the short and even medium term. In the long term, however, it is fraught with the danger of new revolutionary upheavals. This outcome is particularly characteristic of revolutions of the second crisis, including those which resolved the problems of early modernization.

(*c*) In the course of the revolution some constraints may be removed, while others are retained or even strengthened. Moreover, the revolution may give rise to new constraints of its own, which were not present under the *ancien régime*. In these cases the post-revolutionary society's capacity to adapt proves to be inadequate: the necessary changes are hindered and not carried out. Consequently, further revolutionary upheavals remain likely. This situation is typical for cases where:

- the pre-revolutionary crisis is profound and severe;
- social strata and groups linked with the previous system of social relations and the old régime ('rebellious constraints') are strong and active in the revolution;
- the complete removal of constraints is not crucial to the society's survival;
- the period of post-revolutionary instability fails to create the conditions for the development of democracy and the consequent abolition of political constraints.

7. The theory of revolution we have presented makes use of several pioneering works in the field. These include detailed studies of the interconnection between revolution and modernization (Moore 1966; Huntington 1968); of the role of the state in revolution (Skocpol 1979); of the sources of the pre-revolutionary crisis (Goldstone 1991); of the logic of the revolutionary process (Brinton 1965); and other topics. However, we consider our approach to have been distinctive in a number of ways. The basic differences are as follows:

(*a*) Violence is not a necessary criterion of revolution, distinguishing it from all other types of transformation, as most researchers believe. Instead, the criterion is the spontaneous character of social transformation, which takes place under conditions in which the state is weak.

(*b*) Revolution is an economic and social process, not just a political one. Economic factors play a much greater role than has been traditionally recognized. New economic developments shake the foundations of the *ancien régime* and cause pre-revolutionary social fragmentation. A specifically revolutionary economic cycle, with its own logic, unfolds alongside the revolutionary political upheavals. Additionally, government policies actively influence the dynamics of the economy and these dynamics, in their turn, affect the stability of the political régime. Finally, a new élite comes into being on the basis of the redistribution of property that has taken place during the revolution, and to a large extent this élite determines the physiognomy of the post-revolutionary society.

(*c*) A class analysis—the basis of Marxist approaches to this problem—is not applicable to revolution. In conditions of social fragmentation, the basic element of the social structure is a much smaller unit than a class. Furthermore, in the revolutionary period social forces are constantly realigning, as various pro-revolutionary coalitions come together and then dissolve.

(*d*) The successive political régimes of the revolutionary period do not have a clearly defined social nature. They are obliged to manœuvre constantly between different social groups, making all possible efforts to preserve the pro-revolutionary coalition which put them in power. These practical tasks play a much more important role than the pursuit of ideological dogmas in determining the activity of revolutionary governments. Moreover, contrary to the traditional view, we believe that the most ideological governments are not the radical ones, but the moderate ones.

(*e*) It is not the case that a strong state is finally restored by the post-revolutionary dictatorship. The revolution is followed by a period of instability. This generally lasts for a few decades. Not until it has come to an end can the direct consequences of the revolutionary upheavals be regarded as overcome.

2. Contemporary Russia through the theory of revolution

As far as events in Russia are concerned, we maintain that an analysis of the economic and social upheavals of the 1980s and 1990s should be based upon the following premises.

1. A full-scale social revolution has taken place in Russia at the end of the twentieth century. The prerequisites for this revolution were formed in the third crisis of economic growth, and were determined by the contradictions between the new post-industrial tendencies and the rigid institutional system

for resource mobilization which had developed during the Soviet period. This system had inbuilt institutional constraints, associated with the political and ideological monopoly of the Communist Party, the system of centralized planning, the largely extra-economic obligation to work, the generally hierarchical principles upon which society was built, and the system's autarkic tendencies. This meant that Soviet society could not respond to the challenges of global competition; it could not disseminate or assimilate the necessary volume of information, and it was not capable of dynamic structural changes. Therefore the conditions for a revolutionary situation matured, and the crisis of the Soviet system became inevitable.

The shock that undermined the foundations of the Soviet system and activated the processes of pre-revolutionary fragmentation was the oil boom of the mid-1970s. 'Petrodollars' flooded into the country, leading to an uncontrollable redistribution of resources, an artificial rise in living standards, and a very sudden increase in the USSR's dependence on foreign trade and the state of the world market. The subsequent fall in oil prices, and the exhaustion of external sources of support for a system which could not make the transition to an information society, greatly aggravated the crisis, and served as the catalyst for revolutionary changes.

2. The basic characteristics of the recent Russian revolution do not differ fundamentally from those of previous revolutions. Like these other revolutions, it involved:

- a crisis of the state as the starting point of the revolution;
- profound social fragmentation;
- weak state power throughout the entire revolutionary period;
- a revolutionary economic cycle;
- large-scale redistribution of property;
- a succession of moderate and then radical governments followed by a Thermidor.

As in the revolutions of the past, the transformations in Russia had a largely spontaneous character, and their outcomes did not correspond to the objectives proclaimed by the authorities. This was not primarily because the reformers were intellectually ill equipped or made mistakes. It had more to do with the inexorable logic of the revolutionary process and the weakness of the state. The authorities, as in any other revolution, had no stable social base of support and so they were unable to conduct purposeful policies.

It is also essential to take account of the revolutionary nature of these changes when assessing prospects for economic growth in Russia. As our analysis of previous revolutions has shown, the entire revolutionary process is attended by an economic crisis. It stems from the manifestations of crisis in the pre-revolutionary society, the fierce political struggle, the increase in transaction costs, etc. This crisis can only be overcome once the revolution is completed and a strong state is restored. It is therefore hardly surprising that in Russia (unlike, for example, in China, where reforms have been implemented in an evolutionary way) the transformation of social relations has been accompanied by a precipitate fall in production, sharp fluctuations in both macro- and microeconomic indicators, a decline in living standards, and other manifestations of crisis. The experience of other revolutions shows that stable economic growth can only be re-established once the revolutionary process is completed.

3. Although in its fundamental characteristics it resembles the revolutions of the past, the recent Russian revolution, like any other, has its own peculiarities. The main peculiarity of the revolutionary process in late twentieth-century Russia concerns the role of violence in that process. It would be wrong to claim that there were no violent acts whatsoever in this revolution. The conflicts of August 1991 and October 1993 were resolved by forcible methods. However, the extent and role of violence indisputably distinguish it from other revolutions. There have been two main reasons for this.

First, the Russian revolution was not attended by large-scale violence in the form of spontaneous destructive actions by revolutionary masses. Such actions were more a feature of revolutions in underdeveloped, primarily agrarian countries. In those conditions violence was the main means by which the 'common folk' could influence the authorities. There were simply no other instruments by which the authorities could be compelled to make the changes desired by the lower strata. Mass violence is atypical for developed, highly urbanized societies—democratic mechanisms create the conditions in which people can freely express their will; social movements quickly become institutionalized and are able to influence the authorities without spontaneous destructive outbursts. Thus the same effect is achieved in a non-violent form.

Secondly, violent acts, terror, or other forms of forcible repression of opponents were not resorted to by the revolutionary authorities in Russia. As we have seen, there were exceptions to this rule. However, violence did not have a systemic character and was not integral to the politics of the revolutionaries. There is a variety of factors which can explain this, both global ones and those connected with the specific course of the revolution. The most important reason for this is that the transition to a post-industrial society involves a general revival of humanitarian principles, and the value of human life increases. Even under conditions of radical change, violence would have done much to alienate both the mass of the population and the élite. In any case, the revolutionary authorities hardly had to deal with any direct political threat to the gains of the revolution. There was no armed resistance to the changes. The contradictions which propelled the revolution forward were mainly economic and politico-economic in character. The revolutionary authorities did not have to take firm coercive measures as a matter of course. Their commitment manifested itself in their implementation of economic, social, and other changes.

On this basis, we may presume that the limited scale of violence was not merely a Russian peculiarity, but will be a feature of any future post-industrial revolutions.

4. The course of the recent revolution in Russia conformed in general to the logic of earlier revolutions, although it had its own specific features.

At the outset the process of revolution displayed certain peculiarities. The transition from reform to revolution took place during the 'Gorbachev era', without any change of political leadership. For this reason it is difficult to set an exact date for the beginning of the revolutionary process, although it is clear that it began during 1987–8. A feature of the first few years of Gorbachev's rule was that the authorities undertook only fairly cautious reforms, while an expectation of radical change was welling up in society. Paradoxically, by the time the revolution actually began, the initial period of unity among social forces opposed to the old régime was already virtually exhausted. The basic illusions and mistakes of the 'early revolutionary govern-ment' (the moderate government) had already manifested themselves in the period of reforms, and had aggravated economic and social problems and conflicts. When Gorbachev dissociated himself from the traditional ruling stratum—the *nomenklatura*—this unleashed the forces of revolution within society. Social forces within the initial pro-revolutionary coalition had already begun to diverge. The social basis of the government dissolved, and the authorities were less and less able to control what was going on in the coun-try. The fate of the moderates was now sealed, and the conflict between the radicals and the conservatives came out into the open. This clash resulted in the collapse of the USSR, and in the coming to power in Russia of the radicals, headed by Yeltsin.

The radicals' assumption of power in August 1991 did not lead to the destruction of democratic mechanisms, to dictatorship or terror. The radicals, who had neither the opportunity nor the desire to resort to terror or impose ideological stereotypes upon society, were more active in their use of the mechanisms of social and economic manœuvring and attempted to 'buy' the support of social forces. For this reason their policies at first sight appear less consistent than those of radicals in previous revolutions. The need to manœuvre was the main factor determining the choice of the 'voucher' priva-tization model in Russia. The need to supplement the budget and the need to create effective property owners were sacrificed to the necessity of sustaining a pro-revolutionary coalition in favour of the radical reforms, which was already in crisis by April 1992.

The transition to the Thermidor in Russia took place fairly gradually. Moreover, the economic and political processes of Thermidor did not invari-ably coincide. In the economic sphere, the Thermidor can be dated from the end of 1993, when the radical economists were removed from the key posts in government. In the political sphere, it can be dated from the presidential elections of mid-1996. Overall, Russia displayed the same cyclical movement that we have observed in other revolutions, with more radical trends in politics alternating with more conservative trends. Other typically Thermidorian features include a profound state budget crisis, falling living standards for the population, fierce struggles within the élite, and active manœuvring on the part of the authorities between different élite groups.

5. By the year 2000 the conditions for completing the revolutionary epoch in Russia were clearly in place. The existing political régime was rapidly weakening and disintegrating, and 'strong men' were assuming positions of power. There was a partial consolidation of the élite under pressure from internal and external threats, such as wars in Chechnya and Dagestan, an upsurge of terrorism and the danger of international isolation. There was an increase in 'patriotic' and statist rhetoric, the appearance of strong leaders of an essentially undemocratic persuasion, and a diminishing danger of a communist *revanche*. All of these signs indicated that conditions for a post-revolutionary dictatorship were ripening.

The procedures through which the concentration of power takes place in the Russian case have become clear. The parliamentary elections of 1999 brought victory to those political forces which are controlled by Kremlin. Yeltsin vacated the President's post early, and Vladimir Putin was elected President with about 53 per cent of the vote in the first round. His first steps were to consolidate and strengthen his power within the existing legal mechanisms envisaged by the current Russian constitution.

However, in most cases a post-revolutionary dictatorship is unstable. Given the peculiarities of the recent Russian revolution we can assume that 'dictatorship' would take a fairly mild form and would soon come to nothing. Judging by the experience of previous revolutions, conditions in Russia over the next few decades will be characterized by:

- continuing political instability with regular attempts to redistribute property (these will not necessarily be successful);
- opposition between different élite groups and attempts by the authorities to manœuvre between them;
- a gradual reconstruction of the economy;
- a lack of social consensus on a basic system of values and a lack of a stable institutional structure.

As for the final outcome of the revolution in Russia, this will largely depend upon how far the system which emerges from the revolution proves able to respond to the challenges of a post-industrial, information society.

BIBLIOGRAPHY

ADO, A. V. (1977), 'Sovremennye spory o Velikoy Frantsuzskoy Revolutsii', *Voprosy metodologii i istorii istoricheskoy nauki*, 1.

ADONIS, A., and HAMES, T. (1994) (eds.), *A Conservative Revolution? The Thatcher–Reagan Decade in Perspective*, Manchester and New York: Manchester University Press.

ADOV, L. (1999), 'Na dalnikh podstupakh k vyboram', *Ekonomicheskie i Sotsial'nye Peremeny: Monitoring obshchestvennogo mneniya*, 1.

AFTALION, F. (1990), *The French Revolution: An Economic Interpretation*, Cambridge: Cambridge University Press.

ALESINA, A. (1992), *Political Models of Macroeconomic Policy and Fiscal Reform*, Washington, DC: The World Bank.

—— and DRAZEN, A. (1994), 'Why are Stabilizations Delayed?', in T. Persson, and G. Tabellini, (eds), *Monetary and Fiscal Policy*, vol. 2, Cambridge, Mass. and London: MIT Press.

AL'SKY, M. (1925), *Nashi finansy za vremya grazhdanskoy voiny i nepa*, Moscow: Finansovoye izdatel'stvo NKF.

ANDREEVA, N. (1988), 'Ne mogu postupit'sya printsipami', *Sovetskaya Rossiya*, 13 Mar.

ARKHANGEL'SKY, S. E. (1933), 'Rasprodazha zemel'nykh vladeny storonnikov korolya', *Izvestiya AN SSSR*, 7th ser., 5.

ARUTUNIAN, L. A., and ZASLAVSKAYA, T. I. (1994) (eds.), *Kuda idet Rossiya?*, vol. 1, Moscow: Interpraks.

ASHLEY, M. (1961), *Great Britain to 1688*, Ann Arbor, Mich.: University of Michigan Press.

—— (1962), *Financial and Commercial Policy under the Cromwellian Protectorate*, London: Frank Cass.

ASHTON, R. (1936), 'Conflicts of Concessionaire Interest in Early Stuart England', in Coleman and John (1936).

—— (1960), *The Crown and the Money Market 1603–1640*, Oxford: Oxford University Press.

ÅSLUND, A. (1995), *How Russia Became a Market Economy*, Washington, DC: Brookings Institute.

ASTON, T. S. (1959), *Economic Fluctuations in England 1700–1800*, Oxford: Oxford University Press.

—— (1965) (ed.), *Crisis in Europe, 1560–1660*, London: Routledge and Kegan Paul.

AVEN, P. O., and SHIRONIN, V. M. (1987), 'Reforma khozyaystvennogo mekhanizma: real'nost' namechaemykh preobrazovany', *Izvestiya Sibirskogo Otdeleniya AN SSSR: Serya Ekonomika i prikladnaya sociologiya*, 3.

AYLMER, G. E. (1972) (ed.), 1972. *The Interregnum: The Quest for Settlement 1646–1660*, London: Macmillan.

BADOL'SKY, A. (1997), 'Regional'naya elita pozhinaet plody bankovskogo krizisa', *Otkrytaya politika*, 12.

Bibliography

BADOVSKY, D. (1994), 'Transformatsya politicheskoy elity v Rossii—ot "organizatsii professional'nykh revolutsionerov" k "partii vlasti" ', *Polis*, 6.

BAJT, A. (1971), 'Investment Cycles in European Socialist Economies', *Journal of Economic Literature*, 9.

BARBER, E. G. (1967), *The Bourgeoisie in 18th Century France*, Princeton, NJ: Princeton University Press.

BARG, M. A. (1991), *Velikaya angliyskaya revolyutsiya v portretakh ee deyateley*, Moscow: Mysl.

BARKAI, A. (1990), *Nazi Economics: Ideology, Theory, and Policy*, Oxford and New York: Berg.

BARNARD, T. C. (1975), *Cromwellian Ireland: English Government and Reform in Ireland, 1649–1660*, London: Oxford University Press.

BARNES, D. G. (1930), *A History of the English Corn Laws 1660–1846*, London: Routledge.

BAUER, A. (1908), 'Essai sur les révolutions', *Bibliothéque Sociologique Internationale*, 36.

BAUER, T. (1978), 'Investment Cycles in Planned Economies', *Acta Economica*, 21.

—— (1988), *From Cycles to Crisis?*, Vienna: WIIW.

BAUMAN, Z. (1993), 'A Post-modern Revolution?', in J. Frentzel-Zagorska (ed.), *From a One-party State to Democracy: Transition in Eastern Europe*, Amsterdam: Rodopi.

BAZAROV, V. (1919), 'Posledniy s"ezd bol'shevikov i zadachi "tekushchego momenta" ', *Mysl*, 10.

—— (1925), 'O "vosstanovitel'nykh protsessakh" voobchshe i ob "emissionnykh vozmozhnostyakh v chastnosti', *Economicheskoe obozrenie*, 1.

BELL, D. (1980), *The Social Framework of the Information Society*, Oxford: Oxford University Press.

BELOUSOV, A. R. (1994), 'Krizis industrial'noy sistemy', in Arutunian and Zaslavskaya (1994).

BERGSON, A. (1966), *Essays in Normative Economics*, Cambridge, Mass.: Harvard University Press.

—— (1967), 'Market Socialism Revisited', *Journal of Political Economy*, 75.

BESANSON, A. (1989), 'La Russie et la Révolution française', in Furet and Ozouf, (1989).

BESSEL, R. (1996) (ed.), 1996. *Fascist Italy and Nazi Germany: Comparisons and Contrasts*, Cambridge: Cambridge University Press.

BETHELL, L. (1986), *The Cambridge History of Latin America*, vol. 5 Cambridge and New York: Cambridge University Press.

BEVERIDGE, W. (1939), *Prices and Wages in England: From the Twelfth to the Nineteenth Century*, vol. 1, London: Longmans.

BIALER, S, and GUSTAFSON, T. (1982) (eds.), *Russia at the Crossroads*, London: George Allen and Unwin.

BIM, A. S. (1995), 'Sotsial'nye aspekty privatizatsii', in Zaslavskaia (1995).

BINNEY, J. E. D. (1958), *British Finance and Administration 1774–1794*, Oxford: Oxford University Press.

BIRMAN, A. M. (1967), 'Neotvratimost', *Literaturnaya gazeta*, 11 January.

BLACK, C. E. (1975) (ed.), *The Modernization of Japan and Russia: A Comparative Study*, New York: Free Press.

BLUMBERG, A. (1990) (ed.), *Chronicle of a Revolution: A Western–Soviet Inquiry into Perestroika*, New York: Pantheon Books.

BOETTKE, P. J. (1993), *Why Perestroika Failed*, London and New York: Routledge.

BOGDANOV, A. (1918), *Voprosy sotsializma*, Moscow: Knigoyolatel'stvo pisateley v Moskve.

BORCHARDT, K. (1973), 'The Industrial Revolution in Germany 1700–1914', in Cipolla (1973).

BORODKIN, F. M., KOSALS, L. YA., and RYVKINA, R. V. (1989) (eds.), *Postizhenie*, Moscow: Progress.

BOTTIGHEIMER, K. S. (1971), *English Money and Irish Land: The Adventurers in the Cromwellian Settlement of Ireland*, Oxford: Oxford University Press.

BOULOISEAU, M. (1983), *The Jacobin Republic 1792–1794*, Cambridge: Cambridge University Press.

BRENNER, R. (1993), *Merchants and Revolution*, Cambridge: Cambridge University Press.

BRETT-JAMES, N. (1935), *The Growth of Stuart London*, London: Allen and Unwin.

BRINTON, C. (1965), *The Anatomy of Revolution*, New York: Vintage Books.

BROWN, A. (1990), 'Reconstructing the Soviet Political System', in Brumberg (1990).

BROWN, H. P. and HOPKINS, SHEILA V. (1955), 'Seven Centuries of Building Wages', *Economica*, 21.

—— —— (1956), 'Seven Centuries of the Prices of Consumables, Compared with Builders' Wage-Rates', *Economica*, 22.

—— —— (1981), *A Perspective of Wages and Prices*, London and New York: Methuen.

BROWN, K. M. (1989), 'Aristocratic Finance and the Origins of the Scottish Revolution', *English Historical Review*, 104.

BROWN, P. A. (1918), *The French Revolution in English History*, London: George Allen.

BRUMBERG, A. (1990) (ed.), *Chronicle of a Revolution*, New York: Pantheon Books.

BRUNTON, D., and PENNINGTON, D. H. (1954), *Members of the Long Parliament*, London: Allen and Unwin.

BRUTSKUS, B. D. (1922), 'Problemy narodnogo khozyaystva pri sotsialisticheskom stroe', *Ekonomist*, 1, 2, and 3.

—— (1995), *Sovetskaya Rossiya i sotsializm*, St Petersburg: Zvezda.

BUDKOVETS, T. I., and KLYAMKIN, I. M. (1997), *Russkie idei*, Moscow: Institut sotsiologicheskogo analiza.

BUKSHPAN, YA., (1916), 'Zadachi gosudarstvennogo regulirovaniya khlebnoy torgovli', *Izvestiya Osobogo soveshchaniya dlia obsuzhdeniya i obyedineniya meropriyatiy po prodovol'stvennomu delu*, 27.

BURKE, E. (1982), *Reflections on the Revolution in France*, London: Penguin Books.

CALHOUN, C. J. (1982), *The Question of Class Struggle: Social Foundations of Popular Radicalism during the Industrial Revolution*, Oxford: Basil Blackwell.

—— (1983), 'The Radicalism of Tradition: Community Strength or Venerable Disguise and Borrowed Language?', *American Journal of Sociology*, 88.

CALL, T. C. (1953), *The Mexican Revolution: From Political to Industrial Revolution in Mexico*, New York: Oxford University Press.

CAMERON, R. (1993), *A Concise Economic History of the World: From Paleolithic Times to the Present*, 2nd edn., New York and Oxford: Oxford University Press.

CARR, E. H. (1950), *The Bolshevik Revolution, 1917–1923*, London: Macmillan.

CARR, E. H. and DAVIES, R. W. (1969), *Foundation of a Planned Economy, 1926–1929*, 2 vols., London: Macmillan.

CARR, R. (1980), *Modern Spain 1875–1980*, Oxford: Oxford University Press.

CARUS-WILSON, E. M. (1941), 'An Industrial Revolution of the Thirteenth Century', *Economic History Review*, 11.

—— (1959), 'Evidences of Industrial Growth on some Fifteenth-century Manors', *Economic History Review*, 2nd ser., 12.

CHAMBERLIN, W. H. (1935), *The Russian Revolution 1917–1921*, vol. 1, London: Macmillan and Co., Ltd.

CHAMBERS, J. D. (1953), 'Enclosure and Labour Supply in the Industrial Revolution', *Economic History Review*, 2nd ser., 5.

CHAUSSINAND-NOGARET, G. (1985), *The French Nobility in the Eighteenth Century: From Feudalism to Enlightenment*, Cambridge: Cambridge University Press.

CHERLEY, K. C. (1943), *Armies and the Art of Revolution*, London: Faber and Faber Ltd.

CIPOLLA, C. M. (1973) (ed.), *The Fontana Economic History of Europe. Vol. 4: The Emergence of Industrial Societies*, London and Glasgow: Collins/Fontana Books.

CLAPMAN, J. H. (1944), *The Bank of England*, Cambridge: Cambridge University Press.

CLARKSON, L. A. (1971), *The Pre-industrial Economy in England 1500–1750*, London: B. T. Batsford.

—— (1985), *Proto-industrialization: The First Phase of Industrialization?*, London: Macmillan.

CLAY, C. G. A. (1984), *Economic Expansion and Social Change: England 1500–1700*, 2 vols., Cambridge: Cambridge University Press.

COBB, R. (1972), *Reactions to the French Revolution*, London: Oxford University Press.

COBBAN, A. (1968), *Aspects of the French Revolution*, London: Cape.

COHAN, A. S. (1975), *Theories of Revolution: An Introduction*, New York: Halsted Press.

COLEMAN, D. C. (1956*a*), 'Industrial Growth and Industrial Revolution', *Economica*, 23.

—— (1956*b*), 'Labour in the English Economy of the Seventeenth Century', *Economic History Review*, 2nd ser., 8.

—— (1977), *The Economy of England 1450–1750*, Oxford and New York: Oxford University Press.

—— and JOHN, A. H. (1936) (eds.), *Trade, Government and Economy in Pre-industrial England*, London: Weidenfeld & Nicolson.

COLTON, T. J. (1986), *The Dilemmas of Reform in the Soviet Union*, New York: Council for Foreign Relations.

COOPER, J. (1989), 'The Prospects for the Socialist Economy', in Joyce, *et al.* (1989).

CORFIELD, P. (1973), 'Economic Issues and Ideologies', in C. Russell (ed.), *The Origins of the English Civil War*, London: Macmillan.

CPSU, (1987), 'K sovetskomu narodu: Obrashcheniye Tsentral'nogo Komiteta Kommunisticheskoy Partii Sovetskogo Soyuza', *Kommunist*, 7.

CRISP, O. (1976), *Studies in the Russian Economy before 1914*, London and Bastingstoke: Macmillan Press.

CROUZET, F. (1964), 'Wars, Blockade and Economic Change in Europe, 1792–1815', *Journal of Economic History*, 24.

—— (1967), 'England and France in the Eighteenth Century: A Comparative Analysis of Two Economic Growths', in Hartwell (1967).

—— (1972) (ed.), *Capital Formation in the Industrial Revolution*, London: Methuen.

—— (1989), *Historians and the French Revolution: The Case of Maximilien Robespierre*, Swansea: University College of Swansea.

—— (1990), *Britain Ascendant: Comparative Studies in Franco–British Economic History*, Cambridge: Cambridge University Press.

—— (1996), 'France', in Teich, and Porter (1996).

—— CHALONER, W. H., and STERN, W. M. (1969) (eds.), *Essays in European Economic History 1789–1914*, London: Edward Arnold.

CURTLER, W. H. R. (1920), *The Enclosure and Redistribution of our Land*, Oxford: Oxford University Press.

DAHRENDORF, R. (1968), *Society and Democracy in Germany*, New York: Garden City.

DAKIN, D. (1965), *Turgot and the Ancien Régime in France*, New York: Octagon Books.

DALIN, S. A. (1983), *Inflyatsiya v epokhi sotsial'nykh revolyutsiy*, Moscow: Nauka.

DAVIES, J. C. (1997*a*), 'Toward a Theory of Revolution', in Davies (1997*b*).

—— (1997*b*) (ed.), *When Men Revolt and Why*, New Brunswick, NY and London: Transaction Publishers.

DAVIS, C. A. (1970), *American Society in Transition*, New York: Appleton-Century-Crofts.

DEANE, P. (1961), 'Capital Formation in Britain before the Railway Age', *Economic Development and Cultural Change*, 9.

DEUTSCHER, I. (1967), *The Unfinished Revolution: Russia 1917–1967*, London and New York: Oxford University Press.

DE VRIES, J. (1976), *The Economy of Europe in an Age of Crisis, 1600–1750*, Cambridge, Cambridge University Press.

DICKINSON, H. T. (1985), *British Radicalism and the French Revolution, 1789–1815*, Oxford: Oxford University Press.

DICKSON, P. M. G. (1967), *The Financial Revolution in England: A Study in the Development of Public Credit 1688–1756*, London: Macmillan; New York: St. Martin's Press.

DIZARD, W. P. (1982), *The Coming Information Age*, 1st edn., New York: Longman.

DMITRIEV, M. (2000), 'Evoliutsiya ekonomicheskikh programm vedushchikh politicheskikh partiy i blokov Rossii', *Voprosy Ekonomiki*, 1.

DOBROLYUBSKY, K. P. (1930), *Ekonomicheskàya politikà termidoriànskoy reàktsii*, Moscow and Leningrad: Gosizdàt.

DOLGOPYATOVA, T. G. (1995), *Rossiyskie predpriyatiya v perekhodnoy ekonomike*, Moscow: Delo Ltd.

DORNBUSCH, R., and EDWARDS, S. (1991) (eds), *The Macroeconomics of Populism in Latin America*, Chicago and London: University of Chicago Press.

DOROSHENKO, A. (1916), 'K voprosu o regulirovanii khlebnoy torgovli', *Vestnik finansov, promyshlennosti i torgovli*, 52.

DRUCKER, P. F. (1939), *The End of Economic Man: A Study of the New Totalitarianism*, London and Toronto: Heinemann.

DUBIN, B. (1997), 'Rossiyane i moskvichi' *Ekonomicheskie i Sotsial'nye Peremeny: Monitoring obshchestvennogo mneniya*, 6.

—— (1999), 'Vremia i liudi'. *Ekonomicheskie i Sotsial'nye Peremeny: Monitoring obshchestvennogo mneniya*, 3.

DUNN, J. (1972), *Modern Revolutions: An Introduction to the Analysis of a Political Phenomenon*, 1st edn., Cambridge: Cambridge University Press.

DUNN, J. (1989), *Modern Revolutions: An Introduction to the Analysis of a Political Phenomenon*, 2nd edn., Cambridge: Cambridge University Press.

EATWELL, R. (1996), *Fascism: A History*, London: Vintage.

EGLAU, KH. O. 1986. *Borba gigantov*, Moscow: Progress.

EKIRCH, A. (1969), *Ideologies and Utopias: The Impact of the New Deal on American Thought*, Chicago: Quadrangle Books.

Ekonomicheskaya zhizn SSSR: Khronika sobytiy i faktov, 1917–1965. Vyp. 1: 1917–1950 (1967), Moscow: n.p..

ELLMAN, M., and KONTOROVICH, V. (1992) (eds.), *The Disintegration of the Soviet Economic System*, London and New York: Routledge.

ELTON, G. R. (1974), *England under the Tudors*, London: Methuen.

EMSLEY, C. (1979), *British Society and the French Wars 1793–1815*, London and Basingstoke: Macmillan.

ENGELS, F. (1987), 'Anti-Dühring', in F. Engles, *Collected Works*, vol. 25, London: Lawrence and Wishart.

ERSHOVA, N. S. (1994), 'Transformatsiya pravyashchey elity Rossii v usloviyakh sotsial'nogo pereloma', in Arutunian and Zaslavskaya (1994).

Estadisticas Historicas de Mexico (1985), vol. 1. Mexico City: Instituto Nacional de Estadistica, Geografia e Informatica, Mexico.

FACCARELLO, G., and STEINER, P. (1990) (eds.), *La Pensée économique pendant la Révolution française*, Grenoble: Presses Universitaires de Grenoble.

FAL'KNER, S. A. (1919), *Bumazhnye den'gi frantsuzskoy revolyutsii (1789–1797)*, Moscow: VSNKh.

—— (1924), *Problemy teorii i praktiki emissionnogo khozyaystva*, Moscow: Ekonomicheskaya zhizn.

FEIWEL, G. R. (1969), *New Currents in Soviet-type Economies: A Reader*, Scranton, Pa.: International Textbook Company.

FELDMAN, A. S. (1964), 'Violence and Volatility: The Likelihood of Revolution', in H. Eckstein (ed.), *Internal War*, New York: Free Press.

FERRO, M. (1985), *The Bolshevik Revolution: A Social History of the Russian Revolution*, London: Routledge and Kegan Paul.

FINBERG, H. P. R. (1967) (ed.), *The Agrarian History of England and Wales*, Cambridge: Cambridge University Press.

FISCHER, S, and SAHAY, R. (2000), *The Transition Economies after Ten Years*, IMF Working Paper, Washington, DC; IMF.

—— —— and Vegh, C. A. (1996), 'Stabilization and Growth in Transition Economies: The Early Experience', *Journal of Economic Perspectives*, 10.

FISHER, F. J. (1935), 'The Development of the London Food Market, 1540–1640', *Economic History Review*, 5.

—— (1961) (ed.), *Essays in the Economic and Social History of Tudor and Stuart England*, Cambridge: Cambridge University Press.

FLERON, F. J., and HOFFMANN, E. P. (1993) (eds), *Post-Communist Studies and Political Economy: Methodology and Empirical Theory in Sovietology*, Boulder, Colo. and San Francisco: Westview Press.

FLEURY, M., and VALMARY, P. (1957), 'Les Progrès de l'instruction élémentaire de Louis XIV à Napoléon III, d'après l'enquête de Louis Maggiolo (1877–1879)', *Population*, 13.

FOHLEN, C. (1973), 'The Industrial Revolution in France 1700–1914', in Cipola (1973).

FORD, H. (1924), *My Life and Work*, London: Heinemann.

FOUCAULT, M. (1979), *Discipline and Punish: The Birth of the Prison*, London: Penguin Books.

FRANKEL, E. R., FRANKEL, J., and KNEI-PAZ, B. (1992) (eds), *Revolution in Russia: Reassessments of 1917*, Cambridge: Cambridge University Press.

FURET, F. (1981), *Interpreting the French Revolution*, Cambridge: Cambridge University Press.

—— (1996), *The French Revolution 1770–1814*, Oxford and Cambridge, Mass.: Blackwell.

—— and OZOUF, M. (1989) (eds.), *The French Revolution and the Creation of Modern Political Culture*, Oxford: Pergamon Press.

—— and RICHET, D. (1970) (eds.), *The French Revolution*, New York: Macmillan.

GAGNON, V. P. (1987), 'Gorbachev and Collective Contract Brigade', *Soviet Studies*, 1.

GAIDAR, E. (1996), *Dni porazhenii i pobed*, Moscow: Vagrius.

—— (1997*a*), 'Anomalii ekonomicheskogo rosta', in E. Gaidar, *Sochineniya*, vol. 2, Moscow: Evraziya.

—— (1997*b*), 'Detskie bolezni´ postsotsializma', *Voprosy ekonomiki*, 4.

—— (1997*c*), 'Gosudarstvo i evolutsiya', in E. Gaidar, *Sochineniya*, vol. 1, Moscow: Evraziya.

—— (1997*d*), 'Vlast´ i sobstvennost: razvod po-rossiyski', *Izvestiya*, 1 Oct.

—— (1998*a*) (ed.), *Ekonomika perekhodnogo perioda, 1991–1997*, Moscow: IET.

—— (1998*b*), *Pora otbrosit´ illyuzii*, Moscow: DVR.

GALEOTTI, M. (1997), *Gorbachev and his Revolution*, London: Macmillan.

GAMBARIAN, M., and MAU, V. (1997), 'Ekonomika i vybory: opyt kolichestvennogo analiza', *Voprosy ekonomiki*, 4.

GARRATY, J. A. (1973), 'The New Deal, National Socialism and the Great Depression', *American Historical Review*, 78.

GASTEV, A. (1919), 'O tendentsiyakh proletarskoy kul´tury', *Proletarskaya kul´tura*, 9–10.

GERSCHENKRON, A. (1962), *Economic Backwardness in Historical Perspective: A Book of Essays*, Cambridge, Mass.: Belknap Press.

—— (1968), *Continuity in History and Other Essays*, Cambridge, Mass.: Belknap Press.

GIMPEL´SON, E. G. (1973), *Voennyy kommunizm: politika, praktika, ideologiya*, Moscow: Mysl.

GINZBURG, A. M. (1926) (ed.), *Zakonodatel´stvo o trestakh i sindikatakh*, 3rd edn., Moscow and Leningrad: VSNKh SSSR.

GLADKOV, I. A. (1956), *Ocherki sovetskoy ekonomiki, 1917–1920*, Moscow: AN SSSR.

GODECHOT, J. (1951), *Les Institutions de la France sous la Révolution et l'Empire*, Paris: Presses Universitaires de France.

GOLDMAN, M. I. (1983), *USSR in Crisis: The Failure of an Economic System*, New York: W. W. Norton and Co.

—— (1987), *Gorbachev's Challenge: Economic Reform in the Age of High Technology*, New York and London: W. W. Norton and Co.

—— (1991), *What Went Wrong with Perestroika*, New York and London: W. W. Norton and Co.

GOLDMAN, M. I. (1994), *Lost Opportunity: Why Economic Reforms in Russia Have Not Worked*, New York and London: W. W. Norton and Co.

GOLDSMITH, R. W. (1961), 'The Economic Growth of Tsarist Russia', *Economic Development and Cultural Change*, 9.

GOLDSTONE, J. (1980), 'Theories of Revolution: The Third Generation', *World Politics*, 32.

—— (1991), *Revolution and Rebellion in the Early Modern World*. Berkeley, Calif.: University of California Press.

GOLOVACHEV, B. V., and KOSOVA, L. B. (1996), 'Vysokostatusnye gruppy: Shtrikhi k sotsial'nomu portretu', *Sotsis*, 1.

GOODWIN, A. (1979), *The French Liberty: The English Democratic Movement in the Age of the French Revolution*, London: Hutchinson.

GORBACHEV, M. S. (1995), *Zhizn' i reformy*, vol. 1, Moscow: Novosti.

GORDON, L. A., and PLISKEVICH, N. M. (1995), 'Perekrestki rossiyskoy istorii', in Zaslavskaya (1995).

GOSKOMSTAT R. F. (1994), *Pomesyachyne indikatory kharakterizuyushchie ekonomicheskie i sotsial'nye protsessy v RF: Dekabr'*, Moscow: Goskomstat.

—— (1998a), *Kratkosrochnye ekonomicheskie pokazateli Rossiskoi Federatsii: Mart*, Moscow: Goskomstat.

—— (1998b), *Rossiyskiy statisticheskiy ezhegodnik*, Moscow: Goskomstat.

—— (1999a), *Kratkosrochnye ekonomicheskiye pokazateli Rossiyskoi Federatsii: Mart*, Moscow: Goskomstat.

—— (1999b), *Rossiyskiy statisticheskiy ezhegodnik*, Moscow: Goskamstat.

—— (1999c), *Sotsial'no-ekonomicheskoye polozhenie Rossii: Dekabr'*, Moscow: Goskomstat.

—— (2000), *Kratkosrochnye ekonomicheskie pokazateli Rossiyskoi Federatsii: Mart*, Moscow: Goskomstat.

GOUGH, H. (1988), *The Newspaper Press in the French Revolution*, London: Routledge.

GRASSBY, R. (1978), 'Social Mobility and Business Enterprise in Seventeenth-century England', in Pennington, and Keith (1978b).

GREGORY, P. R. (1982), *Russian National Income, 1985–1913*, Cambridge: Cambridge University Press.

GROMAN, V. O. (1925), 'O nekotorykh zakonomernostyakh, empiricheski obnaruzhivaemykh v nashem narodnom khozyaystve', *Planovoe khozyaystvo*, 1 and 2.

GROSSMAN, G. (1971), *The Industrialization of Russia and the Soviet Union*, London and Glasgow: Collins/Fontana Books.

GUREVICH, P. S. (1986) (ed.), *Novaya tekhnokraticheskaya volna na Zapade*, Moscow: Progress.

GURR, T. R. (1970), *Why Men Rebel*, Princeton, NJ: Princeton University Press.

HABAKKUK, H. J. (1962), 'Public Finance and the Sale of Confiscated Property during the Interregnum', *Economic History Review*, 2nd ser., 15.

HAGOPIAN, M. N. (1974), *The Phenomenon of Revolution*, New York: Dodd, Mead.

HAMEROW, T. S. (1958), *Restoration, Revolution, Reaction: Economics and Politics in Germany 1815–1871*, Princeton, NJ: Princeton University Press.

HAMILTON, E. J. (1938), 'The Decline of Spain', *Economic History Review*, 8.

HAMPSON, N. (1983), *Will and Circumstance: Montesquieu, Rousseau and the French Revolution*, London: Duckworth.

HANLEY, S. B., and YAMAMURA, K. (1977), *Economic and Demographic Change in Preindustrial Japan, 1600–1868*, Princeton, NJ: Princeton University Press.

HANSON, P. (1988), *Economics, Sovietology and Mr Gorbachev's Agenda*, Birmingham: University of Birmingham Press.

—— (1992), *From Stagnation to Catastroika: Commentaries on the Soviet Economy, 1983–1991*, New York: Praeger.

HARGREAVES, E. L. (1930), *The National Debt*, London: E. Arnold.

HARRIS, S. E. (1930), *The Assignats*, Cambridge, Mass.: Harvard University Press.

HART, J. M. (1987), *Revolutionary Mexico: The Coming and Process of the Mexican Revolution*, Berkeley, Calif.: University of California Press.

HARTE, N. B. (1936), 'State Control of Dress and Social Change in Pre-industrial England', in Coleman and John (1936).

HARTWELL, R. M. (1967) (ed), *The Causes of the Industrial Revolution in England*, London: Methuen.

HAYEK, F. A. (1991), *The Road to Serfdom*, London: Routledge.

HAZEN, C. D. (1897), *Contemporary American Opinion on the French Revolution*, Baltimore: Johns Hopkins Press.

HENDERSON, W. O. (1961), *The Industrial Revolution on the Continent: Germany, France, Russia 1800–1914*, London: Frank Cass.

HEXTER, J. H. (1941), *The Reign of King Pym*, Cambridge, Mass.: Harvard University Press.

HILL, C. (1958*a*), *Puritanism and Revolution*, London: Secker and Warburg.

—— (1958*b*), 'Recent Interpretations of the Civil War', in Hill (1958*a*).

—— (1962), *The Century of Revolution 1603–1714*, Edinburgh: Nelson.

—— (1968), *Reformation to Industrial Revolution: A Social and Economic History of Britain 1530–1780*, London: Weidenfeld and Nicolson.

HIRSCHMAN, A. O. (1963), *Journeys toward Progress: Studies of Economic Policy Making in Latin America*, New York: Twentieth Century Fund.

—— (1991), *The Rhetoric of Reaction: Perversity, Futility, Jeopardy*, Cambridge, Mass. and London: Belknap Press.

HOLLOWAY, D, and NAIMARK, N. (1996) (eds.), *Reexamining the Soviet Experience: Essays in Honor of Alexander Dallin*, Boulden, CO: Westview Press.

HOLMES, G. (1969) (ed.), *Britain after the Glorious Revolution, 1689–1714*, London: Macmillan.

HOLMES, L. (1993), 'On Communism, Post-communism, Modernity and Post-Modernity', in J. Frentzel-Zagorska (ed.), *From a One-party State to Democracy: Transition in Eastern Europe*, Amsterdam: Rodopi.

—— (1997), *Post-communism: An Introduction*, Cambridge: Polity Press.

HORSEFIELD, J. K. (1960), *British Monetary Experiments 1650–1710*, London: G. Bell.

HOSELITZ, B. F. (1961), 'Some Problems in the Quantitative Economic Study of Industralization', *Economic Development and Cultural Change*, 9.

HOSKING, G. (1990), *The Awakening of the Soviet Union*, London: Heinemann.

HOSKINS, W. G. (1964), 'Harvest Fluctuations and English Economic History, 1480–1619', *Agriculture Economic Review*, 12.

—— (1968), 'Harvest Fluctuations and English Economic History, 1620–1759', *Agriculture Economic Review*, 16.

HOUGH, J. (1982), 'Changes in Soviet Elite Composition', in Bialer Seweryn and Thane

Gustafson (eds.), *Russia at the Crossroads: The 26th Congress of the CPSU*, London: George Allen and Unwin.

——(1990), 'The Logic of Collective Action and the Pattern of Revolutionary Behavior', *Journal of Soviet Nationalities*, 1.

HUGHES, A. (1991), *The Causes of the English Civil War*, London: Macmillan.

HUGHES, E. (1934), *Studies in Administration and Finance, 1558–1825*, Manchester: Manchester University Press.

HUNECKE, F. (1970), 'Anticapitalist Currents in the French Revolution', in Furet and Richet (1970).

HUNT, L. (1986), *Politics, Culture and Class in the French Revolution*, London: Methuen.

HUNTINGTON, S. P. (1968), *Political Order in Changing Societies*, New Haven, Conn.: Yale University Press.

—— (1991), *The Third Wave*, Norman, Okla. and London: University of Oklahoma Press.

HUXLEY, A. (1932), *Brave New World*, London: Garden City.

ICKES, B. W. (1986), 'Cycle Fluctuations in Centrally Planned Economies: A Critique of the Literature', *Soviet Studies*, 38.

IET (Institute for the Economy in Transition) (1997), *The Russian Economy in 1996: Trends and Outlooks*, Moscow: IET.

—— (2000), *Rossiyskaya Ekonomika v 1999 godu: Tendentsii i Perspektivy*, Moscow: Institut Ekonomiki Perekhodnogo Perioda.

ILLARIONOV, A. (1996), 'Bremya gosudarstva', *Voprosy ekonomiki*, 9.

IMF (International Monetory Fund) (1992), *The Economy of the Former USSR in 1991: Economic Review*, Washington, DC: IMF.

Intelligentsiya o sotsial'no-politicheskoy situatsii v strane: dannye empiricheskikh issledovaniy 1989 g. (1990), Moscow: Institut sotsiologii AN SSSR.

Itogi desyatiletiya Sovetskoy vlasti v tsifrakh, 1917–1927, (1927), Moscow: Mospoligraf.

IVANOV, V. N. (1988), 'Nashe sotsial'noe samochuvstvie', *Argumenty i fakty*, 1.

JAMES, M. (1930), *Social Problems and Policy during the Puritan Revolution 1640–1660*, London: George Routledge.

JASNY, N. (1972), *Soviet Economists of the Twenties: Names to be Remembered*, Cambridge: Cambridge University Press.

JENKINS, P. (1987), *Mrs Thatcher's Revolution: The Ending of the Socialist Era*, London: Jonathan Cape.

JOHN, A. H. (1955), 'War and the English Economy 1700–1763', *Economic History Review*, 2nd ser., 7.

—— (1961), 'Aspects of English Economic Growth in the First Half of the Eighteenth Century', *Economica*, 28.

JOHNSON, C. (1982), *Revolutionary Change*, 2nd edn., Stanford, Calif.: Stanford University Press.

Joint Economic Committee (1990), *Measures of Soviet Gross National Product in 1982 Prices*, Washington, DC: US Government Printing Office.

Joint Economic Committee (1993), *The Former Soviet Union in Transition*, vol. 1, Washington, DC: US Government Printing Office.

JONES, C. (1983), *The Longman Companion to the French Revolution*, London: Longman.

JONES, D. W. (1972), 'The Hallage Receipts of the London Cloth Merchants, 1562–1720', *Economic History Review*, 2nd ser., 25.

JONES, E. L. (1965), 'Agricultural and Economic Growth in England, 1660–1750', *Journal of Economic History*, 15.

—— (1968), 'Agricultural and Economic Growth in England, 1660–1750: Agricultural Change', in W. E. Minchinton (ed.), *Essays in Agrarian History*, Newton Abbot: David and Charles.

—— (1969), 'Agrarian Change and Economic Development', in E. L. Jones and S. S. Woolf (eds), *Agrarian Change and Economic Development: The Historical Problems*, London: Methuen.

—— (1974), *Agriculture and the Industrial Revolution*, Oxford: Blackwell.

JONES, J. R. (1972), *The Revolution of 1688 in England*, London: Weidenfeld and Nicolson.

JOYCE, W. (1989), 'The Law of the State Enterprise', in Joyce *et al.* (1989).

—— Ticktin, H., and White, S. (1989) (eds), *Gorbachev and Gorbachevism*, London: Frank Cass.

KAHAN, A. (1989), *Russian Economic History*, Chicago and London: University of Chicago Press.

KATSENELENBAUM, Z. S. (1917), *Voina i finansovo-ekonomicheskoe polozhenie Rossii*, Moscow: Izd. Kulturnoprosvetitelnogo biuro studentov Moskovskogo Kommercheskogo In-ta.

—— (1918), *Obestsenenie rublia i perspektivy deneznogo obrashcheniya*, Moscow: Sovet Vserossiyskikh Kooperativnykh Syezdov.

—— (1924), *Denezhnoe obrachshenie Rossii: 1914–1924*, Moscow and Leningrad: Ekonomicheskaya zhizn'.

KAUFMAN, R. R., and STALLINGS, B. (1991), 'The Political Economy of Latin American Populism', in Dornbusch and Edwards (1991).

KEARNEY, H. F. (1959), 'The Political Background of English Mercantilism 1695–1700', *Economic History Review*. 2nd ser., 11.

KEMMERER, E. W. (1940), *Inflation and Revolution: Mexico's Experience of 1912–1917*, Princeton, NJ: Princeton University Press.

KENNEDY, W. (1913), *English Taxation 1640–1799: An Essay on Policy and Opinion*, London: G. Bell.

KERRIDGE, E. (1953), 'The Movement of Rent, 1540–1640', *Economic History Review*, 2nd ser., 6.

KERSHAW, I. (1993), *The Nazi Dictatorship: Problems and Perspectives of Interpretation*, London and New York: Arnold.

—— Lewin, M. (1997) (eds.), *Stalinism and Nazism: Dictatorships in Comparison*, Cambridge: Cambridge University Press.

KHOLODKOVSKIY, K. G. (1997), 'Konsolidatsiya elit', in Zaslavskaya (1997).

KISELEVA, E. V. (1976), 'K voprosu o prodazhe natsional'nykh imushchestv', *Frantsuzskiy ezhegodnik—1974*, Moscow: Nauka.

KISHLANSKY, M. (1986) *Parliamentary Selection: Social and Political Choice in Early Modern England*, Cambridge: Cambridge University Press.

KLEIN, L., and OHKAWA, K. (1968) (eds.), *Economic Growth: The Japanese Experience since the Meiji Era*. Homewood, Ill.: Richard Irwin.

KLYAMKIN, I. M. (1993a), 'Do i posle parlamentskikh vyborov', *Polis*, 6.

—— (1993*b*), 'Kakoy avtoritarnyy rezhim vozmozhen segodnya v Rossii?', *Polis*, 5.

KNOX, M. (1996), 'Expansionist Zeal, Fighting Power, and Staying Power in the Italian and German Dictatorships', in Bessel (1996).

KOCHETKOVA, O. (1999), 'Ekonomicheslie faktory elektoral'nogo povedeniya', in *Nekotorye politekonomicheskie problemy sovrememnoy Rossii*, Moscow: IEPP.

KOKOREV, V. (1996), 'Institutsional'nye preobrazovaniya v sovremennoi Rossii: analiz dinamiki transaktsionnykh izderzhek', *Voprosy ekonomiki*, 12.

KOKOVTSOV, V. N. (1992), *Iz moego proshlogo: 1903–1919*, 2 vols., Moscow: Nauka.

KONDRATIEFF, N. (1984), *The Long Wave Cycle*, New York: Richardson and Snyder.

KONDRAT'EV, N. D. (1993), *Izbrannye sochineniya*, Moscow: Ekonomika.

KONDRAT'EÀ, T. (1993), *Bol'sheviki-yakobintsy i prizrak termidora*, Moscow: Ipol.

KORDONSKY, S. G. (1989), 'Sotsial'naia struktura i mekhànizm tormozheniya', in Borodkin *et al.* (1989).

KORNÀI, J. (1990), *Defitsit*, Moscow: Nauka.

KOROTKOV, S. N. (1984), 'K voprosu o kharaktere yakobinskoy diktatury', *Vestnik LGU*, 2nd ser., 23.

—— (1988) 'Finansovaya politika Frantsuzskoy revolyutsii: kharakter i itogi', in S. N. Korotkov, *Ot starogo poriadka k revoliutsii*, Leningrad: LGU.

—— (1992), *Finansovaya politika Konventa*, St Peterburg: SPGU.

KOSALS, L. Y., RYVKINA, R. V., and SHUVALOVA, O. R. (1999) 'Peremeny v Rossii v 1993–1997 gg.: mnemie ekspertov'. *Ekonomicheskie in Sotsial'nye Peremeny: Monitoring Obshchestvennogo Mneniya*, 7.

KOSMINSKY, E. A., and LEVITSKY, Y. A. (1954) (eds), *Angliyskaya burzhuaznaya revolyutsiya XVII vekà*, 2 vols., Moscow: Àkàdemiya Nàuk SSSR.

KOTZ, D., with WEIR, F. (1997), *Revolution from Above: The Demise of the Soviet System*, London and New York: Routledge.

KOVAL, T. B. (1997), 'Ekonomicheskaya reforma i obshchestvennoe mnenie', in Mau and Glovatskaya (1997).

KRASILSHCHIKOV, V. A. (1996), 'Zavisimost' i otstalost' v razvitii Rossii', *Mir Rossii*, 4.

KRITSMAN, L. (1925), *Geroicheskiy period velikoy russkoy revolutsii*, Moscow: Gosudarstvennoye izdatel'stvo.

KRUGMAN, P. (1997), *Pop Internationalism*, Cambridge, Mass. and London: MIT Press.

KRYSHTANOVSKAYA, O. (1995), 'Transformatsiya staroy nomenkatury v novoy rossiyskoy elite', *Obchshestvennye nauki i sovremennost'*, 1.

—— and White, S. (1996), 'From Soviet *Nomenklatura* to Russian Elite', *Europe–Asia Studies*, 48.

KUNOV, G. (1923), *Bor'ba klassov i partiy v velikoy frantsuzskoy revolyutsii: 1789–1794*, 3rd edn., Moscow and Leningrad: Gosizdat.

KUZNETS, S. (1968), 'Notes on Japan's Economic Growth', in Klein and Ohkawa (1968).

LABROUSSE, E. (1969), '1848–1830–1789: How Revolutions are Born', in Crouzet *et al.* (1969).

—— (1990), *La Crise de l'économie française à la fin de l'Ancien régime et au debut de la Révolution*, Paris: Presses Universitaires de France.

LARIN, YU. (1923), *Itogi, puti, vyvody novoy ekonomicheskoy politiki*, Moscow: Moskovskiy rabochiy.

—— (1924), *Uroki krizisa i ekonomicheskaia politika*, Moscow: Moskovskiy ràbochiy.

LATSIS, O. R. (1994), 'Replika', in Arutunian and Zaslavkaya (1994).

LAWSON, R. A. (1971), *The Failure of Independent Liberalism (1930–1941)*, New York: Putnam.

LAYARD, R., and PARKER, J. (1996), *The Coming Russian Boom: A Guide to New Markets and Politics*, New York: Free Press.

LEE, M. (1985), *The Road to Revolution: Scotland under Charles I, 1625–1637*, Urbana, Ill. and Chicago: University of Illinois Press.

LEFEBVRE, G. (1962), *The French Revolution from its Origins to 1793*, London: Routledge.

—— (1964), *The French Revolution from 1793 to 1799*, London: Routledge.

—— (1965), *The Directory*, London: Routledge.

LENIN, V I. (CW) *Collected Works*, London: Lawrence and Wishart 1960–.

—— (*PSS*), *Polnoe sobrànie sochineniy*, 5th edn., Moscow: Politizdat, 1960–70.

LEONARD, E. M. (1962), 'The Enclosure of Common Fields in the Seventeenth Century', in E. M. Carus-Wilson (ed.)., *Essays in Economic History*, vol. 2, London: Edward Arnold.

LERNER, À. YA. (1967). *Nàchàlà kibernetiki*, Moscow: Nàukà.

LEVADA, YU. (1997), 'Nashi desiat let', *Ekonomicheskie i Sotsial'nya Peremeny: Monitoring Obshchestvennogo Mneniya*, 6.

—— (1998), 'Fenomen vlasti v obshchestvennom mnenii', *Ekonomicheskie i Sotsial'nya Peremeny: Monitoring Obshchestvennogo Mneniya*, 5.

—— (1999*a*), '1989–1998: desiatiletie vynuzhdennykh povorotov', *Ekonomicheskie i Sotsial'nya Peremenyi: Monitoring Obshchestvennogo Mneniya*, 1.

LEWIN, M. (1985), *The Making of the Soviet System: Essays in the Socialist History of Interwar Russia*, New York: Pantheon Books.

—— (1997), 'Bureaucracy and the Stalinist State', in Kershaw and Lewin (1997).

LINGLE, C. (1998), 'Whatever Happened to the "Asian Century"?', *Intellectual Capital.com: Money, Markets and Management*, 12 Feb.

LIPSON, E. (1931) *The Economic History of England*, vol. 2, London: A. and C. Black.

LOMEYER, A. E. (1918) (ed.), *Voprosy denezhnogo obrashcheniya*. St Petersburg: Tsentral'nyi voenno-promyshlennyi komitet.

LUBLINSKAYA, A. D. (1965), *Frantsuzskiy absoliutizm v pervoy treti XVII veka*, Moscow and Leningrad: Nauka.

MCAULEY, M. (1983) (ed.), *The Soviet Union after Brezhnev*, London: Heinemann Educational Books.

—— (1992), *Soviet Politics 1917–1991*, Oxford: Oxford University Press.

MCDANIEL, T. (1991), *Autocracy, Modernization, and Revolution in Russia and Iran*, Princeton, NJ: Princeton University Press.

MCFAUL, M. (1990) '1789, 1917 Can Guide '90s Soviets', *San Jose Mercury News*, 19 Aug.

—— (1996), 'Revolutionary Transformations in Comparative Perspective: Defining a Post-Communist Research Agenda', in Holloway and Naimark (1996).

MACGREGOR, K. (1996), 'Expansionist Zeal, Fighting Power, and Staying Power in the Italian and German Dictatorships', in Bessel (1996).

MCKAY, J. P. (1970), Pioneers for Profit. Foreign entrepreneurship and Russian Industrialization 1885–1913. Chicago.

MADDISON, A. (1995), *Monitoring the World Economy 1820–1992*, Paris: OECD.

MAGUN, V. S. (1994), 'Trudovye tsennosti rossiyskogo naseleniya', in Arutunian and Zaslavskaya (1994).

—— (1995), 'Trudovye tsennosti rossiyskogo naseleniya', in Zaslavskaya (1995).

—— (1996, 'Revolyutsiya prityazaniy i izmenenie zhiznennoy strategii molodezhi v stolitsakh i provintsii: ot 1985 k 1995', in Zaslavskaya (1996).

MAISKY, I. M. (1957), *Ispaniya, 1808–1917*, Moscow: AN SSSR.

MALLE, S. (1985), *The Economic Organization of War Communism 1918–1921*. Cambridge: Cambridge University Press.

—— (1994), 'Privatizatsiya v Rossii', *Voprosy ekonomiki*, 3.

MANFRED, A. Z. (1950), *Frantsuzskaia burzhuaznaya revolyutsiya kontsa XVIII veka (1789–1794)*, Moscow: Nauka.

—— (1973) (ed), *Istoriya Frantsii*, vol. 2, Moscow: Nauka.

MANNING, B. (1999), *The Far Left in the English Resolution 1640–1660*, London, Chicago and Sydney: Bookmarks.

MARCZEWSKI, J. (1961), 'Some Aspects of Economic Growth of France, 1660–1958', *Economic Development and Cultural Change*, 9.

—— (1965), *Introduction à l'histoire quantitative*, Paris: l'ISES.

MARION, M. (1914), *Histoire financière de la France depuis 1715*, vols. 1–5, Paris.

MARKOVITCH, T. J. (1975), 'La Révolution industrielle: le cas de France au XVIIIe siècle', *Revue d'histoire économique et sociale*, 53.

—— (1976), 'La Croissance industrielle sous l'ancien régime', *Annales: economies, Sociales, Civilisations*, 31.

MARTIN, K. (1954) *French Liberal Thought in the Eighteenth Century*, 2nd edn., London: Turnstile Press Ltd.

MARTOV, YU. (1921) 'Na puti k likvidatsii', *Sotsialisticheskiy vestnik*, 1.

MARX, K. (1976), *Capital*, vol. 1, London: Penguin Books.

—— (1986), 'The Civil War in France', in Marx and Engels (*CW*), vol. 22.

—— (1987), 'Preface and Introduction to "A Contribution to the Critique of Political Economy"', in Marx and Engels (*CW*), vol. 29.

—— (1996), Capital Volume 1, in Marx and Engels (*CW*), vol. 35.

MARX, K., and ENGELS, F. (1976), 'Manifesto of the Communist Party', in Marx and Engels (*CW*), vol. 6.

—— —— (*S*), *Sochineniya*, 2nd edn., Moscow: Gospolitizdat, 1954–62.

—— —— (*CW*), *Collected Works*, London: Lawrence and Wishart 1975–.

MATHIAS, P., and POLLARD, S. (1989) (eds.), *The Cambridge Economic History of Europe*, vol. 8, Cambridge: Cambridge University Press.

—— and POSTAN, M. N. (1978) (eds.), *The Cambridge Economic History of Europe*, vol. 7, Cambridge: Cambridge University Press.

MATHIEZ, A. (1963–4), *La Révolution française*, vols. 1–3, Paris: Armand Colin.

—— (1995), *Frantsuzskaya revolyutsiya*, Rostov-on-Don: Feniks.

MAU, V. A. (1993), *Reformy i dogmy, 1914–1929*, Moscow: Delo.

—— (1995), *Ekonomika i vlast: 1985–1994*, Moscow: Delo Ltd.

—— (1996*a*). 'Ekonomicheskaya reforma i politicheskiy tsikl v sovremennoy Rossii', *Voprosy ekonomiki*, 6.

—— (1996*b*). *The Political History of Economic Reform in Russia, 1985–1994*, London: CRCE.

—— (1997), 'Stabilizatsiya, vybory i perspektivy ekonomicheskogo rosta', *Voprosy ekonomiki*, 2.

—— and GLOVATSKAYA, N. (1997) (eds.), *Piat´ let reform*, Moscow: IET.

—— and STARODUBROVSKAYA, I. (1990), 'Perestroyka kak revolyutsiya: opyt proshlogo i popytka prognoza', *Kommunist*, 11.

—— —— (1991*a*), 'Ot Kornilova k bol´shevikam?', *Nezàvisimaya gazeta*, 25 Sept.

—— —— (1991*b*), *Zakonomernosti revolyutsii, opyt perestroyki i nashi perspektivy*, Moscow: IE AN SSSR.

—— —— (1998*a*), 'Budzhet, banki i neproletarskaya diktatura', *Itogi*, 35.

—— —— (1998*b*), 'O gryaduashchey diktature', *Nezavisimaya gazeta*, 3 Sept.

—— SINEL´NIKOV-MURYLEV, S., and TROFIMOV, G. (1996), 'Economic Policy Alternatives and Inflation in Russia', *Communist Economies and Economic Transformation*. 8.

MAYER, A. J. (1971), *Dynamics of Counterrevolutionn in Europe, 1870–1956*, London: Harper Torchbooks.

MEDUSHEVSKY, A. N. (1998), *Demokratiya i avtoritarizm*, Moscow: Rosspen.

MELYANTSEV, V. A. (1996), *Vostok i Zapad vo vtorom tysyacheletii: ekonomika, istoriya i sovremennost´*, Moscow: MGU.

MEREDITH, H. O. (1933), *Outlines of the Economic History of England: A Study in Social Development*, 2nd edn., London: Pitman.

MICHINTON, W. E. (1968) (ed.), *Essays in Agrarian History*, vol. 1, Newton Abbot: David and Charles.

MILLER, J. (1993), *Mikhail Gorbachev and the End of Soviet Power*, London: Macmillan.

MILWARD, A. (1976), 'Fascism and the Economy', in W. Laqueur, (ed.), *Fascism: A Reader's Guide*, Berkeley, Calif.: University of California Press.

—— and SAUL, S. B. (1979), *The Economic Development of Continental Europe 1780–1870*, London: George Allen and Unwin.

MIRSKY, B. (1921), 'Put´ termidora', *Poslednie novosti*, 3 Mar.

MOORE, B., Jr. (1966), *Social Origins of Dictatorship and Democracy: Lord and Peasant in the Making of the Modern World*, Boston: Beacon Press.

MORRILL, J. (1982) (ed.), *Reactions to the English Civil War 1642–1649*, London: Macmillan.

MOSHIRI, F. (1988), 'Revolutionary Conflict Theory in an Evolutionary Perspective', in Goldstone, J. A., Gurr, T., and Moshiri, F. (eds.), *Revolutions of the Late Twentieth Century*, Boulder, Colo.: Westview Press.

MUNTING R. (1996), 'Industrial Revolution in Russia', in Teich and Porter (1996).

MURARKA, D. (1988), *Gorbachev: The Limits of Power*, London: Hutchinson.

MURRAY, W. J. (1985), *The Right-wing Press in the French Revolution: 1789–1792*, London: Boydell Press.

NAISBITT, J. (1984), *Megatrends: Ten New Directions Transforming our Lives*, New York: Warner Books.

—— (1986), *The Years Ahead 1986: Ten Powerful Trends Shaping your Future*, New York: Warner Books.

NARKOMPROD, (1922), *Chetyre goda prodovolstvennoi raboty*, Moscow: Narkomprod.

Narodnoe khozyaystvo SSSR za 60 let: 1922–1972 (1972), Moscow: Statistika.

Narodnoe khozyaystvo SSSR za 70 let (1987), Moscow: Finansy i statistika.

Narodnoe khozyaystvo SSSR v 1990 g (1991), Moscow: Finansy i statistika.

NEF, J. U. (1934), 'The Progress of Technology and the Growth of Large-scale Industry in Great Britain, 1540–1640', *Economic History Review*, 5.

—— (1937), 'Prices and Industrial Capitalism in France and England, 1540–1660', *Economic History Review*, 7.

—— (1940), *Industry and Government in France and England, 1540–1640*, Philadelphia: American Philosophical Society.

—— (1950), *War and Human Progress: An Essay on the Rise of Industrial Civilization*, Cambridge, Mass.: Harvard University Press.

NELSON, J. M., TILLY, C., and WALKER, L. (1997) (eds), *Transforming Post-communist Political Economies*, Washington DC: National Academy Press.

NEL′SON, P., and KUZES, I. (1996), 'Ekonomicheskaya dialektika i stroitel′stvo demokratii v Rossii', *Sotsiologicheskie issledovaàniya*, 1.

NENÀSHEV, M. (1993), *Poslednee Pravitel′stvo SSSR*, Moscow: Krom.

NEWMAN, K. J. (1970), *European Democracy between the Wars*, London: George Allen and Unwin.

NIKITINA, V. (1997a), 'God za godom: 1989', *Ekonomicheskie i Sotsial′nye Peremeny: Monitoring obshchestvennogo mneniia*, 4 (30).

—— (1997b)., 'God za godom: 1990', *Ekonomicheskie i Sotsial′nye Peremeny: Monitoring obshchestvennogo mneniia*, 5.

—— (1997c), 'God za godom: 1991', *Ekonomicheskie i Sotsial′nye Peremeny: Monitoring obshchestvennogo mneniia*, 6.

—— (1998a), 'God za godom: 1992', *Ekonomicheskie i Sotsial′nye Peremeny: Monitoring obshchestvennogo mneniia*, 1.

—— (1998b), 'God za godom: 1993', *Ekonomicheskie i Sotsial′nye Peremeny: Monitoring obshchestvennogo mneniia*, 2.

—— (1998c), 'God za godom: 1994', *Ekonomicheskie i Sotsial′nye Peremeny: Monitoring obshchestvennogo mneniia*, 3.

NOREN, J. H. (1990), 'The Economic Crisis: Another Perspective', *Soviet Economy*, 6.

NORTH, D. C. (1961), 'Early National Income Estimates of the US', *Economic Development and Cultural Change*, 9.

—— (1990), *Institutions, Institutional Change and Economic Performance*, Cambridge: Cambridge University Press.

—— and THOMAS, R. P. (1973), *The Rise of the Western World: A New Economic History*, Cambridge: Cambridge University Press.

NOVE, A. (1990) 'An Economy in Transition', in A. Brumberg (ed.), *Chronicle of a Revolution*, New York: Pantheon Books.

OBOLENSKY, L. (1920), 'Bezdenezhnye raschety i ikh rol v finansovom khoziaistve', *Narodnoe khoziaistvo*, 1–2.

O'BRIEN, P. K. (1988), 'The Political Economy of British Taxation, 1660–1818', *Economic History Review*, 2nd ser., 41.

—— and KEYDER, C. (1978), *Economic Growth in Britain and France 1780–1914: Two Paths to the Twentieth Century*, London: George Allen and Unwin.

OFER, G. (1987), 'Soviet Economic Growth: 1928–1985', *Journal of Economic Literature*, 25.

O korennoy perestroyke upravleniya ekonomikoy: Sbornik dokumentov (1987), Moscow: Politizdat.

OLSON, M., Jr. (1963), 'Rapid Growth as a Destabilizing Force', *Journal of Economic History*, 23.

—— (1997), 'Rapid Growth as a Destabilizing Force', in Davies (1997*b*).

ORWELL, G. (1949). *Nineteen Eighty-Four*, London: Secker and Warburg.

OSADCHII, P. (1991), 'Tseli i Sredstva Elektrifikatsii Rossii i Eyo Ocherednye Zadachi', Nauchno-Tekhnicheskiy Vestnik, 3.

'Otsenka oktyabrskikh sobytiy 1993 g.' (1997), *Ekonomicheskie i Sotsial'nye Peremeny: Monitoring obshchestvennogo mneniya*, 5.

OUTHWAITE, R. B. (1986), 'Progress and Backwardness in English Agriculture, 1500–1650', *Economic History Review*, 2nd ser., 39.

PALMER, R. R. (1987) (ed), *The Two Tocquevilles*, Princeton, NJ: Princeton University Press.

PAPPE, YA. SH., (1997) (ed.), *Finansovo-promyshlennye gruppy i konglomeraty v ekonomike i politike sovremennoy Rossii*, Moscow: CIPE.

PASTUKHOV, V. (1994), *Tri vremeni Rossii*, Moscow: POLIS-ROSSPEN.

PEARL, V. (1961), *London and the Outbreak of the Puritan Revolution: City Government and National Polities, 1625–1643*, Oxford, Oxford University Press.

PENNINGTON, D. H. (1961), 'The Accounts of the Kingdom, 1642–1649', in Fisher (1961).

—— (1978), 'The Making of the War 1640–1642', in Pennington and Keith (1978*b*).

—— and Keith, T. (1978*b*) (eds.), *Puritans and Revolutionaries*, Oxford: Clarendon Press.

PETTEE, G. S. (1938), *The Process of Revolution*, New York: Harper.

PEUKERT, DETLEV J. K. (1991), *The Weimar Republic: The Crisis of Classical Modernity*, London: Penguin Books.

PILBEAM, P M. (1990), *The Middle Classes in Europe 1789–1914: France, Germany, Italy and Russia*, London: Macmillan.

PIPES, R. (1968), *Revolutionary Russia*, Cambridge, Mass.: Harvard University Press.

POLLARD, S., and CROSSLEY, D. W. (1968), *The Wealth of Britain 1085–1966*, London: B. T. Batsford.

POTYAEV, A. (1919), *Finansovaia politika Sovetskoi vlasti*, Petrograd: Institut Ekonomicheskikh Issledovanii NKF.

PRICE, R. (1975), *The Economic Modernisation of France 1730–1880*, London: Croom Helm.

'Printsipy perestroyki: revolyutsionnost' myshleniya i deistviya' (1988) *Pravda*, 5 Apr.

Privatizatsiya v Rossii: Sbornik normativnykh dokumentov i materialov (1993), Moskva: Yuridicheskaya literatura.

Privatizatsiya v Rossii: poryadok provedeniya v 1994 godu, (1994), Moscow: AKDI.

RABINOWITCH, A. (1976), *The Bolsheviks Come to Power: The Revolution of 1917 in Petrograd*, New York: W. W. Norton.

RADYGIN, A. D. (1994), *Reforma sobstvennosti v Rossii*, Moscow: Respublika.

—— (1997), 'Rossiiskaia privatizatsionnaia programma i ee rezultaty', in Mau and Glovatskaya (1997).

RAKITSKY, B. (1968), *Formy khozyaystvennogo rukovodstva predpriyatiem*, Moscow: Nauka.

—— (1993), 'Rossiya moego pokoleniya', *Voprosy ekonomiki*, 2.

RAUSCHNING, H. (1940), *Hitler Speaks*, New York: Putnam.

RICHARDSON, R. C. (1977), *The Debate on the English Revolution*, London: Methuen.

RIGBY, T. H. (1990), *Political Elites in the USSR*, Aldershot: Edward Elgar.

ROBERTS, M. (1967) 'The Military Revolution', in M. Roberts, *Essays in Swedish History*, Minneapolis: University of Minnesota Press.

ROBERTSON, G. M. (1978), *The French Revolution*. Oxford: Oxford University Press,.

ROBESPIERRE, M. DE (1967), *Œuvres complètes*, vol. 10, Paris: E. Leroux.

ROSEMAN, M. (1996), 'National Socialitsm and Modernisation', in Bessel (1996).

ROSSER, J. B., and ROSSER, M. V. (1996), *Comparative Economics in a Transforming World Economy*, Chicago: Irwin.

—— (1997), 'Schumpeterian Evolutionary Dynamics and the Collapse of Soviet-Bloc Socialism', *Review of Political Economy*, 9.

ROSTOW, W. W. (1971*a*), *Politics and the Stages of Growth*, Cambridge: Cambridge University Press.

—— (1971*b*), *The Stages of Economic Growth*, 2nd edn., Cambridge: Cambridge University Press.

RUSSELL, C. (1973), 'Parliament and the King's Finances', in C. Russell (ed.), *The Origins of the English Civil War*, London: Macmillan.

—— (1979), *Parliaments and English Politics 1621–1629*, Oxford: Clarendon Press.

RUTGAIZER, V., GRAZHDANKIN, A., KOSMARSKIY, V., KHAKHULINA, L., and SHPIL′KO, S. (1990), 'Ekonomicheskaya reforma v glazakh obshchestvennogo mneniya', *Ràbochiy klàss i sovremennyy mir*, 3.

RYZHKOV, N. I. (1995), *Desyat′ let velikikh potryaseniy*, Moscow: Knigà.

SADOUL, Z. (1924), 'Soboleznovaniya', *Izvestiya*, 1 Feb.

SCHLESINGER, Jr., A. M. (1986), *The Cycles of American History*, Boston: Houghton Miffin Company.

SCHOENBAUM, D. (1966), *Hitler's Social Revolution: Class and Status in Nazi Germany, 1933–1939*, Garden City, NY: Doubleday.

SCHUMPETER, J. A. (1970), *Capitalism, Socialism and Democracy*, London: Unwin.

SCOTT, M. F. (1989), *A New View of Economic Growth*, Oxford: Clarendon Press.

SEDOV, L. A. (1995), 'Peremeny v strane i v otnoshenii k peremenam', *Ekonomicheskie i Sotsial′nye Peremeny: Monitoring Obshchestvennogo Mneniya*, 1.

—— (1999), 'Krizis vlasti i puti ee evolutsii', *Ekonomicheskie i Sotsial′nye Peremeny: Monitoring Obshchestvennogo Mneniya*, 4.

SEE, H. (1968), *Economic and Social Conditions in France during the Eighteenth Century*, New York: Cooper Square Publishers.

SERVET, J.-M. (1989) (ed.), *Idées économiques sous la Révolution, 1798–1794*, Lyon: Presses Universitaires de Lyon.

Shagi pyatiletok (1968), Moscow: Ekonomika.

SHAPOSHNIKOV, N. N. (1922), 'O putyakh ozdorovleniya denezhnoy sistemy', *Ekonomist*, 4–5.

SHCHEGOLEV, P. P. (1927), 'K kharakteristike ekonomicheskloy politki termidorianskogo rezhima', *Istorik-marksist*, 4.

SHERWELL, G. B. (1929), *Mexico's Capacity to Pay: A General Analysis of the Present International Economic Position of Mexico*, Washington, DC: n.p.

SHUL′TSEVA, V. (1996), 'Telekommunikàtsii mirà i Rossii', *Mirovaya ekonomika i mezhdunarodnye otnosheniya*, 9 and 11.

SIGOV, I. (1917), *Arakcheevskiy sotsializm*, Petrograd: Volnoe ekonomicheskoe obchsh-estvo.

SIMPSON, A. (1961), *The Wealth of the Gentry 1540–1660*, Cambridge: Cambridge University Press.

SINEL′NIKOV, S. (1995), *Budzhetnyy krizis v Rossii*, Moscow: Evraziya.

—— ANISIMOVA, L., BATKIBEKOV, S., MEDOEV, V., REZNIKOV, K., and SHKREBELA, E. (1998), *Problemy nalogovoi reformy v Rossii*, Moscow: Evraziya.

SKIDMORE, T. E., and SMITH, P. H. (1984), *Modern Latin America*, New York and Oxford: Oxford University Press.

SKOCPOL, T. (1979), *States and Social Revolutions: A Comparative Analysis of France, Russia, and China*, Cambridge: Cambridge University Press.

—— (1994a), 'A Critical Review of Barrington Moore's *Social Origins of Dictatorship and Democracy*', in Skocpol (1994d).

—— (1994b), 'Explaining Revolutions: In Quest of a Social-structural Approach', in Skocpol (1994d).

—— (1994c), 'France, Russia, China: A Structural analysis of Social Revolutions', in Skocpol (1994d).

—— (1994d) (ed.), *Social Revolutions in the Modern World*, Cambridge: Cambridge University Press.

—— and GOODWIN, J. (1994), 'Explaining Revolution in the Contemporary Third World', in Skocpol (1994d).

—— and SOMERS, M. (1994), 'The Uses of Comparative History in Macrosocial Inquiry', in Skocpol (1994d).

—— and TRIMBERGER, E. K. (1994), 'Revolutions and the World-historical Development of Capitalism', in Skocpol (1994d).

SMIRNOV, A. M. (1921), *Krizis denezhnoy sistemy frantsuzskoy revolyutsii*, Petrograd: Pravo.

SMITH, A. G. R. (1973) (ed.), *The Reign of James VI and I*, London: Macmillan.

—— (1984), *The Emergence of a Nation State: The Commonwealth of England, 1529–1660*, London and New York: Longman.

SNOOKS, G. D. (1994), 'Great Waves of Economic Change: The Industrial Revolution in Historical Perspective, 1000 to 2000', in G. D. Snooks (ed.), *Was the Industrial Revolution Necessary?*, London and New York: Routledge.

SOBOUL, A. (1975), *The French Revolution 1789–1799: From the Storming of the Bastille to Napoleon*, New York: Vintage Books.

SOLOMOU, S. (1987), *Phases of Economic Growth, 1850–1973: Kondratieff Waves and Kuznets Swings*, Cambridge: Cambridge University Press.

STALIN, J. V. (1955) 'The Tasks of Business Executives', in Stalin, *Works*, vol. 13.

—— *Works*, 13 vols., Moscow: Foreign Languages Publishing House, 1952–5.

STARR, S. F. (1990), 'The Road to Reform', in Brumberg (1990).

STEPANOV, I. (1918), *Ot rabochego kontrolia k rabochemu upravleniu v promyshlennosti i zemledelii*, Petrograd, Zhizn′ i Znanie.

STERRETT, J. E., and DAVIS, J. S. (1928), *The Fiscal and Economic Condition of Mexico*, Washington, DC: International Committee of Bankers.

STEVENSON, D. (1973), *The Scottish Revolution 1637–1644*, Newton Abbot: David and Charles.

STONE, L. (1957), 'The Nobility in Business, 1540–1640', *Explorations in Entrepreneurial History*, 10.

—— (1966), 'Social Mobility in England 1500–1700', *Past and Present*, 33.

—— (1972), *The Causes of the English Revolution 1529–1642*, London: Routledge & Kegan Paul.

STONIER, T. (1983), *The Wealth of Information: A Profile of the Post-industrial Economy*, London: Thames Methuen.

SUMMERS, R., and HESTON, A. (1984), 'Improved International Comparisons of Real Product and its Composition: 1950–1980', *Review of Income and Wealth*, 2.

SUPPLE, B. E. (1964), *Commercial Crisis and Change in England 1600–1642*, Cambridge: Cambridge University Press.

SUTELA, P. (1984) *Socialism, Planning and Optimality*, Helsinki: Societas Scentiarum Fennica.

—— (1991), *Economic Thought and Economic Reform in the Soviet Union*, Cambridge: Cambridge University Press.

SZAMUELY, L. (1974), *First Models of the Socialist Economic Systems*, Budapest: Akadémiai Kiadó.

TAWNEY, R. H. (1941), 'The Rise of the Gentry, 1558–1640', *Economic History Review*, 11.

TAYLOR, A. M. (1992), 'External Dependence, Demographic Burdens and Argentine Economic Decline after the *Belle Époque*', *Journal of Economic History*, 52.

TEICH, M., and PORTER, R. (1996) (eds.), *The Industrial Revolution in National Context: Europe and the USA*, Cambridge: Cambridge University Press.

THIRSK, J. (1952) 'Sales of Royalist Land during the Interregnum', *Economic History Review*, 2nd ser., 5.

—— (1961), 'Industries in the Countryside', in F. J. Fisher (ed.), *Essays in the Economic and Social History of Tudor and Stuart England*, Cambridge: Cambridge University Press.

—— (1967) (ed.), *The Agrarian History of England and Wales. Vol. IV, 1640–1750*, Cambridge: Cambridge University Press.

THOMPSON, E. P. (1964), *The Making of the English Working Class*, London: Gollancz.

THOROLD ROGERS, J. E. (1884) *Six Centuries of Work and Wages*, 2 vols, London: W. Swan Sonnenschein.

—— (1887), *A History of Agriculture and Prices in England*, vol. 5, Oxford: Clarendon Press.

—— (1888), *The Economic Interpretation of History*, London: Fisher Unwin.

TICKTIN, H. (1989), 'The Contradictions of Gorbachev', in Joyce *et al.* (1989).

TILLY, C. (1993), *European Revolutions, 1492–1992*, Oxford and Cambridge, Mass.: Blackwell.

TILLY, R. (1996), 'German Industrialization', in Teich and Porter (1996).

TINBERGEN, J., and POLAK, J. J. (1950), *The Dynamics of Business Cycles: A Study in Economic Fluctuations*, London: Routledge.

TOCQUEVILLE, A. DE (1967), L'ancien régime et la Révolution. Paris: Gallinard.

—— (1997), *Staryy poryadok i revolyutsiya*, Moscow: Moskovskiy filosofskiy fond.

TOFFLER, A. (1983), *Previews and Premises*, New York: Morrow.

TORTELLA, G. A. (1996), *Latecomer: The Modernization of the Spanish Economy, 1800–1990*, in Teich and Porter (1996).

TOYNBEE, A. (1884), *Lectures on the Industrial Revolution in England*, London: Rivingtons.

TREVOR-ROPER, H. R. (1953), 'The Gentry, 1540–1640', *Economic History Review Supplements*.

—— (1955), 'The Social Origins of the Great Revolution', *History Today*, June.

—— (1959), 'The General Crisis of the 17th Century', *Past and Present*, 16.

TRIMBERGER, E. K. (1978), *Revolution from Above: Military Bureaucrats and Modernization in Japan, Turkey, Egypt, and Peru*, New Brunswick, NJ: Transaction Books.

TROTSKY, L. (1953), *Klassovaya priroda sovetskogo gosudarstva*, London: Fourth International.

ULYUKAEV, A. V., and KOLESNIKOV, S. V. (1992) (eds.), *Ekonomicheskaya politika Pravitelstva Rossii: Dokumenty, kommentarii*, Moscow: Respublika.

UNDERDOWN, D. (1971), *Pride's Purge*, Oxford: Clarendon Press.

—— (1978), ' "Honest" Radicals in the Counties', in Pennington and Keith (1978*b*).

USTRYALOV, N. V. (1921), 'Patriotica', in *Smena vekh*, Prague: Politika.

—— (1925), *Pod znakom revolyutsii*, Harbin: Russkaya Zhizn´.

VASIL´IEV, D. (1994) 'Predislovie', in Radygin (1994).

VCIOM (1997), 'Monitoring Peremen: Osnovnyie tendentsii', *Ekonomickeskie i Sotsial´nye Peremeny: Monitoring obshchestvennogo mneniya*, 6.

VELDE, F. R., and WEIR, D. R. (1992), 'The Financial Market and Government Debt Policy in France, 1746–1793', *Journal of Economic History*, 52.

VISHNEVSKY, A. G. (1995), 'Modernizatsiya Rossii: pozadi ili vperedi?', in Zaslavskaya (1995).

—— (1996), 'Konservativnaya revolyutsiya v SSSR', *Mir Rossii*, 4.

VOLOBUEV, P. V. (1995), 'Chetvertooktyabr´skiy politicheskiy rezhim', in Zaslaavskaya (1995).

VORONIN, S. V., and SHMELEV, K. D. (1922), *Denezhnoe obrashchenie i kredit v Rossii i zagranitsey*, vol. 1, Petrograd and Moscow: Institut Ekonomicheskikh Issledovaniy NKF.

VOROZHEYKINA, T. E. (1995), 'Demokratizatsiya i ekonomicheskaya reforma', in Zaslavskaya (1997).

VOSLENSKY, M. (1980), *Nomenklatura: Anatomy of the Soviet Ruling Class*, London: Bodley Head Ltd.

WALKER, M. (1986) The Waking Giant: The Soviet Union under Gorbachev, London: Abacus.

WALLERSTEIN, I. (1974), *The Modern World-System*, vol. 1, New York: Academic Press.

WARD, A. W., PROTHERO, G. W., and LEATHES S. (1904), (eds.)., The Cambridge Modern History. *Vol. VIII: The French Revolution*, Cambridge: Cambridge University Press.

WCER (Working Centre for Economic Reform) (1998), *Osnovnye tendentsii razvitiya ekonomiki Rossii v 1997 godu*, Moscow: RTsER.

WELCH, C. E., Jr. (1980), Anatomy of Rebellion, Albany, NY: State University of New York Press.

WHITE, S. (1989), 'Reforming the Electoral System', in Joyce *et al.* (1989).

—— (1991), *Gorbachev and After*, Cambridge: Cambridge University Press.

WILSON, C. (1965), *England's Apprenticeship, 1603–1763*, London: Longmans.

World Bank (1996), *From Plan to Market*, Oxford: Oxford University Press.

YANITSKIY, O. N. (1997), 'Modernizatsiya v Rossii v svete kontseptsii "obshchestva riska" ', in Zaslavskaya (1997).

YANOV, A. (1984) *The Drama of the Soviet 1960s: A Lost Reform*, Berkeley, Calif.: Institute of International Studies.

YAVLINSKY, G. A. (1993), 'O novoy politike pravitel'stva', *Voprosy ekonomiki*, 2.

ZAMIATIN, E. (1924), *We*, New York: Dutton.

ZASLAVSKAYA, T. I. (1995) (ed.), *Kuda idet Rossiya?*, vol. 2, Moscow: Aspekt Press.

—— (1996) (ed.), *Kuda idet Rossiya?*, vol. 3, Moscow: Aspekt Press.

Zerkalo mneniy (various years) Moscow: Institut sotsiologii RAN.

ZUDIN, A.YU. (1997), 'Sotsial'naya organizatsiya rossiyskogo biznesa', in Zaslavskaya (1997).

INDEX OF NAMES

SUBJECT INDEX